D1590739

Reflections on the Russian Soul

A Memoir

Reflections on
the Russian Soul

A Memoir

Dmitry S. Likhachev

First published in Russian as "Vospominaniya" by Logos, St Petersburg, 1995

English edition published in 2000 by
Central European University Press

Október 6. utca 12
H-1051 Budapest
Hungary

400 West 59th Street
New York, NY 10019
USA

Translated by Bernard Adams
Translation edited by A. R. Tulloch

Distributed in the United Kingdom and Western Europe by
Plymbridge Distributors Ltd., Estover Road, Plymouth, PL6 7PZ,
United Kingdom

ISBN 963-9116-46-7

Library of Congress Cataloging in Publication Data
A CIP catalog record for this book is available upon request

Printed in Hungary by Akadémiai Nyomda

Contents

The Last of the Russian Intelligentsia

This book, incredible in its sweep of time and space, is the worthy culmination of a magnificent life's work. Written in a style that clashes in many respects with that of the received memoirists of bygone centuries, it is an individualistic confessional of the lost twentieth century of Russia. Its author, Dmitry Sergeyevich Likhachev—literary and cultural historian, religious philosopher, one-time prisoner of the gulag—despite his advanced age took an active part as a Member of the Duma in the dismantling of the Soviet empire and conducted negotiations with the masters of the Kremlin over many years on behalf of the impoverished academic community; an independent, very genuine man, he is described to this day in Russia *as the last of the intelligentsia.*

This epithet has many implications. First and foremost it alludes to that appalling tragedy—something straight from Chekhov's stories and Veresayev's novels—to which Russian intellectuals of the early years or the century were subjected as a result of the dogma and false cant of the Soviet world, which ostentatiously marked them out and encompassed their collective betrayal. Academician Dmitry Likhachev, who died, mourned by both the great and famous and the nation at large, at the age of ninety-three in St. Petersburg in September 1999, was a case in point.

Men of his kidney have long been extinct. Bullets were fired into the backs of their heads on the premises of the erstwhile Rossiya Insurance Company, in the subterranean casemates of the Lubyanka. In 1922 those on the list approved, in part, indeed, personally drawn up by Lenin and Trotsky were herded aboard the *Burgomeister Hagen* and the *Prussia* so as forcibly to rid their country of such spiritual giants as Nikolay Berdyayev, Sergey Bulgakov and Pityirim Sorokin, and deprive them for ever of their life-giving native milieu, more important than anything to the Russian intellectual, and with it the opportunity of exercising influence on the rising generation. To this day the damage has been irreparable.

Many an eminent skull was simply smashed with a club on Solovki, the death-island, in the blatantly programmed anti-intellectual Soviet period. Others were starved to death during the Civil War, worked to death building the White Sea Canal or left to rot in the gulag and in exile. Even those, however, that remained alive and were not expelled from their native land had their former, normal lives turned upside-down. They were deprived of the basic needs of intellectual life, its vivifying cultural orderliness; their family ties were severed, their backs broken. They were compelled to abase themselves in the shadows of worthless men, their foreheads branded 'bourgeois expert' as if they were lepers. But perhaps the worst punishment for the generation of the early twentieth century, outstandingly talented and doomed far too soon to perish, was, contrary to the traditions of Russian culture, not to be allowed to strike root in the blood-soaked Russian soil.

Dmitry Likhachev's epithet *last of the Russian intelligentsia* also hints that in the twilight of this breed he was capable of working miracles, cut off though he was from his fellows. With his steel-rimmed spectacles and his quiet, meticulous speech, this bald, pale academic commanded respect by virtue of his personality and his gentle perseverance, and has left behind him ideals such as the Russian soul will have insatiable need of in a totally different historical situation. He took the helm of the ship of Russian culture and steered it to a hopefully better world.

The world-famous researcher into Old Russian literature was deeply conscious of his charge. For that very reason he worked until the day of his death to arrange in a mighty picture the tesserae of his memories. Profoundly religious, of unquestionable probity, he peopled our world with many hundreds of characters, known only to him and through him: with victims and executioners alike—not infrequently both in the record of a single man—and with heroes both of momentous historical events and of everyday life, without an awareness of whose fate and experience our knowledge of twentieth century Russian and Soviet reality would be all the poorer.

Academician Likhachev has at times clearly been hard pressed to fit his work to the Procrustean bed of his own making. At such moments merely a few adjectival clauses present in this book classmates in school, friends of the family, and the several hundred colleagues who worked beside him in the course of his long life. Sometimes the ageing scholar struggled to abide by the traditions of memoir writing, but compared to his Russian forebears he became a frequent breaker of the mould. The mass of names and facts would have been a foreign body on the pages of *Dichtung und Warheit* type works written in the eighteenth and nineteenth centuries. Details of topography, theatre history and bibliography presented in list form by no means dominate the flowing narrative prose of the Westerniser Aleksandr Herzen, and of the Slavophil Sergey Aksakov, both beloved by Likhachev, who himself disliked 'either ... or' solutions. He portrays through a magnifying glass; Boris Pasternak, too, Likhachev's favourite twentieth-century creative writer, used to shun that sort of traditional depiction of the external world; his reminiscent prose is quite different.

In the history of Russian memoir-writing perhaps Andrey Bely, symbolist chronicler of the early twentieth century, led the way in this area. It was his boundless egoism, however, that encouraged him to rescue on the pages of his unfinished four-volume memoir those values from the treasury of the sinking Russian Atlantis which were important to him personally. Dmitry Likhachev, on the other hand recognises the growing pressure on him to rescue values and in his memoirs, like a teacher standing before his class, calls the roll from time to time, reads aloud from yellowed theatre programmes, evokes the ancient map of the city of his birth, St Petersburg—his passionately beloved 'Piter'—and walks with us those streets in which he once trod the cobblestones with the lively, youthful curiosity which he kept to the end of his days.

In the maddening historical moments of 1917, when each month, each week, even, in the last analysis, each day had its own part to play, the still young Likhachev roamed the streets of the city beside the Neva with a few school-friends in a similar fashion. More than half a century later, in the 1970s, I heard from him in an interval during a Slavists' conference in Zagreb that in those days it had been not so much any sympathy with victorious political parties, as empathy with the people, always defeated and persecuted, that motivated him.

It makes sense that the centre of gravity of the memoir that is now appearing in English is old St Petersburg. There the Likhachev family, her mother coming from an Old Believer background, which clung tenaciously to its own traditions and stood apart from the usual ways of Russian life; herself educated and in no way bigot, and his engineer father, who scorned a commercial world reminiscent of Ostrovsky's plays, and loved music and the theatre. The peculiar family atmosphere fitted in well with the day-to-day life of multiethnic, colourful Petersburg, where the influence of the West entered Russia through the 'window let through into Europe'. In Dmitry Likhachev's life, however, the exciting years of childhood and adolescence were exchanged for a burdensome adulthood. The old familiar bonds of society and culture slackened, and there came prolonged suffering in the Soviet Secret Police prison on the island of Solovki. True, after his release the victim of Stalin's mass repressions, known in the special terminology of the Soviet period as 'unjust persecution', became senior researcher in various academic institutions of renown. He gained the title of university professor and as a result of his research on the *Lay of Igor's Host*, the Old Russian epic, was received into the membership of the Soviet Academy of Sciences. Nevertheless, by his own admission, it was his recollections of the Soviet death-camps that peopled the innermost recesses or his mind to the end of his life. As his eightieth and ninetieth years passed he still constantly felt himself to be the persecuted prisoner of the gulag, and even when he received academic awards he remained the same man as when he had been held captive in that hell of hells.

"The Russian intelligentsia in its entirety endured the sufferings caused by the period of chaos," wrote Dmitry Likhachev, admitting his personal partiality for his maligned and severely decimated generation.

> As an eyewitness of this century, it is my human duty to establish the truth about it. Because all too often one hears the expression 'rotten intelligentsia'. This class is seen as weak *and* wavering, because we are accustomed to believing Marxist ideology...which regards the workers alone as the ruling class.
>
> When we examine investigation documents we find only such statements, mercilessly beaten out of the imprisoned intelligentsia, as support the investigators' accounts. But we have to realise that torture broke not only men's bodies. The worst thing was the situation of their families. The investigators used to threaten prisoners that their relations too would be subjected to torture, and there was nothing to restrain their tyranny. Therefore we have no right to condemn those who, without reading their confessions, authenticated the notebooks that the investigators placed before them...[1]

As doyen of Russian sociologists, Dmitry Sergeyevich published his polished essays on the former speculations of the Russian intelligentsia and their searching for solutions at the turn of the century in a little book entitled *The Intelligentsia*. It is typical of him that he included in it—as it were unexpectedly, inadvertently, but with good reason—details of his memoir concerning the gulag, with what seem to be literary variants. With a harshness that did not previously char-

---

[1] D. S. Likhachev, *Ob intelligentsii,* St Petersburg 1997, p. 11.

acterise the tone of his academic arguments he declared: "It has long been time that we disabused ourselves of the myth which for some mysterious reason has persisted in our minds, that the most merciless period of repression began in 1938–37. I believe that one day statistics of the repressions will show that the wave of arrests, executions and banishments began as early as the beginning of 1918, even before the official start of the Red Terror".

Dmitry Likhachev is here referring to the systematic acts of provocation by the Soviet Russian secret police, the Cheka, in the course of which numerous reputable members of the intelligentsia were charged with involvement in alleged conspiracies in order to intimidate them. It was hoped, and rightly, that fear would breed fear. The authorities took hostages and enclosed them in barrack-cities surrounded with barbed wire and watchtowers. We can judge the repressive nature of the regime from the little-known fact that the expression 'concentration camp' appeared almost at once in the correspondence of Lenin and Trotsky in August 1918. All this was accompanied by intensive brain-washing, scare-mongering and disinformation. By this means the Kremlin legitimised, or at least justified and defended the terror that served to consolidate Bolshevik power. Likhachev recalled this too from personal experience.

> During 1918 and 1919, when we opened the windows of our flat in Lakhtinskaya ulitsa, we could hear all night long volleys and short bursts of automatic fire from the Peter and Paul Fortress.
>
> It was not Stalin that set in motion the Red Terror. Stalin was not creative even in his wickedness. He merely focused it to extraordinary sharpness and when he came to power intensified it to an incredible degree.
>
> What happened in 1930–37 was that the leading politicians of the all-powerful Party themselves began to be arrested. That, I think more than anything earlier baffled the imagination of one's contemporaries. In the '20s and early '30s, when officers, members of the bourgeoisie, professors and especially the clergy and members of religious orders, together with Russian, Ukrainian and White Russian peasants were being shot in thousands, that was all considered natural. Then the party started to 'devour' its own, and only the greyest, the most faceless, remained at the top, those who could hide and adapt.[2]

In this world, Orwellian from the start, according to Likhachev there existed (always semi-illegally) societies concerned with spiri-

---

[2] Ibid., p.134.

tual questions; these lived a life different from that of the authorities, and he was an active member of them. Young people with an interest in the philosophy of religion, for example, formed the 'St Sarafim of Sarov' society, and were almost without exception imprisoned with him. Now, the Russian intelligentsia clung with incredible tenacity to life, and to those values upon which its existence was based and which gave it meaning. According to another contemporary writer of a memoir, Nikolay Antsiferov, circles for mutual instruction were formed in the cells crammed with innocent victims of slander, and later in the gulag.[3] On the remote island of Solovki, however—where human life was not worth twopence, and where the guards could with impunity practise on the prisoners tortures learned from the medieval Inquisition—journals of high quality, even periodicals, were produced. Paradoxically, in the late 1920s subscriptions could be taken out for some of these.[4]

Caring nothing for the well-staffed network of informers, Russian intelligentsia who had plumbed the first depths of hell and returned began, as opportunity arose, to meet regularly[5]. Even the wave of arrests that followed the assassination of Kirov in December 1934 did not completely shatter society. Indeed, the intelligentsia tried to some extent to preserve at least the remains of its integrity even when the Kremlin assigned quotas—to be compulsorily achieved and, indeed over-achieved—for arrests and executions to every region and city[6]. This process applied to the gulag and other Soviet concentration camps too.

Despite all this, there existed around Dmitry Likhachev even in the harshest times a body of friends and pupils, the members or which attempted to acquire the fundamentals of independent thought. The authorities knew of this, and brought untold pressure to bear on his closest acquaintances to make them report on his every move; this went on for years. The scholar, always accessible to people and well-intentioned to a fault, knew a certain amount and guessed

---

[3] N. P Antsiferov, *Iz dum o bylo* [Thoughts of the Past], Moscow 1992, pp. 328–37 and 342–44.

[4] N. Stogov, *Tyuremnaya pechatka 1921–1935 gg* [Printing in Prisons in the Years 1921–1935], Pamyati, New York 1978, pp. 527–85.

[5] R. V. Ivanov-Razumik, *Tyurmi I ssilki* [Prisons and Banishments], New York 1953, pp. 220–23.

[6] *Vlasti I khudozhestvennaya intelligentsiya* [The Authorities and the Artistic Intelligensia], Moscow 1999, pp. 345–50.

much more in this regard, but he could not have imagined in what an invisible glasshouse he was actually living. In the early l990s, when he was hard at work on this memoir—a few chapters were already finished—a prominent Russian politician called him in to his office and laid before him his Secret Police dossier. Likhachev began to read it, and when he had finished the first volume pushed aside the thick bundle of papers. "How am I to go on living in the knowledge that the people I trusted most were those that actually betrayed me?" he asked with tears in his eyes. "If I read all these reports I'd have to re-write my memoirs."

But not a line did he alter. Those that knew him are aware that in old age what he did was motivated through and through by a sort of refined wisdom, a total, resolute honesty. He mulled over a thousand times every comparison, every hypothesis, every conclusion. The titles of his books became bywords: *Laughter as a View of the World, The Poetry of Gardens, There is Nothing I Can Prove*[7]. He shunned the enforced political parallels in Russian literature that had been regarded as the norm since Belinski. If he quoted examples from the seventeenth century he did not care whether there was a 'hidden agenda' in his arguments. Only the censorship of the atheist state did he gladly deceive with a sort of exaltation of an abstract Providence[8].

On another occasion Dmitry Likhachev, pondering the life expectancy of trees, was visibly thinking "God had left him here for a good long time too". "The beauty of old trees", he wrote, is beyond com-

---

[7] D. S. Likhachev, *Istoricheskaya poetika russkoy literatury. Smyekh kak mirovozreniye i drugiye raboty* [The Historical Poetics of Russian Literature. Laughter as a View of the World and Other Works], St Petersburg 1977. *Poeziya sadov. K semantike sadovo-parkovykh stylyey* [The Poetry of Gardens. Towards a Semantics of Park and Garden Style], Leningrad, 1982. *Byez dokatel'stv* [Without Proof], St Petersburg 1996.

[8] D. S. Likhachev, *Razvitiye russkoy literatury X–XVII vekov* [The Development of Russian Literature between the Tenth and Seventeenth Centuries], St Petersburg 1998, vol. 14. This is a slightly revised version of the 1973 edition. The following quotation amply typifies Likhachev's moral views: "I am making no changes to this book and I am not completing it. My work has to do with the practices that have developed in Russian cultural studies in the seventies and eighties of the twentieth century, and we must understand them in the context of their time (the first edition was published in 1973). But I have almost completely omitted my dispute with V. N. Lazarev ... as he is not alive, like other scholars who were involved in that dispute."

pare ... for the most part they fall only in storms"[9]. His fine verses in prose also reveal how much he was preoccupied with mortality. "When death is at the door the English speak of 'joining the majority'", he tells us[10]. Still, when, late last summer, he passed away, St Petersburg and that mighty country bade farewell to a minority of one: the last of the Russian intelligentsia.

Miklós Kun

---

[9] *Poeziya sadov*, p. 341.
[10] *Bez dokazatel'stv*, p. 72.

Foreword to the Russian Edition

At a man's birth his time begins to run. When he is a child it runs as a child—quick, or so it seems, over short distances and slow over long ones. In old age, time seems to stand still. It has lost its vital force. In old age the past, and especially childhood, is quite close at hand. By and large, of all the three ages of man—childhood and adolescence, maturity and old age—the longest and the most irksome is old age.

Our memories open a window on the past. Not only do they furnish us with information about it, but they also present us with our contemporaries' views of events and their experience of life. It is not unknown, of course, for the memory to play tricks on the writer (memoirs devoid of error are rare indeed) or for the writer to show the past in an excessively personal light. Nevertheless, in the great majority of cases memoirists do give an account of things which haven't and couldn't have found expression in any other form of historical source.

*

The principal shortcoming of many memoirs is the smugness of their writers. It is very difficult to avoid this fault: it speaks from between the lines. And if the writer makes every effort to be objective and begins to exaggerate his shortcomings, that too is unpleasant. We may call to mind the *Confessions* of Jean-Jacques Rousseau. They make for heavy reading.

Is there any point, therefore, in writing one's memoirs? Yes, to keep the events and atmosphere of bygone days alive and to preserve the memory of people who otherwise would be forgotten or only remembered in distorted official records. One's attitude to life is conditioned by both trifling and significant phenomena. Their effect on one is obvious and brooks no doubts, and the most important trifles are those that form part of the common man's make-up, his perception of the world and his attitude to it. More will be said in what follows of such trifles and accidents of life. Every little thing must be taken seriously when we consider what fate has in store for our children and for our young people in general. It is natural that in my autobiography of sorts that is now laid before the reader positive influences should predominate, as negative ones are more often forgotten. One clings more firmly to a gratifying recollection than to one of pain.

One's interests take shape for the most part in childhood. Tolstoy writes in *My Life*: "When exactly did I begin? When did I begin to live? ...Was I not living then, in those early years, when I was learning to look, to listen, to understand, to speak...Was that not when I acquired everything by which I now live, so much and so quickly that in the rest of my life I have not acquired a hundredth part of it?"

For this reason I shall mainly turn my attention in these reminiscences to the years of my childhood and adolescence. Observations on these years have a certain general significance, although the years that followed too, especially those connected with my work at the Pushkin House of the USSR Academy of Sciences, are important.

Foreword to the English Edition

My *Memoirs* are first and foremost about all those people I have known, including my acquaintances from all strata of educated Russian society.

I have spent most of my life in St Petersburg, but I served four and a half years in prison-camps, where among the 'politicals' there were tsarist officers, academics, representatives of all sorts of clergymen, ... regular and secular, village priests and bishops—persons of scientific merit, sailors, students, businessmen, etc.

Educated people, who were to be found at all levels of society, struggled bravely against the authorities' attempts to force them to obey them and their sterile ideology. This struggle often consisted of nothing more than continuing to devote themselves to their scientific work, to establishing their philosophic ideas, and to persisting in their religious endeavours or writing their poetry...

Little space is devoted here to the post-Stalin period, not because it is less interesting, but because it is better documented and, it seems to me, other people's conceptions of it are less distorted.

My feeling is that the vast majority of the people whose paths I crossed are no longer remembered, and so I feel obliged to leave at least some trace of them in my *Memoirs*.

The Russian educated classes withstood, in the main, the ordeal by terror that was directed in the first instance at them and at the peasantry. We often conceive of the educated as weak and lacking in resolve because they are accustomed to accept the investigatorial treatment of their 'dossiers', the press and Marxist ideology, which considered only the workers to be the 'dominant class'. In these dossiers, however, there has been preserved only such material as served the purpose of the investigators' versions of affairs; the versions established earlier by the 'organs of enquiry' were more reliable.

Lies and deceit were fundamental to the workings of Soviet power in Russia. That is why the memoirs of ordinary people are of such great significance nowadays, as the nation regains its senses.

I hope that my *Memoirs* will take their place on the bookshelves of those to whom Russia means something.

D. S. Likhachev

xvii

The House of Likhachev

According to archival data[1] the founder of the St Petersburg family of Likhachev, Pavel Petrovich Likhachev 'of merchant stock of Soligalich[2]', was received into the second guild of merchants of St Petersburg in 1794. He had settled in St Petersburg some time before and was obviously wealthy for he soon acquired large premises on Nevski Prospekt where he opened a workshop producing items of gold thread on two looms and a shop directly opposite the Bolshoy Gostiny Dvor[3]. The goods he produced included officers' uniform items of all sorts in silver and applique, braids, velvets, brocades, gold thread, gauze, tassels, etc. Three spinning looms are mentioned. The famous panorama of Nevski Prospekt by V. S. Sadovnikov shows the shop with a sign saying 'Likhachev' (signs of this sort with just a surname were the accepted thing for the very best shops). In six windows along the shop-front were displayed crossed sabres and a variety of goods in gold thread work and braid. There is documentary evidence that the Likhachev workshops were situated in the yard behind these premises.

As we learn from the *Petersburg Necropolis* of V. I. Santov[4], the Pavel Petrovich Likhachev that arrived from Soligalich was born on 15 January 1764 and buried in the Orthodox cemetery at Volkov in 1841.

At the age of seventy Pavel Petrovich, together with his family, acquired the title of hereditary and honoured citizens of St Petersburg. This title was established in 1832 by decree of the Emperor Nikolay I in order to strengthen the class of merchants and craftsmen. Although this title was 'hereditary', my ancestors confirmed their right to it in each subsequent reign by the award of the Order of Stanislav and the corresponding letters patent. The Stanislav was the only Order that could be conferred on commoners. Such letters patent were granted to my ancestors by Aleksandr II and Aleksandr III.

My great-great-grandfather Pavel Petrovich had received honoured citizenship, not merely because of his prominence among the businessmen of St Petersburg, but also for his continual charitable work. In particular, he presented three thousand infantry officer's sabres to the Second Army, which had been campaigning in Bulgaria. I learned of this donation as a child, although family tradition held that the sabres had been presented in 1812, during the Napoleonic War.

1

All the Likhachevs had big families. My grandfather on my father's side, Mikhail Mikhaylovich, owned a house next to the Aleksandr Svirski Monastery, which explains why one of the Likhachevs donated a considerable sum to the construction of the Aleksandr Svirski chapel in Petersburg.

Mikhail Mikhaylovich Likhachev, hereditary honoured citizen of Petersburg and member of the Craftsmen's Council, was the elder of the Vladimir Cathedral[5] and when I was a boy lived in a house on St. Vladimir's Square, overlooking the cathedral. Dostoyevski had a view of the same cathedral from a corner window of his last flat. In the year of Dostoyevski's death, however, Mikhail Mikhaylovich hadn't yet become the elder. That office was held by his future father-in-law Ivan Stepanovich Semenov. What happened was that my grandfather's first wife Praskovya Alekseyevna, my father's mother, died when my father (born in 1876) was about five and was buried in the expensive Novodevichi cemetery, something which Dostoyevski failed to achieve. Mikhail Mikhaylovich's second wife was Aleksandra Ivanovna, daughter of the elder Ivan Stepanovich Semenov. Ivan Stepanovich was one of the officiants at the funeral of Dostoyevski. His obsequies were sung by priests from the Vladimir Cathedral and all necessary preparations were made for the funeral in his house. One record of this remained, which we, the descendants of Mikhail Mikhaylovich Likhachev, found odd. This was a quotation by Igor Volgin in the manuscript of his book *Dostoyevski's Last Year*:

> Anna Grigorevna wished to give her husband a first-class funeral. And even so the obsequies cost her very little; most of the ecclesiastical requirements were free of charge. Furthermore, some of the money expended was returned to her, as is confirmed in the following most expressive letter: –
> 'I have the honour to send you 25 silver rubles which were given to me today for the pall and the candlesticks by a grave-digger whom I do not know, and at the same time to tell you the following: on the morning of the 29th the best pall and candlesticks were sent from the church to the flat of the late F. M. Dostoyevski free of charge on my instructions. Meanwhile the grave-digger, whom I do not know and who does not even live in the parish of the Vladimir Cathedral, took from you on his own initiative money for the hire of the church property; he had neither right nor cause to do so, and in fact I do not know how much he took. As the receipt of the money was unauthorised I return it to you, and beg to assure you of my deep respect for the memory of the departed.
> Ivan Stepanovich Semenov,
> Elder of the Vladimir Church.'[6]

My grandfather on my father's side, Mikhail Mikhaylovich Likhachev, wasn't a merchant in the strict sense of the word (the title 'hereditary honoured citizen' was usually conferred on merchants), but was a member of the St Petersburg Craftsmen's Council. But when I was a boy my grandfather's business no longer dealt with gold thread work.

In fact that side of the Likhachev business suffered badly during the reign of Aleksandr III, who simplified the Russian army uniform and reduced its cost. The Winter Palace archive preserves a petition from my great-grandfather, together with an unequivocal reply. The petition is of interest in itself:

> Petition of the hereditary honoured citizen of St Petersburg, the merchant Mikhail Likhachev of the First Guild, for the payment of a grant of 30,000 rubles for the support of trade in brocade, lace and gold thread work.

The Imperial Court minister replied:

> In view of the existence for almost a century of the firm, and the profit which the activity of grandfather, father and son have brought to the gold thread brocade business in Russia, Vorontsov-Dashkov finds it reasonable to recommend support. From the documents presented by Likhachev it may be seen that trade in brocades, laces and gold thread items has been carried on by the house of Likhachev since 1794, and that representatives of the house have on more than one occasion attained the highest awards and commendations from exhibition committees and customers for the high quality and refinement of their wares. The father of the petitioner, honoured citizen Ivan Likhachev, was granted the right, together with his sons, to name himself purveyor of gold embroidery and gold thread work to the Imperial Court, and to display the Imperial arms on his premises and his wares. For this reason the merit of the firm is quite significant and its remaining in business would be most desirable.[7]

On the document, however, is the annotation: Funds withheld.

This is the reason why my grandfather went into floor polishing. In the *All Petersburg* directories for the two decades prior to the Revolution this was given as his specialisation. I remember that when I was a child there was a polishers' hostel adjoining grandfather's flat and overlooking the yard. He kept a strict eye on his workers' behaviour, all the more so as the business was responsible for anything damaged, broken or simply spoiled where they were polishing the floors. I remember that the business polished the floors in the Admiralty and other court premises. Apprentices were recruited from good, sturdy peasant families and Grandfather looked to see whether a worker knew how to eat at table with peasant decency and whether he could cut bread in peasant fashion. He was reputed to be able to judge the moral qualities of his staff from such indicators. As I have already said, my grandfather was the elder of the Vladimir Cathedral, and in summer he took his holidays at Grafskaya (now Pesochnaya[8]) in a dacha next to the church, where the famous preacher of the day, the priest Filosof Ornatski, often preached.

Mikhail Mikhaylovich's first wife died of consumption, leaving him with four children—Anatoliy, Gavril, Yekaterina and Sergey. There is a photograph of her in a family group and a large portrait, copied from the photograph, in an oval frame, showing my father, as a child of about three, wearing a skirt (as little boys were dressed in those days), sitting with his mother.

In 1904 Mikhail Mikhaylovich moved from his house in Razyezhaya into a big flat in a new house opposite the Cathedral, where he was the elder. Here we used to visit him as a family on St Mikhail's Day, when he invited the Cathedral clergy round, held a service of thanksgiving and entertained them to lunch, as he also did on Christmas Day and Easter Day.

Grandfather was of a serious disposition. He didn't like the women of the house to sit idle. He himself only emerged for lunch from his huge study, where in his later years he lay on a couch by his desk. The picture is engraved on my memory: my grandfather is lying fully dressed on the couch. His slippers are at his side. His beard is combed into two parts like that of Aleksandr II (important people in the nineteenth century were supposed to wear beards and whiskers like the Tsar). From a drawer in his desk he'd take golden ten-ruble pieces and present us with them when we went into his study to take our leave before going home. There was a long crack in the ceiling above him, and when I went to see him I was always afraid that one day it would fall on him.

On the last occasion (it was during the war, in 1916 or 1917) he didn't give me any gold, and I, having grown accustomed to his gifts, didn't leave the study, thinking that he'd remember. Finally, Granddad said to me "Well, what are you standing there for?" and called me 'sonny' in a friendly tone. I said "What about the coin?" Granddad was embarrassed, gave a smile and handed me a gold five-ruble piece in-

4

stead of the usual ten; obviously, his affairs had taken a turn for the worse.

I am saying all this about my father's family, but to this day it remains something of a mystery to me. My great-great-grandfather Pavel Petrovich Likhachev "of merchant stock of Soligalich" had been literate but only just. His writing on documents that remain is very like pre-Petrine cursive handwriting. He must have been very practical in his professional life and it is not difficult to see why he was one of the richest craftsmen in St Petersburg.

His son Mikhail Mikhaylovich took after him, but also moved up the social ladder. His chest was covered with orders, medals and the badges of a number of charitable organisations. Grandfather's ponderous nature was often spoken of in the family, and until very recent times I imagined his family as thankless, suppressed by his despotism. At any show of domestic despotism on the part of my father, my mother would say "Mikhail Mikhaylovich" in condemnatory tone. At the same time, we were surrounded by gifts from Grandfather: a standard lamp with a very expensive onyx base, a green carpet with sunflowers for the big drawing-room, a fire-screen with sunflowers, my father's lovely bronze writing set, and four gold pocket watches for father and his three sons. And more besides. Grandfather didn't forget such details as my mother's liking for green—everything in his gifts that could be so was green. Such pointers show how attentive my grandfather was to our family, despite his apparent authoritarianism.

The Children of M. M. Likhachev

As I have said, Mikhail Mikhaylovich married twice. His first wife, Praskovya Alekseyevna, died of consumption, which in those days killed thousands in Petersburg, and mostly the very young. She died on the first or second of March. My father always dreaded those dates, and did in fact die himself on the first of March during the blockade (we registered his death on the second). We used to visit Grandmother's grave in the Novodevichi cemetery—the most expensive in Petersburg at the time. As a boy my father had planted a birch tree on her grave, and by the time I began to visit it with him the tree was old and its roots were disturbing the earth around the grave.

The little note in Praskovya Alekseyevna's hand, giving a list of her children, was kept in the family as a relic. Her eldest son Anatoli died young. Her daughter Yekaterina married the well-known builder Kudryavtsev, who was responsible for the grand-ducal tomb in the Peter and Paul Fortress. Yekaterina Mikhaylovna and her husband had a private house in the Viborg District, and had two sons—Mikhail and Aleksandr, whom for some reason my brother and I called 'uncle' Misha and 'uncle' Shura, although they were our cousins. Both were brought up by governesses, had a good command of French and German, and became electrical engineers on our father's advice. Aunt Katya's house was run in the grand manner. When her husband died she married his assistant, Sevodnik. He was considerably younger than her and, as they say, 'married her for her diamonds'. At all events he was greedy and unpleasant, and soon took a mistress, who acquired all Aunt Katya's jewellery later on during the blockade of Leningrad. Aunt Katya, to attract her husband, paid close attention to her appearance and had her face lifted (during one of these operations she went into a faint and was unconscious for a long time). Her sons came to unhappy ends. Uncle Shura was an assistant to Professor Hakkel, the 'Russian German', an expert on accumulators, which were important for submarines. During the blockade Shura said something incautious about his teacher in the dining room of the House of Scientists and was taken in several times for questioning. After one of these interrogations he returned home, went up to the attic and hanged himself. Then detectives came to the house to see his widow and prevailed on her not to kick up a fuss: the military authorities were very interested in uncle Shura's work. With uncle Misha things were quite different. He became an electrical engineer and moved to Pavlovsk, married the daughter of one Pandzerzhanski, a former captain in the Black Sea Fleet who had been shot before the war. In Pavlovsk he and his wife were captured by the Germans, and he owed his life to the fact that he spoke good literary German like a native. When uncle Misha's wife, by then a widow, applied to Smirnov, chief of the Leningrad *ispolkom*[9], to be allocated a flat, he rapped out without moving his vast bulk: "Take your request to where your father was shot". And she remained living in Baranovichi[10], where the Germans had relocated them.

I will move on to the only son of Mikhail Mikhaylovich and Praskovya Alekseyevna: uncle Gavril. I never saw him. All that has survived of him is a long, instructive letter addressed to Gavril by my father, in which he wrote that he was prepared to offer him employment but required him to promise to perform his duties to the full and not to give up the job as he had done previously. The fact is that Gavril had a restless spirit. Several times he went off to live in a monastery and went on numerous pilgrimages to places as far away as Athos in search of truth. He was incapable of sitting at a desk and carrying out clerical duties in an organised fashion and would vanish on spiritual quests for years on end. Before the Second World War we received news that he had married, was living in Rostov-on-Don, and that his wife sold newspapers in a kiosk. What he himself was doing we didn't know and we never heard of him again. Obviously, he became neither businessman nor craftsman.

My father had a profound respect for his stepmother, but left home in his teens, began to earn his living by giving lessons and attended technical high school, intending to become an engineer. My grandfather, however, wanted him to go to commercial high school and follow him in the business, which wouldn't have qualified him for admission to the Institute.

Nevertheless, despite a difficult home life, Aleksandra Ivanovna was full of a sense of her personal worth, kept up her appearance and didn't humble herself to her husband, although she obeyed him in everything. She loved the children of his first marriage and called them by their pet names—Serozhenka and Katyusha. Nearest of all to her was her very plain daughter, Vera, a remarkable creature of uncommon meekness, exceptional goodness and the most profound faith. I can speak of her only in superlatives. Her voice was unusually beautiful, and her Petersburg accent, as was the case with all grandfather's family, was beyond reproach. She used to call me Mityusha, and this word was music to my ears. She was entirely devoted to her mother, cared for her selflessly and never complained of her lot. Meanwhile, Aleksandra Ivanovna began to have trouble with her legs because of her sedentary lifestyle. She had one leg amputated, and when, after my grandfather's death, she and Vera moved out of the centre of the city to a second-floor flat to reduce expenses, the other leg was removed also. Aleksandra Ivanovna died soon afterwards, and Vera began helping the poor people of the neighbourhood and asking nothing in return. Many local inhabitants knew her and considered her a saint. Uncle Vasya gave her a little money out of his paltry salary, as did her brother and my father, her half-brother. She had let her largest room to a poor Jewish family with numerous children that had been living in a freezing little room with a door opening directly into the street. Naturally, she charged them no rent. However much the stove was stoked one's feet were cold in that barn of a place. In winter she usually sat with her legs on a high bed. When the blockade began she was one of the first to die of starvation. We were unable to reach her, and only learned of her death in the spring of 1942. Where she is buried God only knows.

My other aunt on my father's side—Manya—was very pretty. I remember my parents arguing over which was the prettier—aunt Manya or my mother's sister Lyuba. These arguments were, of course, less than serious. Aunt Manya, however, remained unmarried; my grandfather kept a very stern eye on his daughters. The future priest-in-charge of the church at Shuvalovsk asked for Manya's hand, but she said "Really, what sort of priest's wife would I be?" and refused him. In order to have a modicum of independence she went off and studied dentistry and for a while had a successful practice in a clinic somewhere near the Liteyny bridge, where she had a dental surgery. And then she moved to the china factory near Novgorod, and was evacuated with it during the war. She became so friendly with the staff and the workers that they came to her for advice on everything, even domestic matters. The only thing that caused her distress on return from evacuation was the distance to church. She had been a parishioner of the Nikolodvorishchenski Cathedral in Novgorod until the priest there, who was very popular with his parishioners, was moved to another parish and the eleventh century church itself was made into a planetarium. Once I went to visit her in the hamlet of Proletarski. She was living in poverty, quite near the Moscow-Leningrad road, in a room which she tried to keep tidy, and while I was there—it was my only visit—she asked me anxiously "I've got this room nice, haven't I?" She copied out the *Meditsinskaya gazeta* [Medical Journal] 'so as to keep in touch', and various books. As she lived there in retirement she was called on by her numerous admirers, and she exhorted them all to do good and taught them to believe in God. "Well, if our doctor believes, then certainly God exists..." She was buried in the fifties in the Proletarski cemetery. Before she died she came to Leningrad and was brought up to see us in Baskov Lane. I took a photograph of her, but it came out badly.

Then there was Aunt Nastya—also pretty and unmarried, like aunt Manya. She had been through higher education, attending a teacher training institute (I don't know which one). She had won gold medals and was completely devoted to teaching. She never used to come to our house, but when we paid family visits to Granddad she'd take me to her room and we'd paint or play table games. She died young, of consumption. The development of the disease was, I think, hastened by an inner dissatisfaction, and the oppressive conditions engendered in the family by my grandfather's ponderous 'mercantile' disposition.

And now to my favourite Uncle Vasya—son of Aleksandra Ivanovna. In the old photographs, from before the Revolution, he looks a real dandy: upturned moustaches, overcoat elegantly flared in the style of the time. There are photographs of him with a walking-stick. And if I added to this that he loved going to the cinema with his wife and daughter, was fascinated by Gipsy singing and especially Varya Pannina, whose records he collected, then one could put a full stop: the portrait is complete. But in fact this exterior was only a shell, and, most probably, came from his quite orderly and middle-class wife. In actual fact uncle Vasya, deep down, was a very religious man. His favourite saint was Serafim of Sarov and his photographs of the Sarov wilderness, which he visited alone, have survived. He collected books about Serafim and owned a complete, unexpurgated copy of Motovilov's book on him. He was also enthralled by the miraculous appearance of an icon of the Mighty Mother of God, which was found in the village of Kolomensk on the very day that Nikolay II abdicated.

At that time he, his wife and daughter Natasha lived in the Petrograd District. He worked in the State Bank and took part in the strike by Bank staff in protest against the disruption of the Constituent Assembly by the Bolsheviks. I seem to remember that the strike went on and on—lasted several months. Uncle Vasya's mother-in-law sold all her most vital belongings for a song at the Sytny market in order to live. He himself was in despair, but he could not, as did many, desert the common cause and find work elsewhere. The family was literally starving, and just at the time when the general famine was beginning after the establishment of Soviet power in 1918.

He always talked to me, as a student, about topics of an ideological nature. He wasn't content with simple answers, but sometimes argued. He thought, reflected, dreamed. He wasn't like everyone else. In all things he was himself. On one occasion he said to me for some reason: "I love big ships and the sound of the cannon being fired from the Peter and Paul Fortress". In those days the cannon was used as a flood warning—one shot for every foot above normal—and also

9

roared at the 'Admiral's Hour'—precisely at twelve noon. The popular saying was that the Admiral in the Admiralty drank a glass of rum at the sound of the cannon.

My beloved seeker after truth died a terrible death during the blockade. He wasn't being given anything at all to eat at home, and came to us at the start of the blockade to ask for a little bread, and brought expensive dolls for the children. One could buy dolls in those days, but bread was completely unobtainable. He went to Uncle Shura and fell on his knees in the hall, begging him to give him a little bread. The miserly Shura gave him nothing.

This wasn't the only instance during the blockade of relatives refusing to feed the head of the family and blaming him for not having provided for himself in good time, for not going to work and for having no cards or passes for the canteen.

I have no idea which mass grave Uncle Vasya is buried in. After the blockade I tried to avoid meeting his daughter, not because I thought that she was wicked. On the contrary, one thing that she did in the '30s filled me with respect for her. The process had been begun to recruit her as a secret collaborator and so she was invited in 'for little chats'. She was threatened, cajoled and promised things—all in accordance with instructions. But on one occasion she appeared with her mother and refused to sign the document about not divulging what had been said. The investigator who had summoned her was furious but she went on to inform him that in future she would not talk to him without her mother being present. He finally gave up and did not summon her again. It took courage to keep to her principles like that.

My father, Sergey Mikhaylovich, left home and supported himself by tutoring, put himself through high school and went to the Institute of Electrical Engineering, which had only just opened in the centre of the city. He qualified as an engineer and worked for the Principal Directorate of Posts and Telegraphs. He was good-looking, energetic, very well-dressed, was a fine organiser and was reputed to be an outstanding dancer. It was at a dance at the Shuvalov yacht club that he met my mother. The two of them won a prize at some ball or other, and my father took to walking up and down beneath her windows every day and finally proposed.

My mother was from a merchant background. On her father's side she was a Konyayev. On her mother's side she was descended from the Pospeyev family, which owned an Old Believers' chapel[11] near the Raskolnichi bridge and the Volkov cemetery; it was frequented by Old Believers of the Fedoseyev sect. The Pospeyev traditions were very strong in our family too. In accordance with their ways we never had a dog in the flat, but on the other hand we all liked birds. The family told the tale of how my grandfather Pospeyev had gone to the Paris Exhibition, where he had caused a stir with his fine Russian troykas. Finally both Pospeyevs and Konyayevs became dissenters and attended the dissenting church where the Museum of the Arctic and Antarctic now stands.

My mother's father Semon Filippovich Konyayev was one of the best billiard players in Petersburg, a cheerful, kindly man, a singer and talker, adventurous in everything, easy-going and charming. He was never hard on anyone, and if he lost everything—he'd worry and be ashamed, and then without fail win it back. His flat was never without visitors and there was nearly always a resident guest. He liked Nekrasov, Nikitin and Koltsov[12], and was a fine singer of Russian folksongs and romantic ballads. My grandmother, who was reserved in the Old Believer way, loved him dearly and forgave him all his losses.

My mother and father were typical Petersburg people. The circles in which they moved played a part in this, their friends at dacha resorts in Finland, their liking for the Mariinski theatre, near which we were always renting flats. In order to reduce expenditure, every spring when we went to a dacha we gave up the lease on the flat in town. Workmen took the furniture into store, and in autumn we rented a new five-room flat, of necessity near the Mariinski, where my parents had, through the good offices of members of the orchestra that they knew and Mariya Mariusovna Petipa, a box on the third circle and season tickets for the ballet.

My Childhood

My earliest childhood recollections go back to the time when I was just beginning to talk. I remember a pigeon landing on the window-sill of my father's study. I ran to inform my parents of this momentous event and just could not explain to them—so I called them into the study. Another memory. We were standing in the kitchen garden at Kuokkala and father had to go to his office in St Petersburg. But I couldn't understand that, and asked him "Are you going shopping?" (Father was always bringing things back from town), but the word 'shopping' was beyond my powers to pronounce, and came out as 'shocking'. I was conscious of my mistake; I had so wanted to say it correctly! An even earlier recollection. We were still living on the Angliiski Prospekt (now renamed Prospekt Maklina). My brother and I were watching the magic lantern: a spectacle to gladden the heart. What bright colours! And one picture I liked in particular: children building a Father Christmas snowman. He couldn't talk either. This thought came into my mind and I loved him, Father Christmas—he was mine, all mine! Only I couldn't hug him as I did my beloved velvety, dumb Teddy, Berchik. We read Nekrasov's *General Toptygin* and nanny made a greatcoat for Berchik so that 'General' Berchik 'brought up' my daughters too during the siege. After the war they made a coat for one of their dolls out of the red lining from the 'general's' greatcoat. No longer ranked as a general but silent and affectionate as ever, he has since 'brought up' my grand-daughter.

When I was two or three I was given a little German book with brightly coloured pictures. It contained the story of 'Lucky Hans'. One of the illustrations was of a garden, an orchard with big red apples and a clear blue sky. It was so delightful to look at that picture in winter and to dream of summer. And another memory: when the first snow fell in the night my room was lit up by the light reflected off the snow in the road below (we lived on the second floor). The shadows of passers-by moved over the illuminated ceiling, from which I knew that winter had arrived with all its delights. Any change makes life so happy; time passes and you wish it to go faster. Smells, too, were another source of delight. One smell I love even to this day—that of laurel warmed by the sun, and box-trees. It reminds me of summer in the Crimea, of the meadow which everyone called *Batareyka* because during the Crimean War a Russian battery was positioned there so as to prevent the Anglo-French forces landing at Alupka. And that war seemed so recent and close at hand, as if it had taken place a matter of days instead of fifty years earlier!

One of the happiest memories in my life is of Mama lying on the couch. I work my way in between her and the cushions and lie down too, and together we sing songs. It was before I even went to primary school.

Children, it is time for school,
Long ago we heard cockcrow.
Dress now quickly, that's the rule!
Bright the sun at your window.

Man and beast and bird, you see,
To their tasks are going all.
For its nectar flies the bee,
Home the ants their burdens haul.

Bright the meadow, gay the lea;
Woken wood is full of sound;
Woodpecker drums on the tree,
Sings the oriole her round.

Fishermen now cast their nets;
Mowers sing and scythe the grass...
God does not love idleness —
Say your prayers, then to your class!

Russian children no longer sing this song, presumably because of the final sentence... But every child used to know it thanks to Ushinski's anthology *Rodnaya rech* [Our Native Speech].

And here is another song that we used to sing:

Green the grass
And bright the sun,
To our porch
The swallows come.
Bright the sun
And sweet the spring...
Soon shall warble
From the road!
Grain I'll scatter
And you'll sing,
Songs from distant
Lands you'll bring.

I remember clearly that I sang the word 'warble' as 'wobble' and thought that someone was ordering someone off the road. It was only

13

when I was on Solovki, reminiscing on my childhood, that I realised the true meaning of the line!

Such was life. Every year in autumn we took a flat somewhere near the Mariinski theatre where my parents always had two season tickets for the ballet. It was difficult to obtain season tickets, but our friends the Gulyayevs helped us. The head of the Gulyayev family played the double bass in the theatre orchestra and was therefore able to obtain boxes as well as season tickets. I began going to the ballet at the age of fourteen. The first performance that I attended was the *Nutcracker*, and what impressed me most was the snow falling onto the stage, and I liked the Christmas tree. Later on I also went to evening performances with the grown-ups. And I had my own seat in the theatre: our box, which we shared for the season with the Gulyayevs, was on the third circle next to the balcony. At that time the balcony seats had iron arm-rests, upholstered with velvet. Between our box and the first balcony seat there was a little wedge-shaped seat where a child could sit—and that was my place. I remember the ballets vividly. Rows of ladies waving fans in an attempt to make the diamonds on their deep *décolletages* glitter. At gala performances the lights were only dimmed, and auditorium and stage were both lit as one. I remember how 'short-legs' Kshesinskaya would fly onto the stage in diamonds which glittered in time to the dance. What a magnificent, splendid sight that was! My parents admired Spesivtseva most of all but were dismissive of Lyukom.

Since then the ballet music of Pugni and Minkus, Tchaikovsky and Glazunov has never failed to raise my spirits. *Don Quixote, Sleeping Beauty* and *Swan Lake, La Bayadere* and *The Corsair* are inseparable in my consciousness from the blue auditorium of the Mariinski; even to this day I only have to walk through the door to experience sensations of spiritual uplift and cheerfulness. In 1914 V. Krymov, a famous balletomane of the day, wrote in his sketch *At the Ballet*:

> The ballet has maintained its traditions until the present. Tradition, both on stage and in the auditorium. Is P. P. Durnovo not a tradition, sitting in one and the same seat on the right side of the stalls for thirty-seven years? Is the 'first ballet season-ticket' not a tradition, by which all the boxes of the *belle etage* are known to all by name, and people in the first and second rows of the stalls all nod to one another and address each other by name?
>
> 'The Yacht-club box', 'the Uhlans' box', 'the Polovtsevys' box', 'Kshesinskaya's box'.

Mikhail Mikhailovich Likhachev. End nineteenth century

Vera Semenova Likhacheva, mother of D. S. Likhachev. 1910

Sergei Mikhailovich Likhachev, father of D. S. Likhachev. 1911

Mariya Nikolayevna Konyayeva, D. S. Likhachev's maternal grandmother

Semen Filippovich Konyayev, D. S. Likhachev's maternal grandfather

D. S. Likhachev's parents. 1900

Family photograph. Front row: Likhachev's grandmother,
author (nicknamed Mitya), his mother;
standing: his cousins A. C. Konyayeva and N. S. Konyayev,
and his elder brother Misha. 1912

Author with his mother and brother. 1911

'Why aren't the Likhachevs here?' 'Where's Bakerina? There's somebody else in her box...'

'Ah, there's Kshesinskaya in her box... hasn't been seen for eighteen months—been in mourning...'

It was considered the thing not to miss a single performance of *Don Quixote*, but at the same time not to arrive for the prologue, in which Don Quixote prepares for his campaign—those who came for that were either new to the ballet or were bringing children to a matinee. To miss the prologue was just as cultured as to stroll in the balcony corridors during an entr'acte without going up to the big foyer where sentries stood motionless outside the royal box whether royalty was there or not (the royal family itself always sat on the right, as seen from the stage, in one of the boxes behind light blue door-curtains).

Everything at home was arranged to fit around the ballet, my parents' principal delight. But when we went to the ballet we had to play at being rich. It wasn't cheap, and we saved on everything. First, we took a flat in the cheap Petersburg District, thus saving the cost of a fare; when the Neva was covered with firm ice we either walked or crossed it by sledge, as this would be several kopecks cheaper than riding all the way from the theatre. In winter, ladies had to wear cloaks when they went to the theatre: brown fox trimmed with blue velvet. Ladies wore sleeveless cloaks so as not to crush their dresses and covered their heads with light knitted hoods (I remember theses distinctly to this day). And one day, as my parents were returning by way of a narrow path across the Neva, my mother, bringing up the rear, fell over and couldn't get up—her arms were trapped in her cloak. She called to father, but he couldn't hear her because of the wind. Fortunately someone was walking behind them and he helped her to her feet. The mishap was discussed at length at home and it was decided that in future we would take flats nearer to the theatre for the winter season. I remember too that my family had a diamond choker made from precious stones so as not to appear financially embarrassed at the ballet. There was a shop (possibly Faberge's) in the Bolshoi Gostiny Dvor that took orders for such work. The shop-assistant brought out a catalogue of chokers and put it on the counter and my parents spent a long time choosing a design which could incorporate a large ruby from a ring given to my father by the Tsar at Alupka as its central motif. The ballet required careful attention, as everyone could see us and many knew us, but didn't suspect that my parents had to walk home...

Once a year we were taken on a trip to Pavlovsk 'to rustle the leaves with our feet', once a year a visit to the Little House of Peter the Great before the start of school (such was the Petersburg custom), trips on the steamers of the Finland Steamship Company, cups of soup and *pirozhki* (pies) as we waited for the train at the elegant Finland Station, meeting Glazunov in the hall of the Dvoryanskoye Sobraniye[13] (now the Filarmoniya Hall) and Meyerhold[14] on the Finland Railway train—these were sufficient to blur the dividing line between the city and art...

In the evening at home we played our favourite numbers game *Lotto* and draughts; father would discuss what he had been reading in bed the previous evening—the works of Leskov, the historical novels of Vsevolod Solovev, the novels of Mamin-Sibiryak[15]. All these were in widely available cheap editions—supplements to *Niva*[16].

The Disappearance of Katerinushka

My nurse was called Katerinushka.

All that is left of her is a photograph of her with my grandmother Mariya Nikolayevna Konyayeva. It's a poor photograph, but it's typical. Both of them are weeping with laughter. Granny's merely laughing, but Katerinushka's got her eyes shut and it's obvious that she can't say a word for laughing. I know why they were both laughing, but I shan't say... There's no need!

Who snapped them during this fit of uncontrollable laughter I don't know. The photograph is an amateur effort and has been in the family a very long time. Katerinushka was my mother's nurse, then my brothers' and we wanted her to help us with our offspring—Verochka and Milochka, but it wasn't to be.

I remember that when I was about six and we lived in Tarasovaya Street she used to sleep in my room, and I discovered to my surprise that women had legs. They wore such long skirts that only their shoes were visible. But in the mornings, when Katerinushka was getting up, I could see, under the screen, two feet in thick stockings of different colours (that didn't matter, because under her skirt they were invisible). I looked at these odd stockings and was amazed.

Katerinushka was like a relation both to our family and to that of my maternal grandmother. If the least thing were needed, she appeared in the house; if someone was seriously ill and needed nursing, if a child was expected and preparations had to be made for its entry into the world—swaddling clothes to be made, nappies, a little horse-hair mattress (for coolness); if a girl was getting married and her trousseau had to be got ready—on all such occasions Katerinushka would appear with her little wooden trunk and settle in, take over all the work, tell stories, talk, joke, sing the old songs with the family in the twilight, reminisce about the old days.

It was never boring with her in the house. Even when someone had died she had a way of bringing quietness, decorum, order, a calm grief into the house. And on good days she'd take part in family games, with adults and children; at *Lotto* (played with tiny barrels) she'd give the numbers comical names as she called them out, she'd talk in old sayings and proverbs (which are not one and the same—these days no one knows any sayings as folklorists haven't collected them, and they were often based on what might be termed abstruse but perceptive and wholesome nonsense.

In addition to our family, grandmother's family and those of her daughters (my aunts) there were other families too for whom Katerinushka was a relation, and when she visited them she was never idle, but liked to keep herself busy. She was of a cheerful disposition and had the knack of making everyone else feel happy and relaxed.

She was a light person. Light in every sense of the word, including on her feet. Katerinushka would go off to the bath-house, leaving her little chest behind and would not be seen again. But no one worried about her very much, as they all knew her ways—she'd be back. My mother would ask my grandmother: "Where's Katerinushka?" and Granny would answer: "She's disappeared." That was how her unexpected departures were described. A month later, a year later, Katerinushka would reappear just as suddenly as she'd disappeared. "Where've you been?" "Round at Marya Ivanovna's! I met her in the bath-house, and her daughter was getting married, and I was invited to see to her trousseau!" "And where does Marya Ivanovna live?" "Over in Shlyushina! I've come to see you. The wedding was three days ago. "

She remembered various amusing stories about my mother. Once they had gone to the circus together. It was the first time that Katerinushka had taken mother, then a little girl, to the circus, and she got so excited that she grabbed hold of Katerinushka's hat and pulled it off her head, veil and all...

How should I define the profession of that dear, ever-toiling woman, who brought people nothing but good (happiness came into the family with her)? I think I'd have to call her a domestic dress-maker. This profession has completely disappeared nowadays, but it was once widespread. A domestic dressmaker would take up residence in a house and work for a number of years: she'd re-cut garments, re-make them, patch them, make underwear, make the master's jackets—her hands were capable of anything. Such a domestic dressmaker would appear in a house and all the old clothes would begin to be transformed and the whole family would discuss what was to be re-made and how, what to throw away, what to give to the Tatar woman (Tatar rag-and-bone men went about from yard to yard buying up all manner of unwanted items for coppers).

Katerinushka died as she had lived: without causing anyone any trouble. She disappeared in 1941, a one-eyed old woman. She'd heard that the Germans were approaching her beloved Ust'-Izhora, left my aunt Lyuba's in Gogol Street where she was living, and just set off for her daughter's in Ust'-Izhora. She never arrived and must have been killed on the way, as the Germans were by then close to the Neva. All her life it had been her custom to help those who needed her, and Ust'-Izhora was never the same again... Katerinushka had disappeared for the last time.

The Petersburg of my Childhood

Petersburg-Leningrad is a city of unique and tragic beauty. If one doesn't understand that, one can't love it. The Peter and Paul Fortress is a symbol of tragedy, the Winter Palace on the other bank, of captive beauty.

Petersburg and Leningrad are quite different cities. Not, of course, in all respects. Leningrad shows through in Petersburg, and there is a gleam of Petersburg in Leningrad in its architecture. But the similarities merely emphasise the differences.

My first childhood impression was of barges, barges and more barges. They filled the Neva, the 'sleeves' of the Neva and the canals, laden with firewood and bricks. Dockers unloaded them with barrows. Quickly, quickly they ran along strips of iron, trundled down to the dockside. In many places on the canals gaps were made in the railings, or they were even removed. Bricks were taken away at once, but firewood was left lying in piles on the banks, where it was loaded onto carts and taken round the houses. At various points in the city, on the canals and the tributaries of the Neva, there were firewood exchanges; here one could buy firewood when it was needed, at all times of the year, and especially in autumn. Birch wood, which burns with great heat, was much in demand. On the Lebyazha dike, by the Summer Garden, big ships used to moor with earthenware—pots, plates and jugs—and sometimes they also had toys; earthenware penny whistles were particularly popular. Sometimes there were wooden toys for sale, transported in from the Onega region on ships and barges that moved imperceptibly.

Barges, skiffs, schooners and tugs plied the Neva but the barges had to be poled along the canals. It was interesting to watch two healthy young men in birch-bark sandals (these gave a better grip than boots, and were, of course, cheaper) going along the wide sides of a barge from bow to stern, leaning a shoulder on a pole with a short cross-piece for a rest, moving the entire mass of a barge laden with firewood or bricks, and then going from stern to bow, trailing the pole behind them on the water. Then they'd repeat their walk from bow to stern.

The architecture was obscured and the rivers and canals hidden from view. Facades were invisible behind shop-signs. Public buildings were usually dark red in colour. The glass in their windows gleamed from the red walls of their courtyards; the windows were well cleaned, and many were the windows and shop-fronts that were smashed during the siege of Leningrad. The Winter Palace was dark red, as were the buildings of the General Staff and the Guards Staff. The Senate and the Synod were red. Hundreds of other houses were red—barracks, warehouses and various office buildings. The walls of the curious Litovski transit prison were red as were those of the palace. Only the Admiralty broke ranks and preserved its independence with its white and yellow walls. The remaining houses were well painted, but in dark shades. The tram wires were afraid of infringing property rights; they weren't attached to the walls of houses, as they are today, but hung from tram posts which lined the streets. And what streets! Nevski Prospekt was invisible for tram posts and shop-signs. Some of the shop-signs were beautiful; they climbed the storeys, as high as the third, everywhere in the centre and on the Liteyny and Vladimirski Prospekts. Shop signs were absent only from the squares, and as a result they seemed even vaster and emptier. But in the little streets bakers' golden *krendeli*[17], golden bulls' heads, gigantic *pince-nez* and so on overhung the pavements. Occasionally there were enormous shop signs shaped like a pair of boots or scissors. The pavements were enclosed by covered entrances: canopies supported on metal columns and extending to the outside edge of the pavement. The pavements were frequently edged by an irregular line of wooden posts although outside many old buildings these posts were replaced by ancient cannon. These posts and cannon protected pedestrians against the intrusion of cabs and carts. But all this impaired the view of the street, as did the paraffin street-lamps, all of the same pattern, with a cross-bar against which the lamp-lighters placed their ladders to light, extinguish, light and extinguish again, adjust and clean them.

And how beautiful the buildings were at street level! The front doors were kept spotless and polished. They had fine shiny brass handles (these were removed in Leningrad in the 1920s in the course of the collection of brass for the Volkhovstroy[18]). Windows were always kept spotless, and pavements swept and decorated with little green tubs or buckets placed under downpipes to catch the rainwater which servants in white aprons would then pour out onto the road. Sometimes a hall porter in his blue uniform with gold braid could be seen emerging from a front door for a breath of fresh air. The gleaming shop fronts fascinated everyone, especially the children who would drag their mothers over to the toy-shop windows to gaze at the tin soldiers and model train sets. Chemists' shop windows were decorated with glass jars full of coloured liquids—green, blue, yellow and red—and, in the evening, when lamps were lit behind them, they could be seen from a long way away. All along the sunny side of Nevski Prospekt ('sunny side' was almost an official name for the smart houses on the Nevski) there was a particularly large number of expensive shops. I remember the windows of Teta with their imitation diamonds. In the middle of the window was a stand with little lamps that rotated ceaselessly; the 'diamonds' sparkled with every colour of the rainbow.

Nowadays there is asphalt, but then the pavements were of limestone and the roadway was cobbled. Limestone slabs were hard to come by, but looked beautiful. Even more beautiful were the huge granite plinths on the Nevski. Those on the Annichkov bridge are still there, though a lot have been removed. In the suburbs the pavements were sometimes boarded. Outside the city, in the country, ditches would be hidden under these boarded pavements, and if the boards wore out one could easily fall into a ditch and get a ducking; in Petersburg, however, even in the suburbs, pavements weren't laid over ditches. The roadways were for the most part cobbled, and had to be maintained by peasants working at night, digging up and replacing the worn-out cobbles. A foundation had to be laid with sand and all the cobbles had to be pounded into it with heavy hammers. The roadmen used to work in a sitting position, and they wrapped their legs and left hand in rags to prevent their fingers and legs from being hit by the hammer. Watching these workers could not but arouse feelings of pity. How well they fitted one cobble to the next, flat side up. This was precision work, the work of artists in their field. The cobbled roads in Petersburg were especially fine, made of granite pebbles of various colours. I liked the cobbles most of all after rain or a flood. A lot has been written about the wooden roadways, and they too had their beauty and convenience. In the flood of 1924, however, they were responsible for many deaths: they floated away and carried pedestrians with them.

The colour of the trams and horse-drawn trams is easily forgotten. There was no colour photography in those days, and they don't figure all that often in pictures: see if you can find one! The horse-drawn trams were quite a gloomy colour, dark blue-grey with grey trimmings. But the electric trams greatly enlivened the city; they were painted red and yellow, and the paint was always bright and fresh.

At first the trams were single vehicles, without 'tails', and could be controlled from either end. When they reached the last stop the conductor used to get off the front platform, take down from outside a big white disc which indicated the front, take it to the rear and re-attach it. During the First World War 'tails', supplementary cars, became necessary because the population had increased. Horse-drawn trams were modified; their top decks were removed, they were painted red and yellow and attached to motorised trams with chains. The white discs that indicated which was the front vanished as well; you could see which was the front, and that was that. Riding in the 'tails', however, was unpleasant as the speed made them rock from side to side and the badly fitting windows rattled terribly.

The trams, incidentally, had open platforms on which it was a pleasure to ride in summer. But in all the years of the war and the Revolution passengers struggled to get into the cars and stood on the steps, holding on to the handrails. Some hung onto the 'sausage'—the thick cable carrying electricity to the second car—and were injured if they smashed into the poles supporting the wires.

The sounds of Petersburg! Naturally, the first thing one recalls is the sound of hooves on the cobbled roads. Even Pushkin wrote of the thundering of the Bronze Horseman 'along the quivering roadway'. But the clip-clop of the hooves of cab-horses was coquettishly affectionate. Little boys playing 'ride-a-cock-horse' (one of the most popular children's games) were experts at imitating this sound by clicking their tongues. Modern film-makers use the sound, but they just don't understand that the sounds are different in wet and dry weather. I remember our returning from the dacha at Kuokkala in autumn, and the square outside the Finland Station being full of that 'wet clip-clop'—the sound in the rain. And then the soft, scarcely audible sound of wheels running on the wooden roads and the muffled, 'artificial' hoofbeat once we'd crossed the Liteyny bridge. And again, the way the drivers shouted at people crossing the street: 'Oi!' Seldom did they shout 'Look out'; that was only when some dare-devil showed off by racing the cab. Draymen used to shake the ends of the reins and threaten the horses (to urge them on) with a kind of sucking sound. News-vendors used to shout out the name of whichever newspaper they were selling and, during the First World War, giving a bit of the latest news. Cries inviting one to buy goods (pies! apples! cigarettes!) only appeared during the NEP[19].

Steamers hooted on the Neva, but in Petersburg there were none of the loud-hailer calls characteristic of the Volga; these were obviously prohibited. The little steamers of the Finland Steamship Line plied the Fontanka with their engines uncovered.

One of the most typical street sounds of Petersburg before the First World War was the sound made by the tram bells and we learned to distinguish the four types. The first was before the tram moved off. At stops the conductor (before the war, always a man in uniform) would get off the platform at the rear, let everyone get on and get back on himself last of all; when he was on the step he'd pull on a cord which ran from the entrance to a bell near the driver. When he heard this signal the driver would move off. This cord ran the length of the tram along a metal bar to which were attached leather loops for standing passengers to hold onto. The conductor could ring to the driver from anywhere in the tram. That was the second type of ring. The driver warned careless pedestrians by means of another bell, operated by a pedal. Sometimes the driver would ring this persistently, and this sound was often heard in streets where trams ran. Later electric bells appeared. For a long time pedal-operated bells were in service along with hand-operated electric ones. The conductor's chest was adorned with rolls of tickets in various colours, which were sold for various 'stages' of the route. In addition there were white transfer tickets for changing to another line at certain designated places along the route. All these routes are shown in old guides to Petersburg. From time to time, when a section of the journey had been completed and new tickets had to be bought, the conductor shouted along the tram 'Yellow ticket stage!' or 'Red ticket stage!' The intonation of these announcements has remained with me all my life; I used to go to school by tram.

The sound of military bands was very often heard in the street. Sometimes, on a festival or a Sunday, a regiment would be on church parade; sometimes it would be the funeral of a general; the Preobrazhenski or Semenov regiments would march every day to mount guard at the Winter Palace. All the small boys would run to the sound of the band; there was a great demand for music. It was particularly interesting when soldiers detailed for a funeral were returning from the cemetery: then they were supposed to play cheerful music. They always played cheerful marches at church parades except, of course, during Lent. There were also 'quiet sounds': the jangling of soldiers' spurs, which were often silver-plated. On the Nevski and in the adjoining streets vendors sold children's balloons inflated with light gas; they were red, green, blue and yellow, and the largest were white with pictures of cockerels painted on them. There was always a stir around these stalls. The bunches of brightly coloured balloons hovering in the air always marked the spot where the vendors were.

In the mornings, from the outskirts of the city, and especially the Viborg District, the sound of factory hooters could be heard, each producing its own distinctive sound. Few people had their own alarm clocks and everyone knew that three shrill blasts meant that it was time to go to work.

Then the first cinemas began to appear. Nobody remembers now that there used to be a cinema called 'Mirage' opposite our house on Ofitserskaya Street. On Saturdays, however, we used to go as a family

23

to the 'Soleil' cinema on the Nevski Prospekt. Apart from the main film (I remember *Napoleon's Hundred Days* and *The Loss of the Titanic*, a documentary film in which the cameraman had been filming all the life of the liner and continued to film the disaster while the light lasted, and then filmed even in the lifeboat), there had to be a comedy and a travelogue. The last was often hand-coloured—every frame, and without fail in bright colours: red and green for foliage, blue for the sky. One day we were in either the 'Parisian' or the 'Piccadilli' on Nevski Prospect—I forget which—and were impressed to see the commissionaires in uniform and actually wearing wigs.

My parents often took me with them to the Mariinski theatre. They had two season tickets for the ballet in a box in the third circle. The performances were festivals, and could be depended on for a festive atmosphere. In the intervals snobbish officers used to let themselves be noticed by the barrier above the orchestra pit, and after the show they'd stand under the canopy of the stage door to look at the ladies.

On Good Friday and for matins on Easter Day we went to the chapel of the Principal Directorate of Posts and Telegraph in Pochtamstskaya Street, as Father was a head of department. We left our coats in the cloakroom and went upstairs. The parquet floors in the church were highly polished. The electric wiring was hidden behind the cornices. Electric chandeliers blazed, and some church-goers, brought up in strict Orthodox traditions, found fault with that, but Father was proud of those innovations, which had been his initiative. When a family (ours or any other) came in, an attendant would immediately bring bentwood chairs for them to sit down on and have a rest at points in the liturgy where it was permitted to do so. Later I discovered that the Nabokov family too used to attend that same church. Vladimir and I met, of course, but he was older than me.

The inequality of the inhabitants of Petersburg was plain to see. When houses were being built the builders carried bricks on their backs, climbing quickly up wooden boards with laths nailed across them instead of ladders. Those who lived in apartment houses also carried firewood up dark staircases on their backs, collecting it from special sawing-benches in the yard. Tatar rag-and-bone men would come into yards along with organ-grinders, and one day I saw a Punch-and-Judy show. What surprised me was Punch's unnatural voice (the Punch-and-Judy man would put a widget in his mouth which altered his voice). The Punch-and-Judy man's canvas booth extended from his waist up, and covered him completely; it was as if he wasn't there.

24

The beauty of Petersburg was not only tragic but also hidden (in the palaces and behind the signs). The Winter Palace was absolutely dark at night, as the Emperor and his family lived in the Aleksandr Palace in Tsarskoye Selo. The gay rococo of the palace lost its coquettish nature and the building was ponderous and gloomy. Over the river from the palace the fortress-prison loomed out of the darkness with its towering cathedral spire, a weather-vane-cum-sword poised menacingly above.

The canals that wound around the regularly laid-out streets destroyed the imperial orderliness of the city. In the Aleksandr Garden opposite the Admiralty there were a number of amusements for children among the palaces (in winter, rides on reindeer, in summer a zoo and ponds with goldfish), under the watchful eye, as it were, of maids and governesses. The Field of Mars threw dust in one's eyes at the slightest breath of wind, and the Mikhaylovski castle seemed to wink with one eye—the one window among the many that was bricked up, that of the room where the Emperor Paul had been strangled[20].

The old Petersburg is recalled by V. Veidle in his book *Winter Sunshine*. The house that belonged to him was on Bolshaya Morskaya Street near the arch of the General Staff building. If one went to the left from the arch the first house was no. 6—the hotel Frantsiya, with the restaurant named Maly Yaroslavets; farther along was a French baker's with croissants and chaussons, the same as one would see in Paris. Then came the Bolin the jeweller's with a doorman standing outside. On the corner was a tobacconist's where messengers stood in their red, peaked caps. Opposite was the Tonet furniture factory which produced light and comfortable bentwood chairs.

Across the Nevski Prospekt was the Smurov snack-bar. On the first floor was the English Shop which sold dark grey English glycerine soap. Opposite was 'Flowers from Nice', even in winter. Obliquely across from the cigar shop was Datsiaro: 'purveyors of all requisites for art'. Above them was Henrikh Zimmerman (for musicians). In the middle, by the windows of the second floor, a cast iron bracket carried the name Pavel Bure and a clock which showed the right time.

Farther along Bolshaya Morskaya Street was the restaurant Kyuba with its heavy cream curtains. This, according to the memoirs of Yuliya Nikolayevna Danzas, was the only restaurant of such *bon ton* that a respectable lady could go to without an escort. Then came Muller's, a shop selling the best trunks and suitcases. In 1916 the decision was taken to evacuate the valuables from the Hermitage—in cases made by this firm. Their custodian was Baron Felkerzam.

In golden letters on the granite facing along Bolshaya Morskaya Street was the sign 'Faberge', with the celebrated tailor Kalina opposite. Farther along the road was the Reformed Church (now transformed into the House of Communications).

Night life—the Petersburg *noctambulisme*—was the norm for the Petersburg intelligentsia. 'Society' didn't go to bed before three and seldom got up before eleven. Night-clubs flourished, and the *Brodyachaya sobaka* [Stray Dog] in particular. This was *le rendez-vous des distingués*.

I remember the years 1917–1950 for their dark and boring colours. If houses were ever painted, it was in one colour; decorative features weren't distinguished or repaired. The military had no smart uniforms. People were shabby and wore old clothes even though they had new things; it was injudicious to wear anything new for fear of being taken for a *bourgeois*. For the same reason people didn't wear white collars, but mostly wore, during the First World War and the Civil War, something akin to a service tunic. Sometimes made of the most unmilitary material, and even more often remade from old *bourgeois* clothes, such as a suit jacket, a frock-coat, a morning-coat or the like. During the First World War people wore short overcoats. I remember seeing Shalyapin[21] getting on a tram at the corner of Vvedenskaya Street and Bolshoy Prospekt, not because it was the first time that I had seen a 'personality', but because his coat was an unusual colour—blue.

When I was told in the thirties that in other countries private cars were of various colours, that one could see even red, yellow and light blue ones, for some reason I couldn't grasp the idea, so accustomed was I to all cars being black.

When, just before my arrest, I ordered myself a suit for forty rubles (a lot of money in 1927, which I had earned for work on books for the Institute of Phonetics of Foreign Languages, then under the personal supervision of Semen Boyanus, who taught me English phonetics) I had the choice of either black or dark blue. I chose the dark blue one, which, when it arrived, turned out to be black anyway. So I never wore it and gave it to my brother Yura instead. When I returned from the camp my parents bought me a suit in coarse woollen material, which I wore until the end of the war.

The weather in Petersburg is very changeable and is always accompanied by some special mood. In winter the snow sometimes falls softly, sometimes it whirls about or is driven into a blizzard. Sometimes it falls as wet flakes, sometimes as dry powder; sometimes it is cold enough to cut your face and at others it will caress it tenderly.

In summer the heat and stuffiness leave one weak and enervated; people stop dead in their tracks and remain motionless without any evident purpose or concern. People go down with sunstroke; a thunderstorm builds up and rattles the hollow tin roofs. The Neva changes colour and ripples appear on its dark surface like gnashing teeth.

Nowhere is there a city so proudly beautiful as Petersburg in spring, especially when the parks abound with luxuriant lilac blossom.

The air is transparent on the windless, sunlit days of early autumn, and every contour of the Neva can be seen. The riverside palaces look like appliqué work, cut out of paper and glued onto the blue cardboard of the sky.

Weather always has a relationship with man. It influences him and determines his mood. Petersburg is like a vast theatrical set, a spectacular arena for the greatest historical tragedies, and sometimes for comic improvisation too.

I am writing all this as I contemplate my childhood impressions, in which changes of weather played a special role, for my parents paid close attention to how I dressed to go out. Sometimes I had to wear a coat with a hood which I could pull right over my head, covering my hat and neck. Sometimes I had to change my galoshes for boots, put on gaiters or warm stockings. It all depended on the weather. The weather has more influence on life in Petersburg than in any other city in Russia. You can go out in one sort of weather and come home in another.

Has the weather changed in Petersburg since my young days? What does one mean by weather? If weather is to include snow and its behaviour on roads, pavements and roofs, then it has not. If it is to include the smoke from a multitude of chimneys, which used to rise vertically into the lowering skies of autumn (and on the other hand, into the very high skies of winter) or be blown across the roofs by the wind, then those weather effects are no longer in evidence. Thousands of tiled stoves and huge kitchen ranges are no longer stoked in our city, samovars aren't lit any more, factory chimneys emit less smoke and steamships none at all. The air in the streets smells different, and the feel of it on the face has changed. Tens of thousands of horses, wafting the warmth of their bodies over passers by, strange though it may seem, made the air of the city less 'official'. I mean what I say: just that, 'less official', less indifferent towards man.

In her *Poema bez geroya* [Poem without a hero] Akhmatova[22] gives a vivid impression of the fancy dress atmosphere of Petersburg, which to no small extent depends on its weather, secretive as it is in its changes and its more delicate subtleties.

Kuokkala

The five-room flat cost half my father's salary. In early spring we would give up the flat, move to a dacha and then rent another flat in the same area near the Mariinski theatre in the autumn. That way the family saved money.

We usually went to Kuokkala, across the Finnish frontier, where dachas were relatively cheap and where the intelligentsia—predominantly the artistic fraternity—of Petersburg lived.

Nowadays there are few that can remember what dacha communities and dacha life were like. I will try to give an account of a place much involved in my childhood—Kuokkala, the modern Repino.

In his *Guide to Finland* K. B. Grönhagen is brief and curt on the subject of Kuokkala:

> Kuokkala (42 km from St Pb.). The station is one *versta*[23] from the coast of the Gulf. The region is densely populated by dacha-dwellers in summer. The boring architecture, however, and the absence of good roads, constitute serious defects in a set of otherwise more or less satisfactory conditions for dacha life. The roads to the north of the station are particularly bad. The region is sandy, covered with pine forest, and in general quite suitable for dacha life. It has shops, a chemist and even a theatre. The best dachas are situated along a coastal avenue and are let for high rentals. To the north of the station are inexpensive dachas, many of them also occupied in winter. There is an Orthodox church.

A curious piece of information follows in small type:

> In the final years of the Russian Revolution (that of 1905 is meant–DSL) refugees from the Russian Government found sanctuary here. After the establishment of a bomb factory in the neighbourhood of Kuokkala (at Haapala), however, the Finland administration, under the law of 1826, was required by the Russian authorities to arrest several of these refugees, who were detained by the Petersburg Department of the *Okhrana* (the Tsarist Secret Police).

Some of my happiest childhood memories are to do with the beach at Kuokkala. I recall as if it were yesterday whole days spent on the beach at our hut. This hut was an indispensable adjunct to a rented dacha. Dachas were let as whole units, and it had not yet entered anyone's head to let or rent a dacha as separate rooms. And so in spring, as soon as we moved out to our rented dacha, the owner would load the hut onto a cart and take it to the beach, where he and my father would pick a spot for 'our' hut. There were often so many huts that they were set up in a double row (naturally, the huts in the less convenient back row were set up for late arrivals).

Deck-chairs, bathing costumes and toys were stored in the hut. Most of all I liked model yachts with keels and sails. For a while I also had a model warship which could be wound up and launched and then would fire a shot when it returned to the shore. The gunfire of this ironclad fascinated me the first couple of times that I tried it, but then it became unrealistic. I much preferred to set the sail and the rudder on a model yacht and make it sail close to the wind. The sea was shallow, and I could follow the little boat a long way...

At noon on the beach we drank milk which had been taken there in the morning in a bottle and buried in the cool sand behind the hut.

If we were lucky we saw gunnery practice at the forts. The nearest fort to Kuokkala was Totleben. A tug would tow a white plate past it on a rope and we could see clearly the guns firing at it. We couldn't see hits, but I liked the sound of the shots very much. It was quite deafening as it echoed across the water, and together with the hubbub of the bathers it composed that symphony of sounds that for me blends with the aural associations of childhood.

Behind the hut my brother and I would dig trenches and play at fighting one another in the company of our friends, hurling pinecones, either soaking them in water or 'baking' them for throwing in the dry sand, so that they remained whole and flew a greater distance.

Farther away still stood a lovely pine forest, above which rose a windmill which at times produced electricity and at others pumped water from the well to fill the cistern of our rich dacha-owning neighbours...

Mother would sit on a bench with the ladies of Kuokkala, and I usually walked up and down, balancing on the rails. The track vanished into infinity—to Petersburg, from where Father was to arrive by train. He would bring huge Pavlovsk strawberries or some other titbits, and sometimes a toy; a hoopla, or a toy yacht or a clockwork steamship (I was particularly fond of playing in the water, and we still have two photographs of me in the sea, ankle-deep in the water, wearing a little Panama hat and shorts, with a toy sail-boat at my feet).

I stared into the distance till I could see it approaching. It gave a refined, foreign-sounding whistle (Russian steam engines have a bass siren). Then it rolled up, its wheels whirling (a favourite game of children of five, like myself, was to imitate the engine, using our elbows like pistons). The coaches stretched out, blue, green and red, though the meaning of the colours was different from the Russian. I'm not sure that I remember correctly now, but I think that the blue coaches were the first class. The Finnish conductors emerged first in their black uniforms and stood by the steps to help the passengers down. Father would appear, kiss mother and tell us who he had travelled with. One day Baron Meyerhold was pointed out to me at the window; he was going to Terijoki[24]. It amazes me that I remember him, and that I remember him as Baron. The average dachniki—the engineers and civil servants—knew him as Baron. Other dachniki were artists: the Pugnis, the Annenkovs, Repins, and the rest. For some reason they represented a race apart in my eyes—Italians, brunettes, celebrities from the world of entertainment.

In the evening, when father had come home from work in Petersburg, we would have supper and then I would run across the main road and buy sunflower seeds and Finnish sweets from a stall owned by a middle-aged widow. When I returned we would go for a walk along the shore. We didn't nibble the seeds but cracked them with our nails (as no one does nowadays) and father would set us problems. One of these was as follows: how could he tell correctly, without looking, when the Tolbukin lighthouse would light up and when it would go out. At first I thought that he did it by the reflection in his pince-nez, but he took them off and did it just the same! He was simply counting the time—he knew the periodicity of its illumination.

The dachas at Kuokkala had fences which were always made of wood and always painted in a wide range of colours. Pedlars and Finnish carts would stop by the fences and cry their wares. The pedlars were often from Yaroslavl, and traded in greengrocery, white bread and pastries. They carried baskets of these wares on their heads, placing a ring of soft material under them. Gypsies would bang on a cauldron and shout "Tinning, soldering..." and a third word which I no longer remember. There was often a Gypsy encampment beyond the

30

Author's mother and his sons with friends on beach in Kuokkala. 1910

Bathing in pre-Revolutionary times

Kuokkala railway station. 1913

On way from Sevastopol to Alpuka. 1911

Author on beach
at Miskhor. 1912

In Crimea with friends. 1912

V. S. Likhacheva with sons in park at Alpuka. 1913

Mitya and Misha Likhachev in park at Alpuka. 1913

Miskhor. 1913

S. M. Likhachev with sons. Miskhor 1912

Misha and Mitya Likhachev. Odessa 1912

Author with mother
and brother in park
at Alpuka. 1913

Revolution 1917. Attack on police archives

boundary of the dacha community. They did good work and delivered orders on time.

When there was no wind, as frequently was the case before an autumn heat-wave, by listening carefully it was possible to hear the distant tenor bell of St. Isaac's Cathedral.

In the daytime heat the beach buzzed like a beehive with the voices of a swarm of children, happy or frightened when they jumped into the water, mischievous at play, but always muffled by the water, swimming about, gently. I can hear this music of the beach even now, and to this day I love it dearly. What a miracle of delight, entertainment, mischief, sociable frivolity, theatrical and festive improvisation was that Kuokkala!

Children ruled in Kuokkala. On the beach one heard a hubbub of children's voices. We went off to the sea for the whole day, taking with us milk and breakfast and missing lunch, which in winter was eaten at one o'clock. As I have said, every dacha family had its own hut, and often its own boat. Landing-stages ran out from the beach into the sea and it was fun to turn somersaults into the water off them. These landing-stages were either private or public, in which case one had to pay. On Sundays there would be a band playing somewhere on the beach, performing in aid of some charity. There were also performances in the Kuokkala theatre. A little band of four retired German soldiers would parade down the streets, stop outside a dacha and strike up—starting a popular Finnish song of the time. If we waved them away they would stop playing, but often we asked them to make a note of when to come and play dance music for a birthday or name-day party which the children from all around would attend.

On birthdays and name-days the children usually lit up the garden with Chinese lanterns, and there had to be a firework display; by the way, Gorki used to set off fireworks and light bonfires at his dacha for no reason other than that he just loved fires.

Fireworks could be bought at a pyrotechnic shop near the city council offices on the Nevski. Children from all the dachas came together for these evenings of fun and would run around Kuokkala in cheerful gangs selling badges for charity (for tuberculosis on Daisy Day and then for the wounded soldiers during the First World War).

The interests and entertainment of children were paramount and adults were happy to take part in children's games. A spirit of mischief showed through in the local theatre, where Mayakovski occa-

31

sionally performed, Repin, Chukovski and Kulbin gave readings, and farces were staged by the young people. Boys sang cheeky songs. Both children and adults (sometimes jointly, in parties of various ages, sometimes in small groups) went for long walks.

And the ethnic groups that lived in Kuokkala! Russians, Finnish peasants who sold cheap dachas (we used to play hide-and-seek and other rowdy games with the Finnish boys), Petersburg Germans, Petersburg French and the Italian Pugni family, headed by the uncommonly temperamental Alberto Pugni, who was forever starting arguments and rowing with genuine sincerity like a desperate Russian patriot.

Almost everyone (apart from newcomers) knew each other and visited one another. Collections for charity were organised and kindergartens set up on a communal basis. Adults and children played together at croquet, hoopla and skittles and the older people played cards in the garden whilst indulging in leisurely conversation. The church was a meeting place where everyone gathered, including Catholics and Lutherans, though they didn't always stay for the whole service but tended to wander out into a meadow where they could sit and gossip. During the war Repin became deeply religious and sang in the choir. Pugni's son-in-law Shtern, who ran a rooming house on the corner of Bolshoy Prospekt and Gatchinskaya Street, also developed a keen interest in religion. He was a German, but at the start of the First World War changed his name to Astrov and embraced the Orthodox faith. Misha Shtern and I were great friends.

People used to dress up. A friend of my mother's, Mariya Albertovna Pugni, a pretty, dark-eyed Italian, wore a gold anklet (by 1914 hemlines had risen and scarcely reached down to the instep). The Annenkov girls embarrassed everyone by wearing trousers in the garden. Korney Chukovski himself, on his return from England in 1915 (where he had been as a member of a delegation), took to walking around barefoot at the same time as wearing a very good suit. And the writers all dreamed up a variety of costumes for themselves: Gorki dressed in his own way, as did Mayakovski and the handsome Leonid Andreyev... One could meet them all on what is now the Embankment in Kuokkala, as they either lived there or were frequent visitors.

Korney Chukovski preserved his impish Kuokkala character to the end of his days. Here is a story that I was told by the old doctor Tatyana Aleksandrovna Afanaseva, of the Academy of Sciences sanatorium at Uzkoye. Chukovski usually lived in room 26 of the central block. On the way back from a walk he caught some of the grass-snakes which were so common in the area. He hung about five of them round his neck and over his shoulders, and then, taking advantage of the fact that doors to the rooms were not locked, tossed them over the patients and took pleasure in observing what a fright he gave them. He would not tolerate interruption when he was working, and so he used to hang a sign on his door saying 'Asleep'. This used to stay there until three in the afternoon, and people coming from Moscow to see him would wait and wait, and often, in the end, go away again. Tatyana Aleksandrovna also told me about how, from time to time, he would sink to his knees and implore his sisters, who took him his medicine (usually herbal preparations for the heart, tranquillisers and sleeping draughts), to take it away again, all the while employing theatrical gestures.

In 1914 the happy and spirited life of Kuokkala was tinged with alarm. A German attack on Finland was expected in September, and the Finnish police boarded up the towers of the dachas (at the turn of the century dachas were invariably built with watch-towers, from which one could see the sea). Gunnery practice could be heard from the fort at Kronshtadt, and the sea somehow gave this a plopping sound—just like bottles of champagne being opened. More and more often tugs were seen towing moving targets past the forts for gunnery practice.

Then in the summer of 1915 some Polish refugees came to live in Kuokkala and they gave me my first lesson in politeness to other nationalities. We boys used to make fun of the Poles with the words *tsoto bendze* [there'll be trouble], which they often uttered in their nervous conversations. And then one day an elegant Polish lady turned to us with a smile and said pleasantly "Yes, boys! *tsoto bendze* for us and for you in this war". We felt ashamed, and although the incident was not discussed among us we stopped making fun of them.

One more lasting impression of Kuokkala. In Holy Week, as in all Russian Orthodox churches, everyone was allowed to ring the bell at any time. One day my two brothers and I went with father (people came to the dachas in early spring) to the belfry and rang the bells. How enchanting it was to hear the sound as we stood directly under the bells!

One event took place in Kuokkala that raised the stock of my brothers and myself among the dachniki. An off-shore wind was blowing (the most dangerous), and my eldest brother Misha took the blue blind from the nursery, set it up in our boat and suggested to a completely 'tame' boy, the grandson of Senator Davydov, that they go for a sail. This boy, Serezha (who later worked as an architect and restorer in Novgorod after the Second World War), went to his grandmother and asked permission to go on the trip. She was a beautifully dressed lady with violet eyes and used to wear a silk dress and sit under a parasol to keep off the sun. She only asked Misha whether Serozha would get his feet wet: naturally, there was always water in the bottom of a boat. She told Serezha to put his galoshes on, and he put on his shiny new galoshes and took his seat in the boat. All this happened before my eyes. The northerly wind was, as always, light near the shore but stronger farther out. The boat was driven along. I was watching from the shore and suddenly saw the blue sail slowly list to one side and disappear. The old lady, just as she was, fully dressed and carrying her parasol, walked into the water holding out her hands towards her beloved Serezha. When she reached deeper water the old lady with the violet eyes fell senseless and might have choked and drowned. On the beach, however, behind a sheet erected as a windbreak, the pro-rector of Petersburg University, the red-headed Prozorovski, was sun-bathing. He had been watching the old lady and when she fell he hurled himself to her rescue. But, oh horror! he was only wearing shorts, and in those days that was considered improper. He picked up the old lady with violet eyes and carried her to the shore, while I ran for home at full speed. On reaching our dacha I slowed down and tried to appear calm. My mother asked me, evidently realising that something was wrong, "Is the sea calm?" I was quick to reply "Yes, but Misha's drowning". Those words of mine have been remembered in the family and recalled hundreds of times. They became our family catch-phrase for when something unpleasant happened suddenly.

Meanwhile what was happening out at sea was as follows: the 'tame' Serezha, naturally, couldn't swim. My brother started to lifesave him and told him to take off his galoshes. But Serezha wouldn't, partly so as not to disobey his grandmother, partly because he didn't want to lose his shiny galoshes with the bronze letters S. D. ('Serezha Davydov'). My brother threatened him: "Do as I say, you fathead, or I'll leave you here". The threat worked, but by that time boats were putting out from the shore.

In the evening my father came home. My brother was taken upstairs for a thrashing, and then my father, not departing from his usual practice, took us for a walk by the sea. As we were supposed to, my brother and I walked ahead of our parents, and the people we met kept saying, as they pointed to my brother: "The life-saver, the life-saver!" The life-saver, however, was walking in a gloomy frame of mind, looking dejected.

I too was praised for my sensible self-control. One day, however, in a particularly strong storm, someone I met told me: "The sea's calm, but four huts have been undermined and knocked over". I quickly ran to the sea to have a look. To this day I have loved storms, but not the treacherous off-shore wind.

And another 'time link'. When the manuscript of these reminiscences was completely finished I leafed through Chukovski's work on Korolenko[25]. It transpired that the latter was extremely fond of playing 'ducks and drakes' and in his day was a champion at the sport. This is a favourite pastime of mine as well, and in the autumn of 1931 the writer's nephew Vladimir Yulyanovich Korolenko and I indulged our passion for the sport on our secret walks in the woods by the Solovki lakes.

The summer life of the dacha community was completely unlike what it is today. The dachniki were constantly socialising and visiting each other. They were all concerned about their reputations, about what people would say about them. They dressed up not merely so as to boast about their tailors, but also to create their personal 'images'. Mariya Albertovna Pugni dressed extravagantly, others with emphatic modesty or 'severely', with an aristocratic flavour.

All this gave rise to a culture. Dacha society culture was a model of Russian culture in general, but on a reduced scale. It owed much to conversation. Everyone's opinions were formulated through conversations with friends, sometimes through arguments which didn't lead to enmity but established the intellectual individuality of the parties.

Preparations for an outing would go on for a week. It was decided what clothes to wear and that dress had to be modest yet smart. Shoes! They were the main problem for the ladies. Sandwiches and snacks were made and drinks prepared. One had not only to feed one's family but also to entertain friends.

I asked a Finnish gardener, on whom I called in 1985 in Komarov to buy some flowers for the cemetery, whether she remembered the Yuliya boarding-house on Tserkovnaya Street, where we had lived, if I'm not mistaken, in 1915. She didn't recall the Yuliya, but we had a chat about the boarding-houses and Kuokkala. This is what she said:

"When the Russian gentry lived here, how happy it was here, how many holidays there were. For Whitsun everything would be decorated with birch-trees–even the trains went around with birch-trees on them. A band used to play on the beach in the evening. They had parties. They used to fly kites in windy weather. Are there any kites now? But in those days children and grown-ups used to love flying them. On St Ivan's day they lit bonfires and barrels of tar. They played croquet. Now croquet's been forgotten. I don't suppose you can even buy the kit. People went to the station to meet the trains, and there were little gardens all round the station, and people were driven directly to the platform. There were lots of horses' traps. Finnish horses are small but quick and tough.

"The Finns liked the Russian gentry... The Russians were polite and amiable."

When the Finns left here in the First Finnish War, Aleksandrovna Yanovna hid—she wanted to stay with the Russians. Between the two Finnish Wars[26] she was moved to Vologda or somewhere. There she married. Her first dacha was taken over by the Fire Brigade, but they gave her another where she cultivated flowers, soft fruit and cucumbers for a living. We were always calling on her, and took our daughter Vera to see her.

I was pleased to talk to her about Kuokkala. My impressions were the same as hers, so I had not been exaggerating.

The Crimea

Time spent in the south played an enormous part in the aesthetic upbringing of our family. My father worked in Odessa in 1911–12, and we spent two summers in Miskhor in the Crimea. I remember the smell of sun-baked laurel, the view from the Baydar Gates (where there was a monastery in those days), the park and castle at Alupka and bathing among the rocks at Miskhor (I discovered later from photographs that this was the place where Lev Tolstoy had bathed after his illness, coming down from the estate of Countess Panina at Gaspre). I was especially fond of a little meadow overlooking the sea, where the flowers were unusually sweet-scented. Everyone called this meadow *Batareyka* and this was where we went most often on our walks. During the Crimean War a little battery had been stationed here to prevent the Anglo-French forces landing at Alupka. Here everything merged for me into one: the feeling of nature and the sense of history. The latter arose in me at the age of five or six, and first of all at the memorials of the siege of Sevastopol, on which I loved to climb, and on the tumulus at Malakhov, where I imagined that I was a gunner at the cannon positioned among the fortifications; even at that age the Russian defeat brought a sense of personal grief.

I look back on the months spent in the Crimea, at Miskhor, in 1911 and 1912 as the happiest of my life. The Crimea was different. It was a kind of 'East in miniature', an ideal Orient. Handsome Crimean Tatars in national dress offered mounts for excursions into the hills. The plaintive call of the muezzin resounded from the minarets. There was a particularly beautiful minaret at Koreiza, against the backdrop of Mount Ay-Petri. And the Tatar villages, the vineyards, the little restaurants! And you could go into any park for a walk, and if the owners were away you could look round the Vorontsov Palace at Alupka, the Panina Palace at Gaspre and the Yusupov Palace at Miskhor if you tipped the servants. There were no special restrictions in the absence of the owners, and as they were almost always away the main rooms (except for those that were strictly private) were open to view.

In those days private ownership of the coastal strip was not permitted. A metalled road ran from Miskhor along the coast to Livadiya, and we used to walk along it in the evenings to the lighthouse at Ay-Todor. No private beaches! The only stretch of beach where one could not walk was from Miskhor to Alupka, because of the cliffs. There was, however, a fine path along the top. All these walks have remained in my memory because of my father's excellent photographs. Now much has gone, including the marvellous path along the coast from Alupka. The 'Royal Path' to Oreanda too has been tamed and altered in appearance.

Perhaps my love of all sorts of memorial places and open-air museums has grown ever stronger since that time—whether it be for the famous monument-cannon in Odessa, the garden museums and little houses of Peter in Petersburg, and the simply lyrical memorials such as that to Zhukovski[27] in the Aleksandr Garden in Petersburg, where I walked most often of all until the watchman's 'evening bell' rang and the garden was shut for the night, or the small monuments to Peter, of which there are a number in Petersburg such as that of him steering a boat on the embankment by the Admiralty. Even then I was impressed by the ancient trees in the Nikitski garden in the Crimea, and in Petersburg, during our unvaried holiday excursions to the Islands, I used to look reverently at Peter's Oak, surrounded by a little iron railing. I would stand in front of that oak and whisper my secret wishes to it, such as my hope of being given a wooden box of tin soldiers, or a 'real' steam engine—like I'd seen at a friend's house. It seems strange but my prayers were answered, and I ascribed their fulfilment not to the thoughtfulness of my parents, who had naturally guessed at them, but to the kindly and almighty oak. Together with my sense of history, paganism awoke in me at a very early age.

A Volga Cruise, 1914

In May 1914 we—my parents, my elder brother and myself—went down the Volga from Rybinsk[28] to Saratov and back. From Petersburg to Rybinsk we travelled by train, but I don't remember the journey, apart from some vague recollections of the Petersburg station. Where the trains arrived and departed, in the covered part of the station, at the very end of the rails, hung an icon at which departing travellers prayed and dozens of blazing candles gave off great heat.

It was the month of May. In the morning Rybinsk greeted us with cold and rain. We went to an outfitter's and bought long stockings for me to put on instead of my ankle-socks. Naturally (children are all the same!) this didn't please me very much. In spring one had to be dressed as lightly as possible, such was the dandyism of boyhood. And there was a further humiliation in the shop: the sales-girl who was about to try the stockings on me said "Give me your foot, miss!" I had been taken for a girl! Horror!

In those days the Volga wasn't like it is today. I'm not referring to the absence of 'seas' and floods, dams and locks. It carried a lot of small craft of various types. Tugs hauled caravans of barges in line astern. Timber floated down on rafts, on which there were huts and even little houses for the raftsmen. In the evening they lit bright bonfires for cooking and for drying their washing. Despite their poverty Russian peasants were very neat.

The Volga was full of sounds. The steamers hooted as they exchanged greetings. Captains passed on news to each other through loud hailers and dockers sang.

There used to be special Volga jokes, in which the main point was that people shouted to one another from great distances and things were misunderstood. But there were also childish tales and onomatopoeias. I remember one such onomatopoeia for cockerels crowing to one another. The first crowed "Been to Kostromá." The second asked "What's it like down there?" The first replied "Take a look yourself". This 'dialogue' gave a good imitation of the intonation of cock-crowing.

And here is a scene that I dreamed up myself in the spirit of Ostrovski. A rich merchant gets on our ship and never stops boasting of his wealth. He greets the oncoming rafts by putting his hands to his mouth like a megaphone: "Whose is that raft?" From the raft comes the inevitable reply "Panfilov's". Then the awful merchant proudly turns to the people on deck and pronounces "That's our raft!"

A similar scene actually did take place. A retired soldier called Foss used to travel on the Volga. He was a man of huge stature and unusually fat. It was said that he tied a pillow on himself under his shirt so as to look even fatter. He used to boast of his friendship with some great prince or other and for that reason thought that he had the right not to pay for anything. At meal-times he ate most of everything. Volga steamers of the time were renowned for their marvellous cuisine, especially the fish (sterlet, sturgeon, caviar pressed, unpressed and new-laid, etc.)

Foss sat at our table in Nizhni in the evening. The passengers were alarmed—there was going to be trouble. The humorists tried to worry us: "He'll eat everything and they'll close the restaurant". The captain, however, knew how to deal with him. He wasn't to be prevented from ordering dishes. The captain presented the bill, and when Foss refused to pay he was invited to leave the ship. He refused. Then all the sailors were summoned and grabbed him by both arms and bundled him off. We watched from the upper deck as they put him ashore; he stood on the landing-stage for a long time yelling invectives at us.

On the landing-stages dockers helped their heavy work along with singing and shouting. I remember one night some heavy item being raised from the hold (the steamer carried cargo as well as passengers) and the dockers shouting rhythmically in unison "Here she comes, here she comes!" And when the object had been moved they shouted "There she went, there she went!" That nocturnal shouting is a lasting memory.

At every stop a little market gathered on the landing-stage. The captain told us what to buy and where—here berries, there baskets, elsewhere caviar, somewhere else walking-sticks. My brother and I were keen to pick ourselves sticks; he chose one with a Turk's head handle and I bought one with a little bird, and we kept them for a long time. They were bought either in Kineshma or Plyos. I remember distinctly that the riverbank where the traders were was very green and leafy and rose steeply upwards.

In Troitsa our steamer stopped right right alongside a green meadow. On a knoll was a wooden church the inside of which was completely decorated with birch-trees, while the floor was strewn with grass and wild flowers. The traditional liturgical singing of the church choir was exceptional. The Volga left an impression of musicality: the vast expanse of the river was full of everything that floated, hooted, sang and cried out. In the towns there was a smell of fish, all sorts of food, horses—even the dust, for some reason, had a scent of vanilla. People went about talking or arguing in loud voices, traders cried their wares to attract customers. Little boys bawled out the names of the newspapers they were selling and sometimes the headlines of particular articles or items of news. In the markets one met Persians, Caucasians, Tatars, Kalmyks, Chuvashes, Mordvins—all in their own costumes, speaking their different languages.

I have no recollection of returning by train but I do remember that the second ship we sailed on was the *1812* and that we met the *Kutuzov*; it was 101 years since the battle of Borodino[29].

We still have pictures of the past, our own snapshots. I remember most clearly of all one taken on the Volga. The captain's daughter and I are sitting on a carpet in his cabin, playing some boring game (she was younger than me and, of course, a girl, and I didn't know how to play with dolls). We were separated from the deck by a grille that stretched from floor to ceiling. My parents called to me "Look! It's Zhiguli! Nightingales are singing!" Through the grille I could see a high wooded bank and hear the trilling of the nightingales, but I did not know how to bring my game with the captain's daughter to a close. For a long time afterwards I regretted not having taken a good look at Zhiguli or listened to the nightingales. This sense of a lost opportunity has remained with me to this day, but at least I can say that I have seen the Volga.

The Philanthropic Society Grammar School

In the autumn of 1914 I started school at the Philanthropic Society Grammar School, the same one where A. N. Benois was once a pupil. It was on the Kryukov canal opposite the Chevakinski bell-tower, not far from the Benois' house—on the tram route to Kolomna. I used to like riding on this with my nurse, on the top deck. What a marvellous view of the city was revealed from up there!

I went there at the age of eight, and went straight into the top preliminary class. My parents had chosen not the school but the class teacher, and that top preliminary class had a remarkable one— Kapiton Vladimirovich! He was stern, imposing, wise, and kind in a paternal way when he was able. He was an educator with a capital E. His pupils treated him with love and respect, but they treated me, however, quite differently, and I immediately found myself in a state of conflict with them. I was a new boy, and they were by then in their second year, and a number had transferred from city schools. They were seasoned schoolboys and one day they set about me with their fists. I put my back to the wall and beat them off as best I could. Suddenly they fell back; I felt victorious and launched a counter-attack. But I hadn't seen the usher, and they had. As a result there was a note against my name in the register: "Fighting with his fellows. Usher Mamay". I was terribly upset at that injustice! Another time they set on me in the street with snowballs and forced me towards a little window from which the very same usher Mamay used to watch the pupils' behaviour. Another note appeared in the register: "Misbehaving in the street. Usher Mamay". And my parents were summoned to see the Headmaster.

How I hated going to school! In the evenings, when I knelt to say my prayers with mother, I added on my own account, burying my head in the pillow: "Please, dear God, let me be ill". And ill I was: my temperature started to go up every day, two or three points over the 37. I was removed from the school and so that I should not miss the year's work a tutor was engaged—a refugee Polish schoolmistress (it was the winter of 1915). She was small and thin, and was paid for teaching me and given lunch. At table she seemed so small that my father, out of pity for her, cut down the legs of the table to make it lower. Later that table always had to be put on the glass 'feet' from under the grand piano so as to regain its original height. I had a second lesson in ethnic sensitivity from that Polish girl. She was teaching me Russian history but strayed from the subject and started to talk about Polish history, and I went and blurted out to her face "There's no such thing as Polish history". I was obviously confusing the concepts of history and history book—and there certainly wasn't a history of Poland in Russian. But the Polish schoolmistress began to curse me and suddenly burst into tears. Even today I feel ashamed of making her cry...

K. I. May's Grammar School and Modern School

In 1915 I went to K. I. May's Grammar and Modern School on Vasilevski island. By then my father had taken charge of the electrical station at the Head Post Office and had an official flat there but today not a trace remains of that station. The yard is deserted and our flat no longer exists. In those days, however, it was a treat for me to go there to see the huge, beautiful wheel being turned by a piston gleaming with oil.

I had to go to May's by tram, but it was amazingly hard to fight one's way on board, as the platforms were crammed with soldiers ('other ranks', as they were called). They were allowed to travel free, but only if they rode on the platform. We lived next to Konnogvardeyski Boulevard, and I enjoyed the Palm Sunday bazaars where one could crowd around the second-hand bookstalls and buy peasant toys and special Palm Sunday toys (such as 'American citizens', devils on safety-pins to fix to one's coat, acrobats on trapezes, 'mother-in-law's tongues' and so on), and stuff oneself with Palm Sunday delicacies.

Holy Week was the best week for children in old Petersburg, and this was the time to get the feel of national rejoicing and the beauty of the folk art that was brought in from the whole area north of Lake Onega.

Petersburg-Petrograd not only stood with its face to Europe, as one felt mainly because of its multiracial population (May's school too was full of Germans, French, English, Swedes, Finns and Estoni-

42

ans), but also behind its back was the whole of Northern Russia with its folklore, its peasant art, peasant architecture, with easy travel by river and lake, and Novgorod not far away.

I grew older, and suddenly was at that age when military disasters are particularly hard to bear. Discussion of military debacles and all the embarrassing squabbling in the Government and the Russian army occupied pride of place in family conversations in the evenings all the more so as everything that was happening was, as it were, right there next door. Rasputin appeared in the restaurants and houses that I could see, past which I walked, soldiers trained in every nearby open space, performances in the Mariinski theatre began with the wearisome playing of all the anthems of the Powers allied to Russia, beginning with the Belgian anthem *La Brabançonne*. National pride was both wounded and inflamed. I lived on news 'from the theatre of operations', on rumours, hopes and dangers.

May's school made a deep impression on both my interests and my experience—I would say, my philosophy—of life. Our form had a broad social spectrum. There was the grandson of Mechnikov[30], the son of Rubinshtein the banker and the son of a hall porter. The teachers also were a mixed bag. For two years the old May's teacher Mikhail Georgevich Gorokhov taught us perspective as if it were a precise science; the geography teacher gave us passionate accounts of his travels in Russia and abroad, illustrating them with slides; the librarian introduced us all to her province. I look back with enormous gratitude on the few years that I spent at May's. Even the polite porter, who greeted us in German and said good-bye in Italian, taught us politeness by example—how much all that meant to us boys!

The teachers didn't compel us to give away the ringleaders of our pranks, and allowed us to play noisy games and to have fun during breaks. In gym lessons we usually played vigorous games such as *lapta*[31], tag and handball. In the holidays we went as a school out to some estate near Strugi-Byelaya Station on the Pskov line[32]. We brought out a variety of form magazines and even wrote and copied our own compositions without the supervision of the teachers.

I regret that I was unable to attend all the evening activities and the school societies—the journey was very difficult on the overcrowded trams.

The Revolution—Outward Impressions

Naturally, neither my family nor I—a boy of eleven or twelve—had the remotest idea of what was going on; but it was going on almost under our noses, as we lived in Novoisaakiyevskaya Street, near St Isaac's Square. The family took little interest in politics.

When, in the early days of the February Revolution, Petrograd police occupied the top of St Isaac's Cathedral and the attics of the Astoria Hotel and opened fire on any crowd that gathered, my parents were indignant at them and became wary of going to such places. When, however, the police were dragged out of their positions and killed by an infuriated mob my parents were indignant at the cruelty of the mob, irrespective of any justification there may or may not have been for the event.

When my father and I used to go to the Nevski to watch the regiments marching with their bands, which they did ceaselessly and without evident purpose, the sound of the marches raised our spirits. But when these same regiments went past in disorganised ranks we were saddened because we remembered how splendidly the Horse Guards had marched on Sundays to their regimental Church of the Annunciation and with what balletic art the commanding officer—a Russified German—had marched at their head. We remembered the gleam of cuirasses and helmets, and the whirling of the drum-major's mace in front of the band.

Yes, before the Revolution... When my father and I walked down Bolshaya Morskaya Street and saw peasants who had come into town to find work building a house, carrying loads on their backs, shod in birch-bark sandals so as not to slip, I almost sighed for pity and we thought of Nekrasov's 'The Railway'. The same thing happened at any place on the embankment where barges might be unloaded of bricks or firewood. Hefty porters trundled their barrows as fast as possible with heavy loads so as to get along the narrow plank slung between the side of the barge and the bank without stopping. We were sorry for the porters and tried to imagine them living on those barges, away from their families, freezing cold at night, missing their children, for whose sakes they in fact earned their bread with heavy work. But when these former dockers and porters, workmen and low-ranking civil servants went to the ballet at the Mariinski theatre on free tickets, filling the stalls and the boxes, my parents yearned for the glitter of diamonds in the hall of the blue Mariinski. The only thing that pleased them at those performances was that the ballerinas danced no worse than before. Spesivtseva, and likewise Lyukom, were just as splendid, making their bows to the new audience as they had to the old. And of course, how remarkable it was! What a lesson in respect for the new spectator the theatre of the day gave to us all!

In the 1920s the operas *Khovanshchina* and *The Invisible City of Kitezh* enjoyed very great success, and in them two most remarkable singers and actors, Pavel Zakharovich Andreyev (husband of Delmas) and Ivan Vasilevich Yershov. Mussorgski and Rimski-Korsakov—especially the former—were not only composers but also philosophers of Russian history. Mussorgski must have had a stroke of genius to place the most penetrating aria, addressed to Russia, in the mouth of the morally dubious character of Shaklovity. If he'd given it to the irreproachable hero it wouldn't have had the same effect. The audience all but died of excitement when Andreyev, in the role of Shaklovity, sang "The nest of the *streltsy*[33] sleeps. Sleep, Russian people. The foe slumbers not", and then, turning to the auditorium, "O thou Rus'[34] of ill-starred fate, thou hast groaned beneath the Tatar yoke, been at the mercy of the whim of the Boyars... There is no longer tribute to pay to the Tatars, the power of the Boyars is broken, but thou, hapless wretch, sufferest and endurest yet..." The audience leapt to its feet when Andreyev ended his monologue with the prayer "Oh Lord, forgive the sins of the world, hear me, grant that Rus' may not perish at the hands of evil hirelings". Andreyev sang that aria as many as three times as the audience called for encores and many were in tears.

Another no less emotional subject was the fate of Grishka Kuterma, sung and acted brilliantly by Yershov in *Kitezh*. The country was full of such Grishkas who had dismantled the churches and betrayed Rus', and as my parents and I were making our way back to the Petrograd District on foot in total darkness, trying to keep to the middle of the road along the rusting tram-lines, it seemed to us that round the corner at every crossroads there lurked the same Grishkas: the people who drank away and sold out everyone and everything.

Later, in the 1930s, Yershov was a frequent visitor to the Academy of Sciences Bookshop. He liked to chat to the Polish woman that ran the shop, Yelena Kazimirovna, whom we nicknamed 'Desperate Kindness'. Yershov, gallant and witty, liked to talk to her, as it were, for the sake of relief from the all-encompassing vulgarity.

Life in No. 1 State Printing-house

My father was genuinely happy and proud when the staff of the electrical department at No. 1 State Printing-house (now *Pechatny dvor*) chose him as their director. We moved from Novoisaakiyevskaya Street in the middle of Petrograd[35] to an official flat in the Petrograd District. It was the autumn of 1917, but the events of the October Revolution seemed somehow remote from me, and my recollection of them is indistinct.

Living at the press taught me a great deal. I am indebted to it for my interest in printing. The smell of a freshly printed book, even today, is for me the finest of stimulating aromas. I had the run of the place, got to know the type-setters, who considered themselves the intellectuals of the staff and wore their hair long in a style known as the *Marksistka*; they often wrote poetry and took pride in their work. My father gradually became a specialist in printing machinery; he was able to understand foreign equipment bought for the printing-house soon after the Revolution.

The printing office had a large theatre, where the leading singers and actors of the city performed for the staff, and where there was once a public debate between A. V. Lunacharski[36] and the 'Renovationist' Metropolitan Aleksandr Vvedenski[37] on "Is there a God or not?"

I remember the paradoxes of the time: after the debate a crowd of believers actually wanted to give the Metropolitan a thrashing, and my father, at the request of the management, saved him by taking him into another street through the back door of our flat. The point was that 'Metropolitan' Vvedenski had given evidence against the popular Metropolitan Veniamin of Petrograd at his trial in the Filharmoniya.

I learned a great deal during my time at the printing office. But not the least influence was, perhaps, the library which my father acquired from the director of OGIZ[38]—Ilya Ionovich Ionov (a person of no small repute in the literary circles of the time) for safe-keeping. This library contained books from the Elzevier and Aldine presses[39], very rare eighteenth century editions, collections of almanacs, albums of the nobility, the Fisherman's Bible, lavish jubilee editions of Dante, editions of Shakespeare and Dickens on very fine Indian paper, a manuscript of Radishchev's 'Journey from Petersburg to Moscow'[40], books from the library of Feofan Prokopovich[41], but most of them were books autographed by contemporary writers (I remember dedications on Yesenin's[42] collected verse, A. Remizov[43], A. N. Tolstoy[44], etc.). My father also received some things as presents—a death-mask of Aleksandr Blok[45] taken by Manizer by a new process which allowed an impression of the whole head, not just the face, to be taken. It was hard to recognise Blok from it: he was completely bald, sick, old. This death-mask has since disappeared.

The library was acquired under the following circumstances. At *Pechatny dvor* we had a huge official flat, in which my brother and I could even ride round on our cycles. Ionov was appointed, as a sort of honourable exile, to the position of trade representative in the USA and, knowing that my father was an honest man and had a large flat, sent us the bulk of his library. But when he returned he went to live in Moscow instead of Leningrad and as soon as my father heard of his return, he packed all the books into crates and sent them off to him in Moscow. There, however, Ionov, who was married to Zinovev's[46] sister, was arrested and his property in Moscow vanished.

The few years that we had the library in our flat were not wasted for me. I delved into it, read, searched, admired the manuscripts and fine editions, the engravings and photographs of important works of art. I lacked education, otherwise I would have been able to extract more for myself from that remarkable library. Much of it I simply ignored.

Ionov himself had had no systematic education. In his youth, while still in grammar school, he had been arrested by the tsarist government in Odessa and had received a life sentence, which he served in Schliesselburg prison. He emerged from there a very sick man with surprising gaps in his knowledge, for which he was frequently ridiculed. People did not realise that despite everything, he was widely read in a number of fields as he had been able to obtain books in prison.

Taytsy, Olgino, Toksovo

After the Revolution, when the Russo-Finnish frontier was closed, we spent the dacha season in various places: Taytsy, Olgino za Lakhtoy and Toksovo. Nowhere, however, was there such an interesting and happy life as in Kuokkala, where there had been a Petersburg dacha infrastructure. There obviously had once been such a community in Olgino, but it had gone before our time. There was a theatre there, dark and gloomy, where on one occasion my favourite school-teacher Leonid Vladimirovich Georg introduced a concert of Tchaikovsky's work. He probably had to do this to supplement his income and was embarrassed to see me and Zheniya Maksimovna, a pupil from another form, there in the hall. I felt infinitely sorry for him.

The only thing that was of interest in Olgino was a huge rock on the shore of the Gulf; it had been split in two, and according to local tradition Peter the Great had stood on it in 1724 and directed the rescue of fishermen caught in a storm. Another local tradition was that the road to Konnaya Lakhta had been cut through the forest to transport the pedestal for the Bronze Horseman to the Gulf of Finland[47].

Dacha life in Olgino was complicated by the domestic problems of the famine period. Early in the morning I would walk to Konnaya Lakhta for milk, for which I would pay or barter. The local Finnish peasants would usually send me packing or drive a hard bargain; they displayed a sense of personal superiority. In winter I dried the leaves of black currant and raspberry for tea, collected sticks for the samovar and driftwood for the bathhouse. Life in Olgino was, perhaps, harder than in town, but such was the force of habit: in summer one had to go to the dacha.

The Toksovo District really was interesting. At one time the King of Sweden had had a hunting lodge there. The house itself had been burnt down, but under the cover of the dense forest traces still remained of its stone foundations. Not far away was the treeless Pontus Hill, on which, the saying went, the Swedish commander Pontus de la Gardie had pitched camp during his campaign against Moscow in the Time of Troubles[48]. On this hill Finnish boys sometimes found Swedish coins, buttons and knife-blades...

In Toksovo there was also the Kommandantskaya Hill, where the Finnish school was and where the commandant of the hunting-lodge had lived. There were still descendants of the Swedes living in Toksovo. The Gaveman family lived in a pretty wooden house (nearer to Lake Heppojärvi), and the two Asalanus sisters occupied another very long, very old, single-storey house; they took in Finnish girls for a fortnight or a month before their confirmation in the church. The girls studied the elements of music and French there. Of course, they later forgot it all, but they went back to their cows with something very important to the rest of their lives: respect for culture and pride in knowing two or three words of French.

It was in Taytsy, where we stayed for the summer of 1917, and in Olgino (1918–19) that I began to take an interest in the history of the districts where we spent the summer in dachas. In Toksovo I began to study and record local traditions seriously but my notes disappeared when the house was searched on 8 February 1928.

In Toksovo my health improved. My parents hired me a boat for the whole summer, a little Finnish one with a pointed bow, and I particularly liked going out in it in bad weather and heading straight into the oncoming waves.

Traces of the suntan that I acquired on the water stayed with me for a long time. When I caught typhus on Solovki the doctor asked me "Where did you get this suntan? You've been in prison all summer, haven't you?" And that suntan was two years old. I consider that I owe my health, my interest in people and my optimistic outlook to the dachas which my parents rented even in the most difficult years.

And nevertheless it is Kuokkala that has always remained brightest in my memories of dacha life...

The Lentovskaya School

For a while after we moved to the official flat on the Petrograd District I still went to school at May's. There I experienced the first school reforms, from the introduction of work experience (woodwork lessons were replaced by sawing firewood to heat the school) to co-education (the girls from the neighbouring Shaffe school were transferred to us) and the rest. Travel to school, however, on the overcrowded trams became completely impossible, but walking there was even harder because of the dreadful food situation in the Petrograd of the day. We ate *duranda* (pressed oil-cake), bread made from oats and bonemeal, and sometimes we managed to obtain a little frozen potato, while for milk we walked to Lakhta and bartered. I was moved to the Lentovskaya school in Plutalovaya Street because it was nearer. And once more I found myself in an excellent establishment. Compared with May's, the 'Lentovka' was poorly off for equipment and premises, but it was amazing in terms of its teaching staff. The school had been founded after the 1905 Revolution from a number of teachers who had been dismissed from official grammar schools on account of their revolutionary activity. They had been brought together by the theatrical entrepreneur Lentovskaya, who put up the money and organised a private grammar school to which members of the intelligentsia with left-wing tendencies immediately started to send their children. The headmaster (Vladimir Kirillovich Ivanov) had a library of revolutionary Marxist literature in his study which, before the Revolution, he secretly allowed trusted pupils in the senior forms to read.

A close link, friendship, 'common cause', developed between pupils and teachers. The latter had no need to enforce discipline by stern measures. They could make a pupil feel ashamed, and peer pressure was such that misdemeanours were never repeated. We were allowed to smoke, but not a single founder-member of the school exercised the right.

I have written a special article on one of the teachers there, Leonid Vladimirovich Georg, but I could do the same for several others: Aleksandr Yakubovski (our history teacher, who was to become a famous Orientalist), Pavel Andreyev (brother of the writer Leonid, our art teacher), Tatyana Ivanova (who taught us geography) and numerous others. The school was near home, and I frequently attended the literature and philosophy societies with their activities which proved so popular among the adults.

One month in the summer of 1921 had huge significance for the formation of my character, my interests and, I would say, my love for the Russian North. The school organised a trip to the North and we travelled by train to Murmansk, then by steam yacht to Archangelsk via the Kola peninsula and the White Sea, then by steamer down the Severnaya Dvina to Kotlas and back by train to Petrograd. This two-week journey played an enormous role in shaping my conceptions of Russia, folklore, wooden architecture and the beauty of the northern Russian landscape. One should travel one's native land as early in life and as often as possible. School trips also foster good relationships with the teachers and are then remembered for the rest of one's life.

In school I acquired the knack of drawing cartoons of the teachers in just a couple of lines. One day, during the break, I was drawing them all on the classroom blackboard, when suddenly in came a teacher. I froze. He, however, came up and joined in our laughter (although he himself was one whom I had drawn) and left without saying a word. A lesson or two later our form master came in and said "Dmitri Likhachev, the headmaster wants you to do your cartoons again on paper for the staff common room." We had clever teachers.

In the Lentovskaya school pupils were encouraged to hold their own views. There were often arguments in class. Since then I have tried to maintain my independence in matters of taste and opinion.

In the opinion of my favourite teacher, Leonid Georg, Pushkin was without equal, although for him all literature was important, and I won't even say on a different level. Incidentally, he also thought very highly of Aleksandr Vvedenski[49] and encouraged him; he was a year or two senior to me in the school, and even then was writing his OBERIU poems.

At different times and in different circumstances I have enjoyed a variety of western literatures. Sometimes I am drawn to Dickens, sometimes Joyce, sometimes Proust, Shakespeare, Norwid[50] ... I find it easier to list the authors whom I don't feel disposed to read. And, of course, I haven't yet mentioned the philosophers whom I like and whose opinions I can share, as it were in fun, temporarily and with pleasure. Philosophical theories and views of the world hold for me an aesthetic value. Philosophers are artists, and we ought not to hide from them behind the shields of our personal views. But the acquisition of philosophical concepts is a very complex question. By being obstinate and indulging in slanging matches we deprive ourselves of a great deal.

Leonid Vladimirovich Georg

Leonid Vladimirovich Georg was one of those old 'teachers of literature' who taught in our grammar and modern schools in the nineteenth and early twentieth centuries. They greatly influenced their pupils and, in return, were regarded with both deep affection and girlish worship.

These old teachers of literature not only shaped their pupils' attitude to life but also educated their taste, their humanity, intellectual toleration, interest in arguments on philosophical questions, sometimes interest in the theatre (in Moscow, the Maly teatr) and music.

Leonid Vladimirovich possessed all the qualities of the ideal teacher. His talent, intellect, wit, inventiveness were multifaceted; he was invariably fair in his treatment of us, was of handsome appearance, had the instincts of an actor, could understand young people and could turn to advantage situations that were sometimes extremely trying for the educator.

I will tell you about these qualities of his.

When he appeared in the corridor, or at break in the hall, or in the classroom, even in the street, he never went unnoticed. He was tall, and his face was intelligent, slightly mocking, but at the same time kindly and attentive. Blonde, pale of eye, regular of features (perhaps his nose was a little on the short side, although straight enough to conceal this defect), he immediately attracted attention. He always wore well-fitting suits, though I never remember his wearing anything new; times were hard (he taught me between 1919–23), and how could he have afforded a new suit on his modest teacher's salary!

His dominant qualities were gentleness and elegance. There was no room for aggressiveness in his philosophy. He was most of all like Chekhov, his favourite writer, whom he often read to us when he had to stand in for colleagues who were frequently ill.

These 'stand-in' lessons were little masterpieces during which he encouraged us to develop an intellectual approach to life and the environment. What did he not talk to us about! He read us his favourite writers, and I recall readings of *War and Peace*, Chekhov's plays *The Seagull*, *Three Sisters* and *Cherry Orchard*, Maupassant's stories, Russian folk tales, *The Bronze Horseman*... Too many to list them all. He brought a French text into class and showed us that learning French could be interesting; he went through some stories of Maupassant, rummaged through the dictionary there in front of us in search of the most expressive translation, rejoicing in this or that feature of the French. And he went out of the room leaving us with a love not only of the French language, but of France. It goes without saying that after that we all started to do our best to learn French. That lesson took place in spring, and I remember doing nothing but French all summer... In other 'stand-in' lessons he told us about listening to Krivopolenova, demonstrating how she sang, how she spoke, how he took notes during the singing. And suddenly we all began to understand that old Russian woman, to love her and to envy Leonid Vladimirovich for having seen her, heard her and spoken to her. The most interesting of these 'stand-in' lessons, however, were those about the theatre. Even before the appearance of Stanislavski's[51] famous book *My Life in Art* he had told us about Stanislavski's theory, which he put into practice not only as an actor but also as a teacher. His tales of productions and famous actors somehow developed organically into studies of some play, which he would stage magnificently with the pupils in school. His staging of Pushkin's *Little Tragedies* was a huge success for him not only as a teacher, nor merely as a great producer (and I have no qualms about that 'great'), but also as a set-designer. With the help of his pupils and using coloured paper he devised remarkably beautiful, under-stated sets for his productions. I remember that in *The Stone Guest* there were cypresses, black or some other very dark colour (green or blue?) represented by sharp-pointed cones, a white column in some interior, also cut out in paper which my father had obtained for him as scrap from *Pechatny dvor*, where we were living at the time.

I remember how he used to train his pupils to be actors: he would make his actors wear their costumes in everyday life. Don Juan would be sitting there in lessons, scowling, in Spanish dress with a sword, and Dona Anna in a long dress. At break-time they walked about and even ran, but only as Don Juan and Dona Anna would have been able to do in such a complex imaginary situation (an actor must play all the time, but if he wants to have fun or do something out of character he is obliged to devise some motivation, establish a corresponding 'situation' for himself). Leonid Vladimirovich taught them to wear the costume first of all—before entering into the part. An actor has to feel completely at ease with a cloak, a long skirt, behave freely with his hat, toss it carelessly onto an armchair, draw his sword easily from the scabbard. Leonid Vladimirovich would surreptitiously keep an eye on a costumed pupil and knew how to upbraid him with a choice remark, always offered tactfully and in good humour.

Leonid Vladimirovich was a follower of the psychologist James[52]. I remember how well he explained James' position to us: "We don't cry because we feel sad, but we feel sad because we cry". This position he was able to subsume into his teaching method. He suggested to one very shy boy that he should change the way he walked. He told him to move more quickly, step out and always swing his arms when he walked. When he met him in the break he would often tell him "Swing those arms, swing those arms". He instilled self-respect in his pupils and demanded from them respect for others, for their fellows. When he enquired into something that had happened in the classroom he never forced us to betray the instigator or the person responsible. He endeavoured to make the culprit own up. The betrayal of a fellow pupil was intolerable in his eyes, as it was, incidentally, to all the good teachers in the old days.

When I was at the Lentovskaya school Leonid Vladimirovich was a tenor, but later he was 'discovered' as a baritone, and, it is said, quite a good one. In those days there was a grand piano in every classroom, requisitioned from the 'bourgeois'. Leonid Vladimirovich would take his seat at the piano and demonstrate to us features of musical form in Tchaikovski, whom he liked very much (in those days it was fashionable not to like Tchaikovski, but he just laughed at the fashion).

Leonid Vladimirovich would use gentle humour to combat bad habits or lack of taste in matters of dress in his girl pupils. When our girls started to grow up and began to pay particular attention to their hair or the way they walked Leonid Vladimirovich would tell us, without naming names, that at that age girls tended to begin waggling their hips as they walked (risking, as he put it, 'dislocation of the pelvis', a condition of his invention), or found themselves bits of rag, and he'd explain the meaning of dress-sense. He even read to us in class about George Brummel[53] from Kuzmin's[54] *On Dandyism*, but not so as to praise dandyism but rather to reveal to us the complexity of what might be called beautiful conduct, nice clothes and how to wear them, and in order to ridicule ostentation and foppishness in the boys.

Many years have passed since then, but how much of his instruction has remained with me all my life! On the other hand, what he said and showed us must not be labelled 'instruction'. It was all spoken extempore, on the spur of the moment, humorously, gently, 'Chekhov-fashion'.

He was able to discover interesting aspects of all his pupils—interesting both for the pupil himself and for those around him. He would tell us about a pupil in another class, and how interesting it was to learn about him from others! He helped each of us to find his true self: in one he would reveal some national characteristic (always a good one); in another a moral point (kindness or love for 'the little ones'); in a third, good taste; in a fourth, wit—and not simply wit, but he could characterise the special qualities of that wit ('a dry wit', Ukrainian humour—and immediately followed an explanation of what constituted Ukrainian humour); in a fifth he would find a philosopher, etc. , etc.

My friend Serezha Eynerling (son of the poet Galina Galinaya) was keen on the Nietzsche school of philosophy, and another friend, Misha Shapiro, on Oscar Wilde. Naturally, Leonid Vladimirovich knew of these enthusiasms and one day told us in class about both Nietzsche and Wilde. He showed us valuable aspects of their attitudes to reality but in such a way as to make it clear to us all that both were interesting, but that we should not be bounded by them. We must be broader in outlook than our teachers. He helped my friends to get off their 'philosophical plateau', for which they remained grateful to their boyhood idol.

For Leonid Vladimirovich himself there were no idols. He was keen on all manners of artists, writers, poets and composers, but his enthusiasms never became idolatry. His very favourite poet was, I would say, Pushkin, and of Pushkin's works his favourite was *The Bronze Horseman*, which he once staged with his pupils. It was rather along the lines of a choral recitation, produced as a theatrical performance with the text, Pushkin's own words, as the most important element. At rehearsals he made us consider how to speak this line and that, with what intonation, what pauses. He showed us the beauty of Pushkin's language, but at the same time his lapses too. Here's an example that I remember from those days: "All night the Neva / Struggled seaward against the storm / Without overcoming their (whose?) mutinous foolishness / And became too weak to quarrel...". He could find similar imperfections, not to say errors, in the most famous works of painting, sculpture and music. He once said that the legs of the Venus de Milo were shorter than they should be, and we gradually came round to his opinion. Did it upset us? No, our interest in art grew as a result.

At school Leonid Vladimirovich organised a system of self-government. For some reason I was against this piece of 'impudence', as it seemed to me. I proved in my class that there is no such thing as self-government and that all those meetings, elections, electoral duties, etc., were all nothing more than a futile waste of time when we ought to have been preparing for entry to high school. For once I began to oppose Leonid Vladimirovich, the affection I felt for him changed into extreme irritation. The whole class refused to take part in this experiment in self-government. Leonid Vladimirovich told my father about what we had done "Dima wants to show us that he isn't at all the person he's been making himself out to be". He was patently angry with me. But he came into our class, quiet and mildly sarcastic as ever, and suggested that we share our opinions concerning self-government with him and put forward our own proposals. He patiently heard us out and raised no objections. He merely asked us what we proposed. We were completely unprepared to offer anything positive, and he helped us, paid attention to what we had to say. We acknowledged that someone in the school had to do the heavy work, saw firewood, haul the pianos (for some reason we often had to move them from one place to another). So he proposed that our class should organise itself as it wished, or even not at all. But he still insisted that the school needed help with the heavy work, for which outsiders could not be brought in, and that seemed acceptable to us. We were, of course, the oldest and strongest in the school; we couldn't, naturally, let little girls from junior forms do our difficult jobs. We would do all that, but we didn't want to be formed into any organisation. To that Leonid Vladimirovich said "But we're going to have to call you something, aren't we?" and proposed there and then that we should be known as 'the independent group' or, for short, 'indgroup'. We agreed. Thus, without our noticing, he'd put an end to all our rebelliousness, and we entered the school self-government scheme as a very important and really valuable part of it.

Leonid Vladimirovich was very poorly off. In those days teachers' salaries were miserly, and sometimes benefit concerts were organised for them. Leonid Vladimirovich refused for a long time to permit this, but finally his actor friends came to the school and performed on his behalf.

Soon after I'd left school he went down with, I believe, typhus, and the attack left him with a weakened heart. I met him on a tram and he appeared to me to have put on weight. He said to me "I haven't put on weight, I'm inflated!" Later came the time when Leonid Vladimirovich was no more than a memory for his pupils. For more than fifty years I have remembered him more vividly than any of my other teachers. I remember that high, very handsome forehead...

The University

My time at University was, of course, of the utmost importance for the development of my academic interests and, at the same time, the most difficult.

56

I entered Leningrad University at a rather earlier age than usual: I would not be seventeen for a few more months. It was one of the first years when entry was regulated according to social class. I was neither working class, nor the son of a worker—but of an ordinary civil servant. Even in those days letters of commendation from influential persons carried weight. It shames me to admit that my father obtained such a letter for me, and it played a certain part in my admission. The University was going through the most acute period of its 'reconstruction'. The 'Red Professor' Nikolay Derzhavin—a celebrated authority on Bulgaria and a future Academician—was actively promoting this if not actually putting it into practice.

There were 'red' professors and plain professors. Actually, there were no professors at all, as this title, together with all academic grades, had been suppressed. Nevertheless it became the convention to divide the professorate into 'red' and 'old' on the basis of whether they addressed us as 'comrades' or 'colleagues'. The 'reds' knew less, but addressed the students as 'comrades'; the 'old' professors knew more, but called the students 'colleagues'. I paid no attention to this convention but went to hear everyone who seemed interesting.

I entered the Faculty of Social Studies. Its official abbreviation FON was also interpretable as 'Faculty of Expectant Girls'[55] but by the standards of modern times there weren't many girls. It merely seemed that there were a lot because one was not used to them: before the Revolution only men had gone to university. The student body was no less varied than that of the 'conventional professors'; some were straight from school, but mostly they were adults from the Civil War fronts, still in military uniform. There were 'eternal students' who had been studying and working for ten years, children of high-ranking members of the Petersburg intelligentsia, educated in their time by governesses and fluent in two or three foreign languages.

There were divisions within the Faculty. There was the Socio-Educational division[56], dealing with historical studies and the Ethnology and Linguistics division, so called at the suggestion of N. Ya. Marr[57], where philological studies were carried out. This division was subdivided into sections, and I chose the Romano-German one, but immediately began to study Slavonic and Russian also.

There was in those years no compulsory attendance at lectures. Nor were there any general courses, as it was considered that there was little factually new that general courses could impart after school. Students could qualify in Nineteenth Century Russian Literature by reading a reasonable number of books. On the other hand, there flourished a variety of courses on particular subjects or 'spetskursy', as they were known. Thus, for instance, V. L. Komarovich lectured on two evenings a week on Dostoyevski, and his lectures, which began at six o'clock, would last until midnight. He would inform us of the progress of his research, present his material like academic papers, and numerous eminent scholars attended his lectures.

In the '20s Leningrad University was an unusual phenomenon in literary studies, and of course just next door, on St. Isaac's Square, was the Institute of the History of the Arts (the Zubovski Institute) with its busy theatrical and artistic life. All this was going on while my academic interests were forming, and there is nothing surprising in the fact that I lost my head and there was a lot that I failed to find time to go to.

I left the University in 1928 after writing two theses, one on Shakespeare in Russia in the late eighteenth century and the first years of the nineteenth, the other on tales of the Patriarch Nikon. By the end of my student days I had to earn a living but there were no official positions to be had, and I took on the job of establishing a library for the Institute of Phonetics of Foreign Languages. The Institute was well off but not very keen to pay me. I worked in the Book Fund, of which Saranchivy was in charge, at no. 20 on the Fontanka. And once more there was an astonishing range of books requisitioned from a variety of private libraries and palaces, rarities, rarities and more rarities. It was a shame to choose all these for the Phonetics Institute, and I tried to take only the unusual or the essential, leaving the remainder, the more valuable, for others to choose from.

What was the principal benefit of my time in the University? It's hard to catalogue everything that I studied or learned there. It wasn't merely a matter of attendance at lectures or classes. There were endless and very liberal conversations in the long University corridor, thesis defences to listen to and lectures to attend—there were a vast number of lecture theatres and meeting-rooms in the city, ranging from the Volfila on the Fontanka, the Tenishevaya hall, the House of Printing and the House of the Arts to the little room in modernist style at the very top of *Dom knigi* where at one time and another Yesenin and Chukovski gave readings as did other prose writers, actors, etc. I used to go to the Great Hall of the Filarmoniya, where one could meet all the current personalities, especially of the musical world.

Most beneficial of my University classes, in my opinion, were not the 'general courses', which counted for little, but the seminars and tutorials at which various texts were read and discussed.

Pride of place goes to the logic classes. From the first year I attended Professor A. I. Vvedenski's practicals, which were held, by an irony of Fate, where Bestuzhev's courses for women had formerly been held[58]. I say 'by an irony of Fate' because he manifestly regarded women as incapable of coping with a course in logic. In those years, when logic was one of the compulsory subjects, he would set students a 'test', strenuously refraining from asking the women questions and occasionally passing ironic comments on the subject of the female mind. But his classes were masterly, and the women, though few in number, did attend them. When Vvedenski's lectures and classes came to an end one of our 'mature' students—as I recall, one who had served in the Civil War—organised a group to study logic in the flat of Professor S. I. Povarnin, author of a famous text-book on the subject. We went there and read in Russian translation Husserl's *Logical Researches*, referring to the German original now and then for better understanding of the text. Povarnin told us more than once: one must know languages, even if not well, even if one is always running to the dictionary, because translators of scientific and technical books are not to be relied on.

Zhirmunski's classes and seminars on English poetry of the early nineteenth century were a real schooling in the understanding of poetry. With him we read various poems of Shelley, Keats, Wordsworth, Coleridge and Byron, analysing their style and content. Zhirmunski gave us the benefit of his vast erudition, making us refer to the dictionaries and anthologies of his contemporaries and we discussed poetry from all angles, biographical, literary-historical and philosophical. He made no concessions to our ignorance of any of the three, our poor knowledge of English, symbolism or simply the geography of England. He regarded us as adults and addressed us as he would his learned colleagues. Not without cause did he address us as 'colleagues' when he greeted us ceremoniously in the University corridor. It strengthened the bond between us. We felt something of the same during the seminars on Shakespeare given by Vladimir Myuller, at the Old French classes of Aleksandr Smirnov, and those of Semen Boyanus on Middle English poetry.

The real pinnacle of the 'slow reading approach' was L. V. Shcherb's seminar on Pushkin, where we would read no more than a few lines or stanzas in a whole year. I can tell you that at the University I had a thorough grounding in 'slow reading', deepened by a philological understanding of the text. We were taught another subject by dear V. E. Yevgenev-Maksimov, who held classes in the manuscript sections of the libraries. He would get us into an archive and then, to our surprise, come along and check, while we were working, to see how we were getting along. Once he took me with him to see the collector Kortanov at Novaya Derevnya as he hoped to obtain some material on Nekrasov from him. He aroused our inquisitiveness and taught us not to be afraid of archives as he regarded a fear of archives in a budding academic as a kind of childish illness to be conquered as soon as possible.

The lectures of Ye. Tarle also drew my attention, but they taught me mainly about the art of oratory and lecturing. I often remembered, in later years, when I'd begun to teach in Leningrad University in the '40s, how Tarle used to pause as if seeking a suitable word, and how the word that he found 'fired' us with its precision and was remembered for life. I would recall too how Tarle used to 'think' as he gave his lectures, how he would amble up and down clumsily, like a bear, beside the rostrum, 'searching' for facts, 'calling to mind' documents, creating a complete illusion of brilliant improvisation. In actual fact his lectures were prepared in detail in advance, down to the pauses in his 'searches for the *mot juste*'.

I turned to Old Russian literature at the University because I considered that as an artistic phenomenon it had been largely ignored in literary studies. Furthermore, Ancient Rus also interested me from the point of view of gaining knowledge of the Russian national character. The literature and art of Ancient Rus' taken together seemed to me a promising field of study. The way that Old Russian literature changed stylistically with the passage of time seemed to me very important. I wanted to establish the characteristics of one period and another on the lines of those recognised in the West—particularly in the works on the history of culture of Emile Mâle[59].

My lifetime has seen not only a flowering of literature (I will not say 'Leningrad' literature, for one should not classify Russian literature into the schools of Leningrad, Moscow, Odessa, Vologda, etc.), but also of the study of the humanities. The world has never seen such a constellation of scholars—of literature, language, history, the Orient—as was in the University of Leningrad and the Institute of the History of the Arts in the Zubov Palace in the 1920s. Alas, I didn't realise at the time how important it was to listen to poets and writers and to see them. For me, therefore, my time as a student of Leningrad University was a time of wasted opportunities. I heard Sobinov[60], but gave my ticket for Shalyapin to a friend and didn't go to meet either Yesenin or Mayakovski. I only spoke once on the telephone to Samuil Marshak[61] (he suggested that I should study children's literature and write for children in Russian).

The Red Terror

Russian culture of the 'Silver Age'[62] (an age, by the way, which lasted only a quarter of a century) was born of conversation and discussion—untrammelled, free, and revealing a speaker's inner thoughts. In these conversations, which by some essential spiritual law had to have not fewer than three participants, new thoughts, new 'revelations' came to life. Talking formulated and honed one's thoughts and cleared the way for further ideas. The fruitfulness of these conversations was dependent on their complete freedom. It was no accident that from 1928 onwards, with the rise to power of Stalin and his dictatorship over the hearts and minds of the people, the persecution of the educated classes and the repression of their meetings and their conversations began.

'Russian conversations', long-drawn-out, lasting past midnight, were a characteristic and very fruitful feature of the Russian culture of the nineteenth and the first quarter of the twentieth centuries.

I would like in these memoirs to give an account of what thinking Russian youth lived on in those years, seen, of course, from the narrow angle of my personal experience. I kept no notes apart from those made on Solovki and immediately on my return to Leningrad. Nowadays I can no longer give precise dates. I can only hope that my memory is accurate.

There is an essential difference between the way that intellectual circles formed in the 1920s and the way that learned societies come into being nowadays. In those days it was sufficient to find a temporary place for meetings, to organise a lecture, present a paper, open a discussion. If a series of public events took place, or a thorny problem dragged on over a number of meetings, and it was sometimes not clear who was convening them, the group had to be named and min-utes kept. A room in a flat, the auditorium of the Tenishevski Insti-tute, a school staff-room, notification by hand-written bills (and often by word of mouth) were quite sufficient.

First came the need, then the modest 'formalisation'. Nowadays, things are quite the opposite: first of all one thinks up a title, the means are found, an establishment is confirmed, etc. Titles are the most exalted—never less than lycee, college, university, academy and the like.

* * *

One of the aims of these memoirs is to dispel the myth that the pe-riod of the harshest repression began in 1936–37. I think that in the future the statistics of arrests and executions will show that waves of arrests, imprisonments and deportations had begun as early as 1918, even before the 'Red Terror' officially appeared in the autumn of that year. These waves continued to break in a constant crescendo right up to the death of Stalin, and it seems that the new wave of 1936–37 was merely the 'ninth wave[63]' ... When we opened our shutters at night in the flat in Lakhtinskaya Street even in 1918–19 we could hear spasmodic shots and short bursts of machine-gun fire from the direction of the Peter and Paul Fortress.

It was not Stalin who started the 'Red Terror'. He merely increased it dramatically and took it to an incredible pitch on coming to power.

The arrests of prominent activists in the all-powerful party began in 1935–37, and that, it would appear, has done more than anything else to inflame the imagination of my contemporaries. While officers, 'bourgeois', professors and, in particular, the clergy, together with Russian, Ukrainian and White Russian peasants were being shot by the thousand in the '20s and early '30s, it all seemed 'natural'. But then there began the 'self-devouring aspect of power', which left the country with only the most nondescript, those devoid of character and those who had gone into hiding or had reached an accommoda-tion.

So while there were people left in the country who could think—people possessed of some spark of individuality—intellectual life in Russia was not extinct, neither in the prisons, the camps nor at large. Having just about made contact in my youth with people of the 'Silver Age' of Russian culture, I had sensed their strength, their courage and their ability to oppose all the processes of disruption in society. The Russian intelligentsia has never been corrupt. When it was exposed to corruption only a small part of it began to participate in ideological campaigns and activities, the struggle for 'purity of line', and by so doing ceased to be of the intelligentsia. This was a small part, and the majority had already been exterminated in the war of 1914–17, the Revolution and the first years of the terror.

My recollections are first and foremost of the people close to me and of the intellectual life of the '20s and early '30s, in so far as that life was accessible to me in those years.

With every passing year of my youth I sensed an encroaching spirit of corruption which sapped the amazing, life-giving strength that came from the older generation of the Russian intelligentsia.

Day and night changed places, as people couldn't sleep at night. They lived in the expectation of hearing a car stop right outside their windows and an 'iron' investigator appearing at the door of their flat accompanied by witnesses, pale with dread...

One always remembers one's youth as a happy time. I, however, and my contemporaries in school, university and intellectual circles have something painful to recall, something which stings my memory and which was the hardest of all to bear in my young days. This was the destruction of Russia and the Russian Church which took place with murderous savagery before our very eyes, leaving no hope, it seemed, of recovery.

Many are convinced that loving the Motherland means being proud of her. No! I was brought up to another sort of love tinged with pity. The failures of the Russian army in the First World War, especially in 1915, wounded my boyish heart. I dreamed only of what could be done to save Russia. Both the ensuing revolutions disturbed me mainly because of what was happening to the Russian Army. News from the theatre of operations became more and more worrying. My grief knew no bounds.

Naturally, there were many conversations in the family about what seemed to be the innate unconcern of the Russians (it was said that they always relied on the 'off-chance'), about German strength in government, about Rasputin, the misconduct in Petrograd of the huge mass of poorly trained soldiery and the repulsive NCOs who were training the new recruits in the streets and squares. I watched these NCOs every day in the vicinity of St Isaac's Cathedral, where we lived—'revolutionaries' who had stayed away from the front, exercising their right to remain in the rear, in Petrograd; their treatment of the recruits was cruel. These 'patriots' actually despised and hated the new intakes of peasants.

When the scandalous peace of Brest-Litovsk was concluded it was impossible to believe that it wasn't treachery plain and simple, the handiwork of the enemies of our Motherland.

Persecution of the Church began almost contemporaneously with the October cataclysm. This was so intolerable for any Russian that many unbelievers began to go to church, distancing themselves psychologically from the persecutors. Here are some data, undocumented and possibly imprecise, from a book of the time:

> On the basis of incomplete data (the Privolzhe and Prikame and a number of other places are not included), over a period of only eight months (June 1918 to January 1919) there have been killed one metropolitan, eighteen bishops, one hundred and two priests, one hundred and fifty-four deacons and ninety-four monks and nuns. Ninety-four churches and twenty-six monasteries have been closed, fourteen shrines and nine chapels desecrated; the lands and property of seven hundred and eighteen parochial clergy and fifteen monasteries have been sequestrated. Four archbishops, one hundred and ninety-eight priests, eight archimandrites and five Fathers Superior have been imprisoned. Eighteen religious processions have been banned and forty-one broken up, and acts of worship have been indecently disrupted in churches in twenty-two towns and ninety-six villages. At the same time desecration and destruction of relics and requisition of church furnishings have taken place.

This was only the first few months of Soviet power. Afterwards the slaughter gathered pace. This was only the start, after which came the declaration of the 'Red Terror' on 5 September 1918, although lynchings and mass executions (those that took place in the Peter and Paul Fortress) had come even earlier.

Then there began yet more provocation of the 'living church', by the confiscation of church treasures, etc., etc. The publication in 1927 of the 'Declaration' of Metropolitan Sergey, who tried to reconcile Church with State and State with Church, was understood by all, Russians and non-Russians alike, within the framework of the facts of the persecutions. The State was 'theomachist'.

Services in the remaining Orthodox churches were conducted with especial devoutness. Church choirs sang particularly well as they were swollen by many professional singers (often from the opera company of the Mariinski theatre). Priests and other clergy officiated with great feeling. My teacher Panteleymon Germanov went to church very frequently, as did my school friend Misha Shapiro, who came from a profoundly traditional Jewish family. At the same time Mariya Yudina was baptised, my school friend Volodya Rakov became a server with Father Viktorin Dobronravov at the church on Petrovski Island, etc.

As persecution of the Church became more widespread, and executions more numerous so all of us felt an ever keener grief for the Russia that was dying. Our love for the Motherland resembled least of all pride in her, her victories and conquests. Nowadays many find that hard to understand. We didn't sing patriotic songs—we wept and prayed.

It was with this sense of grief and sorrow that in 1923 I began my University studies of Old Russian literature and art. I wanted to sustain Russia in my memory as the children sitting round her bed want to retain the image of a dying mother and gather up representations of her to show them to their friends and tell of the greatness of her tormented life. My books are, in essence, memorial notes offered for the repose of Russia's soul: you can't remember everything when you are writing a book—you jot down the dearest names, and for me such names are associated with Ancient Rus'.

The Making of a Philosophy

And I mean 'philosophy', not 'ideology'. This section of my memoirs I will open with a quotation from Act IV, scene iii, of Shakespeare's *Julius Caesar*. The thought that it contains has been my conviction all my life: only a correct philosophy, a correct view of the world, can save a man, both physically and spiritually. The lines are as follows:

Brutus. O Cassius, I am sick with many griefs.
Cassius. Of your philosophy you make no use.

I began thinking about the essential nature of the world, it seems, when I was a child. I remember being excited, as are many children, by the 'mirror effect'. What is there, beyond the world, and can one not look into that part of the mirror world which is hidden beyond the edges of the mirror? All children, it seems to me, go through the curiosity of *Alice through the Looking-glass*. I was also interested in whether or not the things and the world that I couldn't see at a given time were still there. I used to try to look round as quickly and suddenly as possible so as to find out what was happening behind my back when I wasn't looking. From the prayer that I used to say with my mother at night I knew that every child had his guardian angel, and I'd look round without warning to catch a glimpse of him behind my back. The world has always seemed to me, since before my schooldays, something of a riddle.

In the most senior classes of the Lentovskaya school the pupils were intent on working out their own personal views of the world. To have one's own philosophy was very important for the self-assurance of us teenagers, and as we pondered the meaning of everything that existed we reached the definite conclusion that we needed egoism. When one meditates on the general problems of life it is only in conditions of total spiritual isolation that one resolves to take 'evil' decisions. Evil usually arises from thoughtlessness. The emblem of conscientiousness is not simply feeling but thought!

Serezha Eynerling, my closest friend and neighbour in class, was keen on Nieztsche, and called himself a Nietzschean. His Nietzscheanism, however, was a 'kindly Nietzscheanism'. He did not rudely reject the teachings of Nietzsche, nor accept them lock, stock and barrel. He was excited by pages here and there in Nietztsche and accepted the division at the beginning into the Dionysian and the Apollonian.

My other friend Misha Shapiro liked Oscar Wilde and dreamed of a government led by an intellectual aristocracy. There was something about the Venetian Republic that appealed to him, and something in the English ruling class as well. In my last year at school I became friends with Sergey Neustruyev. Of all my friends he was the most sceptical. Scepticism is dangerous. After leaving school he was recruited by the OGPU[64], and at some risk to his freedom he warned me a week in advance of my impending arrest. He died soon after somewhere in the Soviet Far East.

Naturally, not all the class took the making of a philosophy seriously. But all, I venture to assert, were aware of the need to acknowledge their relationship with their surroundings. This was forced upon them by conditions in the country and by the general intelligence of the class.

What is meant by the general intelligence of one's environment is another story. The contents of these moral surroundings comprised a collective psychology that presupposed freedom of the person, a collective morality, a collective super-philosophy that brought together the intelligent people of the world, collective intellectual interests, even freely changing vogues for deep philosophical currents, ways of understanding human reputations, upbringings, proprieties, orderliness and much more, now half forgotten. In a moral environment a philosophy became natural behaviour in the wide sense.

I too established my own 'philosophical system'. To some extent it was an expression of my character, but mainly of my reaction to all the ills that surrounded me. It was a philosophy that took shape as I wrestled with the eternal questions and sought to explain the meaning and purpose of existence.

If time is an absolute reality, then Raskolnikov was right[65]. Everything will be forgotten, will pass out of one's life, and all that will remain will be humanity 'which has been made happy' by the crimes that have passed into non-existence. What is more important on the scales of time: a future that is actually approaching, or a past which is disappearing more and more, into which, as into the maw of a crucible, good and evil go in equal measure? And what consolation is there for a man who has lost his dear ones? How can there be prediction, prophecy? The facts of prediction are there, unquestioned by the unbiased mind. And so on.

I reached the conclusion that time was merely one of the forms of perception of reality. If at the end of the world 'there should be time no longer' (Revelation 10:6), then it does not exist as a sort of beginning, either at its inception or throughout its existence.

An ant crawls, and what has vanished behind it seems to exist no more as far as it can tell. That's how we too, and all living things that have consciousness, perceive the world. And in actual fact all the past, in every tiniest detail of its multi-million year existence, still exists, and the future already exists on the same scale right up to its apocalyptic end.

We look through the window of a racing train. To a child it seems that only what he can see through the window exists. That which the train had raced past is now no more. That which the train is approaching does not yet exist at all.

The prototype of eternity is present also in time. The simplest example is music. At any given moment in a musical performance the last sound is present and the next can be anticipated. Without this 'overriding of time' it would be impossible to perceive music. And this partial fusion in music of past, present and future is a faint reflection of that eternity into which all that exists has been absorbed, and which is picked up by the 'stylus of the present' from the gramophone record of eternity.

The 'record' carrying everything that has happened and that will happen in the future exists in timeless eternity, and the playing of that record, on which everything is 'compressed', takes place in time. Time presents the opportunity to 'listen to the record'.

Is that unimaginable? Yes! Time exists for the opportunity to perceive an infinitely rich eternity. Time, or better, a sense of time, is present in all living things (not just Man, but everything that has life), but it is only a *form* of the perception of an infinitely rich timeless existence.

There is another consideration that made me personally think that time is nothing but a condition of the perception of timeless existence. Of course, if time is an absolute, not a relative, category, then the past is the most enormous field of existence, completely free of the rule of God. The past sets a limit on the omnipotence of God. The past, if it exists, is immutable. And therefore, as I see it, the past is merely a part of that timeless monolith which is coeval with God. The past does not go away or change because it and we are co-eternal, and as a result it is subject to God, established by God together with all that is to come. It need not be resurrected. The resurrection of the dead, which has been promised us and without which there is no moral consolation, follows immediately upon death as a crossing into eternity. We simply flow into the world of timelessness, eternity. And in that world we are with all that has happened, all that we have experienced, all that has been and in fact continues to exist.

God is omniscient! Of what does His omniscience consist? I conceived of this omniscience as follows. Let us consider: what is the number of individual objects that we can define at once, without counting—that is, the quantity of which we can indicate in a single moment. One—no need to count. Two—ditto. Three—ditto. But when we come to four and five we have to count consciously, to deal with them sequentially. The calculation may be carried out with astonishing rapidity, but nevertheless it does take place in our minds. Omniscient God has no need to count anything. He holds 'in His consciousness' in a moment millions and millions. Together with this he retains in His consciousness phenomena of all sorts and of all times in His timeless wisdom. Therein lies the greatness of God, I deduced, compared with ourselves, who require cognition, cognition and time, as forms of the cognition of reality.

But at this point in the course of my reflections there arose an obstacle. I was convinced of the free will of man. Only on that basis could he be good or evil, answer for his deeds. If, however, he did not possess freedom, it followed of itself from the thoughts that I express above that after all there was no such thing as morality, for man had no choice. The soul of man was a timeless datum. Here the greatest secret was revealed, something not to be envisaged in concrete terms. Man exists outside time, as a free being, answerable for himself, and at the same time within the will of God. That, therefore, obviously exists, even if time is acknowledged not as a form of the perception of existence, but as an absolute phenomenon within which God Himself too exists.

The theological teaching on synergy came to my assistance—the union of divine omnipotence and human freedom, which makes man fully responsible not only for his behaviour, but for his very essence, and for all the good or evil that it contains.

In order to approach the understanding of the timeless world, to become nearer to envisaging it, I think, it is most convenient to think of it not as *eternity*, that is, as a sort of existence in time infinitely extended, but as an infinitely great essence, momentary and all-embracing. That is to say, both past and future exist in a single 'momentary state', common to all things as when a dying man sees his life flash before him.

In connection with this view of time as a sort of limited means of perceiving the world, there is also the view of the omniscience of God—the omniscience which displays the divine greatness more clearly than anything. But of that more later.

But why do I continually talk of time as a means of perceiving the world? Time is a form (obviously, one of the forms) of existence. And one can state precisely why this form is necessary. All of the future that stretches away before us is necessary for the preservation of freedom of choice, freedom of will, which exist contemporaneously with the will of God, without which not a hair falls from our heads. Time is not a deception which compels us either to answer before God and our consciences for our actions, which in fact we cannot revoke or alter, or to somehow influence our behaviour. Time is one of the forms of reality, which permits us to be, in a limited way, free. The combination, however, of our limited freedom with the Will of God, as I have already said, is one of the secrets of synergy. Our ignorance is in contrast to the omniscience of God, but is in no way its equal in significance. But even if we knew everything, we would be unable to govern ourselves.

As I recollect my theory of those days on the timeless existence of everything that is, one aspect of it strikes me as interesting—that concerning the laws of nature. As far as I remember, my belief then was that the laws of nature were a reflection of the eternal nature of Time. True existence had neither time nor space. It was all compact, unified, something like a full stop. The laws of nature, from that of gravity to those of behaviour, were in their way 'recollections' of the primeval timeless and spaceless unity of the world. Not only laws, however, but also presentiments, prophecies, and memory itself: all these were elements of that same primeval linking of everything in the world.

The concept of time that I established while still at school was extremely naive. In downgrading time to a mere function of human perception of the world it completely ignored the ontological essence of time as the self-expression of Existence, and came to contradict my Christian self-awareness. To imagine the history of mankind, and the principal event—the incarnation of Christ—as a form of the perception of a timeless phenomenon, would have been not only quite impossible but also blasphemous. The concept of time, however, as a form of the perception of existence played a big part in my youthful life—I might say a 'pacifying' part, enabling me to be steadfast and spiritually poised in all my experiences, especially those concerned with my imprisonment in the DPZ[66] on Solovki. But that was where it began gradually to crumble once I had met Aleksandr Meyer and spent long hours in philosophical discussion with him, of which more later.

Even before my arrest I had presented a paper on my 'conception' to a circle at which there were present not only my teachers but also a group of visiting philosophers. I remember that Ye. P. Ivanov was there. I was much talked about at school, but after a while that 'recognition' changed into an ordeal of self-love for me; when I went up to University I was not 'recognised' because the students were older than me and more experienced, and many were unquestionably cleverer and more able. I took that loss of status badly and tried to retrieve it by an ambitious assiduousness in my work.

I remember one more fact connected with my philosophical searches. In *Khelfernak* (of which I shall write below) S. A. Alekseyev-Askoldov was to present a paper on *The Miracle*. He asked me to take notes for his paper and to lecture him from them. I don't know why he made such a request of me. His pretext was that he wanted to be relieved of the work of writing, but I think that he suggested that I should read him my notes for educational purposes, and because he knew of my philosophical ideas.

Askoldov's paper was in two parts. In the first, he discussed why miracles and direct communication with God had been so common in Biblical times and the Middle Ages and had now vanished completely. In the second, he expounded the idea that miracles were a form of the 'economy' of divine energy. The two parts were interconnected. Instead of taking notes for the second part I presented him with a notebook full of my reflections on it. I took it as a great compliment that he partly agreed with my reasoning. I was at the time in the final year, and Askoldov asked me what I was thinking of going into. He suggested that I should be a philosopher. On hearing that I wanted to study literature he agreed, saying that under the circumstances of the day literary studies enjoyed greater liberty than philosophy, and nevertheless had much in common with it. In this way he supported me in my intention to study on the Arts side, whereas my family felt that I ought to become an engineer. "You'll be a beggar", was my father's answer to all my arguments. I've always remembered those words of his, and was very ashamed when I returned from prison, had no employment, and had to live at his expense for several months.

S. A. Alekseyev-Askoldov

When Sergey Alekseyevich Alekseyev came to teach psychology at the Lentovskaya school in the early '20s, he was very handsome. A big photograph of him with his white beard hung in the window of the photographic studio on the Bolshoy Prospekt, and we would go in groups to look at it and compare it with what he looked like in real life. In those post-Revolutionary days photographers' windows were somewhat akin to our television: they established the popularity of the people in the pictures. As we knew little of Alekseyev's services to Russian philosophy and Russian culture as a whole, we considered him a famous man simply because the whole of the Petrograd District admired his photograph.

He didn't take our class but the one senior to it. None the less I saw him frequently and listened to him in the numerous circles that mushroomed in Petrograd at that time. In the first place there were the philosophical and literary circles in our own school; lots of adults came to their meetings, including Alekseyev himself and other teachers.

Alekseyev always treated us youngsters as if we were his equals in age. He invited me to his house (he and his family, of which I well remember his son the poet, lived in a private house on Kronverk-skaya Street). He not only gave me books to read but also talked to me about his thoughts of music and poetry.

I can't remember him ever laughing or smiling; he was always serious, always thinking. He was often seen on his bicycle, his white beard streaming (he would be going to the Islands for a ride), but even on a bicycle he always looked as if he was deep in thought.

In 1922 he suddenly stopped teaching in our school. What happened was this: the pupils of the senior form had heard about his philosophical views, which they considered simply 'mysticism', and attached threads to the strings of the grand piano in the classroom. During the lesson first one string, then another, began to sound. At first Sergey Alekseyevich couldn't understand what was going on, but he noticed the crafty, grinning faces of the pupils, realised the truth, walked out of the classroom and never set foot in the school again.

In 1928 we were all arrested. All members of circles were being arrested. Alekseyev was, as I recall, simply exiled. When I was released in 1932 I lived in Leningrad but he continued to drift about the provinces. In the mid-'30s he came to Leningrad to stay for a few days with a family from Novgorod. We decided not to meet in either of our flats: people who had served one sentence and continued to meet were being arrested and given second terms. He and I therefore met in the Summer Garden and spent a long time walking along the paths, not infrequently glancing over our shoulders. I told him about my time on Solovki and on the White Sea-Baltic canal and about the fate of people we had both known. He in turn told me about Andreyevski, who was living in exile in Novgorod and on the Volkhovstroy. He said that he 'found consolation in music', loved 'Rimski' (there was a fashion among the Petersburg intelligentsia for using only the adjectival element of double-barrelled titles or surnames, whence 'Rimski', 'Swan', 'Sleeping', 'Spades', etc., as, by the way, Anna Akhmatova used to say).

My meeting with him in the Summer Garden was the last. I never saw him again. I heard later that he had been captured by the Nazis and taken to Germany where he lived in the so-called Russian village, which had a Russian church, near Potsdam. He died, having failed to survive arrest by his Soviet liberators, and is buried there; when I was in East Germany in 1966, however, I couldn't find his grave.

Khelfernak

Right up to the end of 1927 the city seethed with various philosophical circles, student societies and 'at homes' held by well-known people. People came together in the University, the Geographical Society and in their own homes. A range of problems—philosophical, historical and literary—were discussed. Students of literature split into *formalists*, representatives of the formal school, and those who maintained traditional methods of literary study. Disputes took place both in private circles and on official territory—in Leningrad University, in the Institute of the History of the Arts (the *Zubovski*) on St. Isaac's Square, but mostly in the hall of the Tenishevski college. We had our circles in the Lentovskaya school as well and one of them met in the flat of our teacher I. M. Andreyevski from the very beginning of the 20s, and had, as I have already mentioned, the name *Khelfernak*[67].

Khelfernak flourished roughly from 1921 to 1925, with distinguished academics, schoolboys and University students gathering every Wednesday in Andreyevski's two stuffy attic rooms. Among those who came I remember S. A. Alekseyev-Askoldov, M. V. Yudina, Dr Modest N. Morzhetski, V. L. Komarovich, I. Ye. Anichkov, L. V. Georg, Ye. P. Ivanov, A. A. Guizetti, M. M. Bakhtin, Vsevolod Vladimir Bakhtin, A. P. Sukhov and numerous others, and of the younger element Volodya Rakov, Fedya Rozenberg, Arkasha Selivanov, Valya Morozova, Kolya Guryev, Misha Shapiro and Serezha Eynerling. There were too many to list. At meetings a huge book was passed around for people to sign, and at the top of the page the subject of the paper, the date and the speaker's name were written in Andreyevski's distinctive Gothic hand. In 1927, a dangerous time for us all, one of the youngest members of Khelfernak, Kolya Guryev, wrapped this book in waterproof material and buried it somewhere on Krestovski Island.

The papers were on the most varied topics—literary, philosophical and theological. Discussions were lively and Andreyevski's little rooms were never empty.

Andreyevski had a huge and carefully selected library (at that time books were very cheap, and could be bartered for bread, salt, flour or even for things sold by weight!) We were all allowed to help ourselves from his library, even in his absence, so long as we stuck a note acknowledging the loan on a special spike, and didn't keep the book longer than the allotted time. Thanks to this library I managed to become acquainted with the most varied philosophical literature while still at school: and even if I couldn't read a certain book, it was important to just hold it in my hands, to memorise the list of contents and its external appearance and simply to discover its existence. Another huge part in my literary education was played by Ionov's library and the vast one in *Dom knigi*, of which I have written above.

Libraries and cultural circles were the basis of my education.

The Brotherhood of St Serafim of Sarov

In the second half of the '20s Andreyevski's circle Khelfernak began to assume a more and more religious character. This change was no doubt explained by the persecutions to which the Church was subject at the time. Discussion of Church affairs took up most of the circle's time. Andreyevski began to consider the change in the circle's fundamental leanings and tried to find it a new name. All were agreed that the circle, which several members of an atheistic tendency had by now left, should be called a 'brotherhood'. But named after whom? Andreyevski wanted to call it 'The Brotherhood of Metropolitan Filipp', having in mind Metropolitan Filipp Kolichëv, who told Ivan the Terrible the truth to his face and was strangled by Malyuta-Skuratov[68] in the monastery of Otroch near Tver. Then, however, under the influence of Alekseyev-Askoldov we called it 'The Brotherhood of St Serafim of Sarov'.

In the quarrel that broke out in 1927 between the supporters of Sergey and the intransigent Josefans, we, the young intelligentsia, were to a man on the side of Metropolitan Iosif, who had refused to recognise the declaration of Metropolitan Sergey, in which he had stated that there was not and had not been any persecution of the Church.

The actions of the government with regard to the Church were plain for all to see: churches were being closed and desecrated, services were interrupted by the arrival of lorries with bands playing or spontaneous Komsomol[69] choirs singing to a bold Gipsy tune a song composed by Demyan Bedny or someone of the sort, with the refrain:

> Hunt them, hunt them down, the monks,
> Hunt them, hunt them down, the priests,
> Make those speculators run,
> Crush the *kulaks*...

Komsomol members would pour into churches wearing their hats, talking in loud voices and laughing. I don't mean to list everything that was done at that time in the spiritual life of the nation but even the young Jewish intelligentsia were deeply embarrassed by events. My friend Misha Shapiro, who was of a Jewish family of the patriarchal faith, was upset and occasionally went to the chapel in one old people's home where there was a surprisingly good choir.

We had the idea of going to church as a group. One day in 1927 five or six of us went together to one of the churches (later destroyed) in the Petrograd District. We were joined by Ionkin, who was an *agent provocateur* although we did not realise it at the time (see below). He pretended to be religious but didn't know how to behave in church; he was nervous, hung back and stood behind us. At that point I began to have my doubts about him. But then it turned out that the appearance in church of a group of adults unknown to the parishioners caused alarm to the clergy, all the more so as Ionkin was carrying a briefcase. With that our 'group visits' ceased.

When I look back over those years I'm certain that we couldn't have had any other approach to the schism in the church than the emotional one. We were on the side of the persecuted Church and simply couldn't have brought ourselves to make the rational compromises to which part of the Orthodox episcopate was inclined. Had we been politicians, then we might have decided either way. But we weren't politicians fighting for the survival of the Church, merely believers who wanted to be honest in all things and were revolted by the political manoeuvrings, the programmes and the calculating, two-faced formulae that enabled people to avoid giving a straight answer.

I remember one day meeting the senior priest of the Preobrazhen-ski Cathedral, Father Sergi Tikhomirov, and his daughter, at my teacher's flat. He was extremely thin, with a sparse white beard. He was neither voluble nor loud of voice, and probably did his work quietly and humbly. When he was 'taken away' and asked about his views on Soviet power, he replied succinctly: "It's from the Antichrist". Obviously, he was arrested and very quickly shot. That was, if I'm not mistaken, in the autumn of 1927, after the Exaltation of the Cross[70], a festival at which, according to popular belief, the devils, frightened by the Cross, are particularly keen to play tricks on Christians.

As I found out from my dossier, which was shown to me in 1992, Sergi's daughter was called Yuliya. I regret making no notes. I lived in such a significant time! But that's not the point: one should keep a record of everything and everybody; that's our duty. It is obvious that she suffered the same fate as her father.

There were only three or four meetings of the Brotherhood before it was 'officially' closed. At one of the last of these Andreyevski introduced to us a young man who stood in front of us in the pose of the Apostle Bartholomew in Nesterov's well-known painting, clasping his hands together in an attitude of prayer and murmuring something unintelligible but 'inspired' and not addressing anyone in particular. Andreyevski went into raptures over him: "What a religious man, what a religious man!" Meanwhile the piggish eyes of the said 'religious man' were very watchful. As he greeted us he whispered "Serezha" and made an effort to learn the names and surnames[71] of those present. A few days later I met him in the famous University corridor, where the long benches on which the students usually sat to argue over questions of politics and general philosophy had not yet been removed. One could meet a few students there at any time, such as, for example, the handsome Borya Ivanov, a convinced Kantian who later became an outstanding religious thinker.

I went up to 'Serezha' and engaged him in a conversation. As this conversation was drawing to a close he began trying to persuade me to help produce some kind of leaflets. "We'll leave them here in the corridor, and they'll be little fires, little fires, and a blaze will flare up..." I remember his using the words 'little fires' and 'blaze'. One of the students saw me talking to 'Serezha Ionkin' and warned me that he was an *agent provocateur*. In questioning me, Ionkin learned that my father had at one time taught chemistry in the no. 1 Nikolayevski cadet school. "I was a student of his... May I call on you?" I told my father. He replied "Ionkin? I remember all my students' surnames, but I never had one called Ionkin..."

Then I went to see Andreyevski and warned him that our group had been infiltrated by an *agent provocateur*. It was decided that the Brotherhood should dissolve itself. The next Wednesday Ionkin was almost the first to arrive. Andreyevski met us with a frown, sat in a deep armchair upholstered in blue velvet which one of his pupils had given him, and began to speak of the futility of our meetings and his decision to meet no more. He called upon us all to go to whichever church our faith required as often as possible and to read religious literature, then he stood up and shook us all by the hand to say good-bye. Andreyevski's speech had been so convincing and, I might say, wise, that "Serezha Ionkin" believed it and left him in peace, but when he tried nevertheless to accost me in the University (he was at the time very drunk) I snubbed him with a decisiveness that was uncharacteristic of me at that age.

On looking over my dossier in 1992 I caught sight of the statements of one 'Ivanovski', and had no difficulty in identifying him as our Ionkin. 'Ivanovski' was a vile secret agent of the GPU. There is no evidence of his official position in my dossier, but his job of showing us all to be monarchists and raving counterrevolutionaries is clearly revealed. At the same time his complete illiteracy is evident. He had been at Andreyevski's when we had still been proposing to call ourselves 'The Brotherhood of Metropolitan Filipp'. Ivanovski / Ionkin hadn't known who that was, and had reported that we were 'the Brotherhood of Kirill, patron saint of islands'. Obviously he had heard that Metropolitan Filipp, whom he called Kirill, had been Father Superior of the monastery of Solovki, which was situated on islands in the White Sea.

We didn't in fact meet at Andreyevski's for some time after the incident with the *agent provocateur*. It seems to me that Ivan Mikhaylovich was inclined to go over entirely to church affairs, and the diversity that was shown at the meetings of Khelfernak was becoming just a little inappropriate in the light of the events that the Russian Church was experiencing.

We couldn't, however, do without Ivan Mikhaylovich entirely. The need to exchange views on what was happening around us was too great. We would call uninvited at his flat, borrow his books as before, placing receipts on the big spike which was stuck into one of the shelves, and when we found him in we'd try to get his opinion on some affair or other, or listen to him talking about Church affairs. The circle shrank, naturally, but it did still exist, and Ivan Mikhaylovich obviously felt that he had no right to send us away. The meetings began again spontaneously.

The Brotherhood of Serafim Sarovski continued to exist until the day of our arrest, 8 February 1928. Ivan Mikhaylovich, however, did have one slight shortcoming—a touch of boastfulness; he sometimes tried to make it appear that he was head of, or a participant in, some great movement, and for some reason he never mentioned Khelfernak again although he considered that the Brotherhood had existed from the outset. Later he was to affirm that the Cosmic Academy (see below) was, as it were, a branch of the Brotherhood which had assumed its extravagant name for the purposes of conspiracy.

The Cosmic Academy of Sciences

At that time membership of humorous circles appeared less risky. It seemed that no one thought of pursuing people who met for the purpose of spending time with no serious aim in view. Volodya Rakov, who had been in my form at the Lentovskaya school, invited me to visit their KAN[72], the Cosmic Academy of Sciences. In the summer the members of this 'academy' had walked from Vladikavkaz to Sukhumi along the Ossete Military Road, armed themselves in the Caucasus with walking-sticks and proclaimed their faithfulness, friendship, humour and optimism. The members of KAN had their own greeting—*khaire* (the Greek for 'rejoice'), their anthem, their 'conference hall' and their *khartifilaks*[73] (Fedya Rozenberg), their sacred place in Tsarskoye Selo[74] on top of Parnas, etc. Including myself there were nine of us: Fedya Rozenberg, his brother Volodya, Volodya Rakov and his friend Arkasha Selivanov, Andryukha Mikhankov, Petr Pavlovich Mashkov (the eldest of us), Kolya Speranski, Tolya Terekhovko and myself. Of these nine members of KAN, two (Terekhovko and Rozenberg) wrote good poetry, one (Mikhankov) had a fluent command of Latin and Greek, wrote verse in both languages and showed great academic promise, two (Rakov and Selivanov) were good singers, one (Rakov) was a good artist and knew the uniforms of all the Russian regiments of the late eighteenth and early nineteenth centuries. Fedya Rozenberg was always amazingly cheerful, direct and inventive in his ideas. In short, we were typical young men, and met almost every week, entirely openly.

We were awarded 'chairs' in KAN on the basis of the papers we presented. I gave one on the lost advantages of the old orthography, and received the chair of Old Orthography, or alternatively of Melancholy Philology.

These days readers often take my inaugural KAN paper (published in Tver in 1993 in the book *The Unknown Likhachev*) as a completely serious piece of work, but it's enough just to read the title, which is a parody of a work against the Old Russian heretics, to realise that it's a joke, although some of its arguments against the abandonment of the old orthography and its replacement by one that's 'boring', 'doleful' and 'lacking in breeding' are by no means out of line with contemporary thinking. It's an ironic paper in keeping with the carnival spirit that prevailed in the Cosmic Academy.

Volodya Rakov occupied the Chair of Apologetic Theology, and that was quite a serious matter, when one considers that he and his friend Arkasha Selivanov, who held the Chair of Elegant Theology, were profoundly religious. Eduard Rozenberg actually converted from Lutheranism to Orthodoxy and took the name Fedor. On the other hand, Tolya Terekhovko (Chair of Elegant Psychology) was a principled atheist. The same could be said of Petr Mashkov (Chair of Elegant Chemistry). Such deep differences of view didn't prevent us all from being friends, indeed, from being fond of one another, taking pleasure in the choral singing of Russian songs and ballads, in trips together to Tsarskoye Selo and boat-trips on the Neva.

The Cosmic Academy was in its way a masquerade. We proclaimed the principle of 'happy science'—science which not only sought after truth, but a joyous truth, clothed in happy forms. This principle, by the way, has long existed in the world of science. The various University festivals, formal processions, traditional costumes, extravagant titles, ceremonies, excursions and journeys in company—all these had and still have a semi-serious nature. This too is in its way 'happy science', for science itself, which demands the full commitment of one's time and spiritual strength, should not be boring and monotonous.

One of the postulates of this 'happy science' was that the world that science establishes by research into our surroundings must be 'interesting' and more complicated than it was before it was studied. Science enriches the world as it studies it and reveals what's new, hitherto unknown, in it. If science simplifies all that surrounds us and subordinates it to two or three simple principles, that is 'unhappy' science, making the Eternal environment dull and grey. Such is the teaching of Marxism, belittling our surrounding society, subordinating it to coarse materialistic laws which kill morality—in a word, rendering morality unnecessary. Such are all forms of materialism. Such is the teaching of Sigmund Freud. Such is sociology when applied to an explanation of literary works and the literary process. Doctrines of the stages of history fall into the category of 'stultifying' teachings as well. I won't say that my interest in events has led me to avoid this urge to simplification completely, but on the whole I've tried to discover the complex, the interesting, the original and the individual in all those people and subjects that I've studied. And this has been so absorbing as to override all the misfortune that has fallen to my lot, especially in my youth.

In our student circle, which played a particularly significant role in our lives at a time when free philosophy and religion were steadily becoming forbidden, unofficial and unrecognised, this masquerade was not in any way set up with a view to conspiracy. On the contrary, the noisy forms which it took could rather attract attention to our circle, and this is precisely what happened. A telegram of greeting purporting to be from the Pope of Rome to the head of the Academy attracted the attention of over-sensitive organisations...

This 'second life' was created by us all in one other way. One of the Academicians, my class-mate, later a student of the Building Institute (formerly the Institute of Civil Engineers), Volodya Rakov, was a lively (quick and faultless) sketcher and very good at water-colours. He drew all of us, and people whom we knew, in various early nineteenth century settings. He even composed whole tales about us. If the story was a long one, he would make a whole album of it, and present it to the principal hero of the illustrated story. Female roles were played either by Valya Morozova, a member of Andreyevski's circle, or by Tolya Terekhovko's sister. Strangers were not allowed into this 'illustrated world'. Each of the figures in the drawings had his own stereotype. The eldest of us, Petya Mashkov, was usually shown as a Colonel of Hussars; Valya Morozova as a girl playing hoopla or croquet, skipping or bowling a hoop. I was always drawn in civilian dress, sometimes wearing a 'double lorgnette' (one in which the lenses are set one in front of the other for the sake of sharp focus). We waited impatiently for illustrated stories to appear and laughed good-naturedly, especially if we found in them an allusion to a real-life situation. I still have one of those albums in which we all lived a 'second life'[75].

The monotone culture of the 'proletarian dictatorship' ousted the polyphony of intellectual democracy. From the very moment it sank its claws into our country, Soviet power endeavoured to silence all other voices. The country subsided into silence—there were only monotones of praise, a unison, a deathly boredom—and deathly is the word, because unanimity and unison were the equivalent of a death sentence for culture and cultured people.

Arrest and Imprisonment

It was early February 1928. The clock in our flat on Oraniyenbaum-skaya Street struck eight. I was alone at home, and was suddenly seized by an icy dread. I had not the least idea why. I had just heard the sound of the clock for the very first time. My father didn't like to hear the clock strike, and the chimes had been turned off even before I was born. Why had the clock decided to strike for me for the first time in twenty-one years with its measured solemnity?

They came for me on the eighth of February early in the morning; there was a uniformed investigator and Sabelnikov, commandant of our buildings at the *Pechatny Dvor*. The latter was terribly upset (the same fate befell him later), but the investigator was polite and even sympathetic towards my parents, especially when my father turned pale and collapsed into the leather armchair in his study. The investigator took him a glass of water, and it was a long time before I could shake off my feelings of acute pity for my father.

The search itself didn't take long. The investigator checked a piece of paper that he had, confidently approached the bookshelf and pulled down G. Ford's *International Jewry* in its red binding. It all became clear to me: one of my University acquaintances had called for no particular reason a week before my arrest, looked at my books and asked, with a voluptuous smile, whether I had anything anti-Soviet. He assured me that he was terribly keen on such lack of taste and vulgarity.

My mother put some things together (soap, underwear, warm clothes) and we bid each other goodbye. As everyone does in these situations I said "This is madness, it'll soon be sorted out and I'll be back soon". But at the time mass and irreversible arrests were in full swing.

In the black Ford, then quite a novelty in Leningrad, we drove past the Exchange. By that time it was getting light and the deserted city was unusually lovely. The investigator said nothing. Anyway, why am I calling him that? My real investigator was Aleksandr (Albert) Robertovich Stromin, who was behind all the prosecutions of the intelligentsia of the late 1920s, served in Saratov as head of the NKVD[76] and was shot 'as a Trotskyist' in 1938.

After being searched and relieved of my cross, my silver watch and a few rubles, I was taken to a cell on the fifth floor of the DPZ[77] bilding in Shpalernaya Street (on the outside this building has three floors, but for the purpose of preventing escapes the building stands in a sort of tank). The cell was no. 273—the same as absolute zero.

At University I had been a friend of Lev Karsavin, and when I got to the DPZ I found myself, as Fate would have it, in the same cell as the brother of a woman friend of his. I remember that boy: he wore a velvet jacket and sang Gypsy ballads in a fine voice, quietly, so that the warders shouldn't hear. Shortly before I had been reading Karsavin's book *Noctes Petropolitanae*.

The good six months I spent in that cell was the hardest period of my life. It was hard psychologically. But it was a time when I met a huge number of people who lived by quite different principles.

I will mention a few of my cell-mates. In cell 273, intended for one occupant, and into which I was thrown, there was an energetic *nepman*[78] by the name of Kotlyar, a shop-owner of some description. He'd been arrested the previous day (this was the period when NEP was being abolished). He immediately proposed that we clean up the cell. The air there was dreadfully foul and the walls, which had once been painted, were black with fungus. The lavatory seat was filthy and had not been cleaned for a long time. Kotlyar asked the warders for some rags, and a day or two later they threw us somebody's woollen underpants. Kotlyar suggested that they'd been stripped off someone who had been shot. Choking back the nausea in our throats we set about scraping the mildew off the walls and washing the floor, which was soft with filth, but the main objective was cleaning the lavatory. Two days hard labour did the trick, and the result was a cell filled with fresh air. The third person to be pushed into our 'one-man' cell was a professional thief. When I was summoned at night for interrogation he advised me to put my coat on (I had with me my father's warm winter coat lined with squirrel fur). "At interrogations you've got to keep warm—you'll feel calmer". The interrogation was my only one (if you don't count the filling up of questionnaires beforehand). I sat there in my coat as if in armour. Stromin, the investigator (the organiser, as I've already said, of all the actions of the late '20s and early '30s against the intelligentsia, including the unsuccessful 'academic' one) failed to extract from me any of the information that he wanted (my parents were told "Your son's behaving badly"). At the start of the interrogation he asked me "Why are you wearing your coat?" I replied "I've got a cold" (that was what the thief had told me to say). Stromin was evidently afraid of catching influenza, as it was then called, and the interrogation didn't last long enough to be exhausting.

Later we had a Chinese boy in the cell (for some reason there were a lot of Chinese in DPZ in 1928), from whom I tried unsuccessfully to learn Chinese; Count Rochefort (such seems to have been his surname), a descendant of the man who set up the tsarist prison system; a peasant boy who'd come to town for the first time and had taken a 'suspicious' interest in a sea-plane, the like of which he'd never before seen. And numerous others. Interest in all these people kept me going.

For six months our cell was taken for exercise by 'Granddad', as we called him, who had done the same for many revolutionaries under the tsarist government. Once he got to know us he showed us the cells where various famous revolutionaries had been held. I regret that I made no attempt at remembering the numbers. 'Granddad' was a stern veteran, but he took part in the warders' favourite game—passing a live rat back and forwards among themselves with brooms. When a warder noticed a rat running across the yard he would start to sweep it with a broom until it died of exhaustion. If there were other warders present they would join in the hunt and pass the rat from one to another, shouting as they did so, sweeping it towards an imaginary goal. This sadistic sport roused the warders to a rare pitch of excitement. The rat would immediately try to get away, escape, but they would keep on sweeping it, screaming and yelling all the time. The prisoners could watch this through the 'muzzles' in the cells, and compare the fate of the rat with their own.

After six months the investigation was over, and I was transferred to the general library cell. There were many extremely interesting people there, including N. P Antsiferov, although, as he points out in his memoirs, I had already left by the time he arrived. We slept on the floor, even right by the lavatory pedestal, and for amusement, we took turn to present 'papers' with following discussion. The habit of discussing questions of general interest, which members of the Russian intelligentsia never tired of, sustained them even in the prisons and the camps. The papers were all on every kind of extravagant subject, and their theses were in sharp contradiction to accepted views. This was a characteristic feature of all papers delivered in prison and camp. The most impossible theories were dreamed up. I too delivered a paper, my theme being that every man determines his own fate even when events seemed to occur at random. Thus it was that all the Romantic poets died young—Keats, Shelley, Lermontov, etc. They had, as it were, thrust themselves upon death and misfortune. Lermontov had even begun to limp on the same leg as Byron. I also expressed my views on the comparative longevity of Zhukovski. Realists, by contrast, lived long. And we, following the traditions of the Russian intelligentsia, had brought about our own arrests. It was our 'free-will fate'. Fifty years later, as I read A. Sinyavski's *Walks with Pushkin,* I thought "What a typical prison or camp invention his whole idea of Pushkin is". However, I presented more such 'astounding' papers, but on Solovki, of which more later.

The most interesting man in the library cell was the head of the Petrograd Boy Scouts, Count Vladimir Mikhaylovich Shuvalov. I had met him now and then in the streets just after the Revolution in Scout uniform, with his long Scout pole and distinctive hat. Now, in the cell, he was gloomy but strong and smart. He was studying logic. As far as I recall these were notions continuing Husserl's *Researches in Logic.* I don't understand how he was able to shut himself off from the dreadful noise in his cell and concentrate on his studies. He must have had great will power and enthusiasm. When he expounded the results of his thinking I had difficulty in understanding him, although I had studied logic under Vvedenski and, like Shuvalov himself, Povarin.

Eventually he was exiled and I never saw him again. I think that a relative of his, or perhaps his wife, worked on the icons in the Russian Museum.

When you consider, our jailers did some strange things. Having arrested us for meeting at the most once a week to spend a few hours in discussion of philosophical, artistic and religious questions that aroused our interest, first of all they put us all together in a prison cell and then in camps and swelled our numbers with others from our city, interested in the resolution of the same philosophical questions, while in the camps we were mixed with a wide and generous range of such people from Moscow, Rostov, the Caucasus, the Crimea and Siberia. We passed through a gigantic school of mutual education before vanishing once more in the limitless expanses of our Motherland.

In the library cell, where people were sent on completion of investigation to await sentence, I saw Nonconformists, Baptists (one of these had crossed the frontier from somewhere in the West, was expecting to be shot and couldn't sleep at night), Satanists (there really were such people), Theosophists, homespun Masons (they used to meet somewhere on the Bolshoy Prospekt in the Petrograd District and prayed to the sound of the cello; how vulgar, if I might say so!). The OGPU satirists, the 'Tur brothers' tried now and then to show us in a ridiculous and insulting light; they published a piece about us in *Leningradskaya Pravda*, thick with lies, entitled 'Oaken ashes', and one entitled 'The light blue international' about some of the others, and so on. M. M. Bakhtin later wrote in his memoirs about 'Oaken ashes'.

Our relatives too gathered, meeting at transfer points and at various little windows where information about us was given out, or more often was not. They were advised what to hand over, what to give us for when we stopped, where and what to provide for their prisoners. Many made friends. By that time we could guess how much they were going to give and to whom.

One day we were all summoned 'without belongings' to the governor of the prison. In a deliberately lugubrious tone, specially assumed for the occasion, he read out our sentences. We stood and listened. Igor Yevgenevich Anichkov was absolutely priceless. With a markedly uninterested air he looked at the paper on the office wall, the ceiling, anywhere but at the governor, and when the latter had finished reading and was expecting us to hurl ourselves upon him with the usual lamentations "we're innocent", "we shall demand a proper trial and a proper defence" and the like, Anichkov, who had received five years like myself, asked with exaggerated indifference "Is that all? May we go?" and, without waiting for a reply, turned and walked towards the door taking us with him, to the complete bewilderment of the governor and the escorts, who took a while to recover. It was magnificent!

About a fortnight after sentences had been pronounced we were all summoned 'with belongings' (on Solovki the call was different: "Fly out like a bullet with your things") and sent off in Black Marias to the Nikolayevski (now Moskovski) Station. We drew up at the extreme right platform, from which the dacha trains now leave. One at a time we got out of the Black Marias and a crowd that was there to see us off in the twilight (it was an October evening) shouted, as they recognised each of us "Kolya!", "Dima!", "Volodya!". Soldiers who formed the escort, bayonets fixed, drove back the crowd of parents, friends and colleagues from school or work. Two soldiers, brandishing their bayonets, walked up and down in front of the crowd while one escort passed us over to the other, checking off the list. They put us in two Stolypin cars [cars used for prisoner transport], which had been considered terrible in tsarist times but in the Soviet era had gained a reputation for actually being comfortable. When we had finally been crammed into our cages another escort began handing out everything that our relations had brought us. I got a big confectioners' cake from the University library, and some flowers too. When the train moved from behind the bars the head of the commander of the escort appeared (Oh bliss!) and said in a friendly manner: "Look here, lads, don't hold it against us: it's orders. What if we don't get the counting done?" Somebody answered "All right, but why start on the people seeing us off with swearing and bayonets?"

Kem Transfer Point and the Crossing to Solovki Island

Our good fortune consisted in being sent to Solovki, those of us that had been given between three and five years, all together in one car, although in separate cages (the so-called Stolypin cars had bars and a corridor along which the escort patrolled). But we still managed to communicate and share information about our fate, our interrogations—everyone had something to tell. Our principal anxiety was that we might be split up in the camp.

I will not describe in detail the first days at Kem, on Popov island and in no. 13 company at Solovki. I will give these in an appendix, and there is no need to repeat everything. I will merely observe that as I got out of the car one of the escort drew blood from my face with his boot, and they all did their utmost to humiliate us. They shouted at us *"Zdes' vlast' ne sovyetskaya, zdes' vlast' solovyetskaya"* [Here the power isn't Soviet—it is Solovki power] from which came the title of the well known documentary film *Vlast' solovetskaya.*

Beloozerov, who was in charge of the consignment, was a virtuoso at swearing and would move in menacingly close to us and then step back. I couldn't believe that this nightmare was really happening. I remember that one of his most 'pleasant' threats was "I'll make you suck the snot out of dead men!" When I laughed (not, however, because I was feeling cheerful) he shouted at me "Keep the laughing for afterwards...", but he didn't beat me...

I must point out that all that we knew about the commanders came from rumours circulating among the prisoners, and some errors crept into my Solovki notes and thence were confirmed in literature, especially by way of Solzhenitsyn's *Gulag Archipelago* and the work of others to whom I talked about the camp.

Two men took turns to be in charge at Kemperpunkt, Kurilko and Beloozerov. The latter I erroneously called Beloborodov: the prisoners had given him this surname, confusing him with the Beloborodov who had shot the Tsar's family. Neither of them was a Guards officer, as I stated, and neither of them spoke French (except that, knowing a phrase or two, they found great pleasure in showing them off before those unjustly imprisoned). A man who had personally seen Kurilko's work in Petrozavodsk told me in 1989 that Kurilko had served in the Red Army, but that during the upheavals of the Civil War he had served a couple of months or so with the Whites as well. Nevertheless he passed himself off as a Guardsman. And I heard from N. P. Antsiferov after our release that when he and Kurilko were sharing a cell in the punishment block and awaiting execution (which he, fortunately, was spared), Kurilko apparently said before he was shot "I die as a Chekist and a Guards officer". He demanded to be shot not in the back of the neck but in the forehead. It is quite possible that for the two months that he served with the White Army he was in a regiment that bore the title of 'Guards'.

I mention this beause I want my readers to understand that the real Guards officers whom I met in Solovki were, every last one of them, men of honour; they had nothing to do with the bestiality of the Secret Police, were never members of it and couldn't have been, because the only men taken into the Interior Secret Police were 'kitchen-sink artists', amateur criminals, murderers, rapists, etc.

For the night we were herded onto Popov Island to be crammed into a shed and taken over to Solovki island next morning. We had to remain standing all night in that shed. The bunks were occupied by half-naked *urki*[79] (petty thieves) and scruffy teenagers who bombarded us with lice, so that within an hour we were covered from head to foot. As soon as the light went out a black curtain began to descend the walls onto those who were lying on the floor. These were the bed-bugs on the move. And amidst all this hell there was one tiny bit of paradise: on a tiny patch of bunk, watched over by two handsome Kabardians in national dress, lay two old men, a priest and a mullah. As morning approached, when I could no longer stand on my feet because they had swollen during the night (even my boots had become too small), one of the Kabardians, Divlet-Girey Albaksi-dovich (I have never forgotten his name, and am eternally grateful to him) saw the state I was in and gave up his place and let me lie down.

The priest who lay beside me, a Ukrainian by birth, told me "On Solovki you must find Father Nikolay Piskanovski—he'll help you".

Exactly why he would help me and how I didn't grasp. I thought to myself that Father Nikolay probably held some position of importance. A most preposterous idea—a clergyman in a position of responsibility! But it all turned out to be true: Father Nikolay enjoyed a special position because of the respect that he was shown by all the authorities on the island, and help me he did, for years.

Next day we were loaded onto the steamer Gleb Boyki, which sailed for Solovki. A housebreaker by the name of Ovchishnikov was standing by me and warned me "Just take your time, be last on".

This was his second time in Solovki. The first time he'd escaped, but he'd turned up at his girl-friend's place in Leningrad and been re-captured after walking all the way to her house with crampons slung over his shoulder. When he spotted a patrol, he'd put the crampons on and climb the nearest telegraph pole. Naturally the patrol didn't make him climb down: man at work!

Ovchishnikov had been dreadfully beaten up at Kemperpunkt. They'd beaten him for getting the warders and commanders into trouble and for ruining the statistics—it had been considered impossible to escape from Solovki. But even so, the housebreaker remained a human being. We patched him up and he helped us with his experience of the camp. When they started cramming people into the hold he pulled us onto a little platform in the middle of the companionway and advised us to go no lower. And indeed, down below people began to suffocate. We were actually allowed up a couple of times for air. After nine months in prison I breathed the fresh sea air eagerly, and looked at the waves and the barren islands as they drifted past.

Near Solovki we were once more crammed into the bowels of the Gleb Boyki (named after a cannibal, the head of the three-man OGPU committee that sentenced people to death or imprisonment). From the sound of ice against the side of the ship we could tell that we were approaching the landing stage. It was the end of October, and coastal ice was beginning to form. We were called out with our belongings onto the jetty, made to fall in and be counted. Then they started bringing up the corpses of those who had suffocated in the hold and those who had been taken seriously among whom were those who had been crushed until bones broke or internal organs ruptured.

We, the living, were taken to bathhouse no. 2. There, in the cold, we were made to undress and our clothes were taken to be deloused. We tried the water, but there was only cold until an hour or so later when the hot came on too. I began to pour hot water over myself non-stop, so as to warm up. At length our clothes were returned, smelling of sulphur, and we dressed. We were taken to the Nikolski gates, where I took off my student cap, which I had kept, and crossed myself. Until then I had never seen a real Russian monastery, and I perceived Solovki and its Kremlin not as a new prison but as a holy place.

We went through one set of gates and a second and were taken to no. 13 company. There, by the light of 'bats' (lamps that would not go out in the wind) we were counted again and searched.

I remember that after the search there was no way that I could fasten the basket which my parents had bought me; it was very light and very strong, like a suitcase in shape. Nor could I swallow the pastry that I found in it. My throat had swollen so much that I couldn't swallow. I mixed a bit of the pastry with a lot of saliva and, with great discomfort, got it down.

Then something unexpected occurred. The section chief (a low-ranking person in charge of a section of bunks) came up to me personally (probably because I was wearing a student cap and he took me for a student), asked me for a ruble in return for which he cleared everybody off the bunks and gave the space to me and my companions. I literally collapsed onto a bunk and only came to next morning. What I saw was quite unexpected. The bunks were deserted. The only person there apart from myself was a priest sitting quietly on the wide window-sill darning his cassock. My ruble had been doubly effective: the section chief hadn't made me get up and go out to roll-call and then to work. I got into conversation with the priest and asked him what seems a most absurd question: might he know, among all those thousands on Solovki, Father Nikolay Piskanovski? He shook out his cassock and replied:

"Piskanovski? That's me!"

Untidy, quiet and modest, he did an excellent job of organising my fate. But more of that later. Meanwhile, as I looked around I realised that Fr. Nikolay and I were by no means alone. On the top bunks lay the sick, while from beneath the bunks little hands were stretched out to us, begging for bread. And on these little hands too was the index finger of fate. Beneath the bunks there lived *vshivki*—teenagers who had lost their clothes. They had got into an 'illegal situation'—they didn't go out to roll-call, didn't receive rations, and lived under the bunks so as not to be chased out naked into the frost to perform physical work. Everyone knew of their existence, but the authorities had simply crossed them off, giving them no soup, bread or porridge rations. They lived on charity. Or rather, lived until they died! And then they were carried out dead, put in coffins and taken to the cemetery.

These were forgotten street-children, often convicted of vagrancy or petty theft. How many of them there were in Russia! Children that had lost their parents—killed, starved to death, driven abroad with the White Army, emigrated. I remember one little boy who insisted that he was the son of the philosopher Tsereteli. When they were at liberty they slept in tar boilers, roamed Russia in search of warmth and fruit in the cavities under passenger carriages or in empty goods trains. They had sniffed cocaine and other harmful drugs brought in from Germany during the Revolution, so that many of them had burned through their own nose-bones. I felt so sorry for those *vshivki* that I walked about like a man drunk—drunk on compassion. This was not a feeling that I had, but something more like a disease. And I am so grateful to Fate that over a period of six months I was able to help a few of them.

One of my first tasks was to look after my belongings and make sure that nobody would steal them. On one of the first days (perhaps even the very first) I handed over my basket of belongings to one of the people in the clerical companies. Then I learnt how to sleep so that my Romanov fur jacket would not be stolen. I would lie on my bunk, turn my coat upside down, put my bare feet down the sleeves and put my boots under my head for a pillow. Even in my soundest youthful sleep nobody could have robbed me without waking me up.

In the morning I was given my ration of bread and hot water in a big enamelled mug which my thoughtful parents had supplied me with. When I returned from work, soup was ladled into the same mug. We were allocated to work details in the morning while it was still dark, at tables lit by 'bats', and sent in groups to work. I had been declared Class 2 fit by the medical section in Kemperpunkt, and so was sent to comparatively light duties.

I had so many jobs in no. 13 company! I scarcely managed to get the same work twice. Most of all I remember sawing wood for the power station, labouring in the docks, acting as a temporary horse, harnessed to heavily laden sledges on the road to Muksalma, doing electrical repairs in the machine shop (formerly the monastery smithy), working in the Lisi nursery (alongside O. V. Volkov and N. E. Serebryakov) and finally, being a cowman in the farm. Eventually my 'quarantine' was over and I was moved from no. 13 company to no. 14 where Fedya Rozenberg, Volodya Rakov, Tolya Terekhovko and others already were. The call to work in the Criminological office, which A. N. Kolosov had promised, failed to materialise, and I remained on 'General duties'. The 'madhouse' went on.

There was no bunk-space for me in no. 14 company, and I laid my bedding on the floor after everyone had gone to bed. I had stomach pains (I didn't yet know that I'd got an ulcer) and Klein, an architect, whom I had out of ignorance at first taken for the builder of the Fine Arts Museum in Moscow, advised me to obtain a dry ration and to make porridge on the little stove in the cell—he himself used to make semolina porridge in a little saucepan. He was unusually thin, and a few months later he died of cancer.

One day I returned from work and felt something new: a strange headache, and I couldn't even stand. Volodya Rakov gave me his place on the top bunk. I lost my vision and became delirious. A paramedic was called who discovered that I had a temperature of 40 °C and should be moved to the camp hospital. Late as it was my friends went and found the chief clerk of the Medical section, G. M. Osorgin. He authorised admission to the hospital, but how were they to get me there? Fedya Rozenberg, Volodya Rakov and a third person carried me there bodily. Although I was semi-conscious I clearly remember going across the yard, under the archway and turning left into the peace of the surgery.

They dragged me to the bath. This was in a big room and was already full of water. I found it more repulsive than I can say—someone had already washed there and, from the look of things, not recently, as the water was stone cold. It's amazing that I didn't catch my death. Someone told me later that a cold bath is actually beneficial when you've got a temperature. Then I remember lying in a big ward between clean sheets. Despite my high fever I felt well off: there were no lice and the bed was soft. I was worried about my belongings: where were my basket and my fur jacket? Along came Andreyevski;

he lived and worked here as a doctor. My basket was under his camp bed. A diagnosis was soon made—typhus. For about three days I lay in the typhus ward on the straw-covered floor. The ward was in what used to be a storehouse.

While being transferred to the isolation ward I was robbed. I remember the name of the thief and what his job was—Astakhov the paramedic. I remember because Andreyevski asked me to sign a statement that Astakhov hadn't robbed me. I refused, as the statement seemed ridiculous. But it turned out that Astakhov was guilty of a lot of stealing, for which he was later convicted. I actually saw him labouring on some heavy duties. He was an intelligent man (at least, he looked intelligent) and I very much regretted later that I had been partly to blame for, or involved in, his sentence of several months' hard labour.

From the hospital I went to the 'convalescent company', whose members had been excused duties, and were allotted bed in a sort of cellar near the laundry.

When I was next on Solovki, in 1966, this cellar had lost its upper floor and almost ceased to exist. I couldn't imagine ever having slept there, but in my time it could only be reached by way of a staircase. Half a metre above my head was a brick vault in which there was a crack with a permanent draught blowing through. By the exit from the convalescent ward there was a watchman in constant attendance, but he was neither Armenian nor Georgian. I tried to find out who he could be, and asked both Armenians and Georgians, but they couldn't tell me. His post was beside a latrine pail, a big iron one, to which led a short flight of wooden steps from a little platform. He used to give me his hand and help me up. I shall never forget him. But then why should I forget in the small part of my life that remains, if I haven't in the previous 65 years! I remember, I could stand only with a great effort. The man in the next bed was a peasant, the living image of Platon Karatayev. He said to me "I'll teach you something, but promise that you'll keep quiet about it. With this knowledge you'll never go hungry. He told me "People everywhere need galoshes for their *valenki*[80]; you just need to know how to make them". And he taught me. He drew a pattern and showed me how to reduce or enlarge the size. Few people know that the secret of cutting rubber is to do it with scissors under water. You can easily get rubber from drivers and it makes no difference if it is red. Evidently, galoshes were his main hope for future prosperity after returning home.

The Camp Topography of Solovki

From conversations on Solovki in 1929 I remember that the 'population' of the island was greater than that of Belgium. At the same time, huge areas of forest and swamp were not only uninhabited, but also unexplored.

What was there on Solovki? A huge anthill? Yes, an anthill it was; it was hard to so much as force one's way between the buildings. The crush round the entrance and exit of no. 13 company was similar to that of the Preobrazhenski Cathedral. 'Trusties' kept order with truncheons but entry and exit were permitted to everyone as long as they were in possession of a work chit.

At night the spaces between the buildings grew quiet. The bastions and shrines towered upward, firmly supported on massive walls which thickened towards the base.

I will try to describe the layout of the camp. In the Kremlin (as that part of the monastic buildings was called that was surrounded by walls built of gigantic boulders, smothered with orange lichen) was no. 14 company. No. 15, outside the monastery, was for prisoners who lived in the various groupings, such as in the machine shop, the alabaster works or no. 2 bathhouse. No. 16 company was responsible for the camp cemetery. People joked about it, but in some companies in winter corpses lay stripped and naked.

Why were the prisoners divided into companies? I think that here we see a certain influence of prisoners from military units who used to maintain discipline among the first arrivals on the islands. The warders themselves couldn't do anything, least of all organise. The military were at the outset the only organising force capable of accommodating, feeding and keeping basic order among the prisoners on Solovki itself and the islands of the archipelago. Many aspects of life there were organised along military lines.

No. 1 company consisted of the 'privileged'—the commanders and section leaders. It's quarters, behind the sanctuary in the Preobrazhenski Cathedral overlooked the parade ground where general roll-calls took place. Above no. 1 was no. 3 company, the clerical company, with windows on both sides. Where no. 2 was I forget. No. 6, the 'sentry company', basically consisted of priests, monks and bishops. They were entrusted with work that required honesty—watching over stores, issuing parcels to prisoners, etc. and were quartered in the main building, also overlooking the parade ground. No. 7 was the 'artistic' company. This is where the actors, musicians, and educational administrators who carried out the 'rehabilitation' work on Solovki lived. No. 8, 9 and 10 companies were also clerical. No. 11 company was the punishment company, quartered at the Archangel Gates. The prisoners had high, narrow benches to sit on, and slept on the bare floor. This company was formed when criminals began to arrive on Solovki and measures were taken against them by the imprisoned counterrevolutionaries ('*kaery*', in official nomenclature[81]) themselves. Finally, the great increase in numbers made it necessary to form a refectory company. The refectory was a hall, larger than the Garnet Hall in the Moscow Kremlin, used first and foremost as a common canteen for all prisoners but when accommodation in the monastery began to run short it was turned into living quarters and became no. 12 company.

Of all the companies, no. 13 was the largest and most frightening. This was the reception company for new arrivals who were sent to do heavy physical work and had all desire to oppose or protest drilled out of them. All arrivals on Solovki were obliged to spend not less than three months in no. 13 company, which is why it was called the 'quarantine' company.

In the mornings we were fallen in for lengthy roll-calls in the corridors that surrounded the Troitski and Preobrazhenski shrines. We formed up in groups of ten, then we were counted, and the last man in the group, as I recall, shouted:

"One hundred and eighty second complete group of ten."

At times there were three or four thousand, even five thousand men on the bunks of no. 13 company, crammed together cheek by jowl and, of course, we were all crawling with lice. Only on special grounds did anyone at all succeed in getting out of no. 13 company.

I remember the company commander greeted us:

"Good morning, quarantine company!"

And we would count up to three after the final word of this 'greeting' and croak in chorus:

"Good mor . . . ."

Then we would go up in turn to little tables at which sat the orderlies (some of whom had taken part in the terrifying mob violence in Leningrad in 1927) and be detailed for work.

In no. 14 company, quartered beyond the refectory and in the adjoining rooms, lived those who had not yet been allotted to 'teams' after their three months in no. 13 company and were awaiting allocation to logging, peat cutting and various forms of production.

No. 15 company, or the 'combined' company, was for those who lived in various corners outside the boundaries of the Kremlin and was considered the most criminal, that is, the most privileged. Apart from these official companies there were 'teams'—prisoners working in Savvatiyev, Filimonov, on the islands of Muksalma, Anzer and Zaychiki and in the various peat-bogs and the logging camp.

No. 16 company was, as I have already said, responsible for the cemetery.

In addition to the companies there existed separately in the Kremlin a large sick bay, which was usually crammed to overflowing, with its 'team of convalescents' in the basement near the laundry.

That, I think, accounts for all the 'residential' premises in the central Kremlin area.

Apart from the 'residential' premises inside the Kremlin there were also the functional: the bathhouse and drying room; the admin. office which dealt with all the discipline and provisioning of the camp (staffed mainly by the best organisers, former military personnel); the Information and Investigation section, which perpetuated its own existence by inventing variety of 'plots', listening to informers among the prisoners (so-called secret agents who were received into a special wooden house—no longer standing—by the Storozhevaya bastion outside the Kremlin); and the needlework shop, where most of the workers were women. This and part of the sick bay were in the first section of the Kremlin near the Nikolski gates. There was a theatre with a foyer, which also served as a lecture room. Most important, however—there was a museum in the Kremlin. It was actually comfortable in the museum, and remarkable performances by fine actors were given in the theatre, but it was harder to be taken on as an actor there than it is to get into the Bolshoi in Moscow today.

Finally, in the first part of the Kremlin and with a separate exit via the Seldyaniye gates (nowadays disused) was a 'monastery': a couple of dozen monks with a Father Superior, a *skhimnik*[82] (not to be confused with an *otshelnik*[83], who would live somewhere in the forest) and they were allowed to hold services in the Onufriyevskaya church situated in the cemetery. These monks were experts at fishing with nets, they understood the currents and knew the routes taken by the fish and so on. They caught *navaga*[84], but most importantly the famous Solovki herring, which found its way to the table in the Moscow Kremlin, and so was still known as the 'Kremlin' herring. When the Onufriyevskaya church was closed the herring 'disappeared' (perhaps as a mark of the failure of USLON[85] to fulfil its obligations to the monks?). I can't say what became of the monks after that; I don't know whether they were driven away or purged. There was also a monk living on Muksalma, who knew how to handle the cows (there were cows in the Kremlin and on Muksalma, where there was excellent pasture).

There were also smaller units in the Kremlin. There was a tiny room under the great bell-tower, where people were executed one at a time (a bullet in the back of the head), and their corpses carted away before the cleaners arrived to wash the blood off the floor. There was a bakehouse which produced excellent bread with technology dating from the sixteenth century—the times of Metropolitan Filipp. There was a wood-yard (now deserted, where the two remaining bells hang, one Norwegian, the other 'royal'). Hot water for making *kvass*[86] was fetched from a supply near the bakehouse in the monastery's large copper jugs.

Unauthorised entry to any premises was forbidden. People were on duty with sticks, with which they struck any importunate visitors. The only personal communication that I had with members of other companies was at work.

The Nikolski gates were the only way in and out of the Kremlin. Sentries were posted there to check passes on both sides. The Holy gates were only used by the fire brigade[87], whose carts could move quickly in and out through them. People who were to be shot were also taken out that way, as it was the shortest way from no. 11 company (the punishment company) to the monastery cemetery, where executions were carried out.

Outside the Kremlin were the offices of SLON, in the building of the former monastery guest-house, the women's barracks, the machine shop (in the former smithy), the farm, no. 2 bathhouse (where health checks were performed and where prisoner spent hours naked while their clothes were fumigated in the delouser), the alabaster workshop, the rope workshop, the sports ground (for voluntary workers) which was kept by two or three prisoners, the voluntary workers' quarters and canteen (for a number of section commanders). Farther along was the brick works.

What was there in the other parts of the Solovki archipelago? I have to say that I gained a very poor knowledge of the rest of the camp, and that only in my errands on foot to collect information about the teenagers, who had to be formed into the *Detkoloniya*, soon to be renamed *Trudkoloniya*[88] and sadly well known through the visit to Solovki of Maksim Gorki in 1929.

I can't omit a special reference to two other establishments which played a large part in the intellectual life of Solovki: the Museum and Solteatr (Solovki Theatre). All three were intended to conceal the nightmarish conditions of life on Solovki, but I will say nothing bad about them. Not only did they save the lives of many members of the intelligentsia, but also they allowed them, to some extent, to continue to live an intellectual life.

I'm very much afraid that the memoir literature of the '20s and '30s gives a one-sided view of the life of those years and, most of all, of life in prison. Suffering, repression and terror were by no means the whole picture. Intellectual life did go on, to a degree, even in the awful conditions of the camps and the prisons, and that intellectual life was even extremely intense in some cases, when people accustomed to thought and wishing to think found themselves brought together.

In his journal *Solovetskiye ostrova*[89] my schoolmaster, the 'one-term man' I. M. Andreyevski, published an article on nervous and psychic disorders in Solovki. He actually discovered a new psychological illness, victims of which were always trying to improve their position—to get a better place on the bunks, to get a bread ration just a bit bigger than other people's, to gain profitable acquaintances and any kind of influence. Such people were entirely occupied in this way, and they died sooner than the rest. There were, however, people (and not many of them) who retained their human dignity, who thought and gave meaning to their existence on a spiritual level.

Solovki was indeed the place where one came face to face with the miraculous and the revolting, with the monastic past and the concentration camp present, and with people of all levels of morality from the highest to the lowest and most infamous. Here were represented every nationality and profession, past and present. Two epochs were in collision here: one the pre-Revolutionary, the other the coarsely contemporary, highly characteristic of the 20s and early 30s.

Life on Solovki was so fantastic that one lost all feeling that it was real. As the words of one of the Solovki songs went: "Everything's mixed up here, like a strange dream".

A characteristic feature of the intellectual part of Solovki as the '20s became the '30s was a desire to rework the 'criminal and shameful' world of the camp into a world of comedy. If our neighbours in Savvatiyev or Muksalma, where the 'politicals' were held—that is, people who had officially belonged to political parties, or who had joined international organisations for the protection of political prisoners— transformed (not without a little exaggeration) their detention on Solovki into a time of suffering and torment, the real counter-revolutionaries of the central part of Solovki emphasised in every way the absurd, the idiotic, stupid, deceptive, slapstick quality of everything that went on there—the foolishness of the organisation and its orders, the fantastic and dreamlike nature of all the island life (a world of strange dreams, nightmares, devoid of meaning and consistency). The little pages of jokes, mainly compiled by Yu. Kazarnovski and D. Shipchinski, with help from Aleksandr Peshkovski in the magazine *Solovetskiye ostrova* were typical of Solovki. Anecdotes, funny stories, comical nicknames and slang as a manifestation of the same sense of humour smoothed away the horror of being on Solovki. Humour and irony told us that it wasn't real. Real life awaited us on our return... The sensation of the unreality of life was maintained both by the unique atmosphere of the white nights in summer and the black days of winter, and in between by the long mornings (no feeling of daytime) which slid into equally long evenings, the loneliness of the forests and the lethal nature of the swamps, the abundance of dark rocks covered with brightly coloured lichen and mosses. The variety of landscapes on the main island was amazing, and no two islands of the Solovki archipelago were alike.

The Scenery of Solovki

I was enabled to maintain my spiritual health on Solovki by the scenery, or rather by the permanent pass to leave the Kremlin drawn up for me in early 1929 by the chief clerk of the Admin. Section Aleksandr Ivanovich Melnikov, former flag-officer to A. F. Kerenski[90]. After his departure at the very end of that year this pass was regularly renewed, as I had to go to the labour colony on official business.

I used this pass as much and as often as possible; I would walk down the road to Reboldova as far as Glubokaya Guba [Deep Bay], and secretly as far as the Peregovorny kamen [Parley Stone] (where discussions had taken place between representatives of the monastery and the commanders of the English squadron during the Crimean War), down the roads to Savvatiyev and Muksalma, etc. Although access to the coastal strip was strictly forbidden, I sometimes went to the Metropolitan's Gardens, where on sunny days I sunbathed for an hour or two, completely forgetting the risk. On Zayachya Guba [Bay of Hares] by the Metropolitan's Gardens I made the acquaintance of a remarkable family of hares. I was lying half-asleep in the bushes, and when I opened my eyes I saw opposite me, no more than an arm's length away, a delightful female hare and several leverets. They were staring fixedly at me as if at a miracle. The monks had taught the animals not to fear man, and the mother hare had obviously brought her babies to show me to them. I didn't move a muscle and neither did they, and we looked at each other with a mutual feeling of heartfelt goodwill. Such ardent contemplation could not last for ever; I moved and they were gone, but the feeling of an amazing warmth of affection for all living things lasted a long time. All around there grew Solovki birches, stunted and bent by the wind, and the waters babbled as, with the ebb and flow of the tide, they flowed over the flat area of the relatively small pebbles of the Metropolitan's Gardens.

I walked in safety down the road to Reboldova as far as Glubokaya Guba with a slender birch stick in my hand. There, one day, I went for a swim. The water still held a wintry chill, and although I went in without a qualm, once I ducked myself it quite took my breath away and I was scarcely able to crawl out. Here I spotted a cross, half rotted away, with an inscription recording the landing here of Meshcheripov's regiment during the Solovki rising of the late seventeenth century[91]. The cross-bar, held in place by nothing more than a metal nail, was about to fall off. I removed that nail and kept it until the blockade, when, in the confusion of an enforced departure (OGPU made me and my family leave Leningrad), I forgot to take it with me.

The road to Reboldova was amazingly lovely, and one day I walked the whole length of it right as far as Reboldova, from where there was a crossing to Anzer. Near Rebovolda was the beginning of the 'running forest', later cut down. This consisted of ancient pines with thick trunks which the ceaseless wind had bent to the ground so that they looked as if they were 'running' and alive. What could they have wanted them for? Their wood was dense and hard to saw.

The islands differ in landscape. The two Zaytski Islands, Bolshoi and Maly, neither of which has any trees growing on it, acquire their beauty from the dazzling coloured combinations of lichen, rocks and boulders, bushes and polar birches, and the sea, which is never out of sight. It is impossible to lose one's way here. Everything seems wild and desolate, and only the low mazes remind one of the customs that man has invented for himself. Two islands, Bolshaya and Malaya Muksalma, are covered with forest and swamp, hills which fall into the sea, and with rich pasture which cattle have grazed for centuries. An artificial causeway connects Bolshaya Muksalma and the main island. Anzer is magnificent. Its scenery is lush and, one might say, even cheerful. Sandy beaches and beautiful deciduous forests remind one of the south. Its high hill is crowned by the *skit* of Golgotha[92], prophetically foretelling by its very name the unbearable sufferings of the old men that died here, the cripples and incurables, sent here from the whole camp to freeze and starve to death, entombed alive. The central, Bolshoi Solovetski island, has a similar landscape to the others. But it also has three hundred lakes, both large and small, some with their own islands where anchorites had once lived and, suitable for keeping top secret prisoners in a state of total isolation from other people.

Here was a great natural Paradise, but at the same time a great Hell for the wide variety of prisoners who represented the various inhabitants of Russia! Here, in this world of sanctity and sin, the heavenly and the earthly, nature and man were united in an uncommon bond.

Huge boulders served as basic building material, and from them arose bastions and walls, and together with slabs and brick they made the foundations of shrines. Roofs were covered with boards and cupolas with aspen tiles, but icons and books, fretwork and wrought ironwork in sanctuaries testify to man's huge efforts to overcome nature, to set the spiritual above the material, to make of nature a gigantic shrine. The *skity*, as it were, compress distance all over the island. There are anchorites' caves and bronze crosses which have grown right into the trunks of trees. The two-man saws used by the prisoners in logging broke their teeth on these crosses and bronze icons.

There are three hundred lakes on Bolshoi Solovetski island. The biggest of them are linked by canals so as to keep Svyatoye ozero

101

[Holy Lake] full of pure water. The main buildings of the Solovetski monastery stand on the side of this lake, between it and the sea on a narrow isthmus. The difference in level between the lake and the sea is eight metres, sufficient to permit the installation in the monastery of a piped water supply and a sewerage system, the use of various sorts of machinery and the construction of docks, which could be rapidly filled and emptied, for repairing ships. It also meant that it was feasible to build an excellent bakehouse, a wash-house and (exceptional for the sixteenth century) a smithy, to supply the refectory with water, etc., etc. The monastery might serve as a graphic refutation of the false concept of the backwardness in technology of Ancient Rus'. Svyatoye ozero is essentially a gigantic pond, artificially created in order to power the life-support systems of the monastery.

The eight metres of overfall between the sea and the lake, which was formed by a dam, obliged the builders to build extremely thick, virtually indestructible walls which would protect the inhabitants of the monastery from enemies and foul weather and create conditions inside the monastery for cultivating a picturesque little garden, with places everywhere suitable for the spiritual response and prayerful meditation of the aged monks.

The Solovki islands are a place where one's awareness of a creator-God and the transitory nature of all that which is human are constantly maintained by the change of the seasons, the rhythm of the days, the long winter nights, the long evening sunsets and long morning sunrises, the rapid changes of weather, the variety of landscapes, the votive crosses, the shrines and chapels, in which the hard work of peasant and craftsman would have been so holy and pleasing to God.

And at the same time, even in monastic days purely worldly cares burst in upon the peaceful life of prayer and work: a clash with heretics, the presence of exiles, the great Old Believer rising which led to the protracted siege of 1668–76[93], in which many died, leaving their unburied bodies lying on the ice outside the monastery...

My walks to the sea came to an end on the opposite side of the monastery, not far from the Parley Stone[94]. I knew that I had to find a resting-place on some headland not usually visited by Degtyarev, 'chief surgeon' of Solovki. What I didn't know was that he had acquired a little dog with an unusually sharp sense of smell, trained to sniff out people at great distances.

I chose a spot on the shore of a bay on the opposite side from that where Degtyarev, 'commander of the forces of the Solovki archipelago', usually rode on his white horse. I was well hidden behind the rocks. Suddenly I heard the repulsive high-pitched bark of the little dog. Degtyarev, chief executioner of Solovki, was galloping round the bay in my direction. I just had time to pull on my trousers and hurl myself into the forest, carrying the rest of my things under my arm. To my good fortune there was a long strip of swamp in the forest, obviously a former river-bed, across which lay the trunk of a huge fir tree. I jumped onto it and crossed over to the far side. Had it not been for fear of falling into Degtyarev's hands (whence I would have gone straight to the *sekirka*[95]) I would never have had the nerve to cross from one side to the other along that tree-trunk. Degtyarev stopped and, after disrupting the charm of the Solovki forest with a choice curse, didn't follow me, and indeed he couldn't dismount and run after me. Why he didn't start shooting I don't know.

Krimkab[96]

When I was in no. 13 company on general duties Father Nikolay Piskanovski and *vladyka* Viktor Ostrovidov made efforts to have me assigned to some sort of office work, or to something at least a little lighter. One day, when we were carting pig-manure (there's a smell if you like!) a very polite and nice-looking gentleman with a grey beard, wearing a black fur jacket and carrying a home-made birch walking-stick approached us and introduced himself to me. This was Aleksandr Nikolayevich Kolosov. One minute's conversation, and I'd been promised 'permanent' work in the Krimkab. Not, of course, straight away. I left no. 13 company for no. 14, in the refectory, where I went down with typhus, and then after the 'convalescent company' in the terrifying basement with the low vaulting and the cracks I found myself in the privileged no. 3 company. I was greeted by the company commander Baron Pritvits, former commandant of the Peter and Paul Fortress, and given a place in Kolosov's cell, with a camp-bed placed lengthways under the window. I was so weak that I was excused duties and used to sit on my bed alone in the cell. Kolosov was the first to return from work at about eight in the evening, and he looked at me cautiously and with surprise. I didn't at first appreciate the reason for his caution. Then I realised that he was afraid that I might infect

103

others in the cell with typhus. He asked Pritvits to put me in the corridor for a week, but he refused. We settled for my basket of belongings being taken out into the corridor or somewhere. I had already gone through a number of de-lousings, but the basket did present a risk, all the more so as, evidently, Ivan Mikhaylovich Andreyevski (who worked as a doctor) had put my basket under his camp-bed in the medical section and evidently caught typhus from it.

I was very embarrassed at Kolosov's misgivings, and for the first weeks felt that I was something of a monster. In the cell there lived General Osovski and two clerks—Baron M. T. Disterlo and Boris Nikolayevich Afinski. I forget when, but very soon Fedya Rozenberg, who had managed to be allowed in from the corridor, also appeared. Kolosov was the unquestioned chief of the cell. He had the best place and slept on a wooden monastic settee. That was a great advantage. The only table in the cell stood right next to his settee. In the evening and the morning he would put a little mirror on the table and spend a long time in front of it combing his beard and moustache and massaging his face with vaseline. He had a weary look. He wore topboots, blue military trousers with stripes down the sides and a green trench-coat. In the past (during the war of 1914) he had been a military procurator, judge and so on. A sense of superiority was still alive in him, but at the same time his breeding made him a very pleasant man in company. He was always of even disposition and never lost his temper. Only by the quivering of his eyelids could one tell that something was irritating him. He was as good a story-teller as he was a listener. In his free time he read books 'in good taste'—mainly Turgenev, whom he found in the library near the theatre and stocked with books confiscated from prisoners or donated by prisoners on release. At work (the Krimkab[97] was on the third floor of the hotel by the landing-stage) he was able to give the camp authorities the impression of great and important activity. In our working room he would sit for a long time, all the more so as it was comfortable, and read novels, holding a pencil poised in his hand, leaning his elbow on the table. When the camp authorities suddenly came in they always found him in this 'working position', and it was impossible to doubt that he was writing something, that is, working. On Sundays we didn't often have the day off, but Kolosov would 'go out on business', carrying some official message and would go for a walk with his home-made birch walking-stick along the road to Filimon in the direction of Glubokaya Guba. When I got a pass for the whole island from A. I. Melnikov, Kolosov and I would go for walks together, and these walks were most profitable to me. He possessed experience of life, was well-read in classical Russian literature, and was a talented raconteur. When he left for Kem in the autumn of 1929 (his sentence expired in the winter) my walks continued with no less interesting a companion—Vladimir Yulyanovich Korolenko, also a lawyer, and nephew of the writer.

Kolosov had in his trunk a beautifully made cheviot suit, a shirt with a turn-down collar and a tie. When he had to report to the authorities or when the typist Shirinska-Shikhmatova was expected in the Krimkab, he would put on his suit and look magnificent—a real gentleman. When Shirinska-Shikhmatova's appeared he would purse his lips in a certain way and assume all manner of airs. With Yuliya Nikolayevna Danzas, who worked with us in Krimkab (but was not directly subordinate to him as her job was to cut out of the newspapers those snippets of information that were of interest to the authorities), he was less gallant, though he was not averse even in her case to 'showing off', but he made no impression on her.

From all that has gone before one might suppose that Kolosov was less than serious, but in fact he did great things. He produced the idea of establishing the Children's Colony in the Sollager, for adolescent criminals, and with the help of his colleagues, saved some hundreds of former street-children, though he couldn't rehabilitate them. This work began in 1928, and our Children's Colony was the first of its kind on such a scale in the Soviet Union. He was so successful in persuading the authorities of the clear (and significant) advantage of this initiative that it received resources that were very considerable for the time. The man in charge of the Culture and Education department, D. V. Uspenski, took part in the organisation; he was, it was said, a Party activist who had volunteered to be sent to work on Solovki. Barracks were built, some of which are still standing to this day. Every teenager was issued with a camp bed and bed linen. Those that were in the general companies were issued with pea-jackets and shoes, and a uniform was invented for them with special hats called 'Lindenerovki' after one Lindener, a Russified German and former member of staff at the Academy of Sciences in Leningrad, who became the first person in charge of the Colony. His deputy was Zdanevich, former People's Commissar for Justice in White Russia, who was replaced on account of his complete stupidity by Innokenti Serafimovich Kozhevnikov, a hero of the Civil War and Army Commander of the Far East Republic.

Krimkab retained the scientific direction of this colony. The position was very advantageous to us all—and had been devised by Kolosov.

Why was it necessary to assemble all the children in one place? Why could they not have been simply called out of the companies, teams and centres where they were at the time and use made of their personal dossiers, which were in the USLON in the Administrative Section? Because there was a surprising degree of disorder in the camp registry. The teenagers, who had been collected at stations and in the streets, dragged out of tar-boilers and from cavities under passenger carriages and so on, gave different surnames every time they were questioned, gambled away short sentences for longer ones and had identical, if any, comments, noted in their dossiers. I had to persuade the teenagers not to keep changing their surnames until they had been registered with the Colony. They, however, were afraid of colonies, suspected a trick, so that only some of those selected for the colony actually got there. But on the other hand, once the Colony had started operations and talk of the good conditions there went round the islands, the teenagers began to agree to go there willingly, and I no longer had to chase them so much and write reports on them.

The same disorder applied to the adults too. Let us take a case in point. It was decided to rid Moscow of beggars. Black Marias drove round the churches and took the beggars from the porches and then, without trial or even questioning (just surnames would be recorded, year of birth and perhaps a little more), they were packed off to Solovki, and straight from the landing stage to Anzer, and then straight up to Golgotha. The same happened in the 'opposite direction': people were shot—'incorrigibles', those whose faces didn't fit, dangerous persons, as it seemed to the authorities—and then recorded as having died of some disease. Such executions under cover of the Medical Section were not only carried out on Solovki. Usually people to be shot in this arbitrary fashion were not kept long in the punishment cells—not more than two or three days. That's how it was, evidently, in the cases of Osorgin, Pokrovski, Bagratuni, Gatsuk and many more.

The number of persons executed was usually higher than that of those sentenced. It is hard to verify that now, but there is no doubt that it was so.

I will give a separate account of the work of the Krimkab. For the moment I will tell of one incident in my work that was immediately connected with Kolosov. He instructed me to compile a report on the organisation of the Colony and explained precisely what it was to contain. I spent a few days writing it and, I thought, wrote it effectively, persuasively and in a style intelligible to our semi-literate masters. I expected praise from him, but as he read it I noticed the corners of his eyes quivering. He found my report far less than satisfactory and set about correcting it. In it there appeared such things as 'for the reason that', 'having regard to the fact that', 'as is evident from the foregoing' and so on, that is, precisely the sort of phrases that I'd tried to avoid but which, it seems, were called for in order to 'create an impression'. I was dismayed. It was beyond my comprehension. But in general I didn't at once appreciate how much good, and by no means in his own interests, Kolosov did for the Sollager; he was refined, poised, sophisticated, but at the same time uncommonly clever and businesslike in a practical way. Perhaps that style was usual in the ranks of the old tsarist civil service?

It is not surprising that the evening in the autumn of 1929 when we said goodbye to Kolosov in the no. 3 company cell was a sad and memorable occasion. I tried to propose a toast for the first time in my life (with a mug of stewed fruit juice in my hand) and I couldn't do it—I burst into tears, by which he was deeply touched.

There is one other thing about him which I haven't mentioned: his work in the Solovki museum, in which he involved me too.

There was something of the nineteenth century about Kolosov—in his opinions, his tastes, the way in which he responded to outward impressions. Once I was walking with him down the road to Reboldova or Filimon. There wasn't a breath of wind and the day was very bright, frosty and dry. The dazzling, pure white snow reflected the rays of the sun. I compared the weather with that of summer: very different yet so similar. He said, pensively and evidently sincerely: "Yes, great Helios...". He brought everything into the standard schemes and patterns of the aesthetics of the last century. And in this connection he was quite the contrary of Aleksandr Aleksandrovich Meyer, whose absolutely independent turn of mind seemed to anticipate the philosophical enquiries and conceptions of the future.

Professor Arkadi Vladimirovich Borodin was very like Kolosov in 'cultural type'. His specialisation was common law, and his aesthetic ideas were likewise on the level (not at all a bad one) of the nineteenth century. He too was fond of Turgenev and A. K. Tolstoy, and couldn't understand modern poetry or painting. He was rather sentimental and old-fashioned but had great experience of life. I can't

107

remember exactly when he was in the Krimkab but it wasn't for long. Middle-aged people who are fond of Turgenev find that he colours their attitude to life, to beauty, to the Russian language. Kolosov, who read Turgenev and was particularly enthusiastic over *Asya*, used to amaze us. There were few books there but I, too, read *Asya* and understood: this was real life, in which even the unspoken word played a part. And we were in an uncouth and savage nightmare world. The illusory reality of Solovki was materially uncouth. One couldn't believe in the peat-bogs, logging, swamps, bunks, typhus, mosquitos, tree-stumps, 'perches'—all this was beyond the bounds of probability, but Turgenev, with his fateful destiny of a single unspoken word in *Asya* seemed to be real life.

Kolosov's upraised pencil was in its way a weapon, a spear aimed at the prison-camp world of Solovki.

There was not the slightest connection between art and reality. The prisoners, lousy as they were, would watch *The Children of Vanyushin*[98] in the camp theatre and dissolve into tears, forgetful of what they were enduring and what was going on outside. They would sing sentimental ballads and be deeply moved; sometimes the partings they sang about were more painful than the rupture from their families in real life. That is why the Solovki theatre, which had been thought up for the sake of appearances, played so great a consoling part on Solovki. It put on performances for at least six years (from 1926 to 1931 inclusive).

Aleksey Grigorovich Satin, professor of climatology, also appeared to me a man of the nineteenth century, though of a different sort. My conversations with him took place most often on the roads of Solovki. He used to walk about in the vicinity of the Kremlin, noting down meteorological data on the fences. Whether the islands had to supply such data to the mainland I don't know. His opinions often reminded me of Bazarov[99]. He was an earthy materialist, and, like all materialists, a pessimist, with an ironic view of everything and scornful of the comforts of life. He went around in a Caucasian hooded cape and fur hat. When the second outbreak of typhus started in the autumn of 1929 he said calmly: "Your own lice won't let other people's land on you; the best way to avoid typhus is to be lousy." And he was.

He was a kindly man. When my parents were due to come and visit me he gave up his little room on the Quality Control Station for us. He shared this room with a naval officer, Azhayev, who protested, as he didn't want to move out to a cold shed. But Satin simply pushed him out and then moved into the freezing shed himself. But then we had a disaster: the little stove set fire to some dried herbs. I managed to put them out, because I had the presence of mind to run next door for a fire extinguisher. If I had failed it would have been the *sekirka* for me. Satin pretended that the part of the collection of dried herbs that had been burnt was of no value. One more thing: he was a first-class chess-player, and he was jokingly referred to as 'the first chess-player and the last nihilist'.

Thus my ideas that anyone with materialistic views must be a pessimist and an egoist were refuted. The exception proves the rule.

The Diagonal of a Child's Blanket

In 1928, as I think I have already said, people knew what was meant by prison, transport and camp, and knew how to equip those being sent for the journey. Their load should be light and should contain basic essentials. They knew, for example, that prisoners would have to lie on hard bunks, and that this is most painful for the pelvis. So they used to make little mattresses stuffed with human hair, as this is very light and uncrushable. I was given one such, no bigger than a pillow, and a child's very light, fluffy blanket which I could cover either my legs or my shoulders with. I spread it over me cornerwise, one corner on my feet, the other on my shoulders, and put more of my clothes on top—in winter, my fur jacket. I pulled it over my head so as to go off into my private world of recollections of home, University, Petersburg. I especially enjoyed thinking of Petersburg in the twilight—the view from Dvortsovy bridge towards Dvortsovaya Square when, as the half-light of evening gave way to the half-light of night, the garland of yellow street-lamps suddenly blazed out and the grandiose semicircle of the General Staff building was revealed.

I have a particularly clear memory of no. 3 company. To save space the table at which my cell-mates sit has been moved right up to my camp-bed, and the little lamp on it flickers. It will be going out at any moment: it is on until ten o'clock, and after that it goes out for a few seconds as a warning, and you have to get everything done in time to go to bed in the light. The lamp gleams dully through the clouds of *makhorka*[100] smoke (it was said that that was less harmful

109

than the smoke of good tobacco) which just had to be tolerated because opening a window would mean letting the cold in. And it's very seldom comfortably warm; it's either stifling hot because of the huge monastic stove, which cools down slowly over a few days, or it's freezing cold while we wait for permission to take our turn for heating.

Lying under my child's blanket gives me a sensation of home, family, my parents' concern and my childhood nightly prayers: "God bless Mummy, Daddy, Granddad, Grandma, Misha, nurse... Bless and preserve them all". Under my pillow, over which I invariably made the sign of the cross at night, I kept a little silver folding icon. A month later the company commander found it and confiscated it: "Not in regulations". An expression I'm sick of in camp life!

The Visit by Maksim Gorki and the Mass Executions of 1929

Gorki visited us on Solovki in the spring of 1929. He spent about three days there; I can't remember exactly how long, but it would be easy to check from his collected writings.

Rumours had been spread in the West by refugees (there had been escapes from detachments of Sollager on the mainland, and some had reached Finland on foot or by boats carrying timber) of exceptional cruelty on the logging sites.

Gorki's mission was, evidently, to counter public opinion in the West. The point was that the Congress of the USA and the British Parliament had passed resolutions to buy no more timber from the USSR; the full horrors of Gulag logging had been made known by escapees such as Malsagov and others. The bulk export of timber was organised by Frenkel, who had written: "We must get everything out of the prisoners in the first three months!" One can imagine what went on at the logging sites!

Gorki was required to calm public opinion. And he did ... and sales of wood recommenced... Some said later that he'd wished, by his fabrications, to obtain an easing of the prisoners' lot, others—that he'd wanted to induce Budberg-Zakrevska to visit him; she had been afraid to return to Russia with him. I don't know which version is true—perhaps both. Gorki was awaited impatiently.

Finally rumours trickled out of the radio station—Gorki was on his way to Solovki. Not only did the authorities begin to prepare, but so did those prisoners who had any kind of connection with Gorki, as did those who simply hoped to arouse his pity and obtain freedom.

One fine day the steamer Gleb Boyki arrived at the landing stage in Bukhta Blagopoluchiya [Bay of Prosperity] with Gorki on board. From the Krimkab windows we could see him standing on a knoll for quite a long time next to a woman in odd-looking clothes: a leather jacket, leather riding breeches tucked into high boots and a leather cap. This turned out to be his daughter-in-law, the wife of his son Maksim. She was obviously dressed (in her opinion) as a dyed-in-the-wool Cheka[101] woman. The outfit was a deception! Gorki wore a cloth cap, tilted to the back of his head in the proletarian style of the day (in imitation of Lenin). The monastery barouche came for him, pulled by a horse that had been found God knows where. I was amazed. I could point out to this day the very spot where he waited for the barouche...

All we prisoners were delighted. "That Gorki will spot everything, find out everything. He's been around, you can't fool him. About the logging and the torture on the tree-stumps, the *sekirka*, the hunger, the disease, the three-tier bunks, those without clothes, the sentences without conviction... The whole lot!" We began to wait. A day or two before his arrival fir trees were cut down in the forest and erected for decoration along both sides of the road through the labour colony. Every night squads went out from the Kremlin into the Solovki forest to ease the pressure on the Kremlin and the bunks. The patients in the sick-bay were issued clean dressing-gowns.

Gorki rode round the island a little with his leather-clad companion. The first day, I think, he went to the sick-bay. On both sides of the entrance and the stairs the patients were lined up in their clean dressing-gowns. He didn't go upstairs. He said "I don't like parades", and turned towards the exit. He also went to the labour colony where he called in at the last building on the right before the school (now, in the 80s, the porch has been demolished and the door boarded up). I was standing in the crowd outside the barrack, as I had a pass and I was directly concerned with the colony. Some ten or fifteen minutes after Gorki's arrival the commander of the labour colony—the former Army Commander Kozhevnikov—emerged from the barrack with his assistant Shipchinski, followed by some of the boys. At his request Gorki had stayed for a face-to-face talk with a boy of fourteen, who had been called on to tell him the 'whole truth'—about all the tortures to which prisoners were submitted in their physical work. Gorki stayed talking to the boy for no less than forty minutes (I had at the time a silver pocket watch which had been presented to me by my father just before the First World War, and secretly handed to me on the island during his first visit). Finally he came out of the barrack to wait for the barouche and was weeping for all to see, making no attempt at concealment. I saw it myself. The crowd of prisoners was in ecstasy. "Gorki's learned it all! The boy's told him everything!"

Then he went to the *sekirka*. The punishment cell had been transformed: the 'perches' had been removed, and in the middle was a table with newspapers on it. The prisoners who had stayed there (those who looked fairly healthy) had been made to sit and read. Gorki climbed the steps to the punishment cell, went to one of the 'readers', and turned the newspaper round: he had been ostentatiously holding it upside down. After that Gorki quickly left and drove off, probably to have lunch or tea in the Biosad gardens, just outside the camp boundary, where a very small number of specialists lived in comparative comfort.

Gorki went nowhere else on Solovki, as far as I remember. He and his daughter-in-law embarked on the Gleb Boyki and there were entertained by a hapless monk—one of those who, everyone knew, were allowed to drink and who had been got drunk especially for the occasion.

But the boy's life was over. Possibly even before Gorki left, but there was a great deal of discussion about him. "Had the boy ever existed?" If there really had been such a boy, why hadn't Gorki had the brains to take him away with him? They'd have had to let him go... But there had been a boy. I knew all the 'colonists'.

Other consequences of Gorki's visit to Solovki, however, were even more dreadful. And he must have foreseen them.

Gorki must have had the wit to realise that an effort would be made to devolve the blame for every 'irregularity' onto the prisoners themselves. That is a classic method of evading responsibility. Immediately after he had gone arrests and reprisals began. When he and his daughter-in-law and their attendant GPU men reached Popov island and Kem, where they were to board the Gleb Boyki, a party of prisoners were working, loading and unloading, in the wind and cold in just their underwear: at the time, no clothing other than underwear was issued in the camps. It was impossible to conceal this party, stripped to their underwear. Popov island, where the landing stage was (without so much as a roof over it for protection against the weather), was totally barren and windswept. I know that only too well, as we spent two or three hours embarking on the Gleb Boyki (the half-frozen and the living got their turn after the ordinary cargo). When Gorki was there a criminal was in charge of the party of prisoners, a crafty and inventive man, and he devised a way of concealing unclothed prisoners on the bare island. "Fall in!" "Close ranks!" "Closer, closer!" (accompanied by a barrage of filthy language), "Closer still!! You rabble!!" "Squat!" "Sit down, I tell you, on top of each other, you so-and-sos!!" A compact mass of human bodies was formed, shivering from the cold. Then he ordered the crew to bring tarpaulins and sails (the Boyki still had her masts) and they were all covered up. Gorki stood on deck until loading was finished, chatting and joking with the camp staff. Quite a while went by. Only when the steamer had sailed sufficiently far away were the tarpaulins removed. You can imagine what was under them. Arrests began soon after Gorki's departure and both punishment blocks, the *sekirka* and the one in the Kremlin, were crammed full.

I also heard the following story. Before Gorki arrived in the Solovki camp the European Thompson Commission arrived in Kem, having negotiated in Moscow that it would be free to move anywhere at all about the camp and to speak freely to prisoners. The members of the Commission lived in Kem in the flat of one of the camp staff who was evidently away on leave. They collected a lot of material on the mainland, took photographs and made notes. A certain experienced pickpocket, however, was given the job of stealing it all. He organised his cronies and they crowded round the Commission, cut away their camera and stole documents and notebooks from their pockets. For this he was paid by the camp authorities with a few kilograms of flour and other commodities ('the price of honour in our empire'). The Commission left empty-handed—but I don't know whether they'd been on the island.

A second disaster befell Solovki in the late summer of the same year. Anyway, could anything 'new' happen in that fantastic nightmare that was Solovki?

One morning a teenager from the Colony came into the Krimkab and handed Kolosov a big bundle—Whatman paper[102], rolled into a tube. Kolosov unwrapped it, turned pale and sat in silence for a long time. At length he asked someone to go to the premises underneath the Directorate, where since monastic times there had been a printing press, and to ask Molchanov, who was in charge there, to come and see him. I remember that at first the two of them, Molchanov and Kolosov, talked quietly, reading and looking over the big sheet of Whatman paper. Then they called all of us to a conference. The sheet of Whatman paper turned out to be a proclamation of Serafimovich Kozhevnikov's ascent to the throne of All the Russias. Amnesty was promised to all prisoners and there was a proposal to seize the Solovetski ships, take Kem and march on Petrograd.

What was to be done? If this was a joke, then it put at risk the lives of any who read that 'proclamation', including the boy. Anyway, the decision was taken to hurry over to Kozhevnikov and find out what it was all about. The emissary returned looking upset. Kozhevnikov had not taken roll-call in the labour colony. He wasn't there, nor was Shipchinski, and the window of their office was shut. Then, with an expression of suffering (he really was suffering morally), Kolosov got up and went with Melchanov to the Information and Investigation department, one of whose offices was on the second floor of the USLON building. By this time the whole camp was seething. Rumours were not creeping—they were flying. People said that a minelayer had come to the coast of the island and taken Kozhevnikov on board. A search was instituted. No one doubted that this was a well-organised escape. Kozhevnikov had evidently decided before leaving to make fun of the authorities by publishing his 'proclamation'. The whole camp was jubilant. But then the rumour reached us that Kozhevnikov and Shipchinski had tried to kill a sentry at the powder magazine, which was to the right of the Filimon road. That meant that they hadn't escaped, but were in hiding on the island.

Every day there were conflicting reports. They'd been seen! They'd not been seen! Their tracks had been spotted somewhere. Tension in the camp was terrible. After about a fortnight the two of them were caught. They put up a resistance near a firtree under which they'd been living. They had an axe, with which they defended themselves. The order had been to take them alive.

I remember someone shouting "Here they come! Here they come!" We rushed to the Krimkab windows. I could see clearly. First was Kozhevnikov, being dragged along unconscious by his arms, the soles of his feet turned outward, and hauled up the stairs that lead straight to the second floor of USLON. His head was hanging, and there was blood on his bald patch. Behind him came Shipchinski, arms bound behind his back. He was walking proudly, but twitching oddly. What happened at the interrogation I don't know.

It turned out that Kozhevnikov had gone mad and Shipchinski had decided not to abandon him. They'd been living in the forest (it was by then autumn). They'd been fed by the 'cowboy' Vladimir Nikolayevich Degtyarev, who lived in the arboretum. This brave man was short and agile, and wore cowboy gloves and a cowboy hat. He was a former pupil of May's school (where I had been). He'd made up his mind to run off to America even before the First World War, had come back after the Revolution and had paid for it with a ten-year sentence. He was a great eccentric. He refused to enter the Kremlin on foot, and had been given a goat. He led the goat all the way to the Kremlin (when he had to appear there) but mounted it outside the Nikolski gates and as he rode in produced his pass out of his gauntlets for the sentry to check. Why he was permitted to fool about like that I don't know. Probably the authorities liked not only drunkards but eccentrics as well. He was completely honest. When it was discovered that he'd been helping the escapees I imagined that he'd be shot out of hand. But no... Later, after being released, I was walking home from work down Bolshoi Prospekt in the Petrograd District, where trams used to run in those days, when I had a shock: off a fast-moving tram leaped Degtyarev, who ran over to me (he'd seen me from the platform) and told me that he was working as a forester on some plantation in Central Asia. With a friendly shout of "All the best from Alatau!" he rushed after the next tram and vanished. So he was alive! And I was pleased as could be.

It was rumoured also that Kozhevnikov was still alive. He was supposed to have been seen in Moscow, either going into the Kremlin or coming out. His former Revolutionary services counted in his favour, it was said, as did his service in the Civil War and his connections[103], whereas Shipchinski was shot along with many others. The authorities had had a fright and decided to give people a warning. More arrests began. Some case was made about an attempted rising, but later they didn't even bother to cook one up.

Those shot were listed as having died of typhus. The numbers executed on both counts possibly totalled 300 or 400 for a round figure, at least while Kolosov was there—that is, before his release in late autumn 1929. The waste of human lives weighed heavily on me. I was particularly sorry about the frail Shipchinski, who had always been cheerful and unbowed.

The commander of the Culture and Education department, in which Shipchinski had worked (the labour camp came under its aegis) asked him just before a Soviet holiday: "Think me up a slogan to make it clear to everyone that here on Solovki we do everything for those who are from similar social strata—the workers and peasants." Shipchinski[104] came out with "Solovki for the workers and peasants". The commander (the D. V. Uspenski previously mentioned) replied "Well done!" and gave orders for the placard to be written. I'm passing on, of course, only the gist of the conversation that Shipchinski told me about. It is possible that it was actually Uspenski who shot Shipchinski in the back of the head.

Before his execution Shipchinski struck up a relationship with a young lame ballerina (her leg had been broken during her investigation). They had somehow managed to arrange meetings and after his tragic death I felt especially sorry for them both.

In the autumn of 1931 a boy who worked in the registry of the Information and Investigation department asked me whether I might like to see my dossier. I had not as yet been taken to the mainland and the Belbaltlag[105]. He took me late one evening to an office on the second floor of the Directorate, which surprised me by its lack of windows; it was crammed with racks of prisoners' dossiers. He showed me an ordinary school notebook cover containing forms (the article of the criminal code, my sentence, etc.), and on the top of which was written in large letters: 'Connected with insurgents on Solovki'. These dossiers have evidently been preserved in Petrozavodsk. It would be interesting to take a look at that curt comment, which all but cost me my life and rendered me 'in permanent residence' on Solovki for almost the whole of 1931, when all my friends had been transferred to Medvezhya Gora [Bear Mountain] to take part in the White Sea-Baltic Canal project.

In late 1929 there was a second outbreak of typhus on the island. This was an unusual sort of typhus and was not treated. Any cell where cases occurred was sealed until everyone in there was dead. Food and hot water were passed in through the door which was opened just a crack. The theatre was closed, and patients from the general companies lay there like sardines. When one of them began to lose consciousness an orderly would go to him, rouse him and ask "Surname, surname!" This would be written in indelible pencil on a tag which had already been attached to his left hand. The confusion in prisoners' dossiers was terrible. Men, delirious and dying, crawled from where they lay and villains with long sentences swapped surnames with the dying if theirs were shorter.

It has been suggested that the 'Asian typhus' was in fact bubonic plague, for a simple reason: black spots or blotches appeared on the bodies of those who went down with it (I had forgotten that, as I never saw it for myself; one was not allowed to visit them).

In no. 7 company, where I was from the summer of 1929, the first cell on the left was sealed (it overlooked the sea, and Volodya Sveshnikov-Kemetski had lived there at one time). In that cell there happened to be a recently arrived young writer from Moscow, with whom I managed to make friends. He had published a novel which I've been trying to find for a long time—either *Sever i Yug* or *Yug i Sever*[106]. He told me that for Russia the problem of North and South was much more important than that of East and West. He was completely fit at a time when someone in his cell took sick. He was locked in with the rest, and I used to talk to him through the door. When he sensed that he was dying he asked me to give his wife his silver spoon and pushed it under the door. It was smaller than a teaspoon and bent but I remember it better than his face or the face of his wife, who came to Solovki, in disregard of all the camp rules, to her husband's grave in the summer of 1930. He was buried in a mass grave so that it was impossible to ascertain exactly where he lay. I have completely forgotten the surname of that young writer and the title of his first and only book.

In the late autumn of 1929 my parents came to visit me again (two visits a year were allowed). We stayed in the room of a volunteer guard (there were also prisoner-guards) whom my parents had met on the Gleb Boyki, and with whom they had agreed on a certain sum for the hire of his room in the hotel behind the USLON. There was also a photographer's in the hotel for the use of volunteers, where I was photographed three times with my parents on various occasions, and a medical room with the chief medical orderly Grigori Grigoryevich Taybalin. He, incidentally, wrote poetry (a poem on his time in Solovki) and took an old man who spoke no Russian to work for him—'the best singer in Old Bokhara'. From the windows of our room, which overlooked the farm, we could see some soft-looking orientals in silk gowns and silk boots with high heels doing something. These 'basmachi'[107] all soon died, unable to withstand the cold and the work... But their memory lived on: in the winter of 1929–30, as I have said, the terrible Asian typhus struck the island.

I was living with my parents and the arrests were still going on. Towards the end of their stay someone came to see me from the company and said "They've been for you!" I saw it all: they'd come to arrest me. I told my parents that I'd been called to go to work at once, and left. My first thought was not to be arrested in front of them! I went to see Melnikov, in his room above no. 6 company near the Filippovskaya church. I knocked, but he didn't answer. I couldn't go away. I knocked louder and louder, and finally Melnikov opened the door. He was dressed, and sitting by the table was a young woman; I knew her, she'd been picked up for something to do with forging money. That meant he hadn't opened the door because I had interrupted a tryst!

When he saw me he calmed down.

He calmed down and gave me a stern ticking off, the gist of which was: "If they've come for you, it's no good involving other people. They might be next." The door slammed in my face. I realised that I'd made a mistake. He too might be taken out and shot. Apart from the executions resulting from spiteful, false accusations, supposed 'insurgents' were also being shot, as well as prisoners who were simply 'difficult'. Most of the shootings took place on 28 November 1929 in the cemetery behind the Kremlin, but there were also mass executions on other days below the *sekirka*, on Anzer and at Savvatiyev.

Among the events of that night one more thing sticks in my memory. In the summer of 1929, before the executions, Melnikov's wife Olga had been to see him; she was a friend of my mother and they had invited me to tea. I could see that they were upset, and finally Mrs Melnikov asked me, and he confirmed the question: was he (Melnikov) being unfaithful to his family? This question was quite unexpected. I had absolutely no idea. I decided that it must be a joke, and answered it with a joke: "Yes, he ought to be ashamed..." and the like. Afterwards Melnikov gave me a short ticking off: "If you don't know something, say you don't know." Nevertheless the frivolity of my answer had seemed to calm his wife: if there had been anything going on I wouldn't have joked but would have lied in a serious manner. All this flashed through my mind; what terror Melnikov and his lover had endured when I'd knocked frantically on their door!

I went outside and decided not to go back to my parents, but went to the woodyard and hid among the stacks of wood. The timbers were long, intended for the monastery stoves. There I sat until a crowd turned up for work, and then slipped away without being seen. What I went through there, listening to the shots of executions and looking at the stars in the sky—I saw nothing else all night!

After that strange night a transformation took place in me. I won't say that it happened all at once, rather over the course of the next few days, growing stronger and stronger all the time. That night was only the turning-point.

I realised then that every day was a gift from God. I had to live day by day, be satisfied that I was alive for one day more and be grateful for every morning.

Soon came the order to terminate meetings between prisoners and relatives. My parents left a few days before the scheduled end of their visit, as did Osorgin's wife. He went back to the punishment block and I to no. 3 company.

On 28 October the order went through the camp that all were to be in their companies at such-and-such a time in the evening—I forget exactly what. No one was to stay late at work. We realised what it meant, and sat in silence in our cell in no. 3 company. I hid my cap. Suddenly Black, the dog, began to howl on the sports field, which was just opposite our company windows. That meant that the first group was being led out through the Pozharny gates to be shot. Black always howled his farewell to every group. They say that there were cases of hysterics in the escort. Two dandies (dandies by camp standards) from the mainland were doing the shooting, together with the commander of the Culture and Education section Uspenski. It was said of him that he had been made to work at Solovki to keep him out of sight; he was supposed to have killed his father (who some said had been a deacon, some said a priest). He hadn't received any sentence, but had got away with saying that he'd 'killed a class enemy'. He was actually invited to help with the executions—after all, they'd got three or four hundred to shoot.

There was a hitch with one of the parties at the Pozharny gates. A tall, powerful, one-legged professor of ballistics named Pokrovski (it was said that he'd lectured at Oxford) started to hit the escort with his wooden leg. He was knocked to the ground and shot right there in the gateway. The rest went on without a word, as if bewitched, and were shot outside the women's barracks. The women could hear what was going on and understood, and went into hysterics.

The graves had been dug a day before the shootings. The executioners were drunk. One bullet per victim. Many were buried alive, just a thin layer of earth over them. In the morning the earth on the pit was still moving...

In our cell we counted the number of groups led out to be shot, both by Black's howls and the number of revolver shots.

In the morning we went to work. By that time the Krimkab had been relocated to a room on the left of the entrance, next to the lavatory. Someone saw Uspenski in there, using the wash-hand basin to wash blood off his jackboots. They say he had a charming wife...

Osorgin also had a wife. I remember her—a brunette, taller than him. We met by the Storozhevaya bastion and he introduced me. What restraint it took for him not to tell his wife that he was doomed, about what was in store...

And Black ran away into the forest. He wouldn't live with people! They searched for him, especially Uspenski and the commandant of the forces of the Solovki archipelago, the Latvian Degtyarev, nicknamed 'head surgeon' (he usually carried out the individual executions under the bell-tower). One day I saw him running about, wearing a long overcoat, in a crowd of prisoners, shooting at dogs. The injured animals ran away howling. The skirts of his long 'Cheka' coat were flapping against his jackboots... After that night, with Black howling, Degtyarev developed a hatred of dogs. But a prisoner was all but shot for a stone thrown at a seagull.

After the shootings an order was read to the prisoners at roll-calls about execution 'for cruelty towards prisoners' (what impudence!). A number of people were named, of whom some had really been cruel and some were blamed for various evils, while others who had been shot were not so much as mentioned. Executions were also carried out at the *sekirka*. The camp had been cleared of 'superfluous' persons. As I recall, the names of Osorgin, Fitstum, Sivers and many others were not read out. Fortunately, Antsiferov, who had been in the *sekirka* punishment block and on the condemned list, was not killed and was taken back to Kem.

The Solovki Museum

For me, the most noteworthy place in Solovki was the museum. Much about its existence is, if not magical, at least amazing. At the head of the Solovki Local History Society in the mid-'20s was an Estonian, Eykhmans, a fairly cultured man. As things turned out he went from being director of the Museum to being camp commandant and an exceptionally cruel one at that. Nevertheless he preserved his respect for the Museum, and even after he left it retained its special status right up to the tragic summer of 1932. The Preobrazhenski Cathedral had been preserved in part; the fire of 1922 had only touched its domes, and inside there still gleamed the gold of its magnificent iconostasis, constructed with money dedicated by Peter the Great. There were between two hundred and two hundred and fifty icons and the sanctuary was adorned with a canopy of miraculous wrought iron-work. Also preserved was the Church of the Annunciation on the Gates, where the main museum display was. In the magazine *Solovetskiye ostrova* (1926, no. 2 and 3) there appeared an article by V. Nikolski on 'The Iconographic Collection of the Solovetski Monastery'. From that it is clear that in the chancel of the Church of the Annunciation (begun 1596, finished 1601) there had been more than five hundred icons, among which were two that worked miracles— the Sosnovskaya and the Slavyanskaya. Metropolitan Filipp had prayed before the latter when he was Father Superior of the monastery. There was a note on it:

> *The object of devotion of Father Superior Filipp* (71/2" by 91/2" in a basma[108] frame). This icon was ascribed by the monks to Rublev[109] himself. In the left hand of the Mother of God is the Infant. With one hand He touches her cheek, with the other he tries to embrace her (the Vladimir type?). Where this icon is now I don't know. The gates in the Church of the Annunciation were completed in 1633 through the generosity of Aleksandr Bulatnikov, cellarer of the Troitsko-Sergeyevnaya *lavra*[110], and carved by Lev Ivanov, craftsman of the *lavra*".

This miracle was destroyed in the summer of 1932 by the demand of a commission that came to Solovki from Moscow and gave short shrift to all remains of the 'monastic drug'.

The academic output of the Museum was printed first by letterpress in the former monastery print-shop, on the first floor of the USLON building by the landing-stage, later by some duplicating process. In recent years I've been through the Leningrad libraries looking for these latter, but without success.

In about 1927 Nikolay Nikolayevich Vinogradov became director of the Museum. He had a criminal record (article 67) for, it is said, misappropriation of certain valuable exhibits from the museum at Kostroma. In other words, he wasn't a 'political', and therefore the authorities held him in considerable respect. In those years political prisoners weren't 'cloaked' by the criminal code, but rather the opposite took place: there was a tendency to represent political diversion as a criminal act. At first Vinogradov was deputy director, but then—immediately upon his release—he became honorary director of the Museum. That was in the spring of 1929, when he went up to Leningrad to study in the Synod archives the case of Pushkin's uncle Pavel Isakovich Gannibal, who was imprisoned on Solovki after the Decembrist rising. B. A. Modzalevski too had studied this material in his time, but Vinogradov succeeded in discovering something further, and with great enthusiasm presented a paper on Hannibal in the Museum. I too was present on that occasion, and received a block of 'Tip-Top' chocolate which he'd brought back from my parents in Leningrad.

The point, however, was not the chocolate, but that Vinogradov, however murky his past might have been (and from the moral point of view it was by no means beyond reproach), did a very great deal for the intelligentsia on Solovki, and for the young artists and poets in their midst, of whom there were quite a few.

There was no point in his making himself into a cynical antireligionist and at the same time preserving many valuable church items in the Church of the Annunciation and calling it 'the antireligion section of the museum'. He was clearly not a believer, although in his home region of Kostroma he had served for some time as a village priest. A. B. Ivanov worked as his assistant in the Museum; he had a reputation for toughness among the prisoners. He was of dwarfish build and was called 'the anti-religious bug' or even 'the mini-swine'[111].

When Vinogradov was compelled to give up icons to the coffin workshop on Anzer he tried to pick out the least precious, of which he had built up a special reserve.

One evening Vinogradov came up to me as I was sitting in the Museum because I did not want to return to the company (he had wangled permission for me to do this through my friend the chief clerk of the Administrative department, A. I. Melnikov). I was compiling a list of the most valuable icons in the sanctuary. He handed me a document concerning the discovery of the relics of Zosima and Savvatiy, and pointed without saying a word to one important detail: in one of the shrines, when it had been opened, there had been 'observed' the end of a *papirosa* of Soviet date. This clearly showed that before the official discovery someone who had been smoking a Soviet *papirosa* had crawled into the shrine. By this he obviously intended to demonstrate the value of the 'discovery'.

In her memoirs Yuliya Nikolayevna Danzas, writing in France, says exceptionally little about the Museum, calling it 'anti-religious', and likewise Vinogradov and his colleagues, while stating that she had refused firmly to lead anti-religious excursions. Vinogradov would scarcely have made her lead such excursions: he had his evil hench-man Ivanov for that. On the contrary, Vinogradov spared the intelli-gentsia in every way and compelled no one to do anything. He saved Yuliya Nikolayevna herself from 'general' (i. e. physical) work before she went to work in the Krimkab. By the way, when Kolosov (in charge of the Krimkab) had been released and the very existence of the office was in jeopardy, Vinogradov 'did a deal' for me with the commander of the Culture and Education department with a few *rizy*[112], which he was prepared to let go in exchange for my working in the theatre. Thus I became a real object of slave-trade. Fortunately for me the Krimkab was not closed—but more of that later.

A number of people whom Vinogradov had saved worked with him in the Museum: Prince Voplyarski, who was so old that he could no longer do any work, and who had been under threat of extermina-tion on Golgotha. On Anzer there was Yelena Aleksandrovna Anosova and later the art historian and restorer Aleksandr Ivanovich Anisimov and, of the younger generation, the former Boy Scout Dmitri Ship-chinski, of whom Yuliya Danzas writes in her memoirs that he was 'like a typical Komsomol[113] member'. He had, however, always been irreconcilable to Soviet power and a year later 'escaped' into the for-est to certain death with his deranged older friend Kozhevnikov, as I have already said, and was captured and shot. Vinogradov tried to get M. D. Priselkov to work for him, and asked me to have him released from 'quarantine', and he took on numerous others. Every evening before going to bed, he would invite cultured people to leave their company bunks and camp-beds, where the little lamps flickered in the half-light, to hear lectures, work on the Museum card-indexes or simply to chat, and they felt for an hour or two that they were in their proper *milieu*. A. I. Sizintseva is compiling an archival account of Vinogradov in his native Kostroma. Without trespassing on her aca-demic ground, I will say only that his life was stormy mainly because of his burning passion as a collector. He would stop at nothing, and was a great expert on ethnography, antiques, folklore and ancient literature. To his credit are the book *The Tale of Paris and Venus*, published on the recommendation of A. A. Shakhmatov, two monographs on the Solovetski mazes, printed on Solovki, and a number of articles and other publications, in particular an interesting piece in *Solovetskiye ostrova* on artistic forging on Solovki. Before the Revolution he was highly esteemed by Shakhmatov in Petersburg, where he went in the early years of this century (returning later to Kostroma). He was secretary of the magazine *Zhivaya Starina*, worked on the magazine *Russkoye Slovo*[114], and was a member of the Imperial Geographical Society.

There are a few vague allusions to his links with the *Okhrana*[115], but no conclusive evidence that anyone suffered as a result. Perhaps even in those days he combined unscrupulousness with the desire to assist and entertain... Is such a combination possible? If so, Vinogradov was one such. In any case the good that he did must not be overlooked.

I was introduced to Vinogradov, and he gave me the task of compiling a list of the icons. In the evenings I used to sit in the sanctuary of the Church of the Annunciation on the Pozharny (formerly Svyatiye) Gates, making rough sketches of them. I designated the icons provisionally by rectangles, numbered the rectangles, and then separately under the number I indicated the name of the icon and its approximate date (as Kolosov and others showed me). Many icons which have now been published or are preserved in the Museum in Kolomensk are familiar to me, for example the big Byzantine icon (we labelled it 'Italo-Cretan' after N. P. Likhachev) which was entitled 'The Eternal Rock' (the Mother of God is seated on a throne). There was also the 'Saviour Not Made By Hands' of Simon Ushakov and others. All these I drew and noted on paper from school exercise books. If only I had those notes now! They would be important for the history of Solovki.

Vinogradov published either materials or 'Notes' of the Solovki Local History Society on the duplicator. When he found out that I'd written a thesis on tales concerning the Patriarch Nikon for my diploma under Abramovich, he asked me to write to my parents in Leningrad for it so that it could be published in a similar way. The work, however, had been lost, together with my other thesis on Shakespeare in Russia in the late eighteenth-early nineteenth centuries (which I had written with Boyanus, but had not defended).

124

My evening work in the Museum, my talks with Kolosov, Vinogradov and Anisimov contributed much to my understanding of Ancient Russian art, as did my work as a labourer with the archaeologist and restorer Nazimov of Pskov.

I still have a watercolour by a young Ukrainian artist Petrash who arrived on Solovki from Chernigov (there, as in Kiev, a large group of young people were arrested for belonging to two organisations: the SMU and the SVU[116]). The painting was presented to me later in Leningrad by Eduard Rozenberg, and it shows the pier between the Museum building and the fortress wall (a view, I think, from Vinogradov's window).

In so far as I have touched on the question of the fate of our greatest specialist on Ancient Russian art, A. I. Anisimov, I will quote in full my letter about him to the newspaper *Sovyetskaya kultura*, [Soviet Culture] published under the title 'And documents can be wrong' (concerning the note 'By sentence of the Troika', signed by Ye. Konchiny in the column 'Continuation of a theme' of *Sovyetskaya kultura*, 14 April 1990).

The paper returns for a second time to the subject of the fate of the notable art historian and icon restorer Anisimov, whose last works had recently been collected and published by G. I. Vzdornov.

In a document from the KGB of the Karelian Autonomous Republic, referred to in the article, it is stated that for the serving of a ten-year sentence of the Kollegium of OGPU (the 'Troika'). A. I. Anisimov "arrived in the Belomorsko-Baltiski (sic![117]) corrective-labour camp on 16 April 1931". That is not so. I spent several months in the same cell as him in no. 7 company, the cell where the reserves of the Solovki Historical-Architectural and Natural History Museum are now stored. He did not come to Solovki before May 1931 (the month the crossing was opened). He was immediately rescued from 'general' (i. e. physical) work by Vinogradov, and set to work in the Museum.

Anisimov restored a huge, magnificent icon in the Solovetski Museum, in the well-lit choir of the Church of the Annunciation on the Gates. When I was able I used to go see him in the choir and watch his painstaking work. In our cell he was tidy, deliberate, and cooked himself some sort of porridge on the company stove. At the same time he was exceptionally active—a form of behaviour hitherto completely unfamiliar to me. On two or three occasions in the summer of 1931 Vinogradov obtained a pass out of the Kremlin for him, and he brought back berries and greenery from his long walks. He talked a lot and in so doing, as it were, 'fixed' his lectures. One was about the restoration of the icon of the Mother of God of Vladimir, and as an accompaniment he read a poem about it by Maksimilian Voloshin. He spoke in detail of his 'case', the reasons for his arrest. He didn't conceal his annoyance at the sale and removal from the country of works of art. And this is what he felt strongly: if a country does not value its treasures, let them go abroad, but they must be sold to prestigious museums or to known collectors and on no account 'rendered stateless'. The provenance of icons mustn't be obscured. It wasn't right to split up integral collections of icons for sale to different purchasers. The prices of icons were so low that rich people were at one time buying them for fashionable chess-boards, on which the black squares frequently turned out to be ancient art work. Therefore Anisimov, who dealt with foreign purchasers, had been concerned over the ultimate fate of the icons that were being sold and commended them to 'good homes'. These dealings with foreigners actually served as the grounds for his being accused of 'espionage' (for Switzerland, incidentally).

In 1931 labour began to be withdrawn on a massive scale from Solovki and sent to the White Sea-Baltic Canal construction project. Life on Solovki became unbearable. I was not allowed to leave for a long time, and was taken off on the Gleb Boyki's final trip at the end of October or the beginning of November. Anisimov remained on Solovki, but I didn't lose touch with him. In the spring of 1932 a 'commission' arrived there—exactly what kind, I don't know. When they saw the museum they were besides themselves with rage: it was 'religious propaganda'. An icon that Anisimov valued highly and considered a supreme example of the symbolist icons of the late fifteenth century, was smashed to pieces in front of him. Anisimov developed heart trouble. The Museum was closed. Vinogradov went to live in Petrozavodsk and took his personal collection and small items and manuscripts from the Solovetski Museum with him. Some of the shattered museum exhibits were transferred to the Historical Museum in Moscow (the famous canopy from Solovki is now in the village museum at Kolomensk, and the most precious seven-pointed cross from the island of Ki with the three hundred relics has been restored to the Church). The remarkable iconostasis from the Preobrazhenski Cathedralis still there. This was destroyed some considerable time later by order of the commander of the sea-cadet school[118].

Returning to the fate of Anisimov, I will only say that in the autumn of 1932 he was working on the route which the White Sea-

S. A. Alekseyev-Askoldov, teacher at Lentovskaya school.
Photograph taken in 1930s

D. S. Likhachev with parents, and brother Yuri. 1929

Solovki bay. 1928

St. Herman's chapel on Solovki island used for storing food

Solovki railway station with only one passanger car. 1928

Landing stage in front of USLON building. 1928

Typical barrack in Trudkoloniya

Solovki Theatre. 1928

D. S. Likhachev. 1931

Guard in camp of
construction work on
White Sea-Baltic Canal

Steamer Gleb Boyki at USLON landing stage

D. S. Likhachev (second from right) with his wife, parents,
brother and children Vera and Mila. 1939

Family leaving an air-raid shelter

Searching among the rubbles after artillery shelling

Transporting the dead to the mortuary

Make-shift stove

Fetching water from a tap in the street

Pulling the weak on a sledge

D. S. Likhachev, honorary doctor of the University of Oxford

Baltic Canal was to take. The widow of Maksimilian Voloshin, Maria Stepanovna, told me that after her husband's death Anisimov and a number of other prisoners came upon an Old Believers' chapel in the forest where they held the kind of funeral service for 'Max' which the poet himself had dreamed of. It is known that Voloshin died on 11 August 1932, which means that by that time Anisimov had been able to settle in at Belbaltlag sufficiently to obtain permission to go out into the forest. What became of him after that I don't know. Perhaps the documentary evidence of his execution on 2 September 1937, adduced in *Sovyetskaya kultura* by Konchivy, does not in fact mislead us.

I will add to this note one further conversation which took place on Solovki about Anisimov. It was said that at a meeting in Moscow he had failed to honour the memory of Lenin and had remained seated when everyone stood up. That's just like him...

The Solovki Theatre

There was another 'Chekist miracle' on Solovki: the Solovki theatre or Solteatr. This had been established for the sake of appearances—to imitate culture and educational activity, whereas in fact it had no little significance for the intellectual life of Solovki. Alongside the *zhivgazyeta* [Live newspaper] and low-standard concert performances interesting creative work also went on there.

In my years on Solovki the heart and soul of Solteatr, as of the magazine *Solovki*, was Boris Glubokovski, an actor from Aleksandr Tairov's Chamber Theatre in Moscow, son of Nikolay Nikanorovich Glubokovski, theologian and church historian, whose correspondence with V. V. Rozanov was recently published.

I knew Glubokovski well, but not so much as a close friend as an exceptionally high-profile personality, and one that did much for the intelligentsia of the camp. Almost everyone knew him. It is a pity that no photograph of him can be found as he was tall, elegant, good-looking, lively and well-mannered. He dressed in the Solovki style adopted by the few people who had access to the needlework shop: a short black coat with a sash, black riding-breeches, top-boots and a cap worn slightly to one side.

127

He was gifted in many ways and was reputed to have been a member of Yesenin's Bohemian circle. He had been accused of taking part in some White centrist plot but this is highly unlikely, considering the qualities of his somewhat egoistic nature.

Plays performed in the Solteatr included Zamyatin's *Children of Vanyushin* and *The Flea* and Lermontov's *Masquerade*[119]. The full repertoire may be resurrected from *Solovetskiye ostrova* and from the little news sheet *Solovetski listok* [Solovki News], published after USLON had moved to Kem in 1930; Glubokovski was transferred with it.

Glubokovski's show *Solovyetskoye obozreniye* [Solovki Revue] enjoyed exceptional popularity. It sharply satirised the regime and the way of life on Solovki, and even the authorities. One day, one of the 'unloading commissions' was watching it in an intoxicated state, and the hall was crowded with prisoners. Glubokovski (who had also, obviously, had a few drinks) was directing the performance and shouted from the stage: "Sing up so as to make this scum" (and here he pointed at the commission) "feel sick". Now the revue consisted not only of comic numbers but also of melancholy-lyrical ones, which used to reduce many to tears. Glubokovski himself wrote the lyrics (I have noted down what I could) and the motifs he picked up mostly from operettas. But one motif was said to be of his own invention— that of his song *Ogonki* [Little lights] which in the early '30s all Russia was singing. This song ended as follows:

> From the frost, the blizzards and the snow
> We like all the seagulls haste to go,
> From afar the faint lights' glimmer see,
> Solovki, Solovki, Solovki!

The refrain went:

> Boki, Feldman, Vasilev and Bul
> Promised us the moon, and we were fooled.
> Katanyan to Moscow what took he
> But the doleful song of Solovki?
>
> You who made this island our reward,
> Come, we beg you, sit here at our board.
> Never will you lose the memory,
> Four or five years pent in Solovki.

One of the verses suggested the prisoners' future:

> One day as the winter blizzards roar
> We will gather happily once more,
> Old men in their mind's eye then will see
> Solovki, Solovki, Solovki!

Foolish dreams of prisoners in the twenties...

There were other performances too in the Solteatr. I remember Lermontov's *Masquerade* with Kalugin, an artiste of the Aleksandrinski Theatre in Petrograd, as Arbenin. He was understudied by Ivan Yakovlevich Komissarov, king of all the *urki* in the Solovetski archipelago. He had been a bandit and had 'gone to work' at the head of his gang, with his own machine-gun, robbing clandestine currency exchanges, a pupil and comrade-in-arms of the infamous Lenka Panteleyev. But his Arbenin was a real country gentleman...

I can't remember what else was on in the Solteatr. Films were shown. I remember one with a script by Viktor Shklovski[120], with armoured cars moving over the Troitski bridge in Petrograd. There were concerts too, at which performers from among the non-political prisoners beat out a nimble *chechetka*[121] and did acrobatic turns; one pair, Savchenko and Engelfeld, were very popular. The band was conducted by Valgardt, a short-sighted German, later to become an orchestral conductor in Odessa, who was in prison through association with A. A. Meyer. There was an actress who recited Blok's *Dvenadtsat'*[122] in a hysterical voice. There was a good singer, Perevezentseva, who sang settings of Yesenin (I remember *Nikogda ya nye byl na Bosfore* [I have never been on the Bosphorus]) and shamelessly deceived her husband who worked in one of the companies in the Kremlin and attempted suicide out of jealousy. An Armenian professor from Tbilisi, V. Ananov, gave lectures on the history of music in the theatre foyer, as did A. P. Sukhov on psychology and someone else on something else.

I still have a poster for an 'Evening of Memories of N. A. Nekrasov' in the Solteatr on 12 January 1929. I wasn't there, being down with typhus at the time. B. M. Lobach-Zhuchenko opened the evening with a paper. He was a notable camp personality, but unfortunately I hardly remember him. The sensation of something great and significant which stirs me at the sound of his name is, perhaps, evoked by the name itself—long and somehow imposing[123]. This was followed by papers from Glubokovski, P. I. Iogalevich, P. S. Kalinin and Ya. Ya. Nekrasov. The interval was followed by a concert, with readers (including choral verse speaking, then fashionable), a wind band, a quintet and the Solovetski Choir. The most interesting thing is that excerpts were performed from the opera *Kobzar'*[124] by the prisoner Kenel. Like all performances in the Solteatr it started late, at nine o'clock, as the official end of the working day was at eight.

And all that at the height of a typhus epidemic and with the torment of hard labour! Verily, 'The island of miracles'.

"Everything is mixed up here without colour or face" goes the line from Glubokovski's Solovetski song on a theme from *Priestesses of Fire*.

On release from Belbaltlag Glubokovski received, as did many of us, a certificate with a red diagonal stripe. On the strength of that he was given a residence permit in Moscow and taken back into the Chamber Theatre. I learned from a newspaper announcement that he'd died in the mid-'30s from blood poisoning. He'd become a morphine addict and had injected himself through his trousers...

In the winter of 1929–30, when the second, the so-called 'Asian' typhus was raging, people were dropping in their thousands. The theatre was closed and the auditorium became a sickbay, where the sick lay like sardines, almost without attention. On the stage, however, behind the lowered curtain, lectures took place despite the groans and cries audible from the auditorium.

Ananov, whom I've already mentioned, gave several lectures on music; he was a former member of staff at the Rustaveli Theatre in Tbilisi and of the newspaper *Zarya Vostoka* [Dawn of the East]. I too gave a talk on the pre-Shakespearean theatre (I was asked to, although I realised the absurdity of such a subject under the circumstances, but the Culture and Education department needed my lecture for its collection). In spring, when the typhus had abated and the benches and chairs that had been tossed into the orchestra pit were being pulled out, a corpse was found. It was so emaciated that it had dried out and hardly gave off any smell.

It seems to me that the Solteatr with its curtain, which divided the death and agony of the typhus patients from the attempts made at maintaining at least an illusion of intellectual life by those who might next day find themselves on the other side of that curtain, was almost a symbol of our prison-camp life—and not only of life in the camps, but of all life under Stalin.

Inside and outside the theatre the usual theatrical intrigues went on. Groups and cliques of one or another set of actors and producers were formed. I remember that in 1930 or 1931 I placed an enthusiastic review of one performance in the weekly news-sheet *Solovetski listok*, which began to appear after the transfer of *Noviye Solovki* [New Solovki] to the mainland. Without delay, next week there appeared in answer *Retsenziya po blatu* [The String-Pullers' Review], although I'd written sincerely, as I always try to do.

And so, having described something of the wealth of the topography of Solovki, I will now tell you about my 'journeys' in that world, in which encounters with people are the main interest.

Solovki People

Aleksandr Aleksandrovich Meyer

In the spring of 1929 Aleksandr Aleksandrovich Meyer and Kseniya Anatoliyevna Polovtseva appeared on Solovki. He had been given a ten-year sentence—the maximum at the time, which had been commuted from death on 'compassionate' grounds, having regard to his revolutionary past, which still counted for something in those days. I don't recall in which month the two of them turned up. He was in no. 13 'quarantine' company, she in the women's barracks. Nor do I remember which of us it was that secured Meyer's release from 'quarantine'. Two of us in the Krimkab, Volodya Razdolski and myself, had a hand in it as we both had passes to the 'quarantine' area because we had to round up teenagers and place them in the labour colony. We used to call on newly arrived transports and try to release not only teenagers but also all 'deserving' persons. This was no easy task and success did not come all that often. We had to find out who had arrived and obtain requisitions for them for light work of some sort inside the Kremlin, where conditions were significantly better. I remember those whom I managed to release. Among others I got from Vinogradov a requisition for Mikhail Dmitrievich Priselkov to work in the Museum. But to my surprise Priselkov refused to work there: "I'm here for working on history and I'm not going to do any more". Then I got a requisition for him from the priest Viktor Ostrovidov, who worked in the Selkhoz as a book-keeper. Priselkov became a ledger clerk. Obviously Volodya Razdolski obtained the release of Meyer, who was requisitioned by Kolosov and went straight to the Krimkab. Someone assigned Polovtseva to some office in the USLON building by the landing stage, where the Krimkab was too. This gave her the chance to call on Meyer every day and to bring him his lunch in little pans, and also to take part in amazing discussions of various philosophical problems—discussions that had started with Meyer's arrival. He was an unusual man. He never tired of thinking, whatever the conditions. He always tried to place a philosophical interpretation on everything and to write whenever possible—both in exile and prison in tsarist times, and during all subsequent 'losses of liberty' into which the days of 'Great October' had flung him. First of all, however, I will tell you what kind of a person he seemed to us.

I worked with Meyer in Krimkab, in the USLON building at the landing stage opposite the Kremlin, for more than a year. These were the premises of the former monastery guest quarters. The Krimkab was based in a large room near the lavatory on the second floor, with three windows overlooking the open space outside USLON. Meyer sat at a little table by the left-hand window and lived first in no. 3 company, later in no. 7.

For his life before Solovki I will quote the notes to the memoirs of N. P. Antsiferov, published abroad.

Meyer, Aleksandr Aleksandrovich (1874–1939), philosopher. Born in Odessa, son of a grammar school teacher of ancient languages. Studied at the Novorossiski University in Odessa, 1895–96. In 1896 he was arrested for taking part in a revolutionary movement and exiled to Shenkursk. There he kept himself busy educating himself and translating books on philosophy, sociology, logic and psychology. He married an exiled Odessa schoolteacher, P. V. Tychenko (1872–1942), returned to Odessa with his wife in 1902 and tried to continue his University course, but was banned from the city. Before 1905 he lived in Baku, where he was arrested for organising workers' circles, and exiled to Tashkent, where in 1905 he worked on the paper *Russki Turkestan* [Russian Turkestan] and continued his revolutionary activity. In 1906 he was arrested but soon escaped from Tashkent prison, lived for a while in Finland, and from early 1907 in St Petersburg. At the end of the decade he was giving a number of courses in philosophy, aesthetics, history of religion, psychology and other subjects in the People's Universities Association, at the N. V. Dmitriyeva People's University, the P. F. Lesgaft Women's Courses and in other places. From 1909–28 he worked in section of the Rossica Public Library. After 1917 he worked in the *Institut zhivogo slova* [Institute of the Living Word] and the Lesgaft Institute. In December 1928 he was arrested in connection with the 'Voskreseniye circle' (the 'Meyer case') and in 1929 sentenced to be shot, but the sentence was commuted to ten years on Solovki. He worked in SLON, in the Criminological office. In 1930 he was re-arrested (a prisoner being arrested again!—DSL), taken to Leningrad and tried under the 'Academy of Sciences case'. In 1931–34 he worked (again as a prisoner—DSL) as a hydrology technician on the White Sea-Baltic Canal, where he met A. F. Losef. From 1935–37 he was on the Moskva-Volga Canal. He died of liver cancer in a Leningrad hospital and is buried in the Volkov cemetery. Meyer's philosophical and political views underwent a great degree of evolution. In his youth he was a Marxist revolutionary and in 1907 became one of the theorists of the so-called 'mystic anarchism', published two articles in the journal *Fakely* [Torches](St Petersburg, 1907). In 1909 his first book, *Religiya i kultura* [*Religion and Culture*] appeared. At the same time he became a conspicuous member of the St Petersburg Religious and Philosophical Society and drew nearer to the Merezhkovskis[125], who considered him 'quite their man'. Between 1909–17 he travelled widely in the country lecturing, and published no fewer than 50 reviews, articles and pamphlets. Characteristic of his thought during the war is *Vo chto vyerit Germaniya* [What Germany believes in] (1916), a critique of Protestantism, in which he distinguishes three features which he considers fallacious: the rejection of the Christian understanding of personality, the rejection of the Church as preserver of tradition, and the advancement of a principle of national and religious independence vis-à-vis the idea of a Universal Church. To these tendencies Meyer opposes not Orthodoxy (as, for example, does Vladimir Ern), but a sort of coming synthesis of collectivism (the socialist idea) and Christianity. In 1917 Meyer, alone of the founders of the Religio-philosophical Society project concerning the separation of Church and State, took part in the work of the Local Council (he was selected from the Religious-philosophical Society). He published a number of works in which he came out in favour of supporting the Provisional Government and the summoning of the Constitutional Assembly, and against the defeatism of the Bolsheviks. Blok recorded Meyer's anxiety over the fate of the country and the Revolution in his brief notes on Meyer's talk to the Religious-philosophical Society on 21 May 1917 (*Zapisnyye knigi* 1901–1920, Moscow, 1965 pp. 340–341). After October Meyer's position vis-à-vis the Bolsheviks was not as irreconcilable as the Merezhkovskis'. He tried to find good seed in Bolshevist theory and in the course of a few post-Revolutionary years came to believe in the evolution of power.

In her memoirs D. S. Merezhkovski Zinaida Hippius mentions Meyer three times, beginning in 1912, as a family friend and one of the organisers of the Religious-philosophical Society and an 'altogether very interesting man'. Meyer himself says very little about the Merezhkovskis. When he was on Solovki in 1929 he was certain that they were still living in Warsaw, and did not really approve of that.

To me, Meyer seemed an old man although he was only 55. He was thin, emaciated, very nervous, active, seemingly struggling against an inner fatigue. Top-boots which were obviously too big for him (allowing room for warm footcloths), a dark *tolstovka* (long belted blouse), a long face, a scraggy beard, long hair (until it was cropped, as everyone's was) and very lively eyes ... that's how I've always remembered him.

In our Krimkab room with its three windows he was given the best place, as I've said, at the table by the left-hand window. By the right-hand window was the long table belonging to Yuliya Nikolayevna Danzas. Meyer was given a bed on the first floor in no. 3 company, the company I was in, commanded by Baron Pritvits. It wasn't long before the indefatigable Meyer, who was accustomed to giving lectures and presenting papers to the most varied audiences, gave a lecture on some complex philosophical subject. Afterwards the company commander, with an elegant bow, thanked Meyer for the 'marvellous lecture' of which clearly neither he, nor most of those 'listening', had understood a word.

Meyer had had a great reputation in Petrograd. We knew that, along with D. S. Merezhkovski, Z. N. Hippius, N. A. Berdyayev and A. A. Blok he'd been an active member of the St Petersburg Religious-philosophical Society. He'd been friends with the first two and like-minded on many points. He'd been a member of the All-Russia Synod that had elected Patriarch Tikhon in 1918. Together with Blok, Andrey Bely and others he'd been a founder-member of the Free Philosophical Association (*Volfila*) in Leningrad, and then leader of the most highly esteemed circle of the intelligentsia, known as the 'Tuesday Society', because meetings took place on Tuesdays.

Later these meetings were moved to Sundays, and the circle was renamed *Voskresen'ye* (or rather, Stromin[126] the investigator, the famous organiser of 'academic cases', announced on the basis of this name that the aims of the circle were the 'revival of the old Russia'; here he was confusing the meanings of the words *voskresen'ye* [Sunday] and *voskreseniye* [resurrection, revival]).

I'd heard a lot about Meyer's circle from Andreyevski before my arrest. It used to meet on the Maly Prospekt in the Petrograd District, near Spasskaya Street in a wooden house (which is no longer standing) and in other places. One could visit Meyer at any time. The regular members of the circle were at first (until they left) the Merezhkovskis, Polovtseva, the literary expert L. V. Pumpyanski, the artist P. F. Smotritski, the orientalist N. V. Pugulevskaya and her husband, and later L. Orbeli (the future academician), the pianist M. V. Yudina, the painter A. A. Bruni, the schoolmaster I. M. Andreyevski, G. P. Fedotov (util he left Russia) and numerous others. Incidentally, many of Fedotov's ideas originated in Meyer's circle. Our *Khelfernak* was visited by Meyer's people, and vice versa, so that many of the discussions that arose in Khelfernak were continuations of discussions in *Voskresen'ye*. Entry to meetings of *Voskresen'ye* was open to all, and the door was never locked during meetings, but my youthful shyness stopped me attending and, moreover, I didn't care for formality, which Meyer liked. Proceedings opened with prayer, and after the papers (usually short) everybody was supposed to give their opinions in turn, albeit briefly, as to whether or not they agreed. The meetings of *Voskresen'ye* have been described in detail by N. P. Antsiferov in *Tri glavy iz Vospominani* [Three Chapters from My Memoirs] and also in the autobiography of Fedotov which prefaces vol. I of his collected works (Paris, YMCA Press).

Contact with people older than myself (in fact all the imprisoned intelligentsia were older than me) was extremely valuable for me. I didn't 'take lessons from them', but became familiar with their experience of life and received the most varied information on all manner of fields of science, philosophy, literature and poetry. Vladimir Yulyanovich Korolenko—the nephew of Vladimir Galaktionovich Korolenko—used to call in at the Krimkab and kiss the hands of the ladies there, V. Gruzova and Yu. N. Danzas. Georgi Mikhaylovich Osorgin[127] came too (though rarely), and Aleksandr Petrovich Sukhov joined the conversation, as did Ivan Mikhalovich Andreyevski, the scupltor Amosov and our own young people, V. S. Razdolski, A. A. Peshkovski, Yu. Kazarnovski, A. Pankratov and L. M. Mogilyanska. If it had been possible to take notes of everything, what marvellous conversations, discussions, actual arguments, tales and opinions would have been preserved for Russian culture.

Was this the original of Vyacheslav Ivanov's *Bashnya* [The Tower]? Indeed it was better, as everything went on for even longer, and our everyday conversations were conducted under the blessed aegis of our chief, Aleksandr Nikolayevich Kolosov, holding his pencil to his ear and ready at all times to conceal our idleness from the authorities, though at the same time prepared to drive us to the worthy task of saving the flea-infested street-children, those who had been 'sucked in', the 'socially near' and the infinitely unfortunate 'colonists' (teenagers living in the Children's Colony, later renamed *Trudkoloniya* [labour colony])[128].

I remember a lot from my conversations with Meyer after I had received his book *Filosofskiye sochineniya* [Philosophical Essays] (Paris, 1982) from Paris. The later material in this is connected with his reflections on Solovki. He was a man of the Russian conversational culture, belonged to those whose views were formulated in infinitely long Russian conversations. In the Krimkab he had powerful collocutors in Danzas, Gordon, Sukhov, Andreyevski, Smotritski and others, but none was his equal. It was important, however, for the younger element, whom he could instruct and lecture in his fashion, to be there. And all the same there was much in his spoken language that was better, more interesting, more profound than in his writings. He spoke more bravely than he wrote and to write well requires courage.

Meyer had a remarkable quality: he responded with philosophical reflections to absolutely everything in our social life. Everyone found him interesting because he took an interest in them. He gave a very great number of lectures and papers under the most varied circumstances. As a participant in a revolutionary movement in tsarist times, he had lived in constant exile, and circles of one sort or another had always sprung up spontaneously around him. He had lectured in workers' universities and on Lesgaft's Higher Free courses. He had never stopped learning languages. He read Greek and Latin fluently, and German was to him a native, domestic language (his grandfather had been an emigrant from the German part of Switzerland). In fact, he read philosophical writings in all the languages of Europe. Later, his daughter tells us, in exile in the '30s, he translated philosophical works from Latin and Greek for A. F. Losev.

His exceptional erudition permitted him to be one of the most modern philosophers, whose works on language, allegory and myth seem to have been written today. In any case, his *Filosofskiye sochineniya*, published in Paris in 1982, give the impression of having been written with a knowledge of Levi-Strauss, Jung, Malinovski and Losev, who published later—such was the extent to which Meyer's work anticipated theirs.

In his first book *Religiya i kultura*, he declared himself a 'mystic anarchist', but subsequently he drew closer to the Orthodox perception of the world; this brought him nearer to Fedotov, one of the most active members of the Meyer circle.

On Solovki Meyer began two works, *Tri istoka* [Three Sources] and *Faust* (reflections of reading Goethe's *Faust*), devoted to the problems of culture—myth and language.

He also wrote a small note 'Forced Labour as a Means of Re-education' in the magazine *Solovetskiye ostrova* (1929, nos 3 and 4), which irritated those who were prosecuted with him and were in the camp on the mainland. It was said that Meyer had "betrayed the principle of freedom". He had also written, it seems, a work on rhythm in labour (a reflection on his experience of teaching the philosophy of movement on Lesgaft's Higher Free courses).

Meyer read and re-read Kholodovski's translation of *Faust,* which was available on Solovki, but he also knew much of the text in German by heart. He discussed all his ideas with a young philosopher, almost my equal in age, from Rostov-on-Don, Vladimir Sergeyevich Razdolski, who lived in the same cell as me and whose fascination with philosophical thought never failed to impress. We had to hand a 'living bookcase'—such was our nickname for Gavril Osipovich Gordon, whose uncommon powers of memory I will speak of later.

One of the most important topics of our conversations was myth, and another connected with it—words. Both of these are considered in Meyer's book *Filosofskiye sochineniya.*

Meyer's thought was of assistance to me in the further formulation of my philosophy.

What is the meaning of the first sentence of the Gospel according to John: "In the beginning was the Word"? And why does Faust, in translating these words, replace 'Word' with 'Deed' (*im Anfang war die Tat*!)? My own thoughts on this subject seemed to me a continuation of those aroused in me by reading I. O. Losski's book *Mir kak organicheskoye tseloye* [The World as an Organic Whole]. With the help of Losski, and of Meyer on Solovki, I reached my own conclusion that the 'General' always precedes the 'Particular', 'Idea' (the Word) always anticipates its every incarnation. Hence I came to a belief in Reason and the Word.

My views on literary studies, my understanding of reality and of human culture have developed within the framework of complex ideas. One's perception of the world takes a lifetime to formulate, and its nature is precisely expressed both in scientific methodology and in 'scientific behaviour' (the last is a special concept, requiring an equally special explanation).

If the Word is the beginning of action, a generalisation, then in an untruthful word, a cliché, lies a very great danger of which the devil constantly makes use.

Mephistopheles says:

Gewöhnlich glaubt der Mensch, wenn er nur Worte hört
Er müsse sich dabei doch auch was denken lassen.
[People usually believe, when they hear only words,
that they ought to let themselves think as well.]

One of the subjects of the conversations with Meyer that I can recall was that of the myth created in our time. He had raised this topic in his lecture *O prave na mif*[129] as long ago as 1918. Naturally, the idea had expanded greatly in the intervening eleven years. It was uncommonly interesting to look for myths and to investigate them during our 'sessions'. By the way, at the same time I wrote a humorous *Fenomenologiya voprosa* [The Phenomenology of the Question], having Meyer's teaching in mind. Having applied to the word question all the basic idiomatic collocations in which 'question' occurs, I obtained the original 'life-cycle' of this 'question': it comes into being, is revealed, draws attention to itself, gets to its feet, grows to full size, arouses another question, broaches other questions and brings them to birth, then the answer to it is expounded, enlarged upon, the question crawls away to the side, is reconsidered, abandoned, spoken no more, it expires, is gone, the question is exhausted.

As early as the '20s the power of the 'literary formulae' of the mythology of language had begun to occupy more and more space in Soviet reality. 'The power of words' was becoming the most weighty manifestation of 'spiritual bondage'. Therefore the discussion of questions of language and linguistic culture became one of the most important topics of our conversations in Krimkab.

When the order was given that long hair was not to be worn Meyer too had his cropped. He was very ashamed of his new appearance; in my notes, written immediately on release, it says 'he suffered'.

When Kseniya Anatoliyevna Polovtseva was not to hand he couldn't deal with his little saucepans or make his own soup, although he had more food than us as he was teaching Latin to the wife of Golovkin, one of the camp officials (evidently, she wanted to go in for medicine), and reading her the poems of V. S. Kemetski; he was naively enthusiastic over her 'spiritual qualities'. It was partly under the influence of these meetings that he conceived the idea that it was possible to 'handle the camp' by way of persuasion: 'everything that is foul is from the organisation, not the people'. These views of Meyer's were the cause of arguments in the Krimkab, and I've often regretted not taking full and detailed notes of them: much that was in them remains topical to this day.

During the discussion of Meyer's position three causes of the camp nightmare were identified: a malicious ideology, its malicious implementation, and the malicious people that had brought it all to life. And these phenomena threatened to spread throughout the whole country. Meyer insisted that the fault lay with the organisation, but the truth is that it lay also in the drive toward Socialism, and in the people who were forced to implement by evil methods ideas in which there was a certain amount of good. We insisted that the people had been damaged by evil concepts, and that the organisation of the camps was the direct result of an aggressive ideological system—Marxism (or rather, that which passed for Marxism).

Meyer's views were in part reflected in his article 'Rhythm in labour', which was printed in the magazine *Solovetskiye ostrova* and which gave rise to many arguments, of which I have spoken.

Yuliya Nikolayevna Danzas

The complete antithesis of Meyer in the Krimkab was Yuliya Nikolayevna Danzas, who worked opposite him at a huge table creaking beneath a pile of newspapers, from which she took cuttings for the camp authorities. A former lady-in-waiting to the Empress Aleksandra with a doctorate from the Sorbonne, she'd been arrested as early as November 1923 and had spent five years in Siberian prison camps before coming to Solovki.

Quite a detailed account of her life is given in the book *Leonid Fedorov. Zhizn i deyatelnost*[130] by deacon Vasili. She was born in Athens in 1879, grand-daughter of the French emigré Charles Danzas, whose second son Constantine had been Pushkin's second at his duel. Her mother, whose maiden name was Argiropoulos, was of ancient Byzantine stock and traced her ancestry back to the eleventh-century Emperor Romanos Argiros, who had married the last of the Macedonian dynasty, the Empress Zoe. Highly educated, Yuliya Danzas was the author of a number of books and a fine horsewoman. She had lived abroad for a long time to avoid having to discharge her responsibilities as a lady-in-waiting, which she found unpleasant because of the prevailing atmosphere at Court with its spiritualists, its Mitka Gugnivi, Mashka Strannitsa and, most of all, Rasputin.

It is very difficult to write about Yuliya Danzas. She was a complex person, not in the pejorative sense usually attached to the term nowadays, but literally: her spiritual life was concealed by several cultural layers. On the one hand there were her aristocratic descent and her position as lady-in-waiting to the Empress; on the other, her Sorbonne doctorate and her published researches into religious questions. On the one hand she was a ceaseless seeker after truth and a profound religious thinker, on the other an extremely intolerant Catholic who seemed to know everything in her arguments with Orthodox believers or with Catholics of other tendencies, and who was prepared even on Solovki to take a somewhat lofty attitude to the sufferings of the numerous Orthodox clergy and even to write in the camp press about the existence of an Inquisition in the Orthodox Church, thereby lending strength to the anti-religious propaganda. On the one hand she was of refined breeding, yet on the other she was constantly in conflict with her neighbours and speaking the same language as Gorki. And on and on! On the one hand she was a Russian and a patriot who during the First World War had joined the Ural Cossacks and spent time in the front-line trenches, but on the other hand she had suddenly felt herself to be the descendant of a French émigré and, by her anti-Russian pronouncements in Rome, later (in her lecture in the Russicum in the late '30s and early '40s) fell foul of Vyacheslav Ivanov[131] himself. Overall, she was very much a rationalist, but for that reason didn't get on well with people. By virtue of her ancestral (or rather, aristocratic) instinct, however, she made some very interesting and valid comments on people's behaviour.

I remember her as a sickly middle-aged woman who walked with the aid of a stick, and wore a short black sheepskin coat of rustic cut. In January 1933, however, after we'd both been released as shock workers on Belomorstroy, she was living in Leningrad while waiting to leave for her brother's in Germany and had no trouble in coming up to see me and my parents on the fourth floor; she was fashionably dressed, her hat—obviously, chosen with care—just a fraction aslant. At times she was an old lady, but then she was relatively young, with bright blue eyes. So it was later when she was abroad; now a novice nun in a convent, now a young lady who had been in scientific work and journalism and wrote three books after Solovki: two of these—in French, neither dated—dealt with the Soviet prison system: *Bagne rouge. Souvenirs d'une prisonière au pays des Soviets,* and *L'itinéraire religieux de la conscience russe*; the third was in Russian: *Katolicheskoye Bogopoznaniye i marksistskoye bezbozhiye*[132]. In addition, she wrote extensive memoirs about her 'spiritual journey to God', and among her numerous articles was one on the spiritual life of Russian youth. When she worked in the Solovetski museum (before starting work in Krimkab) she had had the services of a very honest young man, the former Scout Dima Shipchinski, who arranged, at great personal risk, meetings between her and Catholic figures.

On Solovki, when she was at work on her newspapers, she constantly chanted Catholic prayers to herself in an undertone, but at the same time there was always a hand-rolled cigarette in her mouth, stuck into a long cigarette-holder. God only knows whether she smoked rough prison tobacco or foreign tobacco which she obtained from God knows where. Nothing was too much for her and she endured everything stoically. No-one knows how much she knew, how many interesting people she remembered, but she lacked sparkle and immediate charm, such necessary qualities for dealings with the young on Solovki. In this respect too she was the antithesis of Meyer. I write that not so as to decry the one to the advantage of the other. My contrasting of these two spiritual mentalities is in no sense a valuation. Yuliya's iron but exclusive character evoked praise in its way. Many censured her afterwards, and even Berdyayev[133], incidentally, responded to her negatively; her devotion to the Catholic faith, however, with the help of which she tried to illuminate the whole of Russian history from Vladimir I Svyatoslavich of Kiev onward (him she considered to have been faithful to Rome) is in its way worthy of respect, although the tendentiousness of her work is obvious.

Yuliya Danzas wrote a lot, after her release from the 'Soviet imprisonment' too, but on Solovki she had little influence on the youth.

The course of her life has been described in her own words, as I have already said, in the book *Leonid Fedorov: Zhizn i deyatelnost* by Deacon Vasili ChCV (sic), which relieves me almost entirely of the need to dwell especially on her most interesting life. I will only say that in detailed interviews she for some reason let drop that during the First World War she'd served in forward positions with the Ural Cossack regiment. Why Cossacks, and why precisely the Ural Cossacks? Her explanation was that she'd wanted to be in the cavalry, as she was an outstanding rider, and with the Ural Cossacks because they were Old Believers and distinguished by a strict moral code. They forgave her being unable to handle a lance (it was too heavy for her), but she was perfectly well able to manage a sabre, she said, and even passed the test. Under the Provisional Government she'd been asked to take command of a women's death battalion. She'd refused, and the command had been given to Bochkareva. I can't understand why there's nothing in her reminiscences of herself about the Court and the Imperial Family, but Deacon Vasili explains in his book that she'd been about to write a novel about the Empress Aleksandra. It's a pity that she kept interesting material back for a novel, because she failed to achieve her goal and as a fiction writer she wasn't a success. This can be seen from her story *Solovetski Abelyar* [The Abelard of Solovki], printed in *Solovetskiye ostrova* under her usual pseudonym Yuri Nikolayev. Fictional form, what's more, is out of keeping with a truthful account. She'd known the Court very well, however, and told many stories about the lives of *gosudar* and *gosudaryna* [the Master and Mistress] (as it was accepted in Petersburg to refer to the Emperor and Empress).

I recall three of Yuliya Danzas' stories of the Imperial Family as being more important. Firstly, I've never come across a reference to the fact that after 'Bloody Sunday' in 1905 the Court went into mourning, and no balls or large receptions were held for some time. It is better known that on 9 January the Tsar and his family were not in the Winter Palace, but in the Aleksandr Palace at Tsarskoye Selo, and so could not be held directly responsible for the slaughter. Secondly, at the start of the war of 1914 Colonel Myasoyedov, head of the East Prussia section of the Border Guard, was hanged for a spy; the German Emperor Wilhelm II used to call on him (or did so just once) to dine after hunting. The Tsar had known that Myasoyedov was neither a spy nor merely a traitor, but under pressure from popular opinion, which accused the Tsarina of sympathy towards the Germans, he confirmed the sentence of death out of cowardice. This filled him with remorse, and he considered all his further misfortunes to be God's punishment for his faint-heartedness. Thirdly, she told me a lot about how terribly the Tsarina used to worry, so afraid was she of attempts at assassination every time the Tsar went out.

Another tale of hers that I remember concerned a quarrel between the Royal Family and the Stolypins. After the attempt on Stolypin's[134] life on Aptekarski Island the Tsar invited him and his family to live in the Winter Palace. They moved in and settled down on the first floor. The Stolypin children used to run about through all the rooms, and, as they played, clambered up onto the throne. Aleksandra Fyodorovna complained of this to Stolypin's wife, who was not distinguished for tact. She went to the defence of her children and, among other things, 'let it be known' that her husband meant more to Russia than did the Tsar. After that other quarters were found for the Stolypins, but the Tsarina could never forget the insult that her husband had suffered, which could not be overlooked by the Okhranka. Stolypin 'fell into disfavour with the Secret Police department', which is possibly reflected in the poor organisation of his bodyguard in the theatre in Kiev, where he was murdered by a terrorist.

Together with her tremendous knowledge and her prodigious courage, there was, if I may say so, also something of the primitive about Yuliya Danzas. Take, for example, her views on poetry. She said that she ranked Lermontov above Pushkin. It seems to me that at no level of poetry should one argue about who is superior to whom. One may only say for which poet one has a personal preference, to which one turns more often. Who is the superior, Derzhavin or Baratynski[135]? And even less is it permissible to apply such value-judgements to the poets of the twentieth century. I will say that even in our student days we were all very fond of Mandelshtam's[136] poems; there were poets in our number who imitated Zabolotski's Stolbtsy, the verses of which were mischievous, which we liked, and Vsevolod Rozhdestvenski was much more in vogue than he is today. I can't say that Bely or Bryusov[137] were known by heart—Blok was, of course, more than anyone, and some of Voloshin[138] and Mandelshtam and Zabolotski, whom I've just mentioned. Pushkin was the best known of the old poets, followed by Baratynski, Denis Davydov and Lermontov. It's very interesting to observe which poets the young know by heart at any given time and whose poetry appeals to them on a spiritual level.

But I digress. Yuliya Danzas's slight primitive quality was also shown in her Catholic position.

No one, I believe, has ever paid attention to the fact that great learning coupled with a lack of power of communication can actually have a negative effect. Learning gives a person confidence in his own convictions and prevents his grasping that which is new or unfamiliar. That sense of superiority towards others which learning can stimulate may, if one lacks creative ability, render communication with others difficult. We could understand that she'd embraced the Catholic faith when she was already a mature and thinking person: she'd felt the need of a firm spiritual support, and it was completely natural in our youthful eyes that she'd turned to the religion of her French forebears. Our Orthodox young people didn't argue with her about Catholicism, and indeed how could they, with their modest grasp of theology? When, however, we read her piece on the Inquisition in the Orthodox Church in *Solovetskiye ostrova* our conversations with her dried up, so to speak. There were two reasons: if the Orthodox Church also had an Inquisition, how did that justify the Catholic one? And secondly, it seemed to us improper to give a trump card to the antireligionists, especially in the camp, full as it was of Orthodox clergy.

144

Gavril Osipovich Gordon

In 1930 Gavril Osipovich Gordon was placed in no. 13 'quarantine' company. A professor of History, former member of State Scientific Council, a man of amazing education, a 'former fatty' (someone who before his arrest had been well-covered but had lost a lot of weight in the camp).

It was always very noticeable when he appeared anywhere, although he hadn't ever occupied the position in life that he deserved—and never did. Our team of young people went at once to his assistance, and before long he was installed in no. 7 company, the artistic one, and came to work straight away in the Krimkab. We went on to take steps to make him less conspicuous: at roll-calls he didn't stand in the front rank and he spoke softly in the USLON corridors. Even from the rear rank, however, he succeeded in making a couple of audible comments which Kunst, the commanding officer, read out to us at roll-calls. These retorts (in the form of ingenious questions or expressions of consent calculated to emphasise Kunst's stupidity) could have enraged any idiot of a commanding officer, and Kunst, cunning and agile as he was, was not specially renowned for wit.

I haven't managed to find anything in print about Gordon apart from his own books and articles. His books were history text-books: *The Chartist Movement*; *The Revolution of 1848*; *The History of the Class Struggle in the West*. Neither these nor his articles give a true impression of the immense breadth of his knowledge. He had a perfect knowledge of Classical Greek and German, was well versed in Latin and French, spoke fluent Italian and could read English, Spanish, Swedish and all the Slavonic languages. He was always trying to learn something new. On Solovki he found the opportunity to study Arabic with the mufti of the principal Moscow mosque, and taught him Classical Greek in return.

His biographical details have been given me recently by his daughter, Irina Gavrilovna, whom I found in Moscow. He was born in Spassk in 1885, and in 1890 the family moved to Moscow, where he attended grammar school and University. In 1906 and 1907 he went to the so-called Summer Schools in Philosophy held by Cohen and Natorp in Marburg. In 1909 he served with the 5th Kiev Grenadiers. In 1914 (just before the war) he travelled round the historic places of Greece and Turkey, about which, by the way, he liked to reminisce to us in the cell. Then followed the usual life of an educated man of the time: he was called up into the army again, took part in various social and academic institutions of the Revolutionary period, lectured in Moscow and the provinces; he became Rector of Tambov University and founded the Tambov Scientific-Philosophical Society. Then he was a member of the Collegium of the People's Commissariat of Education for Soviet Russia, deputy chairman of Volgin's Soviet for Higher Education, member of the Pedagogical Section of the State Academic Soviet, etc., etc.

He was a university in himself for the young people on Solovki; he didn't merely give them information on any subject, but was keen to lecture off the cuff even to one or two, with precise bibliographic details, giving quotations, reciting poems. And of particular importance was the fact that he could quote passages in German from Goethe's *Faust*, in which we were all very interested at the time thanks to Meyer. Volodya Razdolski, who lived in the same cell as me, was surprisingly clever at extracting from Gordon information that he needed or found interesting, and paid close attention to his personal accounts. Later, when I met Gordon in Moscow and Leningrad, he commented on Razdolski's unusual ability, but at the same time regretted that there was so much of the dilettante about him; he 'lacked training'.

Gordon attracted young people with his 'joviality', his immediacy, his complete lack of 'side' (always so tempting in a professor), his lack of restraint and his sincerity. He was for ever getting into arguments and making enemies and this was extremely unsafe in those days.

I remember him turning up in the Krimkab and introducing himself: "No relation to Gordon Byron or to Gordon the chemist..."

Pavel Fomich Smotritski

We would never be able to forgive ourselves if we overlooked Pavel Fomich Smotritski in no. 13 'quarantine' company. He was a notable artist of the *Mir iskusstva*[139] circle, a participant in Russo-Finnish exhibitions, and a friend of the architect who had built Leonid Andreyev's house in the Chornaya Rechka district. The fact that he was so little known, I think, was due to his extreme modesty, a kind of psychological imperceptibility. He drew attention to himself neither by his appearance, nor by his manner, nor by his speech, which was always calm and quiet.

After his regulation period in no. 13 company he was sent, as unfit, to Anzer, where he was put to work as an artist in the camp box-making shop. This workshop was a remarkable establishment. Good carpenters and cabinet makers from among the prisoners worked there, mostly making boxes out of icons. These came from the reserves of the Museum, controlled by Vinogradov. They were from the eighteenth and nineteenth centuries, but judging from the quantity of output I suspect that seventeenth century ones also were used, which at the time were considered of no interest. 'At the time' indeed! In the 1940s (evidently, at the end of the war) a specialist with a doctorate in art history allowed a church to be cleared for use as a hospital. It had a stock of icons dating from the seventeenth and eighteenth centuries, and they were all simply burnt.

The wood of the icons was good and sound (it was said that some of the boards were even cypress), there was no shortage of carpenters, and poor Smotritski, a believer who knew his icons, was obliged to decorate these boxes. I never saw any of them, as they all went off to Moscow.

It was harder to get Smotritski freed from Anzer than to rescue him from no. 13 company, but we managed it, and in the spring of 1930 he began to take part in our conversations in Krimkab, and brought with him some marvellous watercolours. Some of his work was engraved for printing and appeared in *Solovetskiye ostrova*. I remember that his initials were in a circle in the bottom right-hand corner.

Smotritski was rather taciturn, but all his remarks and answers were very shrewd and to the point. I remember one conversation with him. I had mentioned to him that I'd noticed that the writers of the late nineteenth and early twentieth centuries had started to invent special forms of dress for themselves. The first to dress in a special way was Lev Tolstoy (incidentally, at the time we were all going about in *tolstovkas*–garments that not only didn't call for clean collars, but at times didn't require underwear), and then so did Stasov, Gorki, Leonid Andreyev, Blok, Voloshin, Bely, Skitalets, etc., etc. There was only Chekhov, we thought, who didn't design his own outfit. Smotritski considered this and said: "Yes, but Chekhov dressed like a typical doctor". I thought back to my childhood, when I'd often been ill and children's doctors had treated me, and I'd been taken from doctor to doctor. No doubt Chekhov had had a 'doctorly self-awareness' in his dress. Smotritski was perfectly correct.

I've remembered Smotritski for that subtle remark ever since.

Vladimir Sergeyevich Razdolski

Volodya Razdolski from Rostov-on-Don, whom I've mentioned above, was the first person of my own age that I got to know and then befriended in the Krimkab. A former university student, he was interested in philosophy and was even quite active, writing things in secret. He was of striking appearance, with great dark eyes and a perpetual smile which curled his lips as if to accompany thoughts that he didn't express. There was always a lighted pipe in his mouth. He was physically not strong, though he moved quickly. He wore top-boots in which his feet rattled about freely, and which were worn down at the heels, as he walked on his heels in an odd way. He couldn't work, and only read, thought and discussed. If ever Kolosov gave him anything to do he took so long thinking how to go about it that it had to be given to someone else, that is to me or Peshkovski. It seemed that Volodya paid no attention to anything except his own philosophical day-dreaming, and so he called all everyday objects and actions by the same name—doggy. If he'd lost his doggy that meant he'd lost his pipe or his pencil or not finished his assignment or whatever. "Where's that doggy?" he would ask, and leave us to decide for ourselves what the question referred to. In the Krimkab he would either be busy reading some book that he'd managed to acquire and which interested him, or in 'intellectual' conversation with Meyer (if the latter wasn't already being engaged in conversation—always in a whisper—by Kseniya Polovtseva, who brought him his lunch in little cans and saucepans). Volodya's thoughts and conversation were always very interesting, and if he'd gone on living under normal conditions he would, no doubt, have become an engaging thinker. He and I were together in the same cell in no. 7 company after Kolosov had left. He slept on a camp-bed under the window and it was always hard to wake him in the morning. Occasionally he would have too much to drink (when smuggled vodka appeared on Solovki) and then the whole cell would unite to save him from the informers and staff on duty. He would be laid out on his camp-bed and covered with an overcoat, and we would say that he was sick so that he shouldn't be disturbed at roll-call. He was an admirer of Sveshnikov-Kemetski's poetry (he lived in our cell too) and was constantly in conversation with Gordon.

I was no match for Volodya in conversation, but I was a good listener. Volodya didn't really know all that much, but he had the knack of drawing the interesting 'oldies' (such as Gordon, Meyer, Danzas, Sukhov, Bardygin—though the last-named wasn't old at all) into discussions and arguments. He didn't doubt the existence of God, but he wasn't a church-goer.

His mother used to come to see him—he'd lost his father. She was unusually beautiful, despite her enervated features. She had a job, a salary, and sent money to her only son... Volodya introduced us. He was of Ukrainian-Polish descent. His full name was Razdolski-Ratoshski, and his ancestry went back into the mists of time...

When he was transferred to Medvezhya Gora, later than myself, he became attached to the younger element that had surrounded A. F. Losev.

Vladimir Kemetski (Sveshnikov)

Many of the young people on Solovki wrote poetry. In the '20s, by and large, there were few young educated people that didn't. It was the fashion. Some wrote in secret and showed their work to no one; others showed their work but didn't offer it for publication; others still were solemnly printed in *Solovetskiye ostrova*. Of my acquaintances A. Pankratov, Yu. Kazarnovski, D. Shipchinski, A. A. Peshkovski and Lada Mogilyanska belonged to the third group, but beyond doubt the most talented, the 'real' poet was Vladimir Kemetski. That, by the way, was his mother's maiden name, which he used as a poetic pseudonym.

I arrived on Solovki at the very beginning of November 1928, but it was only in the spring of 1929 that I became able to use the Kremlin library and to borrow books. It was a good library as all the books sent to prisoners were left there, and there were a lot of professors and people of higher education. Koch (a young German communist who worked in the library, did not have a single tooth in his head—they'd all been knocked out during interrogation), Boris Brik (a poet), A. N. Grech (descendant of the famous Grech[140] and sentenced in the 'Russian Estates Society' case), Novak (a Hungarian Communist), a little old man called Mebus, compiler of an encyclopedia of Theosophy in two big volumes, and Volodya Sveshnikov. I remember that it was very cold in the library, and Volodya, blue with cold and hunger and dressed in a rustic-style short sheepskin coat with an enormous tear in it (which no one bothered to mend for him) dealt with requests for books and took them to the lectern at which 'readers' stood. He always looked like an offended child. To look at him one would say he was just turned twenty, but in fact he was almost thirty. In late 1929 or early 1930 he was moved into the same cell as me. His poetry was highly esteemed, and people who received parcels used to give him treats whenever they could. His sincerity and immediacy impressed me: his every emotion showed on his face. He often had to hide and protect his feelings, as he reacted at once to any injustice or roughness. There was even a trace of hysteria at times in his outraged cries. At times he would turn his anger even on the people helping him, but all of us in his cell forgave him on account of the talent displayed in his verse. Only a small part of what he wrote got into *Solovetskiye ostrova* in the course of 1930, though there may have been some in 1929 and 1931—I haven't checked. Some of his earlier poems were printed also, written in Berlin and Paris, but they were much inferior, showing a tendency to 'educatedness'. In no. 7 company he wrote *Saga ob Erike, syne Elmara* [The saga of Erik, son of Elmar]. He was thinking of death, and his ancestry on his mother's side went back to the Vikings of Scandinavia. When he was writing poetry he muttered constantly and his face had a strained expression, his lips pursed. I remember his face clearly, and his customary posture.

All that I remember of his pre-Solovetski past is as follows: his parents were White emigrants. His father, Sveshnikov, seems to have been a White officer. He had spent some time with his family in Berlin (whence the Berlin themes of some of his early poems, not all of which, by the way, he wanted to be printed, but he let us see them in the cell). Then the family, like many émigrés, moved to Paris. There Volodya, together with a group of émigré youth, joined Komsomol (an independent one, obviously) and started to agitate for a return to the Soviet Union. His parents were against this, but in 1926 he, together with a group of young people, were allowed back. In Kharkov, where he was living before Solovki, and in Moscow he had a bit too much to say, was openly dissatisfied, and was given five years.

On Solovki he was eternally hungry and went round in a very scruffy condition. One of the camp officials had married a former prisoner, one of the intelligentsia, a friend of Lada Mogilyanska. She was in raptures over his verses that were printed in *Solovetskiye ostrova* and twice sent him *makhorka* and a little food. I can't recall her surname, but she's still alive. He dedicated to her one of his poems that was printed in *Solovetskiye ostrova* in 1930. This magazine was on sale all over the USSR and even abroad; I've been told, for example, that there's a complete set in a library in Helsinki[141]. A schoolgirl in somewhere like Ufa, Perm or Vyatka was captivated by his poems and began writing to him and sending him parcels. She invited him to visit their town on behalf of herself and her parents; later, I was told, she became his wife, but that was wrong. He lived on in terrible poverty in Archangel oblast, where he was shot on 29 January 1938 in Ukhtpechlag. Kem was an intermediary point in his release; everyone was sent there from Solovki if their release date fell during the period when the sea crossing was closed. His best poems belong to this final, most impoverished period of his life, after release from camp. Their principal theme is that of awaiting imminent death.

I managed to find some of his poems in the Berlin magazine *Nedra* [The Depths of the Earth] (vol. 4, 1923–24, p. 314). There is a reference to him in the collection of articles *Russki Berlin*: 1921–23 (YMCA Press, Paris, 1983) and a few poems were printed in *Ogonek* and *Nashe naslediye*.

I spent more than half a century looking for information on Volodya Sveshnikov and his verse apart from that printed in *Solovetskiye ostrova* and *Noviye Solovki*. Finally, after more than sixty years, I received a detailed letter from the historian E. S. Stolyarova which left no hope of any possibility of finding any more of his work. In view of its importance I print this letter in full, as evidence of Sveshnikov's tragic death. It is dated 22 July 1994:

> Dear Dmitri Sergeyevich! I was very pleased to receive your letter about the publication of V. Kemetski's verse (in the first edition of these Memoirs, 1995–DSL). I will do as you ask and write of what I know about him.
>
> Kemetski's poems, both manuscript originals and in typescript (evidently the work of A. Pankratov), came into my hands in the early 1980s from a relation by the name of Pankratova—a sister of the A. Pankratov that you knew on Solovki and who died in 1947. Possibly he and Kemetski were connected by ties of friendship—otherwise how could the poems have come into his possession?
>
> I became, as they say, 'hooked' on the poems. I have no background in literary studies (I read History at Moscow University, worked mainly as an editor and am now a librarian in my retirement), but I was immediately aware of the extraordinary quality of the verse and of the personality of the author. It seemed to me frightfully wrong and offensive that this poet should have no readers, that his verse should be inaccessible to people.

I have tried to trace the course of Kemetski's life from the dates and towns given at the end of the poems. It emerges that at first he lived abroad (Paris and Berlin), then in a few Soviet cities—Moscow, Tbilisi and Kharkov—after which Solovki and Kem, and then Arkhangelsk. There it all ends.

I have tried to discover whether any of the poems were published in this country. After a lengthy search I succeeded: I found three of his sonnets in *Nedra* for 1924. The author was named as V. Kemetski, and so I was disabused of my idea that he had adopted the pseudonym Kemetski on Solovki or in Kem.

I even went to Solovki and tried to obtain information from the staff of the museum there. They had been studying the former prisoners discreetly, purely out of interest, although in those days, before perestroyka, this was not without risk. I conducted a friendly correspondence with Antonina Melnik, who worked in the museum, but unfortunately she was unable to shed any light on Kemetski's fate. I did, on the other hand, sense the sublime beauty of Solovki, which comes through in many of his poems.

I tried without success to clear up a point in Memorial[142]. I wrote to A. Rybakov; in his *Deti Arbata* [Children of Arbat] there is a hero called A. Pankratov, who, as he is being sent to [Kan], meets a poet whose fate reminded me of Kemetski's: he too was young and had returned from Paris to Russia. Rybakov replied, but unfortunately that line of investigation led nowhere.

Then I started to look for people who made a professional study of the poetry of the '20s and came across N. A. Bogomolov. This was was a great step forward, as he was familiar with Kemetski's verse and was able to contact you and send you the material that I gave him. And lo and behold! Your long letter arrived, in which you told me about Solovki, the people you mixed with there, the atmosphere and—oh bliss!—about Kemetski. Thus an insubstantial figure became the real Volodya, the poet Vladimir Kemetski. The day I read your letter was a day of great joy for me.

Then I sent you, through A. Lavrov, all the poems of Kemetski's in my possession. And you did what I had dreamed of for so long: you recommended the publication of a number in *Nashe naslediye* [Our Inheritance]. And there, in volume 2 of 1988, Kemetski's poems appeared with my little introduction. The poet had found a reader. What happiness!

Publication produced two responses. First, a letter from Yelena Pavlovna Zelenina, who had been in Arkhangelsk in the '30s visiting her exiled mother and step-father. There she had met the exiled Yan Glinski, whom she had soon married. Glinski was a friend of Kemetski, who was living in Arkhangelsk after release from Solovki. They often entertained exiled writers and artists, among them Kemetski. The next time that Zelenina met Kemetski was in Moscow, where he visited her on a number of occasions. Later they met in Ufa, where he had evidently moved. She was sorry to tell me that by that time Kemetski was drinking a very great deal and could not bring himself to do anything.

A quite unique response came from Aleksandr Ilich Klibanov. I will add that we became friends and saw each other often right up until his death. He was an amazing person and a great scholar, and had spent thirteen years of his life in the camps. I was helping him prepare his correspondence with his wife for publication, but unfortunately he died before it was done. Their letters were remarkable—and what a document of the period.

He had met Kemetski in 1937, in the hold of a barge taking a party of prisoners to the Vorkuta[143] camps. Kemetski made such a strong impression on him that for the rest of his life he had been able to remember several of his poems. Even before we met he had recorded on tape his recollections of their meeting, and I have a typed transcript of this recording, from which I will quote the following:

"Once my attention was drawn to some noise on the companion-way leading from the hold to the deck. I wasn't far from the spot and quickly slipped off my bunk and went over. A young man of about 25–26, small, thin, fair-haired and, as far as I could tell in the poor light, rather pale, was a few paces ahead of me. In front of him stood a hefty corporal of the escort, fighting to restrain a huge dog which was standing on its hind paws and gnashing its teeth at the little man. He, however, shaking all over with excitement, was saying to the corporal, quietly but with great firmness, with prodigious vigour and with menace in his tone 'Don't come near me... I'll kill you!' He turned round and, with strength that I would not have expected from him, tore a tread off the companionway and, brandishing it, moved towards the soldier. And so fearsome, so menacing was he that not only the corporal but also his dog fell back and vanished onto the deck."

"A few of the others and I went up to this man. He was fearfully excited, quite beside himself. We had a job to get him back and sit him down. It turned out that he had needed a breath of air. He was panting, and told me that he couldn't stand it any longer and had actually wanted the soldier to shoot him so as to have done there and then with the flies and all that floating hell that was our barge."

"A good, friendly and trusting relationship sprang up between us very quickly, and as was usual among prisoners each of us told his life-story, gave an account of the road that had led him there. This young man called Sveshnikov, a member of a famous noble family, told me his story. His parents had left the country during the years of the Revolution, had drifted about and finally settled in France, in Paris, and he with them. He had been noted for poetic ability, apparently, which had revealed itself at once and unquestionably. He had been received at the salon of Hippius and Merezhkovski, where he had been a great success, and he himself had taken a keen interest in the people who had been performing there. He had soon felt, however, that he was suffocating in that salon—suffocating morally, just as much as he was suffocating physically in that barge."

"He had left the salon, broken with émigré circles generally and joined the French Komsomol. But he was a poet, and did not know how to go about political conspiratorial work, was picked up for activities of which the French police disapproved and deported from France. He went to Berlin, where again he joined Komsomol—the Jugendbund—and took part in underground activity, was again picked up by the police and this time—under what circumstances I forget—repatriated to the Soviet Union. He went to live in some big town in the south and found work on the newspaper *Zarya vostoka* [Dawn of the East] (published in Tbilisi—DSL) where he worked as a correspondent and literary reviewer. He lived well and breathed easy. Everything was new to him, everything was interesting. He was at home with his surroundings, and those were some of the best years of his still short life."

"But then something quite untoward occurred. He was accused of penetrating the Soviet Union for espionage purposes, of being a spy, German, French or both, was arrested and packed off to the Solovki concentration camp, where he served several years. He said that outwardly living conditions had not always been hard for him, and that he had had the chance not only of writing but also of having his work printed, under the pseudonym Vladimir Kemetski, in a literary almanac published by bookish prisoners."

"He read me (continues Klibanov) his poems. I can remember by no means all of them, strictly speaking only four. I think that they are very good poems, and that is because their author pours himself forth in them. The poems I remember have, in my view, what might be termed a lyrical-civic character: they point the finger at the German middle class, in which he guessed at the Fascists of the future. I remember a bit of the subject of his poem 'Herr Müller': Herr Müller is enjoying himself. He is a grain merchant, a shopkeeper, a butcher, with a short red neck, inspired by sausage and Bavarian beer. He greedily scents blood in the air, and that arouses his greasy soul. Or something of the sort ... I am speaking of the feeling with which that poem left me. And there were others."

"As we approached our destination we were divided into various squads. I was put into the Capitalism pit, and he into another, and we did not meet again. Sometime in late 1937 news reached me that he was seriously ill, and that was the last I heard of him. "

Now from the Ministry of Security document published in your Memoirs (the reference is to the first edition of these Memoirs, in which all the poems that Kemetski thought possible to publish were included—DSL) it is clear that Kemetski was shot in January 1938, and in May 1957 his case was closed 'for lack of criminal evidence'. I have, indeed, one question: why was the decision that he be shot taken by the Directorate of NKVD for the Arkhangelsk region when Kemetski was a prisoner in Vorkuta?

Oh Lord, why did such a man deserve to live and die like that?

154

I had another response about Kemetski from A. N. Dorrer, sister of the wife of another twentieth century poet, Vladimir Shchirovski. She failed to see the poems published in *Nashe naslediye*; this time the stimulus was different. I remembered that in his poem *Pamyat krovi* [Memory of blood] Kemetski took an epigraph from Shchirovski, and suddenly I came across a selection of Shchirovski's poems in *Ogonek* under the heading *Russkaya muza XX veka* [The Russian muse of the twentieth century], edited by Yevgeni Yevtushenko. I got the address of the publisher from *Ogonek*—A. N. Dorrer, who lived in Kherson, and wrote to her. She replied at once. (Oh, what times they were! How we were all seduced by the changes taking place in the country, how much we were all expecting! What has become of it all?) She did not know very much about Kemetski, but she wrote that he and Shchirovski had been friends and told me about one episode which, in Shchirovski's view, had been the cause of Kemetski's arrest. It had been in Kharkov: "... something happened in 1927, when one night, after they had been drinking together, somewhere in a square Sveshnikov shouted 'I'm going to sell my raincoat and go to Paris!' Apparently he spread his coat out on the paving stones. They were only just boys, you know!" Kemetski and Shchirovski had kept in touch by letter when Kemetski was on Solovki. After he was released he went to visit Shchirovski, who was living in Kerch at the time. Later Shchirovski himself was arrested and released, and later died in the very first days of the war. *Ogonek* was interested in Kemetski's verse, but alas, the times were by then beginning to change...

Then I made the acquaintance of V. B. Muravyov, a former political prisoner, who published verse by poet-prisoners first in *Literaturnaya gazeta* [Literary Gazette] and later in a separate book *Sredi drugikh imen* [Among Other Names]. Kemetski was one of these, and his poems were taken from *Solovetskiye ostrova*. He had become familiar with all Kemetski's work and had decided to publish him in full, but this too was fated not to happen. It seems that I am always that little bit too late.

One day I received a letter from Petrozavodsk, from Yuri Linnik of the Centre for the study of the spiritual culture of GULAG. At his request I prepared a large selection of the poetry of Kemetski and A. Pankrator which was published in the magazine *Sever* [The North], no. 9, 1990. The publisher *Kareliya* proposed to publish a book called *Neugasimaya lampada*, [The Unextinguishable Icon Lamp], into which Kemetski's verse would have gone. And again—disaster! The people in Petrozavodsk had another plan, and that did not come to fruition either. At Linnik's request I sent the autograph copy of Kemetski's *Pesn o vozvrashcheni* [Song of return] for the museum that was being set up, and kept a photocopy for myself. That is the only autograph that I have parted with. The rest I still have.

Then came your book, and my rejoicing. And those, dear Dmitri Sergeyevich, are essentially all the facts that I have. If what I have told you is of interest I shall be delighted. I think that the attempt might still be made to look for Kemetski's published work in the newspapers of those cities where Fate hurled him. One never knows.

There may be information on Kemetski in the Parisian section of the Hippius and Merezhkovski archive or in some Kerch publications (I was told twenty years ago that his poems had been seen in something of the sort), and likewise one ought to look through back numbers of *Zarya vostoka*.

I would like to end my recollections of Volodya with lines from a poem of his dated 1927:

> For you, in every age that seem
> To wander, free to quaff the wine
> Of life, of love, inspired to dream,
> For you I write this verse of mine,
> You that have glimpsed that other flame
> Of life beyond the bleakness here...
> I bid you welcome, festal hour
> Of coming doom, that others dread.
> You bring relief! Though pain as well
> It gives me joy to see you come:
> Now the silent prison cell,
> Then the vastness of the tomb.

Aleksandr Arturovich Peshkovski

It's hard to write about him seriously. Yet there was in him, coupled with his exceptional vulgarity and practicality, a naivety, an ingenuousness and a certain something else that made him attractive. He was working in Krimkab before my arrival, was just a little older than me, and was regarded by Kolosov as his prime assistant, a fact which he liked to display to us. But Volodya Razdolski and I weren't offended by this; "Let him get on with it!" He was exceptionally active and lively—the latter not merely because he was for ever procuring or arranging something (for himself, first and foremost—sometimes for us as well) but also because he suffered from some kind of chorea: he twitched his feet (he wore plus-furs and the fashionable pointed slip-ons known as 'Jimmies'), shrugged his shoulders, rolled his head and in particular came out with ejaculations (words were for ever bursting out of his thoughts, especially when he wrote).

He tried to write verse and prose—his masterpiece was *Kuzma vdova* [The widow Kuzma] and was published in *Solovetskiye ostrova*: in his writings he emphasized individual words with large letters, a habit which seemed an extension of his strange illness. "Arturych stammers when he's silent, and Yurka Kazarnovski when he speaks" was said of them humorously, but Arturych stammered even in print with those deliberately selected words of his. His prose work, with the main character, I believe, Madam Lieberman, was not at all bad.

He was a nephew of A. M. Peshkovski, the authority on Russian syntax. His mother and stepfather, Shvedov, used to come to see him. They were from Tsarskoye Selo (by then renamed Detskoye Selo). His mother was deeply religious, and would go into the Museum and pray fervently before the relics of Zosima and Savvatii that were displayed for desecration.

All the youth of Solovki that wrote poetry gathered around Peshkovski—Pankratov, Kazarnovski, Shipchinski, Sveshnikov-Kemetski and Lada Mogilyanska; one might add that all these were shot later, with the exception of Kazarnovski, who died of drug addiction.

I met Peshkovski in Leningrad after my release from the camps. I told him that I meant to write pieces for children's magazines (for *Koster* [The Campfire] to which I'd submitted a manuscript) about the origins of various words. Imagine my surprise when he immediately, and more quickly than myself, published a series of similar pieces on exactly the same words that I'd mentioned to him, and in the very same reference works and publications. I was very annoyed and never had anything to do with him again. When and how he vanished so soon I don't know, but he couldn't simply be inconspicuous, even in Leningrad. I only thank my lucky stars that I didn't go in for writing in those days and made myself inconspicuous, working as a proofreader first in the printing house Comintern and then as a scientific proofreader in the Academy of Sciences press on Vasilevski island.

Aleksandr Aleksandrovich Bedryaga

After the release of Kolosov, Aleksandr Aleksandrovich Bedryaga took charge of Krimkab.

I still remember him clearly. He had a narrow head, balding and pointed at the top, a small moustache, handsome, friendly eyes and a small mouth, and he always looked ready to turn any conversation into a joke. He went about in a dark tolstovka and top-boots. He was a man of education, like Kolosov, who read literature, pencil in hand, ready to assume the pose of a man writing a report if an official entered.

He'd been a lawyer, but before he was arrested he'd abandoned that profession and become a masseur in the Maksimilianovskaya (private) clinic in Leningrad and lived in the same house as B. D. Grekov. His mother expected him to marry her ward after his release. He'd avoided making a promise, but on Solovki, when he had a bad head after one of his frequent drinking sessions, he would say "I'm going to marry Liza". That meant that he was hung over and had a headache. He didn't think much of me as I was a teetotaller, and to the drinking man a teetotaller is always an enemy, a traitor, a living reproach! He felt affection only for Volodya Razdolski, as he was keen to join him in his drinking. These sessions cost a lot of money, as the vodka was smuggled in.

One incident comes to mind. Bedryaga had drunk himself senseless in no. 3 company and was lying flat on his back on his camp-bed; someone had spread something over him. It was the season when there were no sailings. *Pochtarki* used to come over (comparatively small boats which could be dragged over the ice) bringing smuggled vodka, which was obtained from the boatmen by the man in charge of our island detachment, 'Petya' Golovkin, himself; he was a thoroughgoing drunkard. He knew precisely when the *pochtarki* would arrive. And so, 'Petya' Golovkin had had a skinful and started going round the companies looking for anyone who was drunk, and did the rounds, scarcely able to stand upright himself, and put everyone that was drunk in the punishment cells. Now to go into the punishment cells on Solovki was almost certain death. One had to be tremendously fit to spend all day sitting on the perches, as the narrow, backless benches were called; they were so high that one's feet didn't touch the floor.

And so, drunk as a lord, Petya Golovkin rushed into no. 3 company, where there were prisoners 'of substance', who had the means to buy vodka. When the officer came in the orderly on duty shouted "Attention!", the doors to the cells were opened and everyone had to stand to attention. But Bedryaga was laid out! Golovkin asked the orderly "Who's this?" "Sick, sir!" replied the orderly smartly. Convinced that the 'sick man' would not escape but that the other drunkards would have time to hide, Golovkin hurled himself round the other cells, and meanwhile Volodya Razdolski and I dragged the 'dead body' of Bedryaga out into no. 7 company, right across the square outside the Preobrazhenski Cathedral. When he'd inspected all the cells on both floors Golovkin went back to the one where Bedryaga had been lying and couldn't find him. "Where's he gone?" "Don't know", replied the orderly and truthfully; how could he know, as he'd been making the rounds with Golovkin. Seeing that he'd been fooled, Golovkin let out a howl of rage and set off in pursuit of the 'dead body'. First he went to no. 7 company—that of the artistes and musicians of the Solteatr. In charge here was the Estonian officer Aleksandr Adolfovich Kunst, a good comrade and a brave man. Golovkin burst in and turned on Kunst: "Your company's a shambles, they're drunk!" Kunst knew that Golovkin, especially when drunk, was not a man to trifle with, so he clicked his heels and reported "Quite so, citizen commander[144], a shambles: everything's in order!" Golovkin gave Kunst a wild look and sensed that he'd not been quick enough, and said "Everything in order, you say? Right, let's see you walk along a floorboard" (that was his favourite way of catching a drunk). Kunst was sober and quickly walked down a floorboard. Golovkin tore round the cells (the command 'Attention!' had been given and doors were open) and there in the very first was Bedryaga, lying in the same position. We hadn't had time to cover him with an overcoat. He was taken to the punishment block and questioned: where had he got the vodka and who had brought it over? He was beaten up in front of all the prisoners there but didn't give in. After that all the non-political prisoners on Solovki were very respectful of Bedryaga, and indeed towards the Krimkab, and told me about their lives without restraint; these accounts I wrote down and in so doing acquired a command of literary language (in the cold school in Leningrad we hadn't written essays because our fingers were so cold that they wouldn't bend to write letters). Bedryaga was treated by the doctors who took him from the punishment block to the sick-bay with some kind of 'acute' illness. In general, though, it must be said that the authorities were very 'understanding' towards drunkards, and forgave them crimes for which a sober man in the camp would have risked being shot. This is the sort of thing that Bedryaga was excused: one day when he was under the influence he dressed up in a fireman's helmet and the rest

159

of the uniform, took a fireman's hatchet in his hand and put an electric lamp on his chest (all this he had obtained because there were some in the fire brigade too that liked a drink), went into the crowded Solteatr during a performance and shouted "Fire!". Panic broke out, but fortunately no one was killed. The affair was hushed up and the authorities had a laugh. Another time he got to the 'royal bell', which hung in a low bell-tower in the garden outside the Preobrazhenski Cathedral, and rang it quite hard. This time too it was hushed up; the authorities had a laugh. One could go on and on about what Bedryaga did when drunk. We enjoyed living with him. He knew how to 'pull the wool' and pretend that Krimkab was doing a serious job. Everybody was fond of him. He could certainly play tricks, although he was by no means a clever man.

After he was released Bedryaga couldn't find work. No one would take him on. He went to Dmitrovlag near Moscow and there Dmitri Pavlovich Kallistov took him on as a domestic but he took to drink and eventually hanged himself. It was a shame.

But what became of the Deputy Commandant of the Sollager, 'Petya' Golovnikov (the prisoners called him 'Petya' and forgave him all his bestiality because of his alcoholism). He was transferred to Kem while I was still on the island. The camp newspaper was also moved to Kem from Solovki and one day the whole camp rocked with laughter. A copy of the Kem newspaper had found its way to Solovki, and in it the prisoners read an article by Golovkin on the evils of drink. It was a masterpiece of the journalistic art. Golovkin wrote that as the result of drunkenness one lost one's balance, moved erratically, fell over and could break arms and legs, one worked badly and the next day one had a headache, etc. (he described his personal situation). The higher camp authorities had ordered Golovkin to write this article in the hope that afterwards he would be too ashamed to drink. The article was written, however, not by the semi-literate 'Petya' but by some witty prisoner.

Mikhail Ivanovich Khachaturov

One mustn't imagine the Krimkab as merely a centre for serious philosophical thought. Sometimes, when there was no pressing work on hand, it became a special kind of sitting-room. In our cells we merely slept, drank boiled water and saw to personal affairs, all the more so as the flickering light of the little lamps went out early (at ten o'clock). Movement from cell to cell and company to company was forbidden, but in the USLON building on the landing-stage it was easily achieved. The Krimkab attracted most of all, of course, educated people.

Our most frequent visitor was the extremely perceptive Mikhail Ivanovich Khachaturov. He was in for embezzlement, although in my Solovki notes, for some reason, it says against his name 'theosophist'. He used to relate with special delight how he'd squandered large sums of official money, and then had attempted unsuccessfully to cross the Turkish frontier out of Armenia.

In those distant days the population of the camp was divided into the 'socially near' and the 'ka-ery' (the counterrevolutionaries— prisoners caught under Article 58[145]; the word *kontrik* didn't yet exist). The 'socially near' were given every advantage. They could live outside the monastery walls, take the best duties, and were even recruited into the secret police. Superficially it was so, but the authorities realised that thieves and bandits couldn't really be trusted: they were the very ones who would steal, murder, deceive and disrupt discipline. So there was still a small group who enjoyed a higher standard of living than the rest, although chance, blat and special treatment were the deciding factors. To this group of prisoners, more readily trusted than the rest, belonged those who were there under 'official clauses' (for example, secret agents whose cover was blown and who'd been charged with 'divulging State secrets'), foreign currency speculators, embezzlers, etc. The ever lively, witty and clever Khachaturov had been convicted of embezzlement and attempting to flee the country. At that time it was not yet accepted practice to disguise political cases as criminal. That fashion came in only after the war and the establishment of the Declaration of Human Rights, when the government was obliged to do all it could to reduce the percentage of political cases and political prisoners. Therefore Khachaturov's situation in the camp was relatively tolerable. As a resourceful and literate man, he had been given some suitable job and had set himself up in a tiny little room of the Kremlin, with a little stove and electricity, somewhere near no. 2 bath-house. Inside the room was perfectly comfortable, but on the outside it was littered with firewood and all sorts of rubbish. Everybody in the camp tried to be inconspicuous and not to arouse jealousy in particular. I went to visit him twice, and each time I felt as if I'd returned to normal surroundings.

161

He was a frequent visitor to the Krimkab and did us various little favours, at the same time bringing news, jokes and anecdotes, and we enjoyed seeing him. He was educated and widely experienced. He combined in himself the best features of the Armenian and the dashing Cossack from his father and his mother respectively.

Although he was sentenced to ten years, as a non-political he was transferred from Solovki in 1929 or 1930. I learned of his life in the mainland camp from the unpublished memoirs of Nikolay Vasilevich Zhilov, *Letopis moyey zhizni* [Chronicle of My Life]. Every detail of Khachaturov is dear to me, and so I will take the liberty of quoting at length. The author of the *Letopis* writes:

> The detachment headquarters (of the Belomorobaltiski camp—DSL) was deployed to the hamlet of May-guba, where there were houses, a sawmill and a little experimental factory (I recognise Khachaturov—'little factory' is enough—DSL) making building chip-board, run by the prisoner-engineer Khachaturov. From his surname he seemed to be an Armenian, but from his appearance he was more like a Jew. Grey, silver hair, combed smooth, framed the high noble forehead. With the fine, regular, spiritual features of his clean-shaven face and his huge, grey, slightly protruding eyes he looked like a scientist and reminded one, in a way, of portraits of the critic and publicist N. K. Mikhaylovski. The little factory which Khachaturov ran was an experimental business. The work that it performed in primitive conditions has not yet been achieved on a big scale. An experimental, small two-storey house had been built nearby of the chip-board, and Khachaturov and his wife lived there. At the time this was not the only instance of a prisoner 'living out'.

Later on there is a description of how comfortable Khachaturov's quarters were: a comfortable house, surrounded by blat and friends— just as I was accustomed to seeing him. Although we in the Krimkab weren't entirely free from jealousy, we loved him for his *joie de vivre*.

S. O. Shmidt questioned me about Khachaturov, and I wrote to him roughly what I've said above, and to my surprise I received a letter from Khachaturov's daughter, N. M. Pirumova:

> Please accept my sincere gratitude for the lines of reminiscence of my father, Mikhail Ivanovich Khachaturov, that your memory has retained. For me this has been the first voice from an unknown past. He evidently went to Solovki in 1924 or '25. I was about two at the time and, naturally, didn't remember him. He returned in the spring of 1933 and was re-arrested in August 1935, so he was at liberty for eighteen months in all. He died in the camp at Ust-Chibyu[146] in 1938.

He had been a revolutionary in the past, but on Solovki he accepted religion. I remember his tales of the remarkable thinkers whom he met there, but I don't know their names and this is why I attach so much importance to the surnames you mention.

Lada Mogilyanska

The Russian-Ukrainian poetess Lidiya Mikhaylovna Mogilyanskaya, who wrote in Russian and Ukrainian (in the latter, under the pseudonym of Lada Mogilyanska), arrived on Solovki in about 1930. She was from Chernigov, and was a member of the Kotsyubinski[147] circle. A group of young people used to meet in his house, and of course the authorities had to imagine a counterrevolutionary plot. She had been given ten years although, I'm certain, she had only been interested in the poetry. She was a tall, elegant, short-skirted blonde with her hair in the then fashionable 'foxtrot' style. Her friends received shorter sentences and mostly remained on the mainland (in those days only prisoners with full sentences were taken to Solovki—the only stiffer sentence than ten years was death). Other Ukrainians on Solovki included the artists Petrash and Vovk. Lada worked as a typist in the USLON building, that is, in the same place as Krimkab. USLON itself had by then moved to Kem, but the building had kept its name. Lively, quick, witty, interested in the criminals' songs, she at once made a great impression on our young people. An 'illness' became prevalent which we called 'ladomania'. Some of her Russian verse, I believe, was printed in *Solovetskiye ostrova*. I memorised one of the songs that she wrote, entitled *Stoit frayer na fasone* (more likely, *nafasonen*) to the tune of *Pozabyt, pozabroshen*[148].

I used to like humming that song, and one of the young people placed an announcement in *Solovetskiye ostrova*: "A worker in Krimkab is writing a story entitled *Stoit frayer na fasone*—based on the lifestyle of thieves." This was a joke. I tried to write prose on Solovki but nothing came of it. Lada was shot in Dmitrovlag after the death of Gorki (her poems on his death remain, printed in the camp newspaper).

Aleksandr Petrovich Sukhov

The camp authorities were very keen on arranging various lectures as a means of maintaining the myth that those in the camp were not being punished but corrected. The content of the lectures and the numbers present interested them less. They needed a record of 'educational work' and so we came together now and then in the foyer of the theatre at lectures by experienced lecturers —Ananov from Tbilisi and Sukhov from Leningrad.

I remember the contents of a lecture by Sukhov on suggestibility. He had been investigating the very high degree of suggestibility among the labour camp teenagers and associated it with an innate 'flock' or 'herd' instinct. He explained as heightened suggestibility (in veiled fashion) revolutionary movements evoked by the herd instinct, multifarious campaigns and the ease with which they could spread throughout a country, and obedience to an ideology. I remember one experiment in suggestibility which he carried out on the spot in the auditorium. He asked those present to strike their hands on the table after him, but only after he had struck and not before. At first he struck randomly, then began to strike at regular intervals. We fell into the rhythm, and when he suddenly stopped striking the table several of us carried on, because we had succumbed to the suggestion of the rhythm. I was very interested in Sukhov's attempt to account for historical events by the characteristics of human psychology.

Naturally, the question of Stalin cropped up. The years 1929 and 1930 saw the advent of the cult of Stalin, which for some reason had arisen very rapidly. No one yet knew where that cult was to lead, but Sukhov seemed to guess straight away how third-rate were both Stalin and the cult. He didn't consider that Stalin had achieved absolute power on the strength of his abilities. All Stalin's measures, in his view, were the same as those of Lenin, whom he considered an exceptionally cunning and clever usurper; to come second to him was not failure in the least. In Stalin he emphasised 'secondariness'.

Sukhov's opinions on people were always surprisingly accurate. On a number of occasions we walked together on the Solovki roads, and he talked to me about the various types of human characters, and in particular about the connection between a man's character and his physique, about the theories of Kretchmer and others. One day as we walked he suggested that I carry out the following experiment: build a snowman and observe how passers-by react to it. Those of a pyknik build wouldn't touch it but the long-limbed type would destroy it. The experiment worked. "But," Sukhov explained, "uneducated people came by. " It was harder to observe the dependence of behaviour on physique in the educated... Although, although... Gordon was an obvious picnic type. Of course, I'm not quoting his opinions verbatim: direct speech in memoirs is almost always the invention of the writer.

Another visitor to the Krimkab was Vladimir Sergeyevich Muromtsev—son of the first president of the National Duma. He was a very handsome and imposing man, but excessively dull and, it seemed to me, there was nothing to him. People took an interest in him merely because of his father, but to Sukhov he was an interesting psychological type.

It is hard to realise that, despite the difficulties of Solovki life, Sukhov wrote a novel and read us chapters as they were completed. He had neither chair nor table, but wrote the several sections of his epic work, dedicated to the Russian youth of our age, hunched up on his camp-bed and draped in his sheepskin coat. I know for a fact that Volodya Rakov was the principal hero. I remember that there were in that epic-novel romantic love, Volodya's sub-diaconate and the watercolour albums, in which he gave us all another life in the reign of Aleksandr I, and the tragedy of the ruin of the Church.

Sukhov was released before us, and went off to his 'minuses'[149], having selected for his first town of exile Barnaul.

Sukhov wasn't the only one to try and overcome all the horrors of the camp by occupying themselves with clandestine creative activity. It was a real resistance movement, but not gun in hand—a resistance by creativity, of which the authorities wanted to deprive us all.

One curious detail that typifies Sukhov as a person: when I was allowed , in 1991, to look through the dossiers of the Cosmic Academy, Meyer's 'Sunday' circle and the 'Brotherhood of Serafim of Sarov' I also came across Sukhov's dossier. It turned out that he'd been sentenced (to five years) for organising assistance (clothing, food, money) for us after our arrest. He'd never mentioned this, and we, in accordance with the rules of 'propriety among prisoners' hadn't asked him about the reasons for his arrest.

And as for the others involved in our case, I can add that Valya Morozova, who was eighteen, told the investigator straight out that she wasn't going to say anything about the case of the 'Brotherhood of Serafim of Sarov'. Lyusya Suratova, who was about the same age, likewise staunchly refused to give evidence, and Boris Ivanov simply wouldn't speak. There were some odd lines in his interrogation. The investigator wrote to him on the interrogation form "Are you going to refuse to speak for much longer?" and opposite these words Borya had written "I don't know".

That's the sort of people they were.

Yuri Alekseyevich Kazarnovski

Kazarnovski, whom we all called simply Yurka, stood out among the poets on Solovki not only on account of his youth—he was still quite young at the time—but for the ease with which one could approach him. He had no poetic personality as had, for example, Volodya Sveshnikov-Kemetski. He was not profound, but wrote poetry with an unusual and effective light, witty touch. His parodies of Mayakovsky, Blok, Severyanin[150] and others are to be found in one number of *Solovetskiye ostrova*, his humorous aphorisms in another, and all on themes from Solovki life. He had an inexhaustible memory for poetry. He knew by heart almost all of Gumilev[151] (the Mandelshtam of the day) and Bely. He had good taste, appreciated real poetry and was always trying to impart his own poetic delights. There was not a trace of envy in him and when asked to read his verse he read someone else's which he liked. At one time he was living at Kem and had a disagreement there with a naval officer, Nikolay Nikolayevich Gorski—on romantic grounds. He narrowly escaped being shot in the autumn of 1929 as a result of his close association with Dimka Shipchinski.

A number of his parodies have been printed in *Ogonek*, and I had to clarify who they were directed against. In response to my note I received a seven page memoir of meetings with him in the '50s in Alma-Ata, by which time he had become a hardened drug addict. He was, by the way, the last to see Mandelshtam in the camp at Suchan, and Nadezhda Yakovlevna Mandelshtam tried to extract from him even the tiniest information about her late husband: in vain! By that time Kazarnovski couldn't remember a thing...

The reminiscences that were sent to me were from the old mathematician Gleb Kazimirovich Vasilev, and they were brilliantly written. I hope that he publishes them himself one day.

The Clergy

I'll have to begin far back in time. I find it very hard to remember which of the young people, and to what degree, were religious. Everyone that was more or less involved in the very small circle of the 'Brotherhood of Serafim of Sarov' was a believer. Of the nine members of the Cosmic Academy of Sciences, Tolya Terekhovko and Pyotr

Pavlovich Mashkov definitely weren't. Eduard Karlovich Rozenberg (my friend Fedya) converted from Lutheranism to Orthodoxy. An incomplete ceremony of baptism (only the anointing) was performed in the church on Petrovski Island by Fr. Viktorin Dobronravov, who has now been canonised by the Church in Exile. Eduard's brother Vladimir remained an 'indifferent Lutheran' but he became close friends with Fr. Vladimir Pishchulin when they shared a cell on Shpalernaya. The atheist Tolya Terekhovko also became friendly with a priest on Solovki. Fr. Aleksandr Filipenko, with whom we were in no. 13 'quarantine' company on Solovki, picked out Tolya specially from among us all, and told us all "He's an orphan". Indeed, both his father and mother had committed suicide when he'd been quite a small boy. His sister also committed suicide much later, during the blockade of Leningrad, and he himself got into hospital in Borovichi in the first months of the war and starved. Fr. Aleksandr somehow sensed a tragic quality about him, and, as I said, loved him, pitied him and made no attempt to persuade him to believe in God. Had he done so he would have driven them apart.

There was too a 'special case'. Borya (Boris) Ivanov, son of fairly wealthy parents (so it was said), who had been dragged into our case by the investigator although he'd never been in the circles, developed a religious mania on Solovki. Some villain, who gave himself out to be a monk and a priest, took him into 'service', and 'trained' Borya in 'humility': he relieved him of his nice black sheepskin jacket and gave him his own rags, took the best things out of the parcels that he got from his parents and made him serve him and blow his nose with his fingers (which he never managed to learn to do), etc.

When their ways parted Borya went off to be a medical orderly during the great 'Asiatic' typhus, caught it and died.

The clergy on Solovki were divided into the 'Sergian', who had accepted the declaration of Metropolitan Sergi concerning the recognition by the Church of Soviet power, and the 'Yosiflian', siding with Metropolitan Yosif, who had not. The latter were in the majority, and all the religious youth sided with them. The point was not just the usual youthful radicalism, but that at the head of the Yosiflians on Solovki was the remarkably attractive priest Viktor Vyatski (Ostrovidov). He was very cultured and owned printed works on theology, but in appearance reminded one of a rural parish priest. He greeted everyone with a broad smile (I can't remember him without it), had a straggly beard, ruddy cheeks and blue eyes. Over his cassock he wore a woman's knitted cardigan, sent to him by one of this flock. He somehow radiated kindliness and good cheer. He tried to help everyone and, what really mattered, was able to, so that everyone was well disposed towards him and believed what he said. He worked as a book-keeper in the Solovki farm. It was actually he and Fr. Nikolay Piskanovski who persuaded Kolosov to take me on in the Krimkab, and in 1929, when I came back from the 'typhus convalescent squad', he sent me some spring onions and soured cream through Fedya Rozenberg. Wasn't that tasty! One day I met him looking particularly radiant and joyful. It was on the square outside the Preobrazhenski Cathedral. The order had come out for all prisoners to have their hair cropped and forbidding the wearing of long clothing. Father Viktor, who refused to obey this order, was taken to the punishment block and forcibly shaved and his clothing was cut short.

Another joyous man was Fr. Nikolay Piskanovski. One can't call him 'a man of good cheer', but always, in the most oppressive circumstances, he radiated an inner peace. I can't remember his laughing or smiling, but a meeting with him was always consoling. And not only for me. I remember him telling a friend of mine, who had been in anguish for a year over the lack of letters from his parents, to be patient a little while and that a letter would soon come, very soon. I wasn't present on that occasion and can't quote Fr. Nikolay's precise words, but a letter came the next day. I asked Fr. Nikolay how he could have known about the letter, and he replied that he hadn't known, but it had just been 'a prayer answered'. But there were a lot of such 'prayers answered'.

Fr. Nikolay knew that his wife too had been arrested, and was very worried about his children: what if they were put in the Children's Home and brought up atheists! And then, as he was being shipped out of the camp, he was standing in a line of men as they waited for their ration of boiled water. A line of women was moving towards the same tap from the opposite direction, and when Fr. Nikolay reached it, to his amazement he saw his wife there. The prisoners hid them (it was strictly forbidden for men and women to talk), and Fr. Nikolay learnt the happy news that religious friends had taken the children in.

Fr. Nikolay's life was a complete torment, and perhaps even a martyrdom. Not long ago I received a short account of it from relatives of his, simply written and factual. It bears a striking resemblance in the facts it gives and in its style to the *Zhitiye*[152] of the archpriest Avvakum[153].

Nikolay Nikolayevich Gorski

Another visitor to the Krimkab was a former naval officer, now working in the brickworks, Nikolay Nikolayevich Gorski. In his day he had studied in the Naval College alongside the budding writers Kolbasev and Sobolyov, of whom he praised the former and cursed the latter—precisely for what, I forget. Nor will I say, so as not to encumber the history of Soviet literature with imprecise evidence, and all the more so as Gorski himself might have been in error. After finishing Naval College he served in one of the dreadnoughts, either Petropavlovsk or Sevastopol. When Yudenich[154] attacked, Gorski's ship was on the Neva, and the order was given to fire on Yudenich's positions, but there was delay in giving the coordinates. By then Yudenich, whom the Estonians had deserted at the crucial moment, had started to withdraw, and a number of large calibre shells fell on the advancing Reds. Naturally, a plot was discovered! Some of the crew were shot and Gorski, who had nothing to do with the gunnery, got ten years. I won't vouch for the accuracy of this information; in camp it was not done to question one another about their cases.

Gorski had had an impeccable upbringing and this meant that he was able to sustain entertaining conversation and to write interesting letters. Both skills had been of great assistance to Gorski in his career and we all welcomed him eagerly to the Krimkab and listened to him just as eagerly when he spoke on subjects of which we knew nothing ourselves; he had an extensive education and was interested in everything.

At home in the brickyard Gorski lived as man and wife with, as he put it, 'a nice little thief girl'. As his ten-year term approached its end the authorities began to place great trust in him and gave him command of a little ship, the Pioneer. Incidentally, his co-defendant Poiré was given command of the big tug Neva[155], in which capacity he continued after being released until his Neva was capsized by a huge wave and he drowned, together with his beloved dog, which used to protect him from the entirely criminal crew.

Georgi Mikhaylovich Osorgin

In my mind's eye I have a clear picture of Georgi Mikhaylovich Osorgin. He was of medium build, with fair hair and moustache, and always carried himself in a military manner: an upright bearing, a round hat slightly to one side ("three fingers above the right ear, two above the left"), always cheerful, smiling, witty—that's how I've always remembered him. There was a joke connected with him that went round the camp later: to the question "How are you?" he would reply "A lager kom a lager", thus adapting the well known French mot '*a la guerre comme a la guerre*'. He worked as chief clerk in the medical section and I often bumped into him scurrying between there and the USLON building on the landing stage, along the path between the Kremlin wall and the moat. He did a lot to save unfit members of the intelligentsia from general labour: he persuaded the doctors on the medical committees to lower their classifications of fitness for work, put many in the sick-bay or took them on as medical orderlies, for which it was occasionally necessary to know the Latin alphabet and to be able to tell iodine from castor oil. There was a shortage of medically qualified persons in the camp—there was even one occasion when an orderly wanted to do more to heal a prisoner and painted him all over with iodine: he died. Osorgin was a deeply religious man, and at Christmas and Easter applied to the Information and Investigation Department for a pass to attend church (those who applied were taken in a squad to the Onufriyevskaya church in the cemetery, which had been left for the handful of fisherman-monks). The church was Sergian, and the overwhelming majority of prisoner clergy didn't go there and didn't apply to attend.

He was put in the punishment block before the famous shooting of the autumn of 1929, but thanks to the usual muddle in the camp his wife came to visit him, and obtained permission in Kem. The point obviously was that his arrest was the act of the authorities on the island—they just hated him; his independence, cheerfulness, his refusal to let things get the better of him was a source of irritation to them. The authorities on the island hadn't notified the mainland of their intention to execute him, and in Kem their meeting was authorised.

News of Osorgin's arrest alarmed us all in the Krimkab and then I met him, quite by chance, walking along the path by the Kremlin wall arm in arm an elegant brunette who was slightly taller than him and he introduced her—it was his wife, whose maiden name was Golitsyn. There was nothing about him to indicate that he'd just emerged from the punishment block; he was just as cheerful, happy, slightly ironic as ever. It emerged later that the authorities, embarrassed at the arrival of his wife on authority higher than their own, had let him out on his word of honour as an officer for a period a little less than had been proposed for the visit (there were fewer days left until the date set for his execution) on condition that he should tell his wife nothing of the fate that awaited him. And he kept his word! She didn't know that he'd been sentenced to death by the island authorities. She returned to Moscow and soon left for Paris—at that time any Soviet citizen could obtain a passport for foreign currency.

In 1967 in Oxford, where I'd gone to receive an honorary Doctorate of the University, I told Osorgin's sister Sofiya Mikhaylovna about his being shot. She and his widow (who had remarried in Paris) had been convinced that he'd died of natural causes.

Eduard Karlovich Rozenberg

My greatest and, I suppose, only true friend was Eduard Karlovich Rozenberg. He was more cheerful, had more zest for life, than anyone else that I have known.

He was of medium build, with a large head and big feet, on which—a characteristic detail comes to mind—he wore 'Jimmi' shoes with the pointed toes fashionable in the '20s. It goes without saying that such shoes were not to be had in camp, and what he wore there I can't recall—I merely remember what was typical of him. He had a large head, a wide, intelligent forehead and an almost irrepressible smile beamed from his face. He smiled not only with his lips but with his entire face; his lips, by contrast, he kept straight so as to suppress the smile, giving the impression that he was smiling with his mouth full—full of laughter that was about to burst forth. He was a great practical joker, the founder of our second life in the Cosmic Academy, with its anthem, coat of arms, walking-sticks, footstraps on our trousers, excursions together and cult of Pushkin's Lycée. One of our 'lecture halls' was actually on Litseyskaya Street, but to swear eternal friendship to each other we went to Parnas in the Aleksandr Park in Tsarskoye Selo, where right on the top we had our secret stump of a hundred-year-old oak tree. He taught himself Latin and Greek, made friends easily and bore lightly the cares of his unsettled existence, of which there were many, the greatest of which was increasing deafness. Deafness! Fancy one so sociable being deaf!

He came from Peterhof, where his father was director of the imperial pharmacy—a typical German, stout, neat, quiet, like many a pharmacist. His mother was Finnish, a convert from Lutheranism to Orthodoxy. Eduard was not like a German, except perhaps for his unusual tidiness, a purely German trait. His elder brother Volodya (Waldemar), on the other hand, was a German in looks and ways. He was an enthusiastic yachtsman, which enabled him to be an instructor in a sailing school before he was arrested.

Their father preferred Waldemar and didn't care for Fedya. When, after 1917, the pharmacy ceased to be 'imperial' and became an ordinary municipal one, and his father's salary was reduced, Fedya, then at the local grammar school, had to earn his living as a night-time telegraph operator. Life was rendered difficult by his father's quarrelling with his mother, who had converted to Orthodoxy. Fedya (I'll explain later why we called him that and not Edey) loved his father, but loved his mother more and understood her unhappiness. On leaving school (by then a 'united working class' Soviet school) Fedya and his brother took two rooms in Zverinskaya Street in Leningrad and started work in the Financial Directorate on the Griboyedov Canal. In his free time he went to lectures and meetings at the Institute of the History of Art on St Isaac's Square. It was at that time (about 1926) that on his initiative the Cosmic Academy of Sciences came into being; I joined that light-hearted circle of eight friends in 1927, and I consider that our friendship started in that year.

Cheerful people are often superficial but this was not so of Fedya. His attitude to the world about him was serious in the highest degree, and he loved to help people. He would see to every detail. In particular, when I became a family man he was very keen on our living in a dacha furnished as a German house, and found us one in the German houses of Old Peterhof, in the Lugovoy Park. Zina and I went out to inspect one of his proposals: a big drawing room, full of embroideries, little hangings, little plates with views of Peterhof and Germany, and a centenarian parrot that spoke German and would have to live with us. Another time we went with him and Mikhail Ivanovich Steblin-Kamenski to Novgorod. We went on a motorboat belonging to a Novgorod friend of Fedya's to see Nikolay Lipny, to Khutyn, walked to Voltovo, to the Yuriyev monastery. By that time Fedya had a camera, and took a lot of snapshots, particularly of scenes of our 'drunkenness' (in actual fact our mugs contained nothing more than milk).

I kept dreaming that he would take us to Peterhof by yacht, but he didn't have the time for that.

172

He attended the meetings of Khelfernak at Andreyev's, and later went to two or three meetings of the 'Brotherhood of Serafim of Sarov'. By that time his mother had died and he took the bereavement very hard. At the funeral a dispute broke out between the Orthodox priest and the Lutheran pastor as to who was to conduct the service. Strictly speaking, it should have been the priest according to the Orthodox rite, and so it was. It was natural for Fedya to take an interest in questions of faith, especially at the time when the persecution of the Church was gaining momentum. In 1927 he decided to adopt Orthodoxy. For that he didn't have to be baptised again, it was sufficient to undergo the rite of anointing. I remember him in the church of the Home for Aged Artists on Petrovski Island, where the universally loved Fr. Viktorin was the incumbent; he was later canonised by the Church in Exile after his martyr's death in Siberia. Fedya was terribly excited and couldn't undo his boots for Fr. Viktorin to anoint his feet with the myrrh. The name Fedya was given him by Fr. Viktorin in error. We called him Edey at the time, but the Father misheard it as Fedya (Fedor)—I don't know why, but this suited Eduard uncommonly well. He attended Orthodox services diligently, and had been familiar with them all his life. Always sincere in the extreme, he made no secret of his conversion at work. His colleague Sofiya Levina enthusiastically copied all Church material for the Brotherhood—and in particular, the Epistle of the Bishops of Solovki, directed against the servile policies of Metropolitan Sergiy.

On Solovki Fedya and I were both in the Kremlin, at first in different companies (nos. 13, 14 and 3) and later in the same cell. He used to go off early to work and return late, and I too was very busy. At times we didn't see one another for a few days. We didn't waste time so as to get some sleep, and had to write to one another. Fedya always thought up original ways of doing this. Once, irritated by my untidiness, he wrote in the dirty tea-stain in my enamel mug, which I'd left unwashed "Only to be washed with tea". Another time I received a note in verse pinned to my blanket. I remember that one of the verses began *Otoshchavshi vovse zhivotishkom / Odolzhit' proshu odnim rublishkom.* [Having become quite thin in the tummy, I beg you to oblige me with a ruble] ... Fedya worked under the chief book-keeper on the Solovetski farm, Viktor Ostrovidov, who was occasionally able to let Fedya have some spring onions or a little soured cream, which he unfailingly shared with me and the other occupants of the cell. To this day finely chopped spring onions and soured cream seem to me a dish fit for a tsar.

Vladimir Yulyanovich Korolenko

In 1931 Vladimir Yulyanovich Korolenko appeared on the Krimkab horizon. Before me was a face, slightly ironic, ready to be sociable, but far from round; the mouth was strong, reminiscent of the bow of a rowing boat or the lip of a pot, ready to pour forth some interesting tale—tale, but not conversation, not intimate thoughts. There was in him a sort of invisible wall behind which he would not allow a fellow conversationalist to pass. In essence, we knew only two things about him: that he was a cousin of the writer V. G. Korolenko and that he was a lawyer by profession. He had lost the ring-finger of his left hand, and as a result the whole of his left hand was very expressive: a crab's claw? If ever he was telling us of some event in his legal experience and, as he gesticulated, let fall his left hand, that meant that he was putting a definite full stop to his story. And his stories always did reach a conclusion: reaching a conclusion is probably a habit with the legal profession. In the Krimkab he mostly made for Yuliya Danzas. Those two secretive people found common ground in some higher, 'refined' region. She was glad to see him, because she felt at ease in his company; he didn't bother her about things which she didn't wish to reveal, and into which Volodya Razdolski, thanks to his lack of breeding, was always trying to worm his way.

Korolenko aroused a friendly response in me. He, like myself, had an 'all-island' pass, and we often arranged to walk together. Most often we would go down the road to Savvatiy. In winter he wore an astrakhan cap with ear-flaps of slightly unusual pattern. No one else, I think, could have had one like it. It was part of his personality. Strange? That's how it was.

He too liked boyish amusements. Remembering my childhood on the Gulf of Finland, I used to like playing at 'ducks and drakes' and we used to hold competitions to see who could produce most bounces. I can't remember which of us used to win! He was about fifty, no less, but his ability in this sport was considerable. I remember one evening on the Savvatiyev road. We came to a lake that was sheltered from the wind by thick forest. It was late autumn and the water was covered with a thick layer of ice. Darkness was falling, and the frozen surface looked black. If we tossed a pebble onto the surface of the ice it slid for an uncommon distance and vanished without trace. We became absorbed in this activity, and when it was almost completely dark we began throwing stones upwards. They fell vertically, broke through the ice, under which a white bubble of air formed and began to move away from the bank until it vanished on reaching open water. This charmed us magically into a relaxed state. It seemed that we were setting free those white creatures which formed beneath the black surface of the young ice. We went back to the Kremlin quite late, breaking all the rules governing our passes, but the sentry, with black cuffs on his sleeves, a black collar on his greatcoat and a black band on his cap, let us off. Thus a happy walk ended happily, without any threats of the punishment block...

Korolenko's sentence was death, commuted to ten years. He was therefore not liable to be transferred from Solovki, whereas friends began to request my presence in Medvezhya Gora as an 'irreplaceable' careful worker, of which there was great need.

We decided to leave a permanent record of our presence on Solovki. Korolenko obtained a hammer and chisel, and we set off into the forest down the Muksalma road to look for a suitable stone on which to carve our names, and found one to the right of the road. It was a hilly region, with long hills and a long, narrow lake between them. A boulder lay right on the very top of one hill; as I recall, it was about three or four metres long (very approximately) and about shoulder high (that's more precise). We began to carve our surnames, and it was hard work. We paid two visits to the spot and managed to carve 'Korol' above and 'Likhach' below, in letters about the size of one's palm.

The last time that I went back to the Kremlin I found that I was being transported out. That time I was in luck, and was transferred to Kem. My 'suitcase' was ready packed; it was made of plywood, covered in a stolen sheet and painted brown. It turned out to be very useful, and we kept it until after the blockade, in use by my mother.

I was very sorry that we didn't have time to finish carving our names, and asked Korolenko to finish the job. Later he sent word to me via someone at Medvezhya Gora that the inscription was complete.

And at Medvezhya Gora I was told why Korolenko had a finger missing. He'd cut it off himself as an act of penitence for slandering someone during investigation, or for signing something or behaving unworthily in some way or other. That's why he'd been locked up, and he often said that when he was released he would get a job as a keeper on a lighthouse a long way from people...

Whatever the case, I am very sorry for him, and I thank him for finding some relief in my company...

A Few Fragments

Don't think that the Krimkab, the Museum and Solteatr were the only places where Solovki prisoners gathered for philosophical conversation. I got to know a young man of twenty-five by the name of Chekhovski, who worked at the Quality Control Station (there is now an airfield on the site). One day in the summer of 1929 he invited me to go and visit him. I went up to his place on the first floor, and over tea (made from some kind of leaves) he suddenly asked me about my views on Freemasonry. I replied that I hardly knew anything about it. He invited me to visit him and find out more about it, but I, fortunately, declined.

At the height of the supposed existence of the plot on Solovki 'to seize Solovki and then overthrow Soviet power in the country' I met a group of 'plotters' being driven 'at the double' between the Nikolski Gates and the second gates back to the punishment block from interrogation in the USLON building. The escorts were shouting, cocking their weapons and ordering everyone they met to stand still. And suddenly one of those being 'doubled', who with difficulty could still be identified as a young man, greeted me with just his eyes. I realised—it was Chekhovski. I took off my student's cap and bowed low to his receding figure. Obviously, he'd been denounced, and it is to this that I ascribe the note on my own dossier "Connected with insurgents on Solovki".

In the notes that I began to make on Solovki it states that somewhere around that bay where Degtyarev caught me the graves can be found of those who had been 'operated on', that is, in the Solovki terminology of the time, shot individually. 'Operations' were carried out in the daytime. The victim's hands were tied behind his back with wire and he was dragged by two secret policemen, one to each arm, under the bell-tower (all movement of personnel in the Kremlin yard was suspended). There were two 'olives' (bullets) for each person who was to be shot, then along came a horse with the box, the remains were removed and women were called in to wash down the stairs to the ground floor and everything else. The miserable nag took the corpses off, and that was that.

I remember the name of the commander of the special detachment that carried out the individual shootings of hooligans—Chernyavski, a man with a ponderous voice and excessively smart boots. He shot, among others, a boy of thirteen, whom the secret police couldn't handle.

In my notes there is also a reference: "'Solovki prompartiya case'. Forgery of dry ration coupons. Addition to Hessen: death. My and Razdolski's purchases of dry rations. Hidden in the company. Lots were drawn, I went to fetch. Interest in the company. Smell of stale fish by the kvas-brewery." These days I can't altogether decipher it all, but it's obvious that we were at serious risk of 'ending up in a wooden box', not knowing whether our dry ration coupons were genuine or counterfeit, but hunger drove us to take that chance. The boredom of the monotonous and poor-quality food was really unbearable. You sometimes couldn't keep it down.

In no. 6 company in 1928–29 there were quite a few Roman Catholic priests together with the orthodox clergy. In contrast to the Orthodox, the former were allowed to hold services in their cells, and later they were given the chapel of St. Herman[156] in the forest for their devotions. Many of them worked in the laundry, where they were in charge of the laundresses—mostly prostitutes. They behaved with great dignity, and the prostitutes respected them. In 1929 they were given the status of politicals and released from work. This status was also enjoyed by the anarchists on Bolshoi Muksalom island, where conditions were relatively tolerable, but the Roman Catholics were taken to live in the Trinity 'mission' on Anzer. I was on Anzer once, collecting a group of teenagers for the labour colony, and as I passed their quarters I met the Roman Catholics bringing a container of water on a cart. They looked after themselves.

There is quite a lot about the Roman Catholics in Russia, in Siberia and on Solovki in the book by deacon Vasili that I have already mentioned, where he quotes Yuliya Danzas. Their isolated existence makes them of little interest for my memoirs. I will make one observation, however, which Danzas omits: the situation of the Catholic clergy on Solovki was significantly better than that of the Orthodox. It was considered that the Russian clergy had the right to go to the monastic Onufriyevskaya church in accordance with special lists drawn up in advance by the Admin. department. The only prisoners who went there were those who didn't really understand Church affairs and simply couldn't do without church services. One of these was, by the way, Osorgin, who was, furthermore, friendly with the priest Viktor Ostrovidov.

Even in relatively tolerable conditions as we were in the Kremlin, in the stone buildings left us by the monks, we were constantly ill at ease. The Information and Investigation Department was for ever concocting various cases, political and criminal. People were picked up for having a bit of bread too much, for 'not going out to work', for refusing to saw up crosses in the cemetery to the martial sound of the wind band of the 'musical squad' of no. 7 company. When I fell ill, which, thank God, happened seldom, I could have gone mad from the regimental marches which former officers of the tsarist army selfishly practised.

In summer transport was laid on, sometimes to the mainland, some-times into the interior of the island or to other islands such as Muk-salma, Bolshoy Zaytski and Anzer. I kept my things in readiness, as one wasn't given time to pack. The shout would be "Fly out like a bullet with your things", and those who were slow were beaten with cudgels. At all events you learnt to dress quickly, for whatever purpose,and when you went to bed you left your underpants in your trousers and your shirt in your *tolstovka*. Particular attention went to footcloths, which had to be put on properly without creases that would chafe your feet.

The constant anxiety about being summoned for transport waned only with the closure of the sea crossing. Intra-island moves too were reduced at that time.

Leaving Solovki

In the summer of 1931 they began transferring 'slave labour' from Solovki to the construction work on the White Sea-Baltic Canal, which had opened unofficially. The length of one's remaining sen-tence was taken into consideration. Vladimir Rakov left Solovki, as did Fedya Rozenberg and numerous others, but I was unaffected. By that time Meyer had gone, as had Polovtseva and Sukhov, and life became very dull. Even the colony of juvenile criminals was taken away. Ivan Yakovlevich Komissarov, king of the non-politicals on Solovki, also vanished only to appear later as warden of the famous Colony for juvenile criminals at Bolshevo.

At Medvezhya Gora Fedya moved at once into a good accounting job, as the need for qualified bookkeepers was always acute in the camps. He sent appeal after appeal for me as an 'outstanding specialist bookkeeper' to take charge of the main card-index of Belomorstroy. I was detailed for transport. Downstairs in the musicians' squad the trumpeter Vladimir Vladimirovich Olokhov—sometime colonel of the Semyonovski regiment— was detailed to travel with me. The musicians gave him a ceremonious farewell, with speeches and the playing of the march 'Old friends' (that was, I believe, one of the popular marches of the old army, but under a different title). The only horse on Solovki, which usually pulled corpses, was harnessed up and took our belongings (others too were being transferred). By that time I no longer had my basket (it had been stolen) but my plywood suitcase was ready. It was so strong that it didn't break even when it fell off the very top of the load. We were taken to the quarantine, stripped and made to sit naked in no. 2 bath-house waiting for our clothes to be returned from the delouser. We waited several hours and food was sent to us from the musicians' squad. Then as evening was approaching the order came 'Back to the cells'. We were there another fortnight or so, then came another summons, more speeches (this time shorter) and the march again. Back to the bath-house, and again the order 'Back to the cells'. The Information and Investigation department wouldn't release us.

I mentioned earlier that a boy from the Information and Investigation department invited me one evening and showed me my dossier, on the top of which was the note 'Connected with insurgents on Solovki'.

After being called out for the third time, Vladimir Vladimirovich and I left without speeches and marches, we were finally sent to the mainland. He and I met later in Leningrad on Kamennoostrovski Prospekt, and a young man was leading him by the arm: he was now totally blind. His wife had died and he was living with his daughters. Just before the [Second World] War, when attitudes towards the Russian army had changed, his daughters had handed back the colours of the Semyonovski regiment which they had been keeping. Vladimir Vladimirovich had saved them in 1917, when the rout of the army was taking place, by wrapping them round himself and carrying them from the front; so he told me.

At Kem we had to spend the night at Vegeraksha (it was explained to me that this name meant 'abode of witches' in Finnish)—a terrible place because of the lawlessness that took place there. In the morning we were put in first-class prison carriages with three-tier bunks,

179

and I lay on the top one so as to sleep... Next morning, a day later, we reached Medvezhya Gora [Bear Mountain] (abbreviated to Medgora).

Medvezhya Gora greeted us with sunshine, which we hadn't seen for a long time (since summer) on Solovki, and with clean, recently fallen snow. That day I experienced a real sense of liberation, which was not repeated when I was set free on 8 August 1932.

We were taken to a camp beside Lake Onega and set down in the square in the middle of the barracks. Suddenly I heard a friendly woman's voice call "Dima Likhachev!" It can have been granted to few, I think, to hear such a summons out of a camp transport. It was one of Fedya Rozenberg's colleagues: he'd phoned into the camp from the Directorate of Construction and told her to take me to the barrack. I was given the top bunk in one of the 'improved' railway carriages, but right under the chimney of the little stove. On cold nights this stove was so stoked up that the chimney became red hot, and I had to protect myself from it with my fur jacket and couldn't sleep for the heat. In the morning, however, I had a regal wash. There were iron wash-hand basins in the street, in which the water sometimes froze. I stripped to the waist and revelled in the cold, the air, the light.

I was given a pass which permitted me to go through the 'free' part of Medgora (Medvezhya Gora) to the Directorate building. There Fedya met me and sat me down at the main card-index of the Belomorkanal, but ordered me not to work. For the first few days he did all the work for me, staying until late in the evening, and then allowed me to do something on condition that I didn't touch the accounts so that I should not be shown up as a novice. "An experienced accountant can almost play tunes on the books," he said. He lived in conditions that were almost private by camp standards: not far from the Directorate was a barrack with camp-beds. Volodya Rakov and I used to go to him for lunch, and Volodya usually cooked. We would sit on Fedya's camp-bed and all eat from the same saucepan. Not far away, I remember, was the bed of the former bookkeeper of the Mikhaylovski Theatre in Leningrad, a German named Koppe, and he even had a mincing machine. Fedya often went to 'Koppechka', as he called him, for domestic utensils. In the same barrack I also saw the singer Ksendzovski, Nekrasov, the Minister of the Provisional Government, and the violinist Heifetz. I was told that the latter was the brother of a pianist who had gone to the USA. He was tall and thin and of superior appearance but I never really ascertained whether or not he was the brother of the famous pianist[157].

I usually went to work half an hour early, and in the spacious buildings of the Directorate a fine tenor voice sang before the start of work. It was so remarkable to hear real music after years of a military band practising a routine march right under my cell window in no. 7 company.

My pass gave me the chance to go to the 'free' side of Medgora, to call at a bookstall and one day even to spend some time with Fedya, Volodya Rakov and a former military officer by the name of Radziyevski in a beer-shop, which later served Fedya as the subject for endless jokes. In Medgora I met Yuliya Danzas, became friendly with Mosolov (from a good aristocratic family), who proposed that I should go and work with him on hydraulics and live in a tent (I turned the offer down in the end, but went to a number of hydraulic engineering sites). Yuliya Danzas pointed out to me a former baker who bore a striking resemblance to Nikolay II, and even sounded like him; the master, she told me, was a very fine baritone. The baker had been picked up merely on account of this resemblance, and in the '30s would be shot out of hand for it—that was safer.

Zvanka and Tikhvin. Release.

The second half of my time on the White Sea-Baltic Canal is connected with Dmitri Pavlovich Kallistov.

He'd been sentenced to five years under the KAN case, although we hadn't accepted him as a member. He'd given his inaugural lecture to KAN, but we'd refrained from inviting him to meetings. He'd been packed off to Solovki with us but had only spent a week on the island; he'd been returned to Kem on the next boat, where he'd been put to work in the Solovetski Camps Directorate and had soon obtained permission to live in a private flat. That was measure of his energy and ability.

Kallistov and Oscar Vladimirovich Gilinski, an American citizen serving a ten-year sentence for currency speculation, worked in the goods despatch section.

Kallistov came to Medgora now and then to obtain instructions and despatch notes. He sent me word by a third party to ask whether I was prepared to go and work at Zvanka. I had no clear idea of what the work involved, but I was seduced by the closeness to Leningrad and my parents, and the possibility of seeing them more often and—most importantly—the absence of a camp regime. In those days, the nearer a prisoner came to the end of his sentence, the less strict were the security measures. It seemed to me quite normal to be working at Zvanka in conditions of comparative freedom.

Quite a long time had gone by (certainly, at least a month) when suddenly I was called up and told that Kallistov had come from Zvanka and wanted me to meet him as soon as possible with my belongings. I rushed off to shave and in my excitement cut my face. Seeing me in that state Kallistov laughed: he was pleased.

At Zvanka Kallistov arranged for me to live in the same place as himself, a little cottage belonging to the elderly Matryona Kononovna, not far from Volkhov. There I had a bed with a soft mattress and a soft pillow behind a curtain in the room that served as the dining room. I slept there even in the daytime after night-duty at the station. Our third despatcher, Gilinski, had taken a whole flat near the station, paying in dollars. I seldom saw him; he used to travel from Zvanka not only to Leningrad but also to Moscow, and Kallistov and I did all the duties at the station together. The annoying thing for me was that Kallistov too would often go off to see his wife in Leningrad, and then I had to work the clock round. The work was quite demanding. We had a desk in the same room as the shunting despatcher. Zvanka was a big marshalling point, where goods trains were made up. The shunting despatcher had a big display on which the tracks were shown on which rolling stock was positioned for provisional destinations. Guards, wrapped up to the eyeballs against the cold on the open platform of the rear wagon, were constantly tottering into the despatcher's room in clouds of steam. From their heavy satchels they took out documents for every wagon and put them on the despatcher's desk, and with the shunting despatcher hurrying us along we had to check them all and match them with despatch notes and addresses for the camp. The work demanded total concentration, and by five in the morning one's attention was apt to wane; I used to sleep standing up, never mind sitting down. Once I let a whole train go with a few wagons unaddressed. The mistake could have cost me another sentence. But I got away with it...

It makes me shudder to think how I used to crawl under wagons to take a short cut to rolling-stock standing somewhere on track 21 to check out something that had shown up in the paperwork. Rolling-stock was always on the move in several directions, and those dashes of mine underneath wagons were highly dangerous, but I developed a sort of bravado. I have already said that after the experience of avoiding execution by good luck I realised that every day that I lived was a gift from God. Here at Zvanka, however, I developed a sort of indifference to my fate. "What will be, will be. "

I went to Leningrad twice, and once took a box at the ballet at the Mariinski theatre. I bumped into my University friend Dmitri Lvovich Shcherba in the Aleksandrovski Garden, but as soon as he learned that I'd 'run away from the camp' shied away from me. The second time I was picked up by a patrol just outside Leningrad. I gave a telephone number by which they could confirm that I really was a despatcher at Zvanka, and had the right to go through Leningrad. They checked up, and some kind person at the other end confirmed my story (although, of course, it wasn't true: there was no going to Leningrad without permission). Who that person was that saved me from being arrested (and, that means, another 'case') I don't know, but I remember him with gratitude.

Once a request came to identify the accountants in an approaching prison-train, so as to send them to Medgora. We weren't supposed to re-address consignments of people; they just went through unchecked. But there was obviously an acute shortage of accountants such a switch could save a few people from working as navvies. I set off for the separate track where the cars were standing, went into a car and sensed with particular keenness that air of grief that suffused all the camps. I remember the reply of one educated man of my age to my question about his profession: "Pianist and accompanist. I can speak English, French and German." I told him emphatically "I'm putting you down as an accountant. Remember that!" For some reason I often think of that incident. Who was he, and how did Fate treat him later?

Fortunately I never had any other such jobs allocating people.

In spring Kallistov told me that the despatch section at Tikhvin was being 'strengthened', as the wagons from our distribution point passed through there along the branch line. I couldn't see the point of moving there and opposed the idea. Then he admitted that while we'd been in Zvanka he'd got into serious official trouble and was counting on the move to escape. So we moved. He quickly found us a room there through contacts in the Jewish community. A despatcher called Bakshteyn who spoke good Yiddish had to move with us; Kal-

183

listov pretended to be a *goysher* from Austria and spoke mercilessly broken German, supposedly the Austrian dialect of Yiddish. A pointswoman with two children rented us a nice room.

We moved to Tikhvin, where life had ceased completely: there wasn't a single new building, the water supply didn't work, and the inhabitants, for the most part, were old men and women. But it was a beautiful place, as beautiful as a forest in late autumn can be.

There we met a paymaster who had known the whole Rimski-Korsakov family, and the people who lived in the Korsakov's house; we attended the festival of the Mother of God of Tikhvin and observed the excitement of the pilgrims at a miracle of healing performed in their presence.

My mother and younger brother came down for the summer. He was a marvellous swimmer and used to dive into the Tikhvinka river from the bridge; the local boys nicknamed him 'skipping-rope'.

There was too a family of former 'landowners'—a mother and two daughters. The father had been shot, and the daughters worked as clerks in the station. Their mother tried to maintain some level of education in them, and spoke to them in German (she herself was, I think, a German). Kallistov had lived in Vienna as a boy, and was able to say a few words to them when they met; later he learned to speak excellent German.

Sometimes there would be no consignments for Belbaltstroy all day, and I even went in my brother's boat and rode his bicycle. Once I was knocked off by a runaway droshky. I had no time to realise what was happening, I merely felt the warmth of the horse and next moment I was lying in the sand, which saved me from broken bones and bruises. I continued my riding without care and attention even in Leningrad. Once I turned off Dvortsovy bridge at great speed and almost went under a car. This gave me such a fright that since then I have not ridden a bicycle. Kallistov was significantly more active than me and in summer in Tikhvin he suggested a trip to Staraya Ladoga to visit the twelfth century church and the fortress. Bakshteyn could stand in for us at the station. We had to take the train to Volkhov station and from there the steamer to Staraya Ladoga so we had to leave very early, and, best of all, by a goods train carrying sand for ballast.

As soon as the train moved off the sand started to move about, to fall on us, blinding us, getting into our clothes and our hair, but our main fear was that it would sweep us off the train as it slid about underneath us. We couldn't stop the train, however, and we reached

Volkhov station, badly scared and covered with sand, just as the steamer left.

I won't give a general description of Staraya Ladoga...

We grew tired of walking and called into a local tea-house and the impression that it gave me was the strongest of the day, strange though that may seem! It was a two-storey building not far from the Volkhov. The ground floor was the kitchen and living quarters. We went up the spiral staircase to the second floor and found ourselves in a big, well-lit room with windows on all four sides. There were tables covered with white cloths, and on each a pile of slices of black bread and *sitnik*[158]. People were sitting at the tables in groups of two or three, eating and talking after a hard day's work. There was no wine or beer, and everything was tidy and quiet. We chose a table by the window with a view over the Volkhov, and were each brought a large pot of hot water and a smaller one of freshly brewed tea. We were brought a sugar bowl with lumps of hard sugar, which allowed us to drink *vprikusku*[159] if we wished. How often have I since thought that we used to have such tea-houses everywhere. It was no accident that they were done away with: it was too pleasant to sit and chat in them—or rather, to hold conversations on various subjects. That was too dangerous for the powers that be. Work and keep quiet, believe everything official—that was all they wanted from us.

We left the lovely, clean, tea-house as darkness was falling, and to our surprise witnessed an unusual method of catching fish. Long rowing boats slid silently over the water and in them stood fishermen, one in the stern with an oar, the other in the bow, where a torch was burning, with a harpoon. At first we didn't realise what was going on. The boats were drifting downstream and the figures of the men were completely still. Then we realised that the fishermen were harpooning big fish which were attracted to the boats by the light of the torches.

By morning we'd reached Tikhvin, carrying fresh fish which we gave to our landlady. I've been on many trips since then, but that one I'll never forget...

On one other occasion in Zvanka I'd returned home in the daytime. As always, Matryona Kononovna gave me my food and put out the stove, and I went to bed behind my curtain. I slept heavily, almost in a coma. I was awoken by a terrible banging on the window at my feet, and looking up I saw Kallistov's eyes, wide with terror. He gestured for me to open the door, but I simply couldn't walk. I can't remember how, but he forced the door, came in, opened all the windows, got me dressed and dragged me into the street. He made me walk and walk. My legs were buckling under me, my head was splitting with pain, but I kept walking... Kallistov had saved me from carbon monoxide poisoning. It was my good fortune that he'd arrived in time, had been able to break in and had known how to deal with it.

That was one of those thousands of pieces of luck, thanks to which I'm still alive.

When I was in Tikhvin (it was the summer of 1932, as I recall) the collectivisation of agriculture was in full swing. We had no newspapers, no close ties of friendship in Tikhvin and were badly informed as to what was going on. And then this information came to us in personal form...

One evening Kallistov came home—that is, to the house of the pointswoman where we were lodging—with two pails full of milk, and asked for a jug to pour some out for the children; one pail was for me. He hadn't time to offer much explanation, grabbed a pail from our landlady and we were off with him to the station. On the way he told me "A very long train loaded with cows has arrived, they haven't been milked, and the girls with them are milking them and giving the milk to anybody that wants it".

Then I understood: agriculture was being wrecked, the peasantry destroyed; the cows were doomed. The empty shop counters were no accident.

Right at the beginning of August I received a summons to go to Medgora for my release documents. The canal was considered finished and all that were then due for release were being given early release without restrictions. I didn't know to what extent that applied to me personally or only to my sentence. I went to Medgora, stayed there two or three days and received a document in which it was stated that I, as a 'shock construction worker' was released forthwith and with full rights of residence anywhere in the territory of the USSR, that is, I was free to go home to Leningrad, to my parents!

All the co-defendants in my case were released with me, six months early—Tolya Terekhovko, Fedya Rozenberg, Volodya Rakov and the rest. And so I'd spent nine months in Shpalernaya, three years on the Island and the rest of the time (nine months) on the White Sea-Baltic Canal, at Medvezhya Gora, Zvanka and Tikhvin.

My mother and brother had so enjoyed being in Tikhvin that they implored me to stay there for the whole of August. I refused: I needed to register in Leningrad and find work. I had no confidence in the lasting nature of compassionate liberation by Stalin.

We were back in Leningrad in the first half of August. I had no difficulty with my registration, but finding work was trickier. Leningrad wasn't as it had been in the '20s; people were afraid of employing not only former prisoners, but also their relatives.

The Fate of My Friends after Solovki

And so the real impoverishment of thought in Leningrad began after the camps. People were scattered all over the country. Some had died, some were broken men. All were living in isolation, not daring to speak or even to think. Even their health was ruined.

The most fortunate of all were those who were abroad. Even in the mid-twenties Georgi Petrovich Fedotov, active member of the Meyer circle, had managed to go abroad. His numerous writings on Russian culture and Russian Orthodoxy are well known and there's no point in my writing about them. Those who were somewhat older and survived the war after going abroad—Askoldov-Alekseyev and Andreyevski—published there. Andreyevski published mainly the texts of his lectures given in the seminary at Jourdainville on theology, Russian literature, psychology and Church history. He also took the opportunity to tell the story of his circle, exaggerating slightly, it must be added, his role in the spiritual life of the '20s.

Nor did the philosophical experience of Meyer vanish without trace; in 1982, as I have said, his book *Filosofskiye sochineniya* [Philosophical Essays] came out in Paris. It contains an assortment of articles of various dates, including those that he worked out with us in the Krimkab and others which he wrote in exile in some Volga town. They had been collected, preserved and reproduced as an archive by Kseniya Polovtseva, who had shared his years of exile after the camp.

There was a surprising discrepancy between our fates. Generally speaking, those who had been given five years and came through Belbaltlag were given full freedom and went back to Leningrad (not for long, though—just until passports were introduced), whereas those that had had three years were released with internal exile.

Rozenberg, Terekhovko and Kallistov returned to Leningrad. Rakov too received full freedom, but had nowhere to register and went off to work in Petrozavodsk. Valya Morozova, who had been eighteen when sentenced, also stayed in Leningrad 'on her father's surety'. We used to meet, but not regularly, of course. I had no success in finding work, and everyone else was looking too. I wasn't even taken on as a bookkeeper in the furniture factory on Kamenoostrovski Prospekt. The feeling of being a financial burden to my parents, who were not very well off, was most galling. Finally my father found me a post as a proofreader in the *Komintern* printing house. I had a nasty attack of ulcers and was in hospital for a long time, but that's of no interest. The only person not afraid to visit me there was my University friend Dmitri Yevgenevich Maksimov, who had just begun to study twentieth century literature. I also met my University friend Vladimir Aleksandrovich Pokrovski, who had become disenchanted with literary studies and begun to study mathematics, although he had by then published a small but sound work on Bulgarin[160].

In 1933, driven to despair by my unsuccessful attempts at finding work, I accepted the invitation of Kallistov to go to Dmitrovlag and work as a volunteer. On the way I called on Razdolski in Moscow, on Bolshaya Polyanka. He was living in the premises of a former shop, which was divided up by curtains into cubicles in which there were beds. Volodya's bed was separated by sheets, and we had to sit together on it as there wasn't room for a chair, so in order to evade the unwelcome attention of his fellow inhabitants, we went to talk in a neighbouring beer-shop. On the way he told me that he was working as an accountant, that the owner of the 'shop' wanted to marry him to his daughter, that he had long since given up thinking about anything and had no friends in Moscow. In the beer-shop I became convinced that he was addicted to beer. He quickly became drunk and I had to pay for his beer out of the little money that I had. As we returned from the beer-shop we met the sculptor Amosov, who'd been on Solovki. He was blind drunk and it was impossible to talk to him, even though he recognised us.

At Dmitrov, fortunately, I couldn't get a job. To tell the truth I didn't try very hard, as the camp environment aroused in me a feeling of depression and reminded me of the worst aspects of Solovki. But I did see Meyer, who was working in the accounts section; I spent the night sleeping on a chair at Igor Svyatoslavich Delvig's, an acquaintance from Medvezhya Gora, and went back home. I learnt from

Delvig that he was keen on Gypsy music, and that the only place you could hear Gypsies at that time was in the flat belonging to the painter Serov's relations in Moscow, where he went nearly every day. I met others from my old Solovki days, all working like men possessed, and no one talked about topics of common interest, or they'd decided not to, so as not to get another sentence.

The fate of Gavril Osipovich Gordon was wretched. He received a second sentence as the result of his desire to share a 'discovery' of his with those about him. When the general passport system was introduced he was working in the publishing house which produced the 'Academia' series, and pointed out to his colleagues the article headed 'Passport' in the *Soviet Encyclopedia*, in which it said that the passport was 'a weapon of class oppression' or something of the sort.

At the time of the general terror he wrote to me in Solovki from Sverdlovsk, where he'd been sent after his first imprisonment on Solovki. He'd returned to Moscow, but hadn't been there long. During his second ten-year term he wrote to me from a camp on the Volga, saying that he was living 'excellently', writing the history of the foundation of some reservoir and at the same time compiling his autobiography. His 'excellent' life, however, came to an end in the camp by death from pure starvation.

In the interval between his exile to Sverdlovsk and his re-arrest in Moscow he came to see me in Leningrad to show his younger daughter Irina our city. He stayed with us in Lakhtinskaya Street and put his daughter up with an aunt who lived on Petrovski island in the Savina Home for Aged Artistes—the same one where Fr. Viktorin had officiated in the church, gathering about him many young people. Services were still held in the church, but Fr. Viktorin had been arrested. Gordon surprised me with his knowledge of liturgy. When, however, I met Irina a year later in a delicatessen on Bolshaya Polyanka in Moscow, she was afraid to be seen speaking to me; only recently we met again in 1989 in Uzkoye, half a century later. Aren't human bonds long-lasting! Her father had written *Povest o moyey zhizni* [The Story of My Life]—some 25 *avtorskiye listya*[161]—under incredible conditions in Dmitrovlag. These memoirs, according to her, contained hundreds of names of people who had crossed his path and must be uncommonly interesting.

At the very end of 1933 Yuliya Danzas came to see me at my parents' home on Lakhtinskaya Street. She came briskly up to the fourth floor and told us that she was working in the office of a garage while

189

waiting to go abroad, but she'd agreed to translate Rabelais with L. B. Kamenev[162], who was then in charge of a Moscow literary publisher (I can't remember now exactly what it was called). Since her release from the camp she'd managed to have an interview with Gorki, for whose release from the Peter and Paul Fortress she had petitioned before the Revolution. Gorki had obviously felt obliged to take an interest in what became of Yuliya Danzas. She'd even worked for him just after the October Revolution in the Commission for the Amelioration of the Lives of Scholars. She told us that she'd had a long *tête-à-tête* with Gorki, who'd contrived to dismiss his secretaries (all secret agents) on various errands. He'd promised to help with her emigration in return for her word of honour not to speak or write about her sufferings.

She didn't keep her word. The story is that the Pope himself absolved her from fulfilling her promise to Gorki...

After my release I met N. N. Gorski. He was off on an expedition for some oceanographic institution in Leningrad. His wife, Kambulova, lived not far from us in the Petrograd District, and she came to call as he had told her to. I was quite amazed at her beauty; I could have pinched myself and asked "Can this be?" Soon after her visit, however, I learnt a terrible thing: she'd been given the news of his re-arrest on the expedition and that same day, walking along Bolshoi Prospekt, she'd been run over by a tram and died on the spot.

Gorski called on me both at home and at the Academy of Sciences Press. I arranged for the publication of his little book *Thirty Days on the Drift-ice of the Caspian*. This was a success, the Press liked it, and it ran to a second edition. After the [Second World] War he worked in Novgorod, where he married one of his probationer-students. He was arrested again and ended up in Siberia, from where he wrote to me. He'd built himself a house in the forest out of old railway sleepers, where he was living alone in fearful poverty, and he asked me to buy a typewriter and send it to him. We were living in Baskov Lane at the time, and there was a commission shop not far away where I was able to buy him a portable. It reached him, he started to write and survived. One book was about the seas, another about water (*Water—Miracle of Nature*). He actually won some prize for the latter. After receiving full rehabilitation he lived in Moscow with the wife whom he'd married in Novgorod. I found her a job through my elder brother. I went to see him, but it was hard going; he was paranoid about being persecuted and suspected his wife of watching him (though who could take an interest in a man of ninety?). He died and I never heard of his wife again. One thing I can say: he attributed his longevity to his exceptional vital energy. I was always amazed at the way his eyes gleamed.

Sukhov too was in Leningrad for a short while. I managed to get hold of a couple of tickets for Meyerhold's production of the *Forest*. His company were appearing as guests in the Conservatoire, where there was a fine opera hall (I think that it was here that Delmas was appearing in *Carmen* when Blok fell for her charms). Ilinski[163] was in the cast and the set was aerial. The road along which Schastlivtsev and Neschastlivtsev walked hung in the air on ropes, and Ilinski caught a fish in the air and Gurmyzhski's declaration of love took place on a swing. Sukhov was delighted with every invention of Meyerhold's, and sitting beside him in the theatre was a real treat.

Unfortunately his stay in Leningrad after returning from Biysk[164], where he'd been in exile, was brief. He was expelled to some small town and died of cancer just before the war.

I particularly want to tell you about what became of Fedya Rozenberg. When we both returned to Leningrad from the White Sea-Baltic construction I was living in the communal flat in Lakhtinskaya Street (more precisely, three rooms) to which my parents had moved while I was imprisoned. Fedya often came to see us, as did Valya Morozova, Volodya Rakov, Tolya Terekhovko's sister Zoe, uncle Kolya, uncle Vasya and several of my co-defendants. Fedya brought liveliness, talked about new books, read poems and flirted with Valya and Zoe. I liked all that, but it didn't go on for long. Fedya, Tolya and Volodya weren't given passports. Fedya went off to Murmansk, where he was found work by Sofiya Markovna Levina; Tolya went to Borovichi and Volodya returned to Petrozavodsk. It became dangerous for people to meet together, especially former co-defendants. I'll give an account later of what happened to me. Soon, however, Fedya and Sofiya Markovna came back to Leningrad. During the blockade we no longer had the means of visiting one another. My family and I were compelled to leave for Kazan at the end of June 1942, and we left without even saying goodbye. Despite his deafness Fedya was enroled in a 'Latvian' militia, but was soon released. After the war Zina and I were very short of money and took any kind of work in publishing: we took manuscripts for '*montirovka*'. That meant that we had to cover up the messy places where there were corrections with little patches of paper so as to give the manuscripts a clean and legible appearance. Fedya had something to do with the publications of the Financial Institute, took us under his wing and gave us the opportunity to find additional work as proofreaders.

Fedya had a rare combination of qualities; cheerful to the point, at times, of frivolity, he was exceptionally industrious and had a sense of duty. He would stay at work on occasion until late at night, and at the same time would find time for a joke. He had the soul of a collector. Before he was arrested, when he was working in the tax office, he had collected copies of the tax returns of the most prominent Leningrad writers. The investigator couldn't make out (more precisely, couldn't make up his mind) to what extent it was possible to construct a supplementary charge out of those pieces of information which were taken from Fedya when he was searched. He took away from Solovki all the numbers of *Solovetskye ostrova* that came out while we were there, watercolours by the Ukrainians Petrash and Vovk, drawings by Smotritski, Solovki receipts and kopecks, and various forms, correctly supposing that in the future all these things would be of great value. When, however, some years after the war Fedya was again exiled and had to go unaccompanied to the Luga region, he and Sofiya decided to destroy all those materials. All I have left is one watercolour by either Vovk or Petrash showing the view from Vinograd's window on Solovki.

He managed to build a house in Luga for next to nothing. Kallistov and Arkasha Selivanov ('Arkashon', as we used to call him) went out to see him, but I had no time, to my deep regret. Fedya had changed: he'd become very irritable because of his increasing deafness, and indeed because of all that he'd been through. He began to smoke heavily and developed lung cancer. His suffering was beyond belief, and Sofiya Markovna begged the doctors to hasten his end...

He is buried in the Serafimov cemetery.

We have lost a good and talented man!

The Repression of the '30s

Nowadays it's often said and written that the population of the country was unaware of the scale of the horror of the deeds that Stalin perpetrated. I can testify as an inhabitant of Leningrad who had no connections, avoided making friends and spoke little with colleagues at work (I was doing piecework as a proofreader), that nevertheless I knew a lot.

We knew no details, of course, but we could see how the streets of Leningrad were emptied in 1935 after the murder of Kirov[165]. We were aware that train after train was leaving the stations carrying those who had been arrested and were to be exiled.

In 1932 famine struck in town and country. *Torgsiny*[166] were opened. All the gold that could be found in ordinary families was taken along to them—watches, earrings, brooches, engagement and wedding rings, silver icon-frames, etc. The only things not accepted were small precious stones; they had to be returned. I remember how upset my mother was when the assessor tore out rubies, emeralds and small diamonds and nonchalantly tossed them to one side into a box. It was suspected (and very likely true) that assessors appropriated not a few stones themselves. A great deal of gold was surrendered by members of my family, especially while I was in hospital in the autumn of '32 and the winter of '33: I had to be fattened up after a serious gastric haemorrhage so the famine must have reached the cities too.

We could judge the famine in the countryside from the markets. There peasant women (always only women) with children clinging to their dresses sold embroidered towels for a song: these were family heirlooms, the most precious things that they'd been able to snatch up as they fled collectivisation. They were refugees!

I knew what refugees were from the First World War and the Civil War, but there was no comparison. One of us bought two embroidered towels at market (the woman had begged us so insistently to buy), and with them the woes of others came to our house...

One after another refugee women came asking to be taken on as servants. It was very easy and cheap to find a maid, as long as the woman had a passport for registration purposes. But few had...

That was how Tamara Mikhaylovna came to us. She nursed our children, lived out the blockade and evacuation to Kazan with us, returned with us to Leningrad and helped us right up to her death. She had fled the village of Sychovka in Smolensk province following her father, who had found work as a caretaker in Leningrad. She was our children's second nurse. The first left us after a very short time to get married. But I'm getting ahead of myself. I'll go back to the first half of the '30s, to the destruction of the peasants.

In the winter of 1933 the women refugees from the villages used to spend the nights sitting on the staircases in blocks of flats with their children. Caretakers were soon told not to let them in, but they would arrive late, and in the morning people going to work could see the evidence of their nocturnal sojourn. I could see that someone was living on the top of the stairs where our flat was. There was a big window and a large landing, and a number of families with children spent the nights there. But then came a new order: all staircases were to be locked in the evening. Front doors were mended and locks fitted, caretakers were given door-bells and yard gates were locked; theatres and concert halls stood empty.

Once (it must have been in the winter of 1933–34) I was returning from the Filarmoniya. There was a sharp frost. From the platform of the tram in Bolshoi Prospekt I could see no. 44, which had a deeply recessed entrance. The gate, which had been locked for the night, was at the back (it's still there—with its sign saying 'Kindergarten'). At the outer side of the entrance, almost in the street, peasant women were standing, holding table-cloths or sheets to form make-shift shelters for their children, lying in the recess, to protect them from the freezing wind... To this day I can't forget that sight. Every time I pass that house today I reproach myself with not having gone back and at least taken a bite for them to eat!

There was no escaping the peasants in towns.

One day Tamara, whom we had by then taken on as nurse to the children, brought us some hand-woven linen towels that she'd bought for next to nothing; they were decorated with a red pattern and had obviously been used to adorn the icons in some peasant hut, as was the custom. We had them in the family for a long time, and I could always feel grief in them. I also saw half-burnt *teplushki*[167] in which frozen displaced *kulaki*[168] had tried to light a fire and had burnt themselves. I heard stories of people locked in goods wagons throwing their children out of the windows at stations with labels attached, saying things like "Dear People, Take pity on this little one and look after her. She's called Mariya". As late as the fifties we from the Old Russian Literature Department, attending an 'Old Russian Literature Day' that we'd organised in Vologda, saw a church which had been in its time a transfer point for dispossessed *kulaks*. There were frescos in it, but not one of them had been damaged by those families, children or adults. Those peasants were people of high moral principles.

The stories that circulated were a sign that people knew of Stalin's wickedness. I'll only quote one here, and it bears a sort of 'mark of time'. A peasant woman comes to town and says: "There's a great big terrible man with a moustache hanging up, and there's a sign above him '*Zaem pyatiletku v chetyre goda!*'[169]. It was true, there were posters up with a portrait of Stalin and a slogan urging people to subscribe to the loan 'Five-year Plan in Four Years'. Why they had to urge people was not clear—subscription was compulsory. Korney Chukovski began to make systematic notes of political anecdotes, but when searches were taking place, at the very start of the '30s, he destroyed a big book of them. I was told this by Dmitri Yevgenevich Maksimov, who used to visit Chukovski.

People already knew about widespread arrests in the '20s. When I was arrested my parents were given no end of advice—what to put in parcels, what to buy in preparation for exile, how to protect oneself from lice in prison, where and how to present pleas. Everybody in Leningrad was ready for sudden arrest, the arbitrary nature of which no-one doubted. Therefore the assurances that "It'll be sorted out and I'll be released" were completely empty words. Usually it was the people being arrested who calmed their families in this way, and their relatives pretended to believe them. It was a complete pretence on both sides. Only a tiny minority of those 'taken' had a faint hope of returning home.

There were widespread arrests in the Academy of Sciences Press, where I was working as a scientific proofreader, and a particularly large number in our department, where almost all the staff were 'formers'. After the murder of Kirov I met the manageress of the personnel department—a young woman whom we all called Rorka for short—running along the corridor in the Press. As she passed she tossed at me "I'm making up a list of nobility, and I've put you down." I realised at once that to be on such a list boded nothing good, and I said straight away "No, I'm not nobility, cross me off!" and added that my father was a *lichny dvoryanin*, and that meant that nobility had been conferred on him because of his grade in the civil service, and

195

was not inheritable by his children. Rorka replied something like "It's a long list, and all the names are numbered. Just imagine the work—I'm not going to write it all out again". I told her that I would pay for a typist to do it, and she agreed. Two or three weeks went by and one morning I arrived for work and began to read my proofs. After about an hour I realised that the room was almost deserted; there were only two or three there. Shturts, the principal of the department and the technical editor Lev Aleksandrovich Fedorov were reading proofs as well. I went up to Fedorov and asked "Why isn't there anybody here? Is there a production meeting?" Fedorov replied quietly, without looking up or taking his eyes off the page, "What, don't you understand? They've all been arrested!" I sat back down.

One lady in the press said "If St Isaac's Cathedral isn't there in the morning, pretend it's always been that way". And that's right! Nobody ever noticed anything (out loud, that is!).

It wasn't only members of the nobility who were arrested and exiled. I knew, for example, that all former palace servants and estate workers were evicted from the palace suburbs and exiled from Leningrad. Some continued honourably to serve even under Soviet power and were faithful preservers of palace property and historical traditions. The arrest and exile of these people later caused a colossal set-back to the preservation of the great houses and their estates.

Nowadays the years 1936 and 1937 are merely picked out as 'special'. Mass arrests had begun with the unleashing of the 'Red Terror' in 1918 and later pulsated, as it were, gained in strength—in 1928, 1930, 1934 and so on—seizing not just individuals but whole strata of society and sometimes even whole urban districts in which the 'operatives' of the Terror had to be given quarters, such as the area around the *Bolshoi dom* in Leningrad.

How could one not have known of the Terror? People tried —and still do—to stifle their consciences with 'ignorance'.

I remember the dismal effect on everyone of the order that a list of inhabitants be displayed in gateways; previously there had been lists in every house showing who lived in which flat. There were so many arrests that these lists had to be changed almost daily. One could easily tell from them who'd been 'taken' overnight.

Once it was even forbidden to address as *tovarishch* [comrade] passengers on the tram, visitors to an institution, customers in shops or (for policemen) passers-by. Everyone had to be called *grazhdanin* [citizen]—everyone was under suspicion—and would one call an

196

'enemy of the people' a comrade? Who can remember that order now?

And the informants that appeared! Some denounced others out of fear, some as a result of a hysterical nature. Many emphasised their faithfulness to the regime by denouncements, and even boasted about it!

The Publishing House of the Academy of Sciences of the USSR

The thirties were hard years for me. I went to work as a literary proofreader for *Sotsekgiz*[170], in *Dom Knigi* on Nevski Prospekt, in the autumn of 1932. I hadn't had time to get to grips with the work when I began to have the most awful pains. I paid them no attention, didn't watch what I ate, and carried on going to work. One day I had a bad turn on the tram and was taken for a drunk; people began to tick me off—one so young, drunk at this time of the morning! I somehow got to *Dom Knigi*, went upstairs, sat down at my desk and passed out. Black blood poured from my throat. I was taken, semi-conscious, to the Kuybyshev hospital. My parents were summoned to the admissions ward and told straight that I'd lost a huge amount of blood and there was very little hope. I was saved, however, by the surgeon Abramson (blown to smithereens by a shell during the blockade), who had just begun the first experiments in blood trans-fusion. The donor stood by my side and the blood flowed straight from her into the vein which had been opened on my right arm. I remember it as in a dream. I remember a state of semi-bliss, no fear of death, no more pain. Abramson's efforts kept me in hospital longer than was necessary for my recovery, and so saved me from being exiled from Leningrad. I spent several months in hospital, and after that in the Institute of Nutrition (there was such a thing in Lenin-grad) and passed the time reading anything and everything. Reading, reading and more reading. Then I had to find work once again, and my father found me a job in the *Komintern* [Communist Interna-tional] publishing house as a foreign language proofreader. My pains returned; I would go home, fall into bed and stifle them by reading.

There was no shortage of books. Proofreading was considered demanding work, and was limited to six hours [a day]. At five o'clock I would be home and in bed. Thanks to my father's connections and the possibility of obtaining books from the splendid library in *Dom Knigi*, my reading took a more systematic turn. I read books on art and the history of culture. Sometimes I went to the library myself.

When I was transferred to work in the Academy of Sciences Press in 1934 I had the opportunity of obtaining books from the Academy library. Weariness from proofreading and from poring over manuscripts didn't interfere with my reading in bed at home. I was entirely satisfied with my lot. I made copies, pondered things and communicated with hardly anyone. My only friend was my old University chum M. I. Stelbin-Kamenski. He, unlike myself, hadn't finished his course; he was taking all his exams externally and working in the Press as a technical editor. There were many middle-aged 'formers' among the scientific proofreaders: the two former barons, a grammar school boy, a lawyer, a strange elderly Old Believer, and two men of remarkable culture—A. V. Suslov (a relation of Dostoyevski's wife) and L. A. Fedorov. Dealing with them was a higher education. How important it is to pick one's friends, and mostly among those who are on a higher cultural plane than oneself!

My four years working as a proofreader in the Leningrad branch of the Academy of Sciences Press were not wasted. This work inculcated in me an interest in textual criticism, and in particular criticism of printed matter. I worked with the technical editor Lev Aleksandrovich Fedorov (who died of exhaustion during the blockade) and the future distinguished scholar in Scandinavian studies Stelbin-Kamenski in producing an instructional handbook for Academy of Sciences proofreaders, which was printed in a limited edition in the late '30s. Generally speaking, my work in the Press had many points of contact with my 'printing past'. I was extremely interested in book-design. I had already begun to collect such books as came my way on publishing and printing, on the artistic composition of books, and especially dust jackets, which I preferred to hard, rough bindings. I continued having dealings with printers, in particular with I. G. Galaktionov, the noted collector of books of the Soviet period; what has become of his library? presumably it was broken up after his death?

Yu. G. Oksman has reminded me that he suggested that I should move to *Pushkinski Dom*, where he was Deputy Director, but I categorically refused. And in fact I felt at home in the Press; apart from the poor salary it was quite good. There prevailed an atmosphere of communal endeavour, and in charge was M. V. Valerianov, former compositor at *Pechatny Dvor* (compositors were typesetters of the highest qualification, who carried out at the same time the duties of technical editors and were able to compose elegant title pages by means of composed matter alone—nowadays a lost art). Valerianov took an interest in the work, and therefore also in people. He was by nature wise and intelligent. Long may his memory last.

In the '30s I was immersed in my proofreading work (first in printing houses, later in the USSR Academy of Sciences Press) and literary events passed me by.

Attempts at Writing

It is generally true to say that when I arrived at University I had difficulty in setting down my thoughts in written form. Although I wrote two theses—one on Shakespeare in Russia in the late eighteenth century, the other about tales of Patriarch Nikon, they were couched in childish language and were very poorly organised. I had particular trouble in moving from one sentence to another and it was as if each sentence had an independent existence. No logical progression was in evidence and it was hard to read my sentences aloud; they were 'unspeakable'.

And then, on leaving University, I decided to learn to write, and invented a system myself.

Firstly, in order to enrich my language I read books which were, in my view, well written, written in good prose—scholarly, worthy of an art historian. I read M. Alpatov, Dzhivilegov, Muratov, I. Grabar, N. N. Vrangel (his guide to the Russian Museum) and Kurbatov, and copied passages from their books, for the most part turns of phrase, individual words, expressions and images, etc.

Secondly, I decided to write every day, do classwork, so to speak, and to write in a special way. This I called 'without taking pen from paper', that is, non-stop. I decided—and correctly—that the chief source of a rich literary language is the spoken language. And so I tried to write down my own internal spoken language, to pursue with the pen an interior monologue addressed to a real reader—the addressee of a letter or simply a reader. And such an approach quickly began to pay off. I did this even in 1931, when I was working as a despatcher on the railway in Zvanka and Tikhvin (in the intervals between the arrivals of trains), and in the evenings when I was working as a proofreader. At work I also kept notebooks in which I wrote down the thoughts that I expressed with particular precision, briefly and succinctly.

Later, in 1938, when I'd moved to the Institute of Russian Literature, and Varvara Pavlovna Adrianova-Perets tasked me with writing the chapter on the literature of the eleventh to the thirteenth centuries for the *History of the Culture of Ancient Rus'* (volume 2, which came out only in 1958), I wrote it like poetry in prose. I found it very difficult, and at the dacha in Yelizavetina I rewrote it by hand no fewer than ten times. I corrected and rewrote it time and again, and when it seemed that everything was as it should be nevertheless I would sit down and copy it again, and in the process of copying various improvements would suggest themselves. I read the text aloud to myself, in part and whole, tested the good sense of the whole by excerpts. When I read my text in IIMKe[171] (now the Institute of Archaeology) it was a great success, and from that time I have been much sought after to contribute to various publications. To my great regret my text appeared in printed form badly damaged by editorial revisions, but all the same I was one of a very small number awarded a State Prize—my first—for my work on the history of ancient Russian culture.

While I was out of work I tried not to waste time; I read a lot and also decided to write something about thieves' cant. I wrote about that too when I went to the Academy of Sciences Press and the Academy library became available to me. The idea of such a work was fanned by certain thoughts of Levy-Bruhl[172] and was a typical example of 'camp prose'. I strove to create a paradoxical conception, to stun the reader. Furthermore, it was published in the journal *Yazyk i mysl* [Language and Thought] (Leningrad, 1935, vols. 3–4). I thought seriously about going in for linguistics and attended meetings in the Institute of Language and Thought, which was at the time in the other wing of the building where the Press was. These visits, however, soon had to cease, and this is how it happened.

Elections to the Academy were about to take place. N. M. Karinski, who had maintained his position in the face of Marr, had been nominated. Now, however, he had decided to give in to Marr in some degree, to acknowledge that there was something in his work and thereby to improve his chances of election. What exactly that lecture was about, or on what he 'gave ground' to Marr, I can't remember now, but a lot of people attended it. The circular hall was packed— there was 'nowhere to swing a cat'. I went along after the day's work, very tired, and stood by the door—there were no seats left. The lecture went on and on and I felt I was going to fall asleep. The lecturer's voice now moved towards me, now moved off somewhere and I could scarcely hear it. What he was saying I had no idea. At last the monotonous voice changed, and I heard the lecturer say loudly and attentively "What's the time?" and then the question was repeated, "What's the time?". For some reason no one said anything, so I took out my silver pocket-watch and replied loudly "A quarter to eight".

My God, what happened next! No! I can't tell you. Everyone on the big stage, on which the flower of academic philology was assembled, was literally helpless with laughter. Zhirmunski stretched his arms over the table and buried his face between them. Meshchaninov was not merely laughing, he was in ecstasy (Karinski might still have been in competition with him in the Department). The ever-serious Shishmarev was chuckling into his whiskers. Somebody took out a handkerchief and pretended to be fainting. The hall was choking with laughter. I realised that I'd done something awful and tip-toed out, my eyes dim, and went into the office for a glass of water. Somebody came after me. It turned out that Karinski had been giving examples of interrogative intonation ... and I, with my clear answer, had expressed the general opinion of the tedious lecture.

Later opinion was divided. Some thought that I'd spoken up out of cheek, while others realised that I'd simply not heard what he'd said. I became a sort of celebrity; the linguists exchanged greetings with me, and most of them amicably, smiling, because Karinski wasn't liked. But I didn't go to the meetings again, and didn't go in for linguistics.

My Conviction Quashed

I worked for five years as a 'scientific proofreader' in the Academy of Sciences Press. I won't say that it was a bad job. It gave me the opportunity to stay out of sight, to avoid speaking out on 'tricky problems'.

I was frequently ill and went into hospital during acute periods of illness; it was a duodenal ulcer, and gave rise to suspicion of cancer or something no less unpleasant. These suspicions turned out to be unfounded, my fellow patients were sometimes interesting and the books were for the most part attractive.

The big proofreading room (one of the halls of the Museum of Palaeontology, which had been moved to Moscow) was enlivened by 'former people' who had studied at the Lycee, the Institute of Legal Studies or just the University, and with whom it was possible now and then to look up and exchange a few words. On Sundays the proofreaders organised trips out of the city to the palace suburbs. My ulcer prevented my taking part, and that was a great disappointment throughout my time in the Press. They, of course, knew those suburbs not as readers and strangers; they'd either been there before the Revolution or had heard about them from friends. I missed the opportunity of getting to know the outskirts of Leningrad as one who lived there when they were in full bloom. Though I stayed at home on Sundays and lay in bed I heard a lot about them all the same and tried to read up on them. Fedorov, a man with an encyclopedic knowledge of Russia, was invariably the organiser of these trips out of town, which in summer took in ancient towns and monasteries; he was a technical editor and one of the most cultured men that I've ever met. He died of sheer starvation during the blockade in the air-raid shelter of the Winter Palace.

I'm convinced that had those events, which seemed so dreadful, not taken place, I would have spent the rest of my life as a proofreader and would have eventually ruined my eyesight.

It was during one of my periodic stays in hospital that the issue of passports began in Leningrad. This was one of the most frightening times in the life of the big cities. The people of Moscow and Leningrad lived in a state of tension as they awaited their fate: the decision of the Passport Commission. There were no hard-and-fast rules. In Leningrad passports weren't given to nobility, and in the palace suburbs not even to former palace servants. This last was dreadful not only for the people but also for the palaces too. The palace staff had been honest and had looked after every little thing. The 'cadres' that descended upon them appropriated, stole and 'wrote off' objects of artistic worth of which they had no understanding. Highly valuable knowledge was lost which had been handed on by word of mouth, legends and even certain traditions. With the expulsion of the nobility the cultural complexion of the cities changed. The streets altered in appearance. The faces of passers-by became different; the streets had long since changed their clothes.

Even the Academy of Sciences acquired its own Passport Commission, which held its sessions in the main building. I was very much afraid that I would be called up and questioned and my current views on Soviet power wormed out of me. So when I was taken ill and went into hospital I wasn't in any hurry to be discharged. When I came out I learnt that the Passport Commission in the Academy had finished its work. I thought the danger was past but it was not. I was informed that I was not being given a passport. The date for my departure from Leningrad was set. Passports weren't given to Fedya Rozenberg, Tolya Terekhovko, A. N. Sukhov—to everybody who had a 'record'. My father was fearfully agitated, sought out influential people and (I know because they told me) wept in their presence. Finally he found someone (the secretary of the district committee, I believe) who promised to help but wanted to see me. He lived on Kamenoostrovski (then called ulitsa Krasnykh zor [Street of Red Dawns]) just before the Lidval house, if you approach it from the Troitski bridge. I remember being entertained to tea. There was nothing to talk about. The secretary and his wife, who gave me pitying looks, sat at the table. The upshot of it all was that I was given a postponement for completion of medical treatment.

And at this point Zina came to my aid. We weren't married at the time, only intending. It was well known that as a girl the 'scientific proofreader' Yekaterina Mikhaylovna Mastyko had been friendly with the children of the academician Zernov and the future *narkomyust* Krylenko[173], and Zina persuaded her to go out to see Krylenko. That was not easy. The distance in time between them had to be overcome, as well as that between their social positions. I can imagine how hard it was for Yekaterina Mikhaylovna to show herself to him, old and changed as she was. And furthermore—how was she to pay for the journey and what was she to wear? Money was collected. Zina's blouse was loaned, and they set off. Yekaterina Mikhaylovna came back satisfied and explained: I had to obtain a petition from the President of the Academy, Aleksandr Petrovich Karpinski, and to obey the instructions of Krylenko's secretary when I went to see him. I remember Yekaterina Mikhaylovna saying that she was a former worker, a sensible, good woman. I only know that when talking to Krylenko Yekaterina Mikhaylovna had described me as the fiance of her daughter Kati, whom I'd never set eyes on (she came to see us about ten years later, after the war).

Yekaterina Mikhaylovna was a good woman. When all was said and done, what was Zina to her and what was I, and what was it worth to her, who knew all about Krylenko, to take the risk of reminding him of herself?

I was told how to obtain a petition from the President of the Academy. I had to go to the Karpinskis', a private house in Pyatnitskaya Street, there to meet Karpinski's daughter Tolmacheva, kiss her hand (without fail) and hand her a letter from the Director of our Press, Mikhail Valerianovich Valerianov, requesting him to intervene in my case. So I did, travelling by the cheapest train and going straight from the station to Pyatnitskaya. I rang, and was led up a staircase that was steep and narrow for so luxurious a private house to the first floor, where there was a large sitting-room. I was announced, kissed hands, with faltering voice made my request which I had carefully learnt off by heart, and handed over the letter. Tolmacheva was not surprised, went straight away into a little study off the sitting-room and began to shout into Aleksandr Petrovich's ear "A young man has come, cultured. Cultured! You've got to sign a request for him. Sign!" After that she sat down at a typewriter and I heard its brisk clatter. Without a word she brought me out the letter in a opulent envelope the like of which I've never seen in the USSR. I went straight from her to the *narkomyust*.

Krylenko's ante-room was crowded. A middle-aged woman (or such she seemed to me at the time) came up to me at once as if she knew me, took Karpinski's letter from me (I hadn't had the time to read it properly) and said sternly "Stand here"—indicating a spot where everyone could see me—"and however much Nikolay Vasilevich goes for you, say nothing and don't answer and don't deny anything". I was taken somewhat aback: Krylenko was seeing everyone else in his study. Soon there leaped out of the study (more precisely, rolled) a stout, fleshy, even tubby man who moved like an athlete and set about me at once, as it seemed to me, with his fists. "We've had a revolution! Shed our blood! The fate of humanity's in the balance! And you've been acting the goat! Setting up the 'Cosmic Academy'! Laughing at us, eh? I can't find words to express such ignorance", etc., etc. The tirade lasted some minutes. Then, with the petition in his hand he flew swiftly into his study and the secretary beckoned me to her desk and began to ask me the number of my old passport, my place of work, its address, Valerianov's office telephone number, etc. She told me to stay in Leningrad and to contact her if there was any difficulty—and all in a quiet voice, as if in secret. I went back to Leningrad that same day and waited several months. I wasn't summoned anywhere by anyone.

In the height of summer I was called to the post office and handed an envelope from the Central Executive Committee. It contained a document quashing my conviction.

For fifty years I thought "Well, that's that!", but in 1992 it turned out that that hadn't been rehabilitation.

True, misunderstandings only happened when questions of registration arose, first in Kazan and later in Leningrad...

At first I couldn't understand why that obviously contrived scene in the ante-room had been necessary. When Krylenko was arrested shortly afterwards I realised. He was already being watched and was afraid of damaging accusations of favouring counterrevolutionaries. He'd been demonstrating his total dedication to Soviet Power for all in the ante-room to see. I won't say that that demonstration was particularly pleasant for me, but it achieved its purpose, and I'm eternally grateful to Yekaterina Mikhaylovna Mastyko.

I Fail the Exams

A proofreader's position was, of course, the most suitable, or better, the safest under the conditions of the Terror of the '30s. It was acceptable not to talk and to work in silence, just as long as no mistakes slipped through! There was only one unpleasant incident. I. P. Pavlov decided to publish some slim brochures of the work of his institute—I can't recall the name of the series—and it was given to me, and in the very first sentence I somehow changed the sense. Either I put a comma in the wrong place or I made a wrong correction. Anyway, Pavlov's son came to see the Director, Valerianov, to complain. I was summoned. The son said nothing. Valerianov gave me a mild ticking-off. The meaning of the sentence had definitely been altered. I was extremely abashed, but a day or two later Pavlov's son appeared again and told Valerianov that although the meaning had been changed Ivan Petrovich was not complaining. I realised that this was simply a show of goodwill on the part of father or son, or more than likely both. It was not remarkable that the son had looked at me in silence when Valerianov had been ticking me off—he had also, I thought, felt some sympathy.

That, however, was the one and only unpleasant incident directly connected with my work.

In 1935 my first serious article appeared in the journal *Yazyk i myshleniye* [Language and Thought]: *Cherty pervobytnogo primitivizma vorovskoy rechi* [Features of the primordial primitivism of thieves]. It evoked a devastating review entitled *Vrednaya galimatya* [Harmful rubbish] by Mikhail Shakhnovich in *Leningradskaya pravda*. After articles like that arrest usually followed, but the linguists (Abayev, Bykhovskaya, Bashindzhagyan and others) took an interest in my work. I decided to chance my luck and took the post-graduate admission examination for the Institute of Oral Culture. By then my co-defendant Kallistov, who had an identical certificate of release from the Belomorobaltiski camp with no further restrictions, had been accepted as a post-graduate student of Leningrad University. How is he better than me, I thought, forgetting that he'd had the support of the Dean of the Faculty of History, Boris Dmitrevich Grekov.

I'd had an article published. The linguists knew me. I'd submitted a second article to the same journal and it had been proofread.

By then my future wife and I had decided to marry. What had I to lose if I wasn't accepted? I had to try my luck.

That, however, wasn't the point. My application went in. I attached my certificate of release as a shock-worker in Belbaltlag. This was a famous construction, and the favours bestowed by Stalin on those that had taken part in it were widely known and 'respected' by the Party powers. Nevertheless, evidently, the Party authorities that were in charge of everything decided not to accept me—or rather, the opinion of Shakhnovich in *Leningradskaya pravda* meant more to them than those of academic linguists.

That summer my mother took a room in the *Novoye Druznoselye* [New Friendly Settlement] at the Siverskaya station. I obtained leave, but there was no time to prepare for the examinations. Nor was there anyone whose advice I could seek.

The first examination was political—what the subject was called I forget. The secretary of the Party organisation and the scientific secretary of the Institute were present. The examiner asked me what I'd read on the subject. I replied, Bukharin's *Alphabet of Communism*, forgetting that I'd also read Engels' *Dialectic of Nature* and a bit of Marx. Another question followed, and my answer was obviously unsatifactory. The questioner, distorting his face into a smile (I've forgotten the examiner's face, but the smile has remained in my memory like that of the cat in *Alice in Wonderland*), said "Well, I can tell you've read your Bukharin". Perfectly satisfied at that, the examination board broke off the interrogation (that was what I felt it to be). There were no more questions.

I was prepared for the result, but decided all the same to go forward for a second interrogation, this time on my special subject. Just out of curiosity.

I presented myself a day or two later. The chief examiner was an extremely well-known linguist whose name I will not quote. With a pained expression in his voice and eyes averted he asked me which linguists I had studied with at University. I named first Zhirmunski, followed by Yakubinski, Shcherba, Boyanus, Brim, Larin, Obnorski... The pained expression became worse.

"I'll ask you a very simple question, a schoolboy question: what is an adjective (give a definition) and indicate the types of adjective." The question was an obvious time-waster, I didn't answer it but apologised for troubling them, excused myself and left. As he said goodbye, the examiner emphasised once more "I asked you a question which any schoolboy could have answered".

A few months later my examiner came to the Press and I was invited by the technical editor to resolve certain problems over his article, which I had just proofread. I ignored my examiner's greeting, and he was forced to hide his smile of uncomprehending scorn. How many sorts of smile there can be on a human face!

Some time later I met Zhirmunski, and I remember the first words that he spoke: "I hear you've been knocking at the door of our Institute without success..." He didn't say that I'd 'ploughed', 'failed the exams', 'not passed muster'... or anything else. 'Knocking at the door without success!'... A year or two later, having been arrested himself, he suggested that I should go and join his department of the Institute of Literature, but by then I'd become interested in Ancient Russian Literature.

I Leave the Academy of Sciences Press

When I started to work there the head of the proofreading room had been Shturts, a Party member and a man who tried very hard to obliterate his German antecedents. Clearly, he was constantly reproached at Party meetings for his 'choice of staff'. None the less they were grammar school pupils, lawyers, the two Barons and me, with my past. He tried twice to have me dismissed, but the Director, Valerianov, wouldn't permit it. The first time was when Shakhnovich's article with the expressive title 'Harmful rubbish' appeared in *Leningradskaya pravda*: Shturts went to Valerianov and asked that Lihachev be dismissed 'as he wasn't interested in the work of a proofreader' (I couldn't be dismissed for the content of Shakhnovich's article, so Shturts had thought up a formula). The second time it was because I was three days late back from leave (I myself had miscalculated the dates of my summer holiday). Valerianov refused, but bearing in mind my months of idleness I found it rather unpleasant to realise that my immediate superior was anxious to have me dismissed. Anyway, Shturts was replaced by Mastyko, thanks to whom my conviction had been quashed, and things improved for me. But then came 1936, and the arrests of Party members began. After the nobility had been removed the arrests in our Press affected first of all the editors. Adonts, the editor-in-chief, was arrested; he was notable because after Petrograd had been renamed Leningrad he once refused, in the capacity of censor, to pass the book *Petrografiya* and suggested instead the title *Leninografiya*. He was basically a very decent man, but very unintelligent. Kuzmina was taken from the editor's chair, then Misha Smirnov, who managed to find work with another publisher, and then one by one everyone that sat in that chair. I remember it well, that chair; it had come from the Academy conference hall, where the furniture had been designed by Quarenghi. The hall had later been rearranged by Rossi[174], who planned more sumptuous furniture which, by the way, was taken to the Neskuchny palace in Moscow, where the suites were gradually broken up. Even in the early nineteenth century Quarenghi furniture was spread throughout the offices of the Academy. One chair in the style of Louis XVI, very elegant and alien to the taste of our Soviet institution, stood at the editor-in-chief's desk, and when people began to vanish from it one after another (we didn't even have time to remember who they were), it acquired the soubriquet of 'The Guillotine'. The execution of Louis XVI was brought to mind, in whose period style the chair was made. And then the most unpleasant thing happened to me. Valerianov, to whom I was indebted for both my position as a 'scientific proofreader' and for his subsequent protection against attempts to dismiss me, asked me temporarily to take the editor's chair so that the work of the Press should not stop. I raised every conceivable objection: I wasn't a Party member (and the work was of a strictly Party nature), I'd been in prison, I had no experience, etc., etc. Valerianov asked me to do it for two months, for which time, on the suggestion of the editor-in-chief in Moscow, my position would be entitled 'organising editor'. I had to recruit the editors who were Party men, and they would then sign manuscripts for printing.

In the end I couldn't prevail against Valerianov's insistence. I took my place in the 'Guillotine' and began looking at manuscripts with which to fill the void in the Academy printing works. I had to read them all and study the comments that had been written on them. If a manuscript bore no publisher's comments a reviewer had to be found for it (the Press didn't rely on the comments of academic boards). There were sharply hostile comments on only two manuscripts: *Yazyk zheltykh uygur*[175] by Corresponding Member Malov and another book (I forget the author's name), devoted to the languages of the peoples of Dagestan.

I did succeed in doing a bit of good. I authorised a fee for M. D. Priselkov for editing *Obozreniya russkikh letopisnykh svodov* [A Survey of Collections of Russian Chronicles] and published my Solovki friend Gorski's booklet *Thirty Days on the Drift-ice of the Caspian*, which ran into a second edition. It's hard to remember now what I did manage to achieve.

The promised two months slipped by as did two more, but I was kept on and the danger grew constantly. I remember in detail my last conversation with Valerianov. I told him that I was definitely going to give notice. I had nowhere to go, but the danger was very real.

A few days later the *raykom*[176] sent two people to the Press: Dayev as editor-in-chief and Barabanov as an editor. Neither of them had had anything remotely to do with editorial work or publishing. Dayev, who was designated not only editor-in-chief but also villain-in-chief, sat down beside me and suggested that I should go on working with him there so that he could 'learn the ropes'.

In this situation I committed an error: I really thought that there was no longer any threat to me. Dayev, however, decided to 'work me over', and keep a keen eye on me. He reported to the *raykom* that the Press was getting slack, and gave as an example all the negative reviews in the light of which manuscripts either didn't go into production or were corrected. He gave out all the negative comments as his own. Naturally, someone in the *raykom* put forward the suggestion that I be dismissed. I was summoned to the office and it was put to me that I should come off the permanent staff and be employed on a free-lance basis. It was summer, we'd taken a room at Vsevolozhskaya, and at first I felt quite at ease, as I didn't have to travel into town every day as previously. A month went by, however, and then I realised that Dayevhad no intention of offering me any further contracts. Then I decided to go and work for the Department of Ancient Russian Literature at the Pushkinski Dom under Varvara Pavlovna. More of that later, but for now I'll only say that I crossed Dayev's path after the war. The Director of the Academy of Sciences Press enquired of me whether it was worth taking on Dayev. I had to tell him the whole story of how I was sacked. Did I do right? The Director was a good man, and it was unfortunate that he died soon after being appointed.

Novgorod

Zina and I took a holiday in Novgorod on the advice of V. L. Komarovich. This was just before our daughters were born, in the summer of 1937. We took a room with Baroness Tizengauzen on the very edge of the city. There was a marvellous view from the window over the Krasnoye pole and Nereditsa with the bell-tower right on the horizon. Komarovich had had this very room before us.

I'd taken a telescope with me, and when we weren't out walking—early in the morning or before sunset—I enjoyed the view of Nereditsa. I remember, I could see on the white walls the shadows of the swifts as they flashed about in all directions as evening drew on. In the evening, if we weren't too tired from the day's walking, we liked to stroll on the Krasnoye pole. There were lots of geese feeding on the grass in the field, and at evening they returned home, to stand outside the gates of the houses on the Slavna honking for their owners to let them in. Sometimes we would walk to the Kremlin in the evening, sit by the monument to the Millennium of Russia[177] and admire the golden dome of St Sofiya, thickly gilded and polished mirror-smooth, in which the clouds were reflected as they ran across the sky. One could watch that dome for ever, as one can watch running waves. In the daytime we went for long walks, every time to a new monument. We walked considerable distances—to the village of Volotova with its famous fourteenth century church, to Khutyn, to the Kirillov monastery, where Blok's sister and step-mother (his father's second wife) are buried in the Novokirillovskoye cemetery. I went by myself to Lipna and to Skorovodka, where at the time Olsufyev and his wife were cleaning the frescoes. We went to the Yurev monastery, to Peryn and Arkazhi–the only monasteries that we didn't visit were those at Kolmovo and Vyazishchi, where there were OGPU prisons and their victims.

When one considers that Zina was at the time 'near her time', our walks were heroic in their way, unless one takes into account the visits to the ice-cream shop near the church of St Paraskeva Pyatnitsa at Yaroslavovo Court. We've never tasted such ice-cream since... It was magnificent.

We returned by steamer past the Arakcheyev barracks and some lovely wooded countryside; when I passed that way later in a motor-boat with Senkevich there were no woods left anywhere, the villages had been demolished and only scattered ruins remained of the churches. Granin, who was at the time taking part in surveys for the 'Travellers' Club', said with a sigh "How can anyone live in villages like that! Such monotony!" In 1937, however, that 'monotony' hadn't yet arisen. Zina and I sailed all the way to Chudovo and waited there all night for the morning train back to Leningrad. Our daughters were born on 4 August.

I went to Novgorod twice more before the war, with Fedya Rozenberg. On the second of these trips we were joined by Steblin-Kamenski. Fedya had an accountant friend in Novgorod who owned a motor-boat, and in it we went to Lipna, Peryn and the Yurev monastery. I still have two photographs from the last trip; in the one we're having breakfast on the river bank outside the Yurev monastery, and in the second we're drinking milk in the village of Volotova.

Thus by the time the war began I knew Novgorod quite well, and I liked it very much. This fact influenced my choice of subject for my doctoral thesis: 'Collections of twelfth century mss in Novgorod', and in 1945 my small book *Novgorod the Great. The Cultural History of Novgorod from the Eleventh to the Seventeenth Century*, written mainly in Leningrad during the blockade, was published.

From the occasional copy of *Leningradskaya pravda* that came my way in 1942 (it was quite impossible to obtain it regularly; I think it was only published for *Obkom*[178] workers, in small format) I reckoned that the front line passed through the necklace of churches behind the

Krasnoye Polye. Our artillery positions were near Nereditsa. Kovaleva and Volotova were naturally exposed to German shelling. I was deeply grieved that nothing remained of those priceless churches.

Now I come to the main point about Novgorod in my recollections... At the end of the war my family and I were living in Kazan, and I was working in the Institute of Russian Literature as before. The Institute began to be 're-evacuated' to Leningrad. I was not included, as politically unreliable, in the list of those to be sent back—perhaps I'd been crossed off. Dear Viktor Andronikovich Manuylov, then in charge of the Institute in Leningrad, made a special request for me. The Germans were still close to Leningrad. Our train stopped for the night somewhere at a station with the dismal name of *Dno* or *Mg[l]a*[179]. I spent quite a long time in Leningrad. My passport was stolen, my money, my military identity card, my coupons—all my papers. I had to get them all replaced, go before the medical board and so on. I can't remember whether it was during that visit or my next, in January or February, that Novgorod was liberated. In May the road there was open, and Maynulov suggested that I go there to see what was left. The train went slowly, uncertainly, and I saw German corpses, stripped and unburied, lying in the swamps near Leningrad, which had not yet been cleared of mines. I had to change in Chudovo, and went to see if Nekrasov's house was still there. It was! That was a miracle. There was also a brick building of Soviet construction which had been a hospital under the Germans. Right by the hospital walls they'd made a cemetery, and on every grave was a plastic wreath; on some there was a red arm-band with a black swastika on a white circle. On some people had defecated...

I reached Novgorod in the morning. The train stopped in an open space—that was Novgorod. Then I looked around for St Sofiya and sundry churches. On the adjacent tracks were standing trains disgorging collective farm families. Representatives of collective farms were touting for their services, bribing them with various good things: private houses, a shop within easy reach, etc. While I was there a train came in with other families. These were the families of former Novgorod people[180]. My God, what a howl went up when they saw that the Novgorod that they'd been dreaming of all that time no longer existed. It was a lament that I had to record: "Our lovely Novgorod, what have they done to you? What's left of you..." and so on. The whole train of red goods wagons wept, children wept and women flung themselves face down on the ground...

I picked up my briefcase and set off in search of somewhere to stay. The earth bank on the Sofiskaya embankment was riddled with trenches and German dug-outs in which people were living. Here and there smoke was rising and women appeared fetching water from the river Volkhov in buckets. There were lines up with washing drying on them. One couldn't tell where the streets had been. They were cobbled and overgrown with grass, quite tall for May. When I reached the Torgovaya embankment I had to feel with my feet where the roadway was and where soft earth. There was no trace of the former presence of streets, and one could fall down all sorts of holes and well-shafts. I was walking along like a blind man. But I was lucky on the first day: I found the *Dom krestyanina* [House of the Peasant]. Half of the early nineteenth century building was gone, but the roof was left on the remaining half and camp-beds had been set up for people on missions, almost touching one another. I slept there in my clothes.

And what did I see in Novgorod? The Kremlin, compared with everything else, was almost intact. The Russian Millennium monument had been destroyed, and various statues had been marked with white numbers; evidently the intention had been to remove them for a collection somewhere. There were no cupolas on the drums of St Sofiya. I walked through the grass around the cathedral and found the gilded ball from under the cross on one of the small cupolas. I picked it up. The thick layer of gilt was clearly visible. On one of the buildings on the other side of St Sofiya was a sign: *El viva Salamanca*—this was where the Spanish had been. Obviously, the Spanish troops had had their own areas. St Yefim's bell-tower had lost its wooden top, which had so suited it. The museum, however, was beginning to function; its former director, Tamara Konstantinova, had picked up some mahogany furniture in the ruins of Novgorod houses for her office. I gave her the ball, but unfortunately it was of no interest to her.

I looked in at a few buildings in the Kremlin. Everywhere was full of empty boxes of the chemical hot-water bottles used by the German soldiers to keep warm, and with boxes of another sort of chemical— for use against either lice or bed-bugs.

On their sides on the bank of the Volkhov lay the bells of St Sofiya, which had been pulled out of the water by a tank; the lugs of the tenor, the sound of which the Novgorodians had so loved, had broken off as it was pulled out.

There had been an Officers' Mess in the Granovitaya palace during the occupation and there were still a few German signs up. Our forces hadn't shelled the Kremlin, but of course it had been pleasant to feel safe; the walls of the Granovitaya were thick enough. The side of the road where the Sofiskaya church stood had been surfaced with stones taken from one of the churches; the Germans had demolished it to make not only roads, but also their fortifications.

I went into the Yurev monastery. The church on Sinichya Hill was intact, but the most precious monuments had been removed. I saw them in the Yurev monastery. The Spanish hadn't been satisfied with modest graves for their dead, as had the Germans, but had raised tombs with stolen stones. The cemetery was where a spring, said to be holy, rises under its precious canopy. The Yurev monastery had been used as stables by an Estonian cavalry unit and across the road lay the bloated corpse of a horse over which I had to climb. Behind the Cathedral of St George was a gun emplacement, from which telephone wires ran up the staircase of the Cathedral. On the top landing there were bits of bone, and the staircase walls, on which the artists of the Spanish school had painted naked women over the remains of twelfth century frescoes, were pock-marked with bullet holes.

Most terrible of all, however, was a church, with blue cupolas and golden stars, standing at an angle to the Volkhov. It had been the Nazis' principal defensive point. The floor was littered with grenades and machine-gun cartridges. Here the Germans had succeeded in beating off one of our attacks, which had cost us dear. Thousands of Soviet soldiers had gone under the ice.

I also went to my beloved necklace of churches on the Krasnoye pole. Our trenches were to be seen everywhere, near Nereditsa (access to there was particularly dangerous, as the area hadn't been cleared of mines; I walked choosing every spot I trod on), in Kovaleva cemetery and at Lipna, where one of our strong points had been. The churches everywhere had been equipped as observation posts, and for that reason had come under heavy artillery fire. The trenches round Kovaleva wound between the graves, entered burial vaults, were protected with tombstones. One such stone I picked up, inscribed 'to Mother Mary'. Had there been a nunnery at Kovaleva?

I remember a terrible gash in the western side of the church of the Saviour on the Ilin, caused by our shell. The point was that our artillery didn't fire on the churches of Novgorod—there had been a special order to that effect—and the Germans knew that, and sited their observation and fire-control posts in the topmost points of historical monuments. The observation post in the church of the Saviour-on-the-Ilin posed a special threat to our troops as they advanced from the east. One solitary shell was fired at the observation post but unfortunately its impact wrecked a fresco by Feofan Grek. Of course, this wasn't the bombing of Milan by the Americans, in which the monastery of Santa Maria delle Grazie was destroyed, while by some miracle Leonardo da Vinci's 'Last Supper' was preserved, but all the same the loss is a bitter one to admit. The church at Volotova, which I had particularly liked, had been demolished to head-height, and a few bits of valuable fresco remained. If prompt action had been initiated at Volotova much could have been saved, but the Grekovs, who restored Kovalevo, didn't establish a school of pupils and didn't see to Volotova. To see a mound of rubble where there had stood so magnificent a church, to see the monastery of Skovoroda in ruins, with its frescoes unpublished (the ones that had been cleaned by the Olsufiyevs), to see Kovalevo in ruins—all this was dreadful. In Khutyn the frames of the cupolas were still in position, but I didn't manage to get there.

Before leaving Novgorod I went to the place where the Tizengauzen house had been. I remembered what life had been like there, our holiday, the marvellous *ukha*[181] that Tizengauzen had made us (she was the daughter of a priest, and her husband had been the baron until his arrest had worked in the Novgorod branch of Gosbank).

I remembered too how she used to put a pillow on the windowsill in her bedroom (the house was directly on the pavement), lie down and talk to the people that went by—everybody knew everybody.

That quiet provincial life, which even the mass arrests that began in 1936 couldn't disrupt—where is it now?

The Blockade

"... only that which is no more exists.
The future may not be:
the present can and must be changed;
only the past is not subject to mutability:
memory preserves it..."

Zhukovski

I believe that nothing ceases to be, but that everything outside the sphere of our consciousness remains. Time, as we conceive of it, does not exist.

This notebook is for our children—and mine.

On Wednesday 26 June 1957 Mama[182] and I decided to go from Zelenogorsk to town, not, as usual, by train or bus but by steamer from the Zolotoi beach. The steamer service to Leningrad had only just begun, and we felt like taking a look at the Gulf of Finland from the Gulf itself. I've lived on the shores of the Gulf since I was a child, but I've only been on the sea in a small boat (and that very seldom) or a steamer—two or three trips from Leningrad to Peterhof. So off we set for the landing-stage at Zolotoy beach and went right by those dachas in one of which we'd been planning in the early spring of 1941 (or more exactly, late winter, as there was still snow on the ground) to take an upstairs room for the summer. Planning we had been, but take it we did not ... but a Mrs Shiryayev did. Mama and I asked one another "What if we'd taken that dacha ... would we still be alive?" And so there arose in us the idea of writing for our children as much as we could remember of the events of 1941 and '42.

We shall write without any pretence at being systematic, nor of being especially stylish. If I forget something, Mama will correct me. Mama's memory is better and more accurate than mine—especially for figures.

Saturday 29 June 1957

And so, we didn't take the dacha at Terijoki in 1941, we took one at Vyritsa. A broad, straight street led from the station to our dacha, intersected at right angles by other streets, which were named after Russian writers. One of these was I. A. Krylov, who sheltered us in his

216

street, lined with young pine trees, in a new house not far from the little river Oredezh.

They say that the dacha's still there.

It was a cheap dacha. That was what mattered, as I was working as a junior member of staff at the *Pushkinski Dom* and wasn't earning much. Indeed, we were still taking manuscripts at the Press for montage and had even introduced to such work one or two refinements (instead of gluing little bits of paper over the words and passages struck out we started to paste them out with gouache, to speed up the work), but even so our earnings were very small. I remember that our cheap dacha contained a room and a balcony. There were other dacha dwellers living in the house, which had only recently been built. I defended my thesis on 11 June, but was promoted only in August, when my salary increased sharply. We had a nanny, Tamara Mikhaylovna. I went frequently to the dacha and sometimes even stayed there two or three days, taking work with me.

It was a good summer. We would go down to the river and choose a spot with a little beach, where there was room for just our family, and would sunbathe and swim. The bank was steep, and a path led along it above our beach. Then one day we, on our beach, heard snatches of a terrifying conversation. Holiday makers were walking along the path and talking about Kronshtadt being bombed, about some aircraft or other. At first we wondered if they weren't reminiscing about the Finnish campaign of 1939, but their excited voices disturbed even us. On return to the dacha we were told that war had broken out. By evening in the garden of the recreation centre we heard the radio; there was a loudspeaker on a tall pole, and in the space in front of it a lot of people had gathered. Everyone was very gloomy and silent. Next morning I went into town. My mother and Yura had heard about the war on the radio; she told me that he'd turned pale. In town I was struck by the same gloom and silence. After Hitler's blitzkrieg in Europe no one expected anything good. Everyone was surprised that literally days before the war a very great quantity of grain had been sent to Finland—it had been in the papers. People were more talkative in *Pushkinski Dom*, though they looked around. A. I. Grushkin talked most, making fantastic suggestions, but all 'patriotic'.

What happened during the first days of the war I can't remember. Then 'directives' came out: the scientific establishments of the Academy of Sciences were to be 'mothballed', and cut-backs began which went on until the spring of 1943, with members of staff being mobilised as volunteers, while rumours of evacuation circulated. Those concerning the evacuation of the *Pushkinski Dom* changed several times a week.

The papers gave a confused account of the situation at the front, and people lived on rumours. These spread everywhere: in the canteen, in the streets, but they weren't given much credence–they were too gloomy. They were later proved correct.

Rumours of evacuation frightened the children, and indeed orders for their evacuation were given. Women were employed to accompany them. As it was forbidden to leave the city on one's own initiative, everyone that wanted to escape got themselves attached to a children's group. We decided not to send our children away and not to be separated from them. It was obvious that the evacuation of children was completely disorganised. And indeed, we later discovered that the majority of children had been sent to the Novgorod region–right into the path of the advancing Germans. It was reported that in Lyuban the 'ladies' who had been accompanying them took their own children and fled, abandoning other people's children to wander about about, hungry and in tears. Little children couldn't give their surnames when they were picked up, and so lost their parents for good. Later on, in 1945, many unfortunate parents openly demanded that those in charge of the evacuation be prosecuted, including the 'city fathers'.

Evacuation was compulsory, and we hid in Vyritsa, determined to stay there till the last moment. Next door to us were M. P. Barmanski and his sons' families. We conferred and jointly hid our children from being evacuated; we, our daughters and he, his grandchildren.

But the Germans advanced rapidly. Dozens of anti-aircraft balloons appeared above the city. People were on duty round the clock on the roof of *Pushkinski Dom*, and it became more difficult to get to the dacha. On the last occasion I travelled back from Vyritsa in a train consisting entirely of first-class carriages. The windows had all been broken, as German aircraft had attacked it just outside Vyritsa, where the deafening bombing raids on the airfield at Siverskaya could be heard. German Messerschmidts had twice flown low over our dacha, suddenly appearing just above the trees, their engines roaring terribly, and just as suddenly vanishing.

One morning I went home to Lakhtinskaya Street after being on night duty at *Pushkinski Dom* and found Zina and the children there. It transpired that Barmanski had brought them back from the dacha, deciding that life in Vyritsa 'had had it'; first he'd moved his own children out, then he'd returned especially for mine and brought them and their belongings back; all that was left in Vyritsa were the grandfather clock, the wash-tub, the children's beds and a few other things.

Only in Russia has there existed such a quantity of eccentrics and 'originals'. Mikhail Petrovich Barmanski, who played such a great part in the life of our family, was of their number.

In the First World War he'd been an officer and had retained his military bearing, his moustache and his demanding nature towards himself and his subordinates alike. He went about dressed like a labourer: quilted jacket, kersey boots, and then—an army greatcoat that had belonged to his son, killed in the Great October Revolution. He had been red-headed, but I only remember him being completely grey. He considered it unacceptable to show favour to his 'bag of bones', and ate dried vegetables or porridge, went about on foot in his brownish boots. He even called on us at the dacha, eagerly ate something vegetarian and left after asking two or three philosophical questions 'of principle'.

He was a pensioner when he died, well turned eighty, and in his latter years he used to say "One thing I want to live for: to see the end of the film". By 'film' he meant the history of the Russia of his time. He took a keen interest in everything that went on and simply couldn't understand "what it was all leading to".

He worked hard and was poorly paid, but spent as little as possible on himself: such was his rule. He helped his relations and the poor, lent to his subordinates (in his last years he was in charge of the proofreading room of the Academy of Sciences) and never asked for anything in return.

He looked at people sternly, often askance, but when he smiled it was so sincere and pleasant that those who had deserved his smile would be left with an enduring feeling of profound gladness within them.

In 1941, when we were still living at the dacha in Vyritsa, he learned that the Germans were quite close (in the papers it said that "fighting was raging in the Pskov region"); he went to Vyritsa (I was in town and knew nothing about it) and brought all my family out— Zinaida Aleksandrovna and the children. He didn't waste time looking for me (the telephones weren't working) but did it all himself. There's a model of true goodness.

He died as he'd lived, without causing anyone any trouble.

V. L. Komarovich and his family had been staying at Siverskaya and moved from there ten days later, by which time the Germans were quite close. Those ten days were fatal for Komarovich: they hadn't managed to stock up with anything...

By the time we got back to Leningrad from Vyritsa there was a coupon system in operation. The shops were steadily emptying. There was less and less on sale despite rationing: tinned goods and expensive foods had vanished, but in the early days the bread ration was generous. We couldn't eat it all, as the children ate rather little bread. Zina didn't even want to buy it all, but I insisted: it was becoming obvious that there would be shortages. Confusion was growing constantly. And so we dried the bread on the windowsill in the sun. By autumn we had a big pillowcase full of black rusks, which we hung on the wall because of the mice. Later, in the winter, the mice died of hunger. In the frost, in the silence of early morning, when most of us were in bed, we would hear a dying mouse scamper convulsively over by the window and then expire; it hadn't been able to find so much as a crumb in our room. Meanwhile in July and August I had emphasised that there would be famine, famine! And we'd done our best to establish a little reserve for winter. Zina used to stand in queues at unlit shops, the windows of which were protected by boxes made of planks and filled with earth.

What did we manage to buy in those first weeks? I remember that we had coffee, but very little pastry. How I remembered later those weeks when we were laying in supplies! In winter, lying in bed and suffering terrible remorse, I thought of one thing until my head hurt: there, on the shelves in the shops, had been tinned fish—why hadn't I bought it? Why had I bought only eleven bottles of cod-liver oil in April and fought shy of going a fifth time to the chemist's to get another three? Why hadn't I bought a few vitamin C and glucose tablets? These 'why's' were terribly tormenting. I thought of every uneaten bowl of soup, every crust of bread thrown away, every potato peeling, with such remorse and despair as if I'd been the murderer of my children. But all the same, we did the most that we could, and believed none of the reassuring announcements of the radio.

Zina takes over

I will add to what your father has written. That year we'd gone out to the dacha late, as Father was defending his doctoral thesis. We went out on the 19th by hired van, with all our belongings. We had a nice room and a verandah, on the small side but square. Tamara slept up-

220

stairs, in the attic. The weather was fine and the children soon began to pick up. We had only nine days of enjoyment: we went bathing in the stream, walked in the woods and lay on the grass in our yard by the verandah. When we went swimming the girls lay on my back and I swam. After war was declared I stayed on without Tamara, as she'd gone into a factory but still lived in our flat at 9/12 Lakhtinskaya Street.

We stayed at Vyritsa until 18 July. Granny came to see us for a few days and M. P. Barmanski took us back home. That was a Sunday, towards evening. He helped me get the things together and we went into town with the children. Now I can't remember how we all travelled. I remember that I'd previously sent two big trunks into town—maybe Tamara helped. The children's beds were left at the dacha, and some crockery and the settee. All through the blockade the children slept on grown-ups' beds, and Nina Urvachyova gave us a bed. It was hard to get milk in town. I used to get up very early and stand in the crowd outside the market gates. Finally these opened and we all rushed for the milk stalls. At first I got two litres, but then less and less. Some of it I gave to Granny, who stayed at home with the children. I had to queue with the children as well, because until the introduction of ration cards they gave food for them: an extra kilo of groats. Ration cards were introduced and we started drying bread (rye-bread and white) on the paraffin stove. It was only because Mitya advised me to buy all the bread and to dry it, because there was famine coming, that we had a stock of rusks. That was our salvation when the bread ration went down to 250 grams and then 125. When ration cards were introduced the ration was 600 grams for workers and 400 for dependants and children. I remember that we had a stock of potatoes and butter. We kept the potatoes in the kitchen and the butter outside the door. I noticed that these stocks were going down, although we hadn't touched them, and we decided that it must be our neighbours the Kesarevs, and started keeping everything in our room. We had a stock of a few bottles of cod-liver oil, which was important for the children.

I continue writing

I had bought eleven 100-gram bottles of cod-liver oil in the chemist's on the corner of Bolshoi Prospekt and Vvedenskaya Street; it was then in a two-storey building.

Life gradually took on fantastic shapes.

The evacuation slowed by degrees and stopped. We had no need to hide our children. Bombing raids started, and there was talk of nothing else. Every day they began, always at the same time, but as the enemy was so close that there was no chance of giving warning of the approach of aircraft the air-raid sirens were only heard when bombs were already falling on the city.

I remember one of the first night raids. The bombs whistled over our fourth floor. After the sound our house shook, something screeched in the attic and we heard an explosion. Next day we saw that the bombs had fallen on the intersection of Geyslerovskaya Street and Rybatskovsksya Street—not all that close to us. A policeman on point-duty had been killed. A bomb had demolished the corner of a building where there had been a little restaurant which Blok used to frequent. It had blocked an underground shelter and burst a water-main, drowning the people who were taking shelter there. After that we decided once and for all not to go down to our basement. Firstly it was pointless, and secondly walking down from the fifth floor and back up took a lot of energy. The first to stop going was Grandfather (my father). He stayed in bed, but the Kesarevs persisted in going to the shelter and carrying with them a suitcase (the Kesarevs were a married couple who shared our flat). All the same, we were looking after a ground-floor room which overlooked the yard and for a while spent the nights there. Its owner was a single woman who worked in Kronstadt and kindly gave us the key, and we felt safer there. In so far as it was possible we tried to lead a normal life, and even went for walks in the Botanical Garden. We've still got photographs of us and the children taken there by my brother Yura. A few minutes after they were taken an air-raid started, but in the garden we felt entirely calm even while it was going on. I used to wear a grey coat, and because of that I was almost taken for a spy, as light-coloured clothes were not usual in the USSR and were the mark of the foreigner. It happened at the Vitebsk station when I was on the way to the dacha at Vyritsa. Some little boys had been following me and went to tell someone about me. Fortunately the train left quickly or I would have had to be extremely late home. By the way, a word about spies. Spy-mania rose to an incredible pitch in the city. Spies were seen everywhere. One only had to take an attache case to the bathhouse to be stopped and 'checked'. That's what happened, for example, to M. A. Panchenko, our scientific secretary. There were a lot of stories going round about spies. There was talk of signals from rooftops to German aircraft; there were supposed to be some kind of automatic beacons that started to signal immediately a raid began—they were inside the chimneys of houses (and so were only visible from above), on the Marsovo Pole and elsewhere. There may well have been an element of truth in these rumours. The Germans certainly knew everything that went on in the city.

On 8 September we were leaving the clinic on Kamenoostrovski Street. It was evening, and a marvellously beautiful cloud rose above the city. It was white as white could be, and rose up in thick, particularly massive clumps like well-whipped cream. It grew, gradually turned pink in the sunset and finally assumed gigantic, menacing proportions. Later we learnt that the Germans, on one of their first raids, had destroyed the food depot at Badayevo. The cloud had been the fumes of burning oil. The Germans persistently bombed all the food depots. They were even then preparing for a siege, while at the same time the removal of food from Leningrad was being accelerated and no efforts were being made to disperse it, as was done by the British in London. The Germans were preparing to blockade the city, and we—to hand it over to them. The evacuation of foodstuffs from Leningrad stopped only when the Germans cut all the railways, at the end of August.

Preparations for the surrender of Leningrad were also made by burning the archives. Ash—paper ash, which is especially light—flew about the streets. Once, on a clear autumn day as I was leaving *Pushkinski Dom,* I was greeted on Bolshoi Prospekt by a veritable shower of paper ash. This time books were burning; the Germans had bombed the book store at *Pechatny Dvor*. The ash veiled the sun and its light dimmed, and the ash, like white smoke, rose like an evil cloud over the city and seemed to portend imminent disaster. Meanwhile the city had become crowded; people had fled there from the outlying areas, as had peasants. Leningrad was encircled by a ring of peasant carts, which weren't allowed into the city. The peasants lived in camps with their cattle and their weeping children, who began to freeze to death on cold nights. At first people went out to them for milk and meat—they slaughtered the cattle. By the end of 1941 all those groups of peasants had frozen to death, as had the refugee women who'd been packed into schools and other public buildings. I remember one such overcrowded building on the Ligovka. I don't suppose that now anyone that worked there knows how many died there. Anyway, the first to die were those driven by 'internal evacua-

223

tion' from the southern parts of the city; they too were without belongings or stocks of food. One had only to look at them to see the full horrors of evacuation. That's how it was.

Putilov[183] workers were installed in the remaining flats in our block. One day on my return from *Pushkinski Dom* I saw a number of buses on Lakhtinskaya Street. A lot of women and children were getting, but hardly any men. I discovered that the Germans had suddenly advanced towards the Putilov works, and were mortaring the area. The inhabitants were moved out at once, but later all those families from the southern part of Leningrad froze to death. I'll tell you later about one of them, the Kolosovskis, who lived on the landing next to us. When the front stablized near the Putilov factory people from Leningrad began to go out that way—to collect the vegetables from their gardens under German fire. The Komaroviches too used to go for cabbage stalks, which gave them the opportunity of stocking up a little.

V. L. Komarovich was the only one of our friends to call on us in Leningrad. Otherwise only relatives called; uncle Vasya used to come, who began to starve early on, and we gave him and Komarovich ryebread rusks. Uncle Vasya brought the children dolls, for which he'd paid a high price—dolls one could buy but not food, not at any price. Vasya told us that he was so hungry that he'd been to see his nephew Shura Kudryavtsev and had knelt before him, begging for just a little to eat, and Shura hadn't given him anything although he had supplies. Later both Vasya and Shura died, the latter not of hunger but a death no less terrible. I'll tell you about that later.

Komarovich was always making predictions. He loved to consider the impending fate of the world, and passed some very interesting opinions. I remember him before the war on Kronverkski Prospekt; he was reading a newspaper report about the sinking of a British battleship[184]. Everybody was sure that the Germans were going to win, but he said, standing in front of the paper, "The British Lion is old and experienced. He won't be easily beaten. I think that England will win in the end". I remembered those words because from that time on I started to think the same myself. Another visitor was Petya Obnovlenski, who was inclined to panic and thought only of how he could get his hands on some food. His house was bombed. During the raid his family had gone down into the shelter, and he'd stayed under the stairs. The bomb fell right down the staircase and the steps began to fall in on him, but by a miracle he wasn't killed, as in falling they formed a kind of vault above him. He escaped with his ribs badly crushed, and was dug out as was his family from the shelter. They were unhurt, but Petya was taken to hospital and discharged a few days later. Thanks to this incident, however, they all remained alive, and this is how: Petya 'had a brainwave': he reported to the authorities that their passports had been destroyed when they were bombed, and he began to get ration cards with his old passport as well as the new one. There were very many similar incidents in the city. People obtained ration cards for those that had been evacuated, called up, killed or starved—most frequently the last.

I remember being for some reason in a paying clinic on Bolshoi Prospekt in the Petrograd District. A number of people, picked up in the street, were lying on the floor in admission. Warmers had been put on their hands and feet. Meanwhile they should have been fed, but there was nothing to feed them with. I asked what could be done for them, and was told that they would die. "But can't they be taken to hospital?" "No point, there's nothing to give them there either. They need a lot of feeding up, they're so emaciated." The staff took the corpses off to the cellar. I remember that one was quite young, but his face was black—the faces of the starving turn very dark. The nurse explained to me that the bodies had to be taken downstairs while they were still warm because when they cooled down the lice crawled off them. The city was alive with lice; people who are starving have no interest in hygiene.

What I witnessed in the clinic on Bolshoi Prospekt was the first convulsions of famine. Those who were starving were those who couldn't obtain ration cards—refugees from the suburbs or other towns. They were the first to die, living as they did crammed together on the floor in stations and schools. Thus one man had two ration cards and another none. There were countless refugees with no ration cards, but there were quite a few with more than one.

A particularly large number of ration cards got into the hands of caretakers, who collected them from the dying, received them for evacuees, collected their belongings in their empty flats and exchanged them, while it was still permissible, for food. Mama bartered her dresses for duranda or cattle-cake that saved Leningrad for the second time; the people of Petrograd had eaten it in 1918–20 when the city was starving, but there was scarcely any comparison between that famine and the one about to strike!

Trams were still running in the city. One day in August or early September I saw soldiers being taken by tram from the south of the

225

city to the north: the Finns had broken through and were advancing full speed on Leningrad and there was no one to stop them. But stop they did, on their old frontier, and didn't advance any farther. After that not a single shot was fired at Leningrad from the direction of Finland, nor did any aircraft come. Polly Shiryayev, however, and her children had to leave Terijoki on the very first day of the war. She had to send them by themselves, and they went off with a school group to Tetyushi, near Kazan. We too would have had to part with our children if we'd taken that dacha in Terijoki.

Now I'll tell you about what happened in the *Pushkinski Dom*. In August and September the canteen and the academic dining room, centres of gravity for meeting and conversation, were still open. News emanated from these places where people met one another and ... stopped meeting.

In July the registration of volunteers began. All the men were registered. They were called in turn into the Director's office, where L. A. Plotkin held court with the secretary of the Party organisation, A. I. Perepech. I remember Panchenko emerging pale and shaking: he'd refused. He'd said that he wouldn't go as a volunteer, he was going to be called up to serve with the regular army. Later he was sitting in the office saying "I feel that I'll be killed". I heard that. He was branded a coward and treated with scorn, but a few weeks later he was called up as he'd said. He fought as a partisan and was killed in the forest somewhere in the Kalinin area. Plotkin, on the other hand, who had registered everyone, obtained exemption on medical grounds and in the winter escaped from Leningrad by plane; a few hours before his departure he enrolled a 'good friend' of his, a teacher of English, onto the Institute staff and got her on the plane too.

We *belobiletniki*[185] were enlisted into the Institute self-defence detachments, issued with double-barrelled shotguns and drilled in front of the History Faculty building. I remember B. P. Gorodetski and V. V. Hippius among the marchers. The latter walked in a comical fashion on his toes, leaning his whole body forward. Our instructor laughed silently like everyone else at the determined figure of Hippius as he strode along on tip-toe. But Hippius, at whom we were laughing, was already doomed...

In the yard of the Physiological Institute hungry dogs barked frantically (later they were eaten and saved the lives of numerous physiologists). Bunks were immediately put up for us all in the Library Institute which was to serve as our barracks. Hippius and I were told

226

our places. We went, saw and ... walked away. The chaos was total, and it was obvious that there was no sense in spending the night there. Soon even training stopped: people were exhausted, they didn't report for duty and began to die 'untrained'. Part of the staff went out of town to help with more sensible tasks such as constructing defences.

The most terrible thing was the gradual dismissal of one's colleagues. By order of the Presidium, prompted by our Director P. I. Lebedev-Polyanski, who lived in Moscow and had no idea what went on in Leningrad, a 'reduction of staff' took place. Every week notices of redundancy were posted. Our department lost Pokrovskaya and Skripil. All the girls in the office were made redundant and I was transferred to office work. Dismissal was terrible, as it amounted to a death sentence: if you were made redundant you had no entitlement to ration cards and couldn't get work. Pokrovskaya was saved by becoming a nurse, and Skripil left town in the middle of winter.

Later, in Kazan, we heard about these redundancies and registrations of volunteers. Many academic colleagues died senselessly in the Kirov volunteer division, which was untrained and unarmed. Yet more died as the result of senseless redundancy, as there were no ration cards for the redundant. All the ethnographers died, the librarians suffered badly and many mathematicians perished, young and talented people. The zoologists, on the other hand, survived—a lot of them knew about hunting.

But to return to the subject. 'Firemen' and 'signallers' gathered in the canteen, armed with double-barrelled shotguns, drank tea, had some soup made with green cabbage leaves (not from the head, but the hard outer ones) and talked endlessly. G. A. Gukovski talked a very great deal. It emerged that he was Russian on his mother's side (from Novosadskiye), Orthodox, born in Odessa and had been to Venice. He was in a panic, as was Aleksandr Izrailevich Grushkin. The day the Germans came close to Leningrad he appeared in the canteen wearing a peaked cap (worn somewhat to one side) and a shirt belted in Caucasian style, and greeted us with a salute. He told us confidentially that when the Germans came he would pass himself off as an Armenian.

The Director of *Pushkinski Dom* didn't come down. His family had been evacuated and he'd moved into the Institute to live; now and then he would request a bowl of soup or some porridge in his study. Finally he fell ill with stomach trouble, questioned me about the symptoms of an ulcer and asked me to call a doctor. A doctor came from the University clinic, went into the room where he was lying with his distended stomach, sniffed the foul air in the room and pulled a face; as he left he was angry and swore: a starving doctor had been called to the overfed Director!

I remember the University clinic well: that's where I obtained my certificate for white bread. That kept us going. In September my ulcer pains started but soon passed off. The clinic windows were boarded up and the doctors saw their patients by electric light. Later they stopped seeing people as the electricity was cut off. The windows were also boarded up in the academic dining room at the Academy's Museum of Anthropology and Ethnology. One had to have special ration cards to eat there. A lot of members of staff had no ration cards and came ... to lick the plates. One of these was a nice old man by the name of Yakov Maksimovich Kaplan, a French translator. Officially he worked nowhere, took translations from the Institute, but was given no ration cards. At first V. L. Komarovich managed to get ration cards for the academic dining room, but then was refused them. He was by that time bloated with hunger. I remember him coming up to me, after this refusal, as I was eating at a little table where a little oil-lamp was burning and all but shouting at me with a strange show of passion "Dmitri Sergeyevich, give me some bread, or I shan't make it home!" I gave him mine. Later I called at his flat on Kirovski Prospekt and took him a glucose tablet and some dog-rose powder (I'd managed to buy some earlier at the chemist's). He was carrying on a peevish conversation with his wife. She (Yevgeniya Konstantinovna) had come from the Writers' Foundation offices, where they'd also been refused access to the dining room as non-members of the Writers' Union, and was criticising him for not having been able to join the Union earlier. Vasili Leonidovich put on his coat to go to the dining room himself, but his weakened fingers wouldn't obey him, and he couldn't fasten the buttons. The first muscles to go were those that were not used, or were used the least, so people's legs were the last to let them down. Many who lay down never got up again. I had been to Komarovich's before, too, and sawed him some firewood—one had to think of fuel, and firewood was not being delivered to the city.

Although the bombing had stopped people expected it to start again. They had plywood for the windows, which were criss-crossed with sticky paper. I too had taken a few sheets of plywood home, cut to fit our panes and they came in handy in 1945. And I stuck bandages, not paper, on the glass; that was supposed to be better. The photographer's glue was so strong that in 1945 we had difficulty in washing it off.

I often had to do night duty at the Institute and this was particularly unpleasant when the Germans were bombing the Petrograd District. The telephones had been cut off as early as July 1941, and it was impossible to find out whether my family was dead or alive. I had to wait for the end of my shift. Every single bomb seemed to me to have fallen right on our house. It was only when I turned into Lakhtinskaya Street and saw that the house was undamaged that I was set at ease, but I had to go all the way home, up to the fourth floor, to learn how the twenty-four hours had passed: they had seemed infinitely long.

Getting about was becoming more and more difficult. I was a 'signaller' and sometimes had to go to a colleague's flat to wake him for an extra duty. I had a night pass which my brother Yurt had obtained for me; he and his wife had left us and moved to a room that he'd found on Kirovski Prospekt in the flat belonging to Messel, the Director of *Skoraya pomoshch*[186]. I saw the city in the daytime and at night, in the early morning and the evening, during air raids, in the dark, when there was almost no one about, as people were reluctant to leave their flats.

My father continued to go to work in the Komintern (Communist International) printing house. He put out fires in the neighbouring archive, did his shifts, ate badly. At home he chopped wood on a block for our *burzhuyki*[187]—his experience of the earlier famine of 1918–19 in Petrograd served him well. One day I met him by the Admiralty and we were walking home (there were no trams) over Dvortsovy bridge when shelling started. The shells burst quite close with a deafening roar. Father walked on, not hurrying and not looking round; we merely took each other more firmly by the arm. The marks of 'those' shells are still there on the granite of the embankment by the bridge. I'd always known that my father was no coward, but that day I saw how steady he could be; he was the most inconsistent and short-tempered man that ever I knew.

Zina takes over

All the women in the block of flats used to be on watch in the street, sitting by the front door. In the evening we had to see to it that the windows were blacked out. Everyone in the block got to know everyone else while on watch, and everyone talked about where to get food. While I was on watch I made the acquaintance of a woman who offered to let me and the children sleep in a ground-floor room overlooking the yard. That was at the end of September. I remember that terrible explosion in Geyslerovskaya Street that Father mentions. I was sleeping on the folding bed in the middle of the room, and when that bomb went over I felt as if I were flying through the air with space all around me. We didn't go down to the air-raid shelter, and I didn't go there once all through the war. For about three weeks we went down to the ground floor, and then we stopped doing even that. I remember shopping with ration cards, but there was very little food to be had and we had to queue for hours, sometimes whole days, during air-raids to get food. I used to shop for the whole family and my grandparents. At the end of October I'd got all the food and was making my way home, feeling pleased. I'd got Dutch cheese instead of oil. Sergey Mikhaylovich kissed my hand and said that if it hadn't been for me he wouldn't have had any food. That's how I used up all the ration cards, except the December ones which could not be exchanged for oil.

We used to barter things. Komarovich told us that there was no alternative and that we should have no regrets. He came to see us and we gave him tea and bread, and he said "Nowadays bread's like gingerbread". Your father and I were very depressed and he tried to cheer us up. "Don't worry, Dmitri Sergeyevich, you and I'll do great things." Later on, however, he fell ill and in February he died. He advised us first of all to barter women's clothes so I took my dresses to the Sitny flea market and bartered my blue crêpe de Chine for a kilo of bread. It was a poor deal so then I bartered my grey dress for 1,200 grams of cattle-cake, which was better. We then stewed it, put it through the mincer and made pancakes of it.

And how did we make soup? We got 300 grams of meat. Your father cut it up into tiny pieces, we pounded the bones in the mortar and then made a big saucepan of soup.

Winter began very early and was bitterly cold. We had firewood, thanks to the efforts of Sergey Mikhaylovich but the caretaker refused to bring any up and advised us to take all we could into the flat.

I continue instead of Zina

I too remember that Komarovich advised us to barter women's clothes. He said "Zhura's finally realised what the situation is, and she's given permission for her best shoes to be bartered". Zhura was his daughter, who was a student at the Theatre Institute. He sometimes complained of her egoism (I remember him saying "You don't know what it means to have a sixth-form grammar school girl in the house!") Fashionable women's clothes were the only thing that could be bartered: the only people who had food were waitresses, sales girls and cooks.

Anyway, cattle-cake is not all we ate. We also ate carpenter's glue. We boiled it, added strong spices and made a jelly. Your grandfather (my father) was very fond of it. I found the glue in the Institute—eight sheets of it. One I kept in reserve, uneaten. While the glue was boiling the smell was terrible.

I hand back to Zina

We put dried roots in the glue and ate it with vinegar and mustard. Then we could just about get it down. It was amazing, I boiled the glue like a jelly, and poured it into plates where it set. And we ate semolina porridge. We'd used the semolina to clean the children's white sheepskin jackets, so it was full of strands of wool and was grey with dirt, but we were all glad of it. At the start of the war we bought several bottles of vinegar and packets of mustard. It's interesting that when we were being evacuated and were selling our belongings the bottles of vinegar fetched 150 rubles each—the same as the writing set.

How did we heat the house? Sergey Mikhaylovich had bought firewood as early as spring, but there hadn't been time to saw it up and split it, and when the war broke out the caretaker refused to do it. People began walking off with it, so we decided to bring it up to the fourth floor and put it in the kitchen, under the window, then sawed it up. Sergey Mikhaylovich then chopped it up for the makeshift stove that we cooked on. At first we lit the tiled stove in the living room. Unfortunately it was damaged and we had to call someone in to repair it and pay him in wine, which we could get for ration cards and then normally barter for bread. When Yura and Ninochka were evacuated they gave us their amazing stove. We put it in the living room and used it for both cooking and keeping warm by. We bartered my gold watch with Ninochka's friend Ronka for 750 grams of rice. It was a gold watch, foreign, flat, but it didn't go. Granny bartered her gold bracelet for three kilograms of butter and gave us one without Grandfather's knowing (he was beginning to be pathologically greedy—the consequence of malnutrition).

So I continue the tale

Our story is like a children's game: each of us writes a continuation without knowing what has gone before; the result is nonsense, which makes amusing reading. In what we're writing, however, there is nothing amusing. It was such a horror that now it is hard to recall because the memory's defence mechanism rejects the most terrifying things.

I remember two speculators calling. I was in bed, as were the children. It was dark in the room, which was lit by torch bulbs and electric batteries. Two young men came in and began to jabber out "Got any cut-glass? Drawing instruments? Cameras?" They wanted other things as well. Finally they bought something off us. By then it was February or March. They were frightening, like worms in a grave. We were still moving in our dark tomb, but they were ready to eat us.

Before that, in the autumn, Kallistov had called. He asked in fun whether we would sell him some puppies or if we knew of anyone who wanted to find a good home for any. The Kallistovs were by then eating dogs, salting down their meat. Kallistov didn't slaughter them himself—that was done in the Institute of Physiology. In any case, by the time that Kallistov came to see us there were neither dogs, cats, pigeons nor sparrows left in the city. There had been a lot of pigeons in Lakhtinskaya Street, and we saw them being caught. Pavlov's dogs in the Institute of Physiology too were all eaten. Kallistov got some of their meat. I remember meeting him on the way to the Institute of Physiology with a dog. He was walking quickly; dog meat is said to be rich in protein.

At one time we got ration cards for the 'diet canteen', which was the other side of Vvedenskaya, I think—in Pavlovskaya Street, near Bolshoi Prospekt. It was dark in the canteen; the windows had been boarded up. There were oil lamps burning on some tables, and the people having 'lunch' were gathered round one, cutting out the coupons required. A theft occurred: the lamp was put out and thieves snatched the cut out coupons and ration cards off the table. My coupons were stolen as well. There were terrible scenes. Some starving people had literally crawled to the canteen, others had been carried

232

up the stairs to the first floor where the canteen was, as they couldn't climb them by themselves. Yet others couldn't close their mouths, and saliva dripped from them onto their clothes. The faces of some were bloated, flooded with a bluish fluid, while those of others were thin and dark. And their clothes! The starving weren't so much tormented by hunger as by cold—a cold that came from somewhere inside them, insurmountable, incredibly painful—and so they wrapped themselves up as best they could. Women wore the trousers of their dead husbands, sons and brothers (the men were the first to die) and wound themselves in scarves outside their coats. They took the food away and didn't eat it in the canteen; they were taking it to their children or to people who could no longer walk. They carried containers slung over their shoulders on cords, and into them went everything, first course and second. Two ladles of porridge, and for soup—only water. It was considered to be advantageous to get cooked food against ration cards, as it was almost impossible to use them any other way.

As I left that canteen one day I saw a fearful sight. On the corner of Bolshoi Prospekt and Vvedenskaya Street there was a special military school for young people. The students there were starving, as was the case everywhere, and dying. Finally the decision had been taken to close the school, and now those who could were leaving. Some were being supported by their mothers and sisters who took hold of them by the arms as they staggered; they were wrapped in coats that hung off them like clothes-hangers; they fell and were dragged. There was snow on the ground by that time, which, of course, no one was clearing, and it was terribly cold. Farther down the street from the school was a food shop where bread was being issued. Those who had been given their issue always asked for some extra, which they ate on the spot. They jealously noted the weights by the light of the oil-lamps (it was particularly dark in the shop as the windows were covered with boards and earth) and a robbery characteristic of the blockade took place. Small boys, suffering particularly from hunger (teenagers need more food) flung themselves on the bread and began to eat at once. They didn't try to run away, only to eat a bit more before it was taken off them. They'd turned their collars up in advance, expecting a struggle, lay down on the bread and ate and ate and ate. And other thieves lurked on the staircases of the blocks of flats and robbed weakened people of their food, their ration cards, their passports. It was especially difficult for the elderly. Those whose ration cards had been taken couldn't get them replaced. It was enough for someone so enfeebled not to eat for a day or two for them to become unable to walk, and when their legs ceased to function—that was the end. Usually a family didn't die all at once. While there was at least one in a family who could walk and buy bread the rest, the bedridden, could be kept alive. But it only took the last mobile member of the family to fall in the street or on the stairs (a particular problem for those living higher up) and the rest of the family was doomed.

Corpses littered the streets, and no one gathered them up. Who were the dead? Perhaps that woman had a child still waiting for her in a cold, dark, empty flat. There were very many women who fed their children and denied themselves the little that was essential. These mothers died first, leaving the child alone. That was how our colleague in the Press, O. G. Davidovich, died. She'd given everything to her child, and was found dead in bed in her room. Her child was under the covers with her, pulling at his mother's nose to 'wake her up'. But a few days later her wealthy relatives arrived in Davidovich's room to take away ... not the child, but the few rings and brooches that she'd left. The child died later in an orphanage.

The soft parts were cut off corpses that had fallen in the streets. Cannibalism had begun! First the corpses were stripped, then sliced to the bone, but there was scarcely any flesh on them; these naked, dissected corpses were a terrible sight.

This cannibalism can't be condemned out of hand. For the most part it was unconscious. Those who dissected the bodies seldom ate the flesh themselves, but either sold it without saying what it was or used it to feed their dependants and keep them alive. The most important thing in food is protein, and that was nowhere to be found. When your child is dying and you know that only meat will save it—you'll cut some off a corpse...

There were, however, villains that killed people to get their flesh and sell it. The following was observed in the huge red building of the Philanthropic Society, on the corner of Zeleninaya Street and Geyslerovskaya Street. Someone seemed to be trading in potatoes. The purchaser would be asked to look under a settee, where the potatoes were kept, and when he bent down there came a blow with an axe to the back of the head. The crime was spotted by a purchaser who noticed blood on the floor which had not been cleaned up. A lot of human bones were discovered.

In this way one of the staff—Vavilova—of the Academy of Sciences staff was eaten. She went for some meat (she'd been told an address where things could be bartered for meat) and didn't come back. She died somewhere near the Sitny market. She'd looked comparatively healthy. We were afraid to take the children out into the street even in daytime.

There was no electric light, no water supply, no newspapers (it was spring before the first was pasted onto fences—a little bit of a page, as I recall, once or twice a week), no telephones, no radio! But all the same people still kept in touch with each other. A certain General Kulik was expected, who was supposed to be coming to hand over Leningrad. Everyone said with secret hope "Kulik's coming".

Despite the lack of electric light, water, radio and newspapers, the authorities of the State were 'watching'. G. A. Gukovski was arrested and made to sign[188] something, then B. I. Koplan and A. I. Nikiforov were put inside. V. M. Zhirmunski too was arrested. He and Gukovski were soon released and flew out. Koplan, however, starved to death in prison, and his wife, the daughter of A. A. Shakhmatov, died at home. Nikiforov was released, but he was so emaciated that he died soon after at home (and he'd been a *bogatyr*[189], a fine specimen of Russian manhood, who'd always bathed in winter in the hole in the ice outside the Exchange). Others who died were V. V. Hippius, N. P. Andreyev, Z. V. Evald, Ya. I. Yaspinski (the son of the writer), M. G. Uspenskaya (daughter of the writer)—all of them colleagues at *Pushkinski Dom*. The list is too long to repeat.

I remember the death of Yasinski. He was a tall, slim, very good-looking old man, who reminded one of Don Quixote. He lived in the *Pushkinski Dom* library. He had a folding bed, a put-you-up, behind the book-stacks. He had no one at home, and was unable to go there. He lay there behind his books and now and then went into the lobby. His mouth wouldn't shut and saliva trickled from it, his face was black and his completely white, unkempt hair framed it in eerie contrast. His skin was taut over his bones, and the skin by his mouth was especially terrible. It became thinner and thinner and failed to cover his teeth, which protruded and gave his head the appearance of a tortoise. Once he emerged from behind his book-stacks with a blanket over his shoulders and asked "What's the time?" He was told. He asked again " Is it day or night?" (the voice of those suffering dystrophy became indistinct, as the muscles of the vocal cords atrophied). He asked in the lobby, but there weren't any uncovered windows, they were all 'boxed up', and he couldn't see whether it was light or dark outside. A day or two later our Deputy Director on the domestic side, Kanaylov, turned him out of *Pushkinski Dom*. Kanaylov (what a name![190]) drove away everybody that tried to settle down to die in *Pushkinski Dom,* so as not to have to remove the body. Several of our ancillary staff—porters, caretakers, cleaning women—died, who had been drafted in, torn from their families; then, when many hadn't the strength to reach home, they were thrown out to die in thirty degrees of frost. Kanaylov kept a close eye on all that weakened, and not a single person died on the premises.

I was once present at the following scene: one of the cleaners was still quite fit and had taken ration cards from the dying for herself and Kanaylov. In came one of the workers, who was dying (the two of them had thought that he wouldn't be able to leave his bed); he looked terrible—saliva was running from his mouth, his teeth protruded and his eyes were staring. He appeared at Kanaylov's door like a spectre, like a semi-decomposed corpse, and in a hollow voice spoke two words: "Ration cards, rations cards!" Kanaylov didn't immediately catch what he said, but when he realised that he was asking him to give back his ration cards he gave a fearful roar, swore at him and struck him. The man fell over, and I can't remember what happened next. He too must have been thrown into the street.

The folklorist N. P. Andreyev died as follows. In addition to his own shift at the Institute he undertook to do that of his colleague M. K Azavodski, who had felt ill and asked Andreyev to stand in for him. He came to his colleague's aid, all the more so as Azavodski's son had just been born, right there in the air-raid shelter, and went on duty. The double turn exhausted him severely, and his daughter had gone away to work as a hospital nursing sister (that was another way of remaining alive) and wasn't there to help her father. One day Andreyev arrived at *Pushkinski Dom* on his way home from the Gertzen Institute and asked for someone to go with him, as he couldn't make it alone. He lived on Vvedenskaya Street in the house where B. M. Kustodiyev had once lived and A. M. Astakhova went with him but it took them an age to reach the flat, and twice called in on other people for a rest. In one flat Andreyev was given some sugar to eat and this gave him the strength to reach home. There were still people capable of hiding lumps of sugar—lumps of life—from themselves and their family. Food had an amazing effect: you had only to eat a little bit of sugar to feel clearly that strength was flowing back into you. Food cheered and inebriated. It was little short of a miracle! A few days later I went to see Andreyev to take him a flight ticket. Someone

236

in the Institute hadn't made use of it (one of those who had earned the goodwill of the authorities), and the ticket had to be given to Andreyev a few hours before the plane was due to leave. It was dark when I called round at his place. I remember going through the completely deserted streets, along the path down the middle of the roadway in my Romanov sheepskin jacket and with Orlov's walking-stick. On Bolshaya Pushkarskaya Street I fell and gave my knee an awful crack, but I got up (those who were severely debilitated couldn't get back up—they could only walk). I reached Andreyev's house and kept on knocking till he came to the door, which was difficult for him as he was by then unfit to travel and died a short while later. After his death his wife came round from Staro-Nevski (she was young and lived apart from him) and looked for his bank book, in which he had quite a lot of money...

The literary expert B. M. Engelhart died in a mystical, terrible way. I recall telling the story of his death many times in Kazan, but now I've forgotten it; the memory, as I've already said, purifies itself of the most dreadful recollections.

Corpses lay in the street opposite the Institute of Literature, near the Birzhevoy bridge (where one woman's body lay for about two months), in the burnt-out building of the University's Mytinsk students' hostel (I remember two children's bodies on the ground floor), on the Kronverkski—opposite the *Narodny Dom*, where in spring a mortuary was set up, to which, at the beginning of March, we took my father's body on a children's sledge.

I soon gave up walking about and only went out to collect my salary and ration cards. One day my father went for my ration cards as he was going to the printing works for his own and called in for mine on the way home. How I later regretted letting him go! Every such 'journey' took a very great deal out of him and brought death closer.

Zina saved the whole family. She queued from two in the morning to 'utilise' our food-ration cards (only very few managed to find in the shops those items they were allowed on their cards) and then she took the sledge to the Neva for water. We tried to obtain water from the snow on the roof, but it was too expensive in terms of fuel for the amount obtained. Expeditions for water went like this: a child's bath was placed on the sledge, and sticks were put in it. These were needed to stop the water splashing too much; they floated and prevented waves forming on the water. Zina and Tamara (she was living with us in the loft off the kitchen) fetched the water from a spot near the Krestovski bridge. The route taken by the inhabitants of the city in their quest for water was a sheet of ice, as any water that was spilled froze at once in the temperature of minus thirty. Many sledges slid off the middle of the road onto their sides and spilled all their water. Everyone had the same baths and sticks or buckets with sticks: sticks were the discovery of the age! Hardest of all, however, was to scoop up the water and then to climb back up from the Neva onto the embankment. People crawled on all fours, clinging to the slippery ice. No one had the strength to cut steps. In February, actually, a few points were set up where water could be obtained: at the fire brigade on Bolshoi Prospekt, for example. A water-hole was opened there but the ice built up around it so that people had to crawl flat on their stomachs up the ice mound and lower the bucket into the well. Then they had to slide back down clutching tight hold of it.

In December, if I remember correctly, we had a few chances of escaping by lorry across Lake Ladoga. This road over the ice was known as the Road of Death (and not at all the 'Road of Life', the sugary term used by later writers). The Germans shelled it, snow blocked it, and lorries often sank through holes (they went at night, of course). The story was told of a mother who lost her mind: she was travelling on the second lorry with her children in the first, and before her eyes it sank beneath the ice. Her lorry quickly went round the hole in which her children were struggling under the water and roared on without stopping. How many people died of starvation, were killed, fell under the ice, froze or vanished without trace on that road! God alone knows! The husband of the folklorist A. N. Lozanova died there. She was pulling him on a child's sledge as he could not longer walk. She left him on the other side of Ladoga with the luggage on the sledge and went to get bread but when she returned there was neither sledge nor husband nor luggage. Robbery was rife and the weak had their possessions stolen and they were pushed under the ice. At every step one encountered villainy and nobility, extreme selfishness and self-sacrifice, thieving and honesty.

This was the road taken by our villain Kanaylov. He took a few more healthy men onto the Institute staff and proposed that they be evacuated along with himself, on condition that they took nothing with them of their own but carried his cases. These were, incidentally, not his cases, but were from the Onegin bequest, which had come to us by from Onegin, a bastard son of Aleksandr III who had been a lover of Pushkin and collector of books. These suitcases were

238

of yellow leather, and into them were heaped antiques from *Pushkinski Dom* and bundles of marvellous carpets (we had, for example, a late eighteenth century light blue French carpet). Off went Kanaylov with his henchman Yekhalov, also a villain of the deepest dye. He had previously been a trades union activist (or leader), appearing at meetings, calling them and making inflammatory speeches. Then he came to us as bursar and stole. The whole company succeeded in crossing the ice of Lake Ladoga.

But at some railway junction Yekhalov persuaded the workers to help him, got into a train with them and all the carpets (not the train that Kanaylov intended travel in), waved goodbye to Kanaylov and left. There was nothing that Kanaylov could do; now he works in Saratov, I believe, as a member of the city council, has a position of responsibility—but he won't venture back to Leningrad. Yekhalov, however, did come back. He even decided to offer his services to *Pushkinski Dom* immediately after the war, but he was summoned to the Leningrad Academy of Arts and told that he was wanted on a criminal charge. He disappeared from the Academy, but somehow found work allocating flats somewhere on Vasilevski Island. As the person in charge of flats he acquired a number for himself, took bribes and in the end was arrested. Before that he also turned up in Kazan and walked around in a military uniform (he was never in the forces) with a walking stick, pretending to have been invalided out.

After the departure of Kanaylov M. M. Kalaushin took over the Institute. Redundancies ceased; on the contrary, a number of people were engaged—among them our Tamara. Kalaushin himself had previously been one of the first to be dismissed. He'd been working as a hospital porter, and when he turned up to start work at the Institute before Kanaylov left I scarcely recognised him. His face had become puffy, covered in blotches, and quite deformed. In the Institute he organised something with the ration cards, took on V. M. Glinka, approached V. A. Manuylov and later appointed Steblin-Kamenski. The four of them kept the Institute going until 1945, and when Kalaushin left Manuylov remained in charge.

Whenever I went into Kalaushin's office he was eating. He ate bread, dunking it in vegetable oil. He obviously still had the ration cards of people who had flown out or set off along the 'road of death.'

Even before Kaynalov and Yekhalov left, submariners from the boats moored in the Malaya Neva had been let into the Institute. The point was that the remains of our fleet, the icebreakers, the turboelectric Vyacheslav Molotov—all of them had been brought into the Neva and moored on the left bank under the protection of the surrounding buildings. The Vyacheslav Molotov was by the Admiralty, the icebreaker Yermak by the Hermitage and so on. This was not without risk for the two most precious buildings in the city. Our submarines weren't nice neighbours either, and not only because they might attract the German bombers our way.

The ships' crews were allowed into our museum and they promised to give the management a bowl of soup each. For this reason their rooms were furnished with all the best furniture. Turgenev's sofa, Batyushkov's armchair, Chaadayev's[191] clock, etc.—everything was handed over to the sailors for the proverbial mess of potage. The latter was certainly in evidence, and seemed unusually tasty. Furthermore, the sailors had permission to use the library. They owed us nothing but ran a cable from the submarines and gave themselves and the management real electric light! And then it started... At night shadows drifted about the museum, broke into cupboards, looked for treasure. The collection of albums of the nobility suffered in particular, as did many cupboards in the library. And in spring, when the Neva thawed, the sailors left the Institute one fine day without warning, taking with them everything that they could. After they'd gone I found on the floor a gilded plaque: Chaadayev's clock. The clock itself had gone. On what ocean floor is it now?

Malnutrition led to kleptomania even among Institute staff. One of the office staff even stole the wall-clock from the Institute, as well as the baize cloth from the conference table and other things. Then she went to work in the hospital and wasn't seen again in the Institute. She'd been a friend of Kanaylov.

In winter uncontrollable fires broke out. Houses burned for weeks, as there was no means of putting them out. Enfeebled people couldn't look after their makeshift stoves. In every house there were debilitated people who couldn't move and were burnt alive. There was a dreadful incident in a new house on Suvorovski Prospekt (the house is still standing, opposite Akhmatova's. It had been converted into a hospital and a bomb landed on it. The bomb was of the combined high-explosive/incendiary type, and it crashed through every floor, destroying the staircase. A fire started downstairs so that it was impossible for people to get out. The wounded hurled themselves from windows: it was better to be smashed to pieces than burn to death.

In our block a family of Putilov workers froze to death. Our care-taker Trofim Kondratyevich was obtaining ration cards for them and went about at first quite healthy. As we later discovered the following incident took place on our landing, in the Kolosovskis' flat. A woman whom Zina knew had taken in the children of the dying Putilov workers (I've said above that children often died later than their parents, who had often given them their food); she obtained rations cards for them but ... kept them locked up and gave them nothing to eat. The enfeebled children couldn't get out of bed but just lay there quietly and quietly died. Their bodies were left where they lay until the start of the following month, when new ration cards could be obtained for them. In spring that woman left and went to Arkhangelsk. What she did was also a form of cannibalism, the most terrible form.

The corpses of those who died of starvation hardly decayed at all; so desiccated were they that they could last a long time. The families of the dead didn't bury them as they were drawing their ration cards. Nor was anyone afraid of the corpses and the relatives of the dead didn't go into mourning or shed any tears. The doors of flats wouldn't shut, because ice accumulated on the stairs just as it did on the roads (water being carried up in buckets splashed or was spilt by enfeebled people, and froze at once), and so the cold permeated all the flats. That was how the folklorist Kaletski died. He lived somewhere near Kirovski Prospekt. Someone called to see him and found the door ajar: evidently the inhabitants had been trying to chip away the ice in an attempt to shut it, but had failed. In the cold rooms, under blankets, furs, carpets, lay the corpses—desiccated, not putrefied. When had they died?

In the queues people kept hoping. After Kulik they expected someone else to come to Leningrad. We had no idea what was happening elsewhere in the country; we only knew that the Germans had not reached everywhere, and that Russia still existed. The Road of Death led there, to Russia, aircraft flew there, but scarcely any food came from there—not for us, at all events. Yura and Ninochka, his second wife, went off along the Road of Death in a lorry that was specially equipped for survival. Before they left Yura promised to send us food and my father waited for this food with fearful impatience, thinking all the time of Yura sending some smoked sausage. He talked about food constantly, reminiscing about meals on the Volga ships, and when he had some soup (more precisely, what we called soup) he snorted loudly. This snorting annoyed me, as by then

241

I was gripped by the irritability that comes with malnutrition, and I didn't realise that his snorting was indicative of heart trouble. The smoked sausage he was waiting for was another source of irritation for me.

Now I'll tell you about our way of life in the flat in Lakhtinskaya Street. We tried to stay in bed as much as possible, piling on ourselves as much warm clothing as we could. We were lucky that our windows were intact. Some of the panes were covered with plywood and criss-crossed with bandage. Nevertheless it was light in the daytime. We went to bed at six in the evening. We read a bit by the light of electric torches and oil lamps (I'd remembered how we made oil lamps in 1919 and 1920, and the experience came in handy), but it was very difficult to sleep. The cold seemed to be internal and went right through you—your body produced too little heat. The cold was more awful than the hunger. It aroused internal irritability; it was like itching inside, and the itching seized your whole body, made you toss and turn from side to side. All you could think of was food, and you thought the most idiotic thoughts about it: if I'd known sooner that there was going to be a famine! if only I'd stocked up with tinned goods, flour, sugar, smoked sausage!

Zina and I worked out how many days we could last on our reserves. If we used a sheet of carpenter's glue a day that would last so long, if we used a sheet every two days then it would last longer. But then came the complaint: why hadn't I eaten up my helping at such-and-such a time? It would have come in handy now! Why hadn't I bought biscuits in the shop in July? I'd known by then that there would be a famine. Why had I only bought eleven bottles of cod-liver oil? I should have gone to the chemist's again, or sent Zina. And so on like that, endlessly, with terrible anger against oneself, and again the internal tickling, again the tossing and turning.

In the morning the *burzhuyka* was lit. We fuelled it with books, using the bulky volumes of reports of the sessions of the State *Duma*. I burnt them all except the proofs of the last sessions, as that was a great rarity. One couldn't put a whole book into the stove, as it wouldn't burn: it had to be torn up and thrown into the fire page by page. The pages had to be crumpled and from time to time the ash had to be cleared, as there was too much chalk in the paper. In the morning we said our prayers, the children too. We taught the children poetry; they learnt by heart 'Tatyana's dream', the 'Ball at the Larins', Pleshcheyev's 'Home from school the children came, Red their faces from the frost...'[192], Akhmatova's 'My Tatar grandmother gave me...' and other things. The children were four and knew a lot already. They didn't ask for food, only watched jealously when they sat down to table that everyone got a fair share. They would sit at the table waiting for an hour or an hour and a half, however long it took their mother to do the cooking. I used to pound bones in the mortar, and we cooked them over and over again. Porridge was completely liquid, more so than ordinary soup, and to thicken it we put in it potato flour, starch and 'used' semolina with which the children's rabbit-fur coats had been cleaned. The children laid the table themselves and sat themselves down in silence, watching quietly as the 'food' was prepared. Not once did they burst into tears or ask for more; of course, everything was shared equally.

The heat from the *burzhuyka* made the room warmer at once. Sometimes it became red hot. How pleasant that was!

People went about dirty, but we used to wash, devoting to the purpose a glass or two of water which we didn't throw away: we washed our hands in it until it was black. The lavatory didn't work. At first we could flush it, but then it froze up somewhere down below. We used to go through the kitchen into the loft. Others used to wrap up their doings in paper and throw them out into the street, so that it was dangerous to walk near houses, but paths were trodden out down the middle of the roads. Fortunately, for serious matters we went once a week or even once every ten days. That was to be understood, as the body converted everything, and there was not enough for it to convert. It was lucky for us that we were on the fifth floor, with easy access to the loft... When the weather grew warmer in spring there appeared brown stains on the ceiling in the corridor: we'd been going at defined places.

The stove became blocked from the burning of paper—Zina's mentioned that already. Fortunately we found a stove-man who cleared the deposit in the stove and combined the flues into one, so that we could light it again.

*

There has been a break in my writing of some three weeks. We are at the dacha in Zelenogorsk (Listvennaya 16, dacha 132) and there's been a heat wave, which has removed all thoughts of the blockade. Sunshine, bathing, the happy atmosphere of a contented life!

243

No! Hunger is incompatible with productivity, or with any sort of contentment. They can't exist side by side. One of the two—either hunger or contentment—must be a mirage. I think that real life is hunger, and the rest a mirage. In the time of famine people revealed themselves, stripped themselves, freed themselves of all trumpery. Some turned out to be marvellous, incomparable heroes, others—scoundrels, villains, murderers, cannibals. There were no half-measures. Everything was real. The Heavens were unfurled and in them God was seen. The good saw Him clearly, and miracles were performed.

God said: Inasmuch as thou art not cold nor hot I will spew thee out of my mouth (I think that comes in the Apocalypse)[193].

The last thing to die in a man was the brain. When arms and legs had ceased to function, fingers wouldn't do up buttons, there was no strength left to close the mouth, the skin grew dark and taut over the teeth, when the face became a skull with bared, grinning teeth, the brain went on working. People kept diaries, wrote philosophical essays, scientific works, thought sincerely, from the heart, showed unusual resolve, not yielding to pressure, not giving in to vanity and vain glory.

The painter Chupyatov and his wife starved to death. As he died he painted; when he had no more canvas he used plywood and card-board. He was a 'lion' painter of ancient aristocratic lineage, an ac-quaintance of the Anichkovs. They gave us two of the sketches that he did before he died: a fiery apocalyptic angel, full of serene wrath at the evil doing of the wicked, and the Saviour, in whose image there's a trace of the exaggerated forehead of the dystrophic citi-zens of Leningrad. The Anichkovs kept his best picture: a dark Len-ingrad yard, like a well, darkened windows stretching downward, not a single light showing in any of them; in it death has overcome life, although life, perhaps, is still alive but lacks the strength to light an oil-lamp. Above the yard, on the dark background of the night sky, is the Protective Veil of the Mother of God. She inclines her head, looking down in horror as if seeing everything that is taking place in the flats of Leningrad, and spreading out her vest-ment, on which is portrayed an ancient Russian shrine (perhaps the church of the Veil on the Nerl, the first church dedicated to the Veil).

This picture must be preserved. In it the spirit of the blockade is more vividly portrayed than anywhere else.

V. L. Komarovich died. That was hard to believe. He'd been to see us in September, so cheerful and active, had taught us how to barter things for food and had made consoling forecasts.

I was told of his death by T. N. Kryukova (his pupil at Nizhegorod University) and I. N. Tomashevskaya. This is how it happened. He was already bedridden when the decision was taken to evacuate the Theatre Institute. Zhura (his daughter, a student at the Institute) and Yevgeniya Konstantina (his wife) decided to go and to leave him behind as he wouldn't have stood the journey. They intended to leave him in a newly-opened clinic for dystrophics of the Writers' Union. The position was beginning to improve a little in Leningrad, and clinics were opening for starving writers and academics, in which they were taken from their families (they couldn't feed everybody) to be fattened up somewhat. In the *Dom Pisatelya* preparations were in hand for an establishment for dying writers, and I. N. Tomashevskaya was to be the dietician there. The opening of the clinic was postponed, but the Road of Death convoy had to leave. And so Zhura and Yevgeniya Konstantinovna, his daughter and wife, took Komarovich from the flat, fastened him to the seat of a Finnish sledge and took him over the Neva to Voynova Street. At the clinic they found Tomashevskaya and begged her to take him in. She firmly refused: the clinic was to open in a few days' time—what was she to give him during that period? And so his wife and daughter abandoned him, leaving him in the semi-basement where the cloakroom is now, and went away. Then they came back in secret, peeped in at him, left there to die. What they went through—he too! When Tanya Kryukova was attending to him in the clinic after it opened he said to her "You know, Tanya, those wicked women came peering at me, hiding from me!" Tomashevskaya had found Komarovich and took bread from her own husband and son to feed him; when feeding was organised in the clinic she did her level best to save his life, but his dystrophy had reached the irreversible stage in which the patient no longer has the will to eat and can't: the system consumes itself, eats itself away. He dies of exhaustion however much he's given to eat. By the time Vasili Leonidovich died there was food for him to eat. Tanya took care of him; he looked like an immensely old man, his voice was a croak, his hair completely white. But the brain dies last of all, and he was working—working on his doctoral thesis! He had a briefcase with him containing drafts; I later printed one of his chapters (on Nikol Zarazski) in the *Transactions of the Department of Ancient Russian Literature* (vol. V, 1947). The chapter was perfectly 'normal', and no one would imagine that had been written by a dying man who scarcely had the strength left to hold a pencil, a man dying of hunger! But he could feel death: every footnote bears a date—he was counting the days. And he could see God: his footnotes aren't merely dated numerically, but also by the Church feast days. His papers are now in the archives of *Puskinski Dom*, where I deposited them after they were handed to me by Kryukova and I'd extracted the chapter on Nikol Zarazski. Kryukova took him meat twice—meat, of which she and her husband were so short themselves. Her husband also died later. February, however, the month when Komarovich died, was still a month when men were dying. Women began to be the majority of those dying in March. Kryukova was still alive in February, and in March she left the city.

What later became of Zhura and Yevgeniya Konstantinovna? Could they go on living after all that? First they went to either Saratov or Samara. They were both in the theatre, where they met B. M. Eykhenbaum, who'd managed to leave Leningrad a few weeks after them. They rushed to him (it was in the theatre!) and asked "What's the news about Vasili Leonidovich?" He never saw them again and was unable to tell them any more. People said that they'd been in the northern Caucasus (in either Pyatigorsk or Kislovodsk), been captured by the Germans and had gone off with them. I was assured that they were no longer in the land of the living[194].

There were a lot of incidents such as that involving Komarovich. The Modzalevskis left Leningrad, leaving their young daughter dying in hospital, and so saved the lives of their other children. The Saltykovs left Leningrad in spring, leaving their mother fastened in a sledge on the platform of the Finland Station as the public health authorities wouldn't let her through. The dying were left—mothers, fathers, wives, children; those whom it was 'pointless' to feed ceased to be fed; people chose which child to save and left them in feeding clinics, hospitals, on station platforms, in freezing flats, in order to save themselves; the dead were searched—their gold was wanted: gold-filled teeth were broken out, fingers cut off for rings, men and women alike; corpses were stripped in the streets to provide warm clothes for the living; bits of desiccated skin were cut off them to boil up for soup for the children; people were prepared to cut off flesh for their children; those that were left behind remained in silence, kept diaries and notes, so that later someone at least should know how millions died. Were the renewed German shelling and air-raids frightening? Whom could they frighten? There were no satisfied people. Only people dying of hunger live a real life, are able to achieve the greatest villainy and the greatest self-sacrifice, fearless of death. And the brain dies last: when there have already died in some conscience, terror, mobility, feeling—and in others egoism, the instinct of self-preservation, cowardice and pain.

The truth about the blockade of Leningrad will never be printed. It's made into pap. Vera Inber's *Pulkovski meridian* is Odessa pap. There's something approaching the truth in the notes of Erisman, director of the hospital dissecting-room, which were printed in *Zvezda* in 1944 or '45. There's something approaching the truth too in a few 'confidential' medical articles on dystrophy. There aren't very many and absolutely everything in them is 'politically correct' ...

In his article *Kto sochtët... (Leningrad. Blokada Deti)*[195] (in *Nash sovremenik*, 1986, no. 8 p. 170) Viktor Karamzin states "During the blockade 632,253 citizens of Leningrad died". Rubbish! The very idea of counting to the last one! On the basis of what documentary evidence, and who did the counting?

Who indeed will make the reckoning ... of those who slid beneath the ice, were picked up in the streets and immediately taken to the mortuaries and the mass graves? The inhabitants of the suburbs and the surrounding villages that fled into Leningrad? And those that sought salvation from the oblasti of Pskov and Novgorod? And all the others—the refugees that had no papers, who died without ration cards in the unheated accommodation allotted to them: schools, higher educational establishments, colleges, cinemas?

Why underestimate, and obviously, on such a gigantic scale as a factor of three or four? In the first edition of his Memoirs G. Zhukov states that about a million died of starvation, but in subsequent editions that figure was omitted under the influence of the frenzied demands of the former Head of the Leningrad Supply Department.

In August 1942, however, it was stated at a meeting of the City Council that by then, on documentary evidence alone (taken from registrations), about 1,200,000 persons had died; this I have from Professor N. N. Petrovich, who was present at the meeting.

I have some notes on the subject to add to that villainous supplier's account.

Mortality reached its apogee in February and March, although the bread ration was slightly increased. I didn't go to work, occasionally went out for bread. Zina brought in the food and bread, enduring the terrible queues. There were two sorts of bread: blacker and whiter. I read that one should take the whiter sort, and so we did. But it was poor stuff! We would really have liked a crust. People looked greedily at the bits used as makeweight, and many asked the shopkeepers for them and ate them in the street. When Zina brought him his bread ration my father used to look closely to see if there had been any bits; he was afraid that she might have eaten them on the way. But Zina always tried to have less than the rest of us. The Stelbin-Kamenskis used to eat half their ration on the way home. People used to chew groats and eat dried meat because they couldn't wait to get home. They picked up every crumb off the table with their fingers. A special movement of the fingers developed, by which people from Leningrad recognised each other in evacuation: they squeezed breadcrumbs on the table onto their fingers so that these fragments stuck to them and could be put in their mouths. To leave breadcrumbs was simply unthinkable. Plates were licked out even though the 'soup' in them had been completely liquid and devoid of solid content; people were afraid of leaving any *zhirinka* in them (that was a Leningrad term in those days, like *dovesochek*[196]).

That was when a mouse actually died of starvation on our window-sill...

In February my father was bedridden and bloated, and got up only for food. Zina or I used to light his little stove. It became cold in his room—there was no heating downstairs. Long puddles would form when there was heat, as the frozen window-panes thawed. He would think about the restaurants on the Volga ships (he'd been for holidays on the Volga by himself now and then) and of the sausage that Yura was going to send. His heart began to give out, and at the end of February he had severe pains in the region of his heart and left shoulder. We managed to persuade an elderly doctor, who lived in the house opposite, to visit. He could scarcely climb to our fifth floor flat, but my father refused to be examined (he didn't care for medicine or doctors) and the old doctor went away and wouldn't accept the bread that we pressed into his hands. The old doctor soon died, as did his wife. He advised us all the same to warm some water and put father's hands in it, and this we did several times. There were no medicines, as there was no one to make any, but all the same some at least of the chemists were open, selling fragrant toilet water (all the eau-de-Cologne had been drunk). We went to the chemist in Geyslerovski, opposite Lakhtinskaya, and bought a few bottles of toilet water, but my father lay there, groaning with pain—though not much, as he was a very patient man. He died at about eight in the morning of the first of March. He'd been sleeping on the settee in my mother's room (for the last days he was afraid of being left alone, and he was afraid of the month of March), and he was feeling pretty bad when I went to see him early that morning. There was a tiny electric torch burning at his side in the darkness—it ran off the door-bell batteries. From time to time he would raise himself and put his hand on the battery, and the light of the tiny bulb would go out, then shine forth again. Then I went out to finish my coffee. He knocked on the partition, and when I returned he was quite poorly. Nevertheless he got up to go to the lavatory and I couldn't persuade him to go back to bed. He was scarcely able to get there and back. He wouldn't use the chamber pot. He just kept on repeating *"Tsaritsa nebesnaya!"* [Heavenly mother]. You children in the next room didn't understand that Granddad was dying. He breathed a last sigh, and I covered his eyes with big eighteenth-century ruble coins—all that he had from his mother, Praskoviya Alekseyevna, who'd died when he was five. A sighing sound came from his chest—air escaping from his lungs.

What followed was terrible. How were we to bury him? We had to give a few loaves of bread for a grave. Coffins were not being made at all, and there was a trade in graves. It was difficult to dig graves in the frozen ground for the ever mounting number of the bodies of the thousands that were dying. And the grave-diggers sold graves that were already 'in use', burying someone, then taking up the deceased and burying another, then a third, a fourth, and so on, tossing the first-comers into a mass grave. Thus we'd buried uncle Vasya (my father's brother), and in the spring we couldn't find even the grave in which he'd enjoyed his 'eternal rest' for just a day or two. It seemed to us dreadful to be paying in bread, but we did the same as everyone else. We laid father out, washing him with toilet water, sewed him into a sheet, tied him up with white cord (not hempen, but made of something else) and began to worry about having the death certified. Downstairs in our clinic at the corner of Kamenoostrovski and the river Karpovka there were little tables at which sat women who took the passports of deceased persons and issued death certificates. There were long queues at these tables. They didn't put the cause of death as 'starvation' but thought up other things—such were their orders! Some disease was certified for my father and, without seeing him, they issued the death certificate. The queue moved quickly, although it became no shorter...

Zina, Tamara and I carried my father's body down from the fifth floor and put it on a pair of children's sledges joined by a piece of plywood. We tied the body on with white cords and took it to the *Narodny Dom*. There, in the garden, where he loved to go to the outdoor theatre in summer, he was laid among thousands of other bodies; some of them were also sewn up in sheets, some were not; some were clothed, some were naked. That was the mortuary. Before that we had said the burial service over him in the Vladimir Cathedral. We poured handfuls of earth into the sheet, one for him, one for a woman who had been saying the service for her son, who had died she knew not where. So we committed him to the earth. From time to time lorries came to the mortuary, loaded on the bodies in piles and took them to the Novoderevenskoye cemetery. So he lies in a mass grave, but in which, we don't know.

His death certificate is dated the second of March, and we buried him on the third or the fourth.

I remember a lorry arriving at the mortuary as we arrived with father. We asked for him to be put on straight away but the workmen wanted money, and at the time we hadn't got any. We were afraid that while he lay there he would be stripped, the sheet torn, his gold teeth broken off. The lorry didn't take him...

After that I several times saw the lorries that carried the bodies going down the streets, but now carrying bread or rationed foodstuffs. They were the only ones running in our silenced city. Bodies were carried piled high, and in order to get more on some of them round the sides were placed upright, as firewood was carried. I remember one lorry that was loaded with bodies frozen into fantastic positions. They had been petrified, it seemed, in mid-speech, mid-shout, mid-grimace, mid-leap. Hands were raised, glassy eyes open. Some of them were naked. I remember the body of a woman; she was naked, brown, thin, upright in the lorry holding in the other bodies, preventing them from falling off. The lorry was going at speed and her hair was streaming in the wind, while the bodies behind her back bounced and jumped over the pot-holes. She was making a speech, calling out, waving her arms—a ghastly, defiled corpse with open, glassy eyes!

I didn't weep for my father—people generally didn't weep in those days. But while he'd been alive, weak though he'd been, I'd always felt in him a kind of defence. He'd always been my father even when we argued and I was angry with him; I always felt in him a stronger man. With his death I felt a sudden dread of life. What would become of us? Although my father had for a long time been unable to do anything I'd always felt subordinate to him. Now I felt that I was number one, responsible for the lives of my family—Zina, the children, my mother—to an even greater extent than before. Father's room stood empty, his little red settee was empty where he'd slept. The furniture which he'd bought so carefully for the family had been orphaned.

Two or three years before his death he'd set aside money for his colleagues to hold his *pominki*[197]. He'd told me that there were without fail to be celebrations after his death, and he recalled happy funerals of certain of his friends at the press. He had been loved for his cheerful disposition and his fervent morals. There were a lot of tales about him, many of which I heard after the war. But there he was dead, and no one knew except ourselves and the few indifferent, weary people who'd taken back his passport and certified his death, and the workmen who'd refused to put his body on the lorry.

Later still, when we'd moved to Kazan, I often thought that I could see my father's back, or his peaked cap on some passer-by. To this day I often dream of him, especially before unpleasant events. He's sorry for me, and I weep in sorrow for him. In my dreams I weep for him, embrace him, hug him to me. In March my heart turned to ice, but it thawed in Kazan, where I thought about my father an especially great deal, and understood him...

Again a break in my writing. I find it irksome to set about describing death after death.

*

Aleksandr Alekseyevich Makarov died, Zina's father. Zina managed to go twice on foot to see him when he was still alive. The third time she went he was no longer of this earth. The neighbours said that for the past few days he'd not wanted anything and had stopped eating. In his sideboard there was a slab of chocolate and other things to eat. Obviously, he'd been keeping those till last...

My uncle Vasya died. They all fell out in his family and used their own ration cards. His strength gave out and he could no longer fetch bread. He died in the same room as his wife and daughter. They were left alive, and he'd fallen out with them. They say that before he died he didn't really understand what was going on, cursed and swore. He has no grave, just as there are none for the others.

In March a feeding clinic for dystrophics began to operate in *Dom Uchenykh*[198]. Its main point was that they took people in that had no ration cards. My family still had cards, but Kalaushin and Manuylov sent me there through the Institute of Literature. Zina took me there by sledge on which there was a bed, with pillows and a blanket. It was terrible being away from home, as shelling and bombing had started, there were a lot of fires, and no telephones. I was only supposed to be going for two weeks, but anything might happen. Was it a parting for ever? The patients' rooms in *Dom Uchenykh* were heated a little, but all the same it was very cold. The rooms were upstairs, but for meals one had to go downstairs to the dining room, and that movement up and down the dark stairs was very tiring. We ate in the dark dining room by oil lamps and couldn't see what was on our plates. We could just make out the plates and see that something had been poured or put on them. The food was nourishing. Only there did I realise the meaning of 'appetite'. I had an appetite like never before: my body was reviving! In the intervals between meals I lay in bed under the covers and waited in torment for the next, went, ate that and began waiting again.

There was shelling on a number of occasions, with the shells bursting on the Neva ice. The river was clearly visible from the clinic windows as the plate glass panes were intact. It was odd that large plate glass panes didn't break as easily as ordinary glass during shelling. One day I had to cross the Neva to go to *Pushkinski Dom* for some reason, and I saw a woman who'd been killed in the bombardment. She was lying right there by the path, half-covered with snow, her hair spread out, and had been lying there for some days in a pool of blackened blood. A few people in the clinic died; their dystrophy had reached the irreversible stage. They didn't want to eat, and lay there, black, their paper-thin lips now covering, now revealing their teeth. A few scientists stole or forged the coupons for which they were given breakfast, lunch and dinner—such forgery wasn't all that difficult. A Doctor of Science was caught doing this, an astronomer or a chemist, I think.

Eventually my short stay in the clinic came to an end. Zina came for me with the sledge and we carried it through the puddles—spring was here.

At home I not only started to collect material on medieval poetry (I still have my notebooks), but also to write. The point was that M. A.

Tikhonova had been called into the Smolny and invited to organise a team for the speedy writing of a book on the defence of Russian towns. She suggested me as a member of the team, and I went with her to the Smolny, which was not an easy journey for me. From Ploshchad Smolnogo to the main building everything was covered with camouflage netting. Inside it smelled like a dining room, and the people looked well-fed. We were received by a woman whose name I forget, who looked plump and healthy, whereas my legs were shaking from climbing the stairs. She ordered us to do the book in some phenomenally short length of time. She said that writers wrote about one and the same subject, but their work moved slowly, and she (!) wanted the book done quickly. We agreed, and in May the booklet *Oborona drevnerusskikh gorodov* [The Defence of the Ancient Russian Towns] was ready. It came out in the autumn of 1942. I had written the chapters 'Azov—mighty city', 'Pskov' and something else. More than half the chapters were mine, while Tikhanova wrote the chapter about the Troitsko-Sergiyevna Lavra, the introduction and the conclusion. We handed the manuscript in at *Gospolitizdat* to Peterson, who later died in detention in connection with the 'Leningrad case'. I remember that it was well-written—dystrophy didn't affect the working of the brain.

In spring a newspaper, the *Leningradskaya Pravda*, started to appear, though not daily and in reduced format. We only managed to get an occasional copy. It was from the papers that I learnt of the loss of the palace of Pavlovsk and the church at Volotovo; the destruction of both these monuments was described, though they weren't named. Pavlovsk had been destroyed by our own bombers (the German staff was quartered there), while we'd had an artillery observation post in the church, and it had been wrecked by German fire. Later, when I was in Novgorod in 1944, I noticed that the same had happened to Nikola Lipny—our forces had been there. In the book *Pamyatniki russkoy kultury, razrushënnye fashistami* [Monuments of Russian Culture Destroyed by the Fascists]—we've got a copy at home although it was later banned—the trenches at Nikola Lipny are clearly visible, and they're ours. The destruction of the palaces of Leningrad (in particular the Yelagin, which was set on fire before our eyes by the cooking-stoves of units quartered there), of Novgorod and Pskov upset me considerably.

At home things became markedly better. Granny and Zina used to go to Ronka the speculator, from whom they got oil, rice and whatever else in exchange for gold. The oil certainly kept us going. Granny gave us part of the food she bartered and gave the children things to eat. We learnt a poem with the children—Pushkin's *Chto piruyet tsar veliki v Peterburge gorodke* [What does the great Tsar feast on in the city of Petersburg]. The children enjoyed reeling it off, and I enjoyed the parting words of Peter's enemies. Different wars, different statesmen.

There were rumours that the Germans had taken Tikhvin. A mob on Bolshoy Prospekt looted a bread-shop. New policemen appeared, well fed, from somewhere the Vologda region and elsewhere.

I bumped into Kolya Guryev, who was helping to deliver bread to a bread-shop, for which he was given bread in excess of his ration. Soon afterwards he left Leningrad by the Road of Death and died like thousands of others. He's said to have got out of a train and disappeared. When his mother, brothers and wife died I don't know.

Tamara went off to dig trenches around the hamlet of Perya and was there a long time. Seed for kitchen gardens began to be distributed through official organisations. I remember being given a packet of radish seed. We made a kitchen garden in the flat by inverting the dining table, unscrewing the legs and filling it with soil from the square in Lakhtinskaya *Street*; we put it by the window and planted the radishes. We ate the leaves as a salad, for the vitamins. In May we ate orach and were surprised at how good it tasted. People in the country had eaten it from time immemorial when they were hungry, and our situation was significantly worse; obviously, we liked even that. People dug up dandelion roots in the squares, stripped off the bark of oaks to stop their gums bleeding—all the oaks that died in Leningrad!—ate buds, boiled up grass porridge. What didn't they do! But strangely enough there were no epidemics that spring, apart from the dystrophic diarrhoea which afflicted almost everyone—but we escaped.

We gave up our coupons for high-calorie diet. This was issued at the Academy dining room (where it still is, next to the Institute of Ethnography). We had to go and take it in two doses. Even so a lot of people didn't go away but sat right there on the embankment so as not to waste their strength. I remember pieces of glucose being issued, and after you'd eaten it your strength returned at once. It was amazing, almost a miracle. By then a few trams had started running. The fuel for the power station was taken from wooden houses that had been demolished; in that way Novaya Derevnya was dismantled.

The tram ran along Bolshoy Prospekt on the Petrograd Side, along Pervaya Liniya, Universitetskaya Naberezhnaya, over Dvortsovy bridge and down Nevski Prospekt. The other routes weren't yet running. Once, as I was getting on a tram, I got badly hurt. I was lifting my foot to step onto the platform when the tram set off. I found it hard to get on, as trams ran only rarely, but I wanted to. I didn't let go of the handrail as the tram picked up speed; finally I made an attempt to jump aboard, but hadn't the strength. I fell and was dragged. At once a terrible weakness came over me, and for a long time—several weeks—I could hardly move my legs; my knees shook.

In the dining room I would meet people that I knew, and every time I thought "That one's still alive". People would encounter one another there with the words "You're alive! I'm so glad!" They learnt with alarm from one another that so-and-so was dead, such-and-such had left town. People kept counting each other, counting up those that were left, as at roll-call in the prison camp.

But now something unforeseen happened: I was summoned to the police, to the military department, but not on military matters. Interrogations were beginning, demands: the Leningrad of the blockade echoed Solovki of the north. I was called a number of times into Staro-Nevski, where the *Sirotski Dom* used to be. When threats were no use (and they were serious) I was summoned to the police in Petrozavodskaya Street, my Leningrad residence permit was crossed out in indelible ink and I was required to move out, family and all, in a few days' time. The investigator took his leave of me in the police-station yard, watched me going and shouted in menacing fashion "So you don't agree?" I won't describe all those interrogations, threats and 'tempting' offers and promises, etc.

Scarcely a reader of *Oborony drevnerusskikh gorodov* will guess the situation in which its author found himself. Scarcely will he think of the difference in the situations of the besieged. We were doubly besieged, within and without. But our book was read in the trenches round Leningrad, as I was told by Arkasha Selivanov, who had been in the 'Oranienbaum pocket'.

I remember one particularly unpleasant 'visit'. I was leaving the flat with a bundle of books (we were beginning to sell everything we could, and books could be sold at *Dom Knigi*) when I ran into the investigator; he summoned me to Staro-Nevski, as I hadn't answered notices to attend. It took me a long time to get there; I was there all day, and everyone at home was very worried. There was great, decisive pressure being put on me. Then the investigator played a scene, pretending that I was being arrested. He called in a Red Army man and he took me to the basement. Fortunately, I didn't believe his threats and didn't lose my resolve. No one that had survived the horrors of the blockade was frightened of anything any more. It was hard to put the wind up us.

We started to sell everything we could in haste. I decided that we had to live, and anything else we would get. We fastened advertisements of our sale of goods to fences and purchasers came in a constant stream. They bought at bargain prices chandeliers, carpets, the bronze writing set, malachite boxes, leather armchairs, the settee, the standard lamp with the onyx base, books, postcards with views of towns—every single thing that my father and mother had gathered together before the Revolution. Only part of my books (the full set of Russian annals, separate volumes and a few odds and ends) I took to *Pushkinski Dom* for safe-keeping. For this I enlisted the help of the caretaker in the house opposite—'uncle Vanya'—and he took them in his barrow for a loaf of bread.

There was quite a to-do on the main staircase over the leather armchairs. A lady Party member, whom we didn't know, bought them for 600 rubles and left us a deposit, but then along came a second purchaser who gave us a little more. We sold to the latter and decided to return the Party lady's deposit—but she came back at just the moment when the chairs were being carried out. She made such a fuss that the new purchaser and we both withdrew. We met her later when we came back to Leningrad and could have recovered the chairs from her and given her back the money, as then (in 1944-45) a decree had been promulgated under which anything bought during the blockade at robbery prices had to be returned. But ... knowing her excitable nature we didn't ask for the return of our memorial armchairs, in which my father had so loved to sit.

I later saw the picture entitled 'Winter' by, if I'm not mistaken, the Italian painter Massena, in 1944 in the commission shop in Sadovaya, near the public library. It had been reframed and the picture itself had been varnished and a great florid signature added, saying Krzhitski. They say that during the blockade there was a whole workshop that restored old paintings, gave them signatures of famous artists and resold them. Fortunes were made on the empty stomachs of the citizens of Leningrad. Shargorodski, our lawyer and deputy director of the Institute, advised me to reclaim the painting through the courts, but this time too I didn't bother. Although the painting had been a memory from my childhood days I had no energy and didn't feel like taking legal action. The painting is of a winter sunset. A sledge road leads right to the blue horizon, half-hidden in snowy storm-clouds. In the foreground is a peasant cottage with a barrel above the door—it's an inn, and outside are a number of sledges with horses harnessed, waiting for the peasants who've gone inside. There's rather a pessimistic mood about it all...

I hand over to Mama

When we decided to go—and without money one couldn't—we started to sell our belongings. We felt as if we would never return to Leningrad, that it would all be gone, and so we had to sell all our things even if we didn't get much for them. We put up notices (hung them on fences) advertising the sale and people came and bought things as if it were a shop. If there was shelling in the city no one came. Once a young man came along and bought my bronze writing set for 150 rubles; beside it were two bottles of vinegar, and he bought those too for 150 rubles—such was the price of food, even vinegar! I'd bought a few bottles when the blockade was beginning. The shops had been empty—there was only mustard, vinegar and salt on sale, so that's what I bought. The vinegar and mustard helped us to eat the jelly made from carpenter's glue. To flavour it I used to boil it with celery, which I had drying for the winter as there were no root vegetables on sale before then. I remember some of the prices we got for our things, or more precisely for Mitya's father and mother's things. The walnut chest of drawers with a mirror fetched 1,000 rubles; the dressing-table the same. That was very good, but the rest of the things fetched much less. In Granddad's room there was a nice little upholstered couch; we sold it for food, and for tiny amounts, something like 300 grams of soy sweets, a kilo of rice and half a kilo of sugar or the like. The two armchairs in the study, like the two father's got only better, softer, we sold for 600 rubles the pair—300 each. The plush couch fetched 450 rubles, and later we bought a worse one for 1,700. Altogether the sale realised about nine or ten thousand. When we got to Kazan that amount lasted us about three months. For part of the money we bought potatoes off Basevich, a friend of Mitys's brother. He sold us six sacks for which we paid

2,000 rubles. When we left we took only soft things which we sewed up in bales and covered in the oil-cloth off the kitchen table. It amazed us that our bales didn't get lost. Tamara and I went to look for them among other similar bales that were tipped out on the bank on the other side of Lake Ladoga. What a job it was to haul them over and load them into the goods wagons in which we rode to Kazan!

I've left space for Zina and continue to write

Communications with the 'mainland' were gradually being restored, as were communications between people. An enquiry arrived from Misha—were we alive? He sent it through some organisation that he was working for. A man came from there and promised us a lorry to take our things to the station. That was quite a job! Misha had been told of Grandfather's death. People were registering for evacuation in the big hall of the Academy of Sciences, and there I met Kallistov, who was also preparing to leave. We all registered, and I registered Tamara, our nanny. By then she was working in the Institute of Literature—Kalaushin had given her a job as a laboratory assistant. One could take a limited quantity of luggage (I forget how many kilos) and only in soft packaging, that is to say in sacks. People were being despatched from the Finland Station to Borisova Griva Station, and from there over Lake Ladoga in steamers and barges. The city was becoming more and more deserted. The police hurried us along, but the train was rescheduled. The police harrassment drove me to go and see the procurator (in Panteleymonovskaya Street) and report that it was illegal to force us to leave. All this played dreadfully on my nerves. Furthermore, on Bolshoy Prospekt we met Lyubochka, wife of my cousin Shura (Aleksandr Petrovich) Kudryavtsev. He'd been a Doctor of Technical Science, specialising in something to do with marine engineering—he'd trained as an electrical engineer. They'd managed to get through the blockade (Shura was stingy, prudent and economical), and in spring he'd started going for lunch to the *Dom Uchenykh*, and there in the dining room he'd 'opened his big mouth', saying that scientists were losing touch. He'd been summoned like me, given a fright over these words and ordered 'to serve'. It seems that he'd eaten humble pie and agreed, but then had gone to their old flat, which had been bomb-damaged and where they no longer lived, and hanged himself. The investigator who had frightened him had

258

had a fright himself, as Shura had been a military specialist and therefore a man who was needed; he went to see Lyubochka and persuaded her not to say anything, etc. Such was the value placed on defenders of the city.

Before we left, in May and June, the shelling grew much worse. Once our whole flat shook and there was a tremendous roar, and we heard window-panes falling into the street. The sound of falling glass was very characteristic of Leningrad under shelling. The streets filled with fragments of glass and it was quite impossible to walk in galoshes: they were cut to shreds. On that occasion the explosion was very loud. Granny gave a shriek, gathered the children and rushed into the corridor, but it was obvious that if we'd heard the bang we hadn't been hit. Then Granny ran downstairs; there hadn't been another explosion, but that single heavy shell had done a lot of damage. It had hit a two-storey house on the corner of Lenin Street and Bolshoy Prospekt (the house is no longer there) where there was a bread-shop on the ground floor, and had gone right through from top to bottom and exploded in the shop. Dozens of people had been killed, and everything was awash with blood.

When we walked in the street we usually chose on the side from which shells came, the west, but during shelling we didn't take cover. The German shot was clearly audible, then at the count of eleven came the explosion. When I heard a shot I always counted and when I reached eleven I prayed for those it had killed. The wife of Sergeychuk, who ran the dining room, had her head cut off: she was in a tram, which was very dangerous, as the old Leningrad trams had benches along the windows. The glass would be shattered by an explosion and decapitate those sitting there. The next time I was in Leningrad (on a mission from Kazan in 1944) I heard a lot of tales of such tragedies in trams. And in 1945 there still stood outside the Labour Exchange a tram with the windows blown clean out. A shell had fallen on the track underneath it, the track had been torn up and the tram tipped to one side. It remained there for a long time.

The shelling of Leningrad has been well described in the memoirs of the artist A. P. Ostroumova-Lebedeva.

By the time of our departure we'd sold almost everything. A few books and children's toys remained unsold. Zina made little black rucksacks for the girls, to put their favourite dolls in; the rest we gave to the kindergarten which had opened downstairs in our house. What a tragedy it was when the woman in charge of it came and took the dolls! The children cried, threw themselves on their knees and ran down the stairs after her; it took ages to calm them down.

Vasya Makarov, Zina's brother, used to come and see us, and one day he brought some black curds from the store on Kushelevka, which had been burned down in 1939 during the Finnish campaign (it was said, a Finnish aircraft had set it alight). It had been a food store, and now, in the spring of 1942, people were searching the ruins and extracting remnants of food from beneath the charred remains. He'd paid 200 rubles for the curds; they were black and shiny, smelt of earth and stuck painfully in one's throat, and afterwards I had stomach-ache—the only time during the war. Vasya bought our study furniture (everything but the armchairs) and other things, and we asked him to sell the remaining books.

I surrendered the lease on the flat to the ZhAKT[199] but I couldn't get it sealed; there wasn't time. The lorry couldn't be detained. We sent our soft bales to the station on the lorry—luggage was being received at the Moscow station. Then we spent the night in the empty flat and next day, with the very smallest bundles over our shoulders we set off for the Finland station. It was a fine day, the 24 June. We left our flat with the feeling that we would never return; it seemed inconceivable to return to the city in which we had seen so much horror around us. Perhaps that's why we didn't even have the flat sealed, and weren't even very anxious about it. Vasya came to see us off. The children wore their little grey coats (the ones they were photographed in at the Botanical Gardens in autumn 1941) and had their rucksacks. Tamara had bought in advance a sewing machine from old Mrs Obnovlenskaya and carried it wrapped up in a blanket—but without its cover, as hard bales were not allowed. We went by tram, and took a last look at the long-suffering city.

At the Finland Station we were, for the first time, given a satisfying meal of wheat porridge and a big piece of sausage, to give us strength for the journey. There was a hard road ahead, and weak citizens of Leningrad had died on it in their thousands. We ate in the open, then took our places in the carriages that used to take us to the dacha. It was terribly crowded. Stratanovski joined us; he'd lost his wife, who had died comparatively early, in the winter, and he was alone. He looked distraught as he begged us to make room for him in the carriage. The train moved with murderous slowness, stood for a long time in stations; some of the people were sitting, some standing crammed together, and all the seats were packed.

In the night—a white night—we arrived at Borisova Griva, where we were given soup. It was rich and plentiful. We greedily ate this real food. The mosquitoes were eating us alive; we saw the scenery and it was beautiful. We didn't sleep. I talked to the Hebraist Borisov, who later died on the journey from dystrophic diarrhoea. Kallistov, Olimpiada Vasiliyevna, her sister Lyalya and Bobik were on the same train as us. Kallistov joked "I'd have liked to see the Boris who had a mane like that"[200]. We decided to stick together.

Our luggage had been taken to Borisova Griva. We searched for our bundles by their labels and stacked them together in the open. Then the loading of the steamer began. We were allowed on board only once after passports had been checked, but what could we carry at one attempt in our weakened arms?

Kallistov and I, aided by Zina and Tamara, were hard put to persuade the sentries checking documents to let us through a second time, and we went three times each, dragging our bundles up the jetty to the ship. When we came back with the last bundles the ship was moving, with Granny, Zina, Tamara and the children on board. Kallistov and I jumped for it, risking falling into the water, but fortunately landed on board the overloaded vessel. Another minute and we'd have been left ashore. Goodness knows when we'd have seen one another again in that case! I can't tell you how upset Zina had been.

It was a fine day and we sailed in full view of any aircraft that might have appeared, but thank God none did. It was only when we moored on the other side that we felt relatively safe, but at that moment there was an air-raid. The jetty was empty in a flash, but they were only reconnaissance aircraft, and the Germans didn't bomb us.

We were given an *izba* in which to spend the night, but we didn't sleep the second night either, as there were peasants living there and one of their children had a terrible cough and kept choking. He obviously had whooping-cough. Granny wouldn't let him near and he was upset and said, pointing a finger at her, "She says I've got 'hoofing-cough'!"

We were given a few days' food supply, ate again from our aluminium dishes, and ate a lot, although the feeling of hunger didn't leave us for a moment.

I remember looking for our bundles again. All the luggage had been dumped in a heap on the sand, and hundreds of us passengers

261

walked round and round these massed belongings looking for our own things with name-tags giving our surnames and the name of our organisation. It took us a long time to find them, because everyone had so many bundles, but nothing had been lost.

Then we were loaded into goods-wagons with bunks. There weren't enough boards for the bunks and we had to find some. Kallistov, Stratanovski and I found some, but still there weren't enough. There were big gaps in the bunks, and it was very uncomfortable to sleep while the train was in motion. We slept on top with Tamara and Stratanovski underneath. The Kallistovs slept on the other side of the teplushka on the top. Our bundles were put under the bunks and in the middle of the car. The first long stop was at Tikhvin, where again we had some porridge with a lot of butter and had time to go and look around the town, where Kallistov and I had been in 1932. It had suffered desperately. There was no one living there, but the Germans hadn't damaged the statue of Lenin outside the *Gostiny dvor* in the square.

On the way we bought wild onions from local people, and at the stations we went for *kipyatok* [boiling water] and rations. We were well fed everywhere, and we ate and ate, couldn't get enough.

There was a lot of difficulty on the journey, and I won't go into it. All that is another story, another age. It requires separate treatment.

Were the people of Leningrad heroes? Not just heroes: they were martyrs...

Two Letters about the Blockade of Leningrad

It was only in 1992 that I was sent copies of two letters written by me in the autumn of 1942 in Kazan, to where my family and I had been evacuated. They were to my 'co-defendant' in the 'Cosmic Academy' case, Valentina Galaktionovna Morozova-Keller, a member of the Andreyev circle. In my book *Kniga bespokoystv* [Book of Anxieties] (Moscow, 1991, pp. 89 et seq.) I give an account of this affair, for which I was given five years on Solovki, while Valya, still a minor, was released into the custody of her father.

The letters were written with the blockade fresh in my mind.

Letter no. 1

29 December 1942

Dear Valya! I'll describe to you how we lived then. In the summer of '41 we were living in the dacha at Vyritsy, and I'd just defended my thesis. We had some money and I'd suggested a nice bit of a break. I went into town once a week and spent the rest of the time bathing at Oredezhi. We had an excellent dacha. I was on the beach at Oredezhi when I heard that war had been declared, and my heart missed a beat at once. I went into town, and in the Institute there was alarm, talk of evacuation to Tomsk, duties on the roof, people being sent to dig trenches, volunteer detachments. My family were still at the dacha when the Germans actually bombed Siverskaya and German aircraft machine-gunned dacha trains. I still wasn't inclined to take them into the alarmist atmosphere of the city, from which children were being evacuated without their parents, and where there were queues for food, etc. We left the dacha at the last moment. At the end of August the Germans cut all the roads to Leningrad and advanced on Srednaya Rogatka; armed motorcyclists burst into the square at Avtovo, circled round and raced away again. Here they were halted, but it was obvious that a siege was in prospect. We like others made frantic efforts to get in supplies, and we managed to buy about ten kilos of potatoes, twelve kilos of groats and pasta, one kilo of butter and we dried two big sacks of rusks. In a chemist's which stayed open all evening I bought seventeen 100 gram bottles of cod-liver oil for the children, and in another ten blocks of vitamins and glucose the size of bars of toilet soap. With those reserves our winter began. As before I spent alternate nights on the Institute roof, on watch, and all the house-work fell on Zina. The bread ration was sharply reduced on 9 November. The bread became black as [illegible], and moist like clay because of the duranda in it. Air raids started. We spent the night in a small room on the first floor, which we were allowed to use; we reckoned that it was less dangerous downstairs. Zina and the children had their own beds and I slept on the floor. At first it was very frightening, and there were air-raids every evening, beginning at precisely the same time. In the daytime German reconnaissance planes left smoke trails across the sky to show where the next bombing was to be—or so the people of Leningrad thought, as they had never seen the white track of a high-flying aircraft. It was terrifying to wait for evening if a cross had been placed above our region in advance. Once a German dropped four bombs all at once on the tram crossing near your place. The bombs whistled right over our roof, and when they went off our whole house 'danced' and cupboard doors opened unaided. Gradually we got used to it and didn't waste our strength on going downstairs, especially after a number of cellars full of people were flooded with water from broken mains. Petya Obnovlenski was trapped under the stairs [illegible], but fortunately the stairs fell in such a way that he was merely crushed and broke some ribs. Soon shelling joined the air-raids. Father's work-place was hit by shells. He put out the fire (the printing house of the former Synod was burnt, and the Central Archive on Angliskaya Naberezhnaya). For some reason shells often hit trams on Nevski, and there were many casualties from broken glass. The Germans used to shell in the evening, although the streets would be full of people going home from work. They shelled the squares (Truda), bridges (Dvortsovy), crossroads (the corner of Vvedenski and Bolshoy). There were instances of shells hitting queues, of which there were a lot, shops and a kindergarten that was out for a walk. For my sins I had to be constantly outside the house on watch, doing drill or waiting in the dining-room queue. There were a lot of people at the Institute day and night, sleeping in their clothes on Pushkin's and Aksakov's settees, where Gogol had sat, on Turgenev's settee and on the bed in which Blok had died.

The city swarmed with rumours, with people that had come in from the suburbs, and with spies that had been caught. By degrees the fever subsided. The trams stopped running, a lot of people could no longer go to work, and a number left by air. The most senior person that we had was the *zavkhoz*[201], who became very nervy from hunger, shouted at our colleagues and dismissed members of staff. It would have been terrible to be left without work or ration cards, but no one could calm him down. Thus November passed, and our rusks kept us going. In December, however, we too felt hungry. It was unbearably cold at work; the water supply froze and the lavatories didn't work. By that time I could no longer walk, and I got a sick note. These were issued without a glance, without examination, to all and sundry.

Electricity was cut off. Paraffin ran out. It was a good thing that we had a stock of firewood and a *burzhuyka*. We rationed what we had left. We had soup—little more than water—four times a day. We went to bed at six in the evening and stayed there until nine or ten in the morning. Occasionally Zina started queuing in the evening, and she queued about two hours in the afternoon as well for bread. She and Tamara took a sledge to the Neva near Krestovski Island for water. We tried melting snow, but the whole street outside our house was covered with filth. Once Fedya Rozenberg, my friend and co-defendant from Solovki, came to see us on his unsteady legs, and Kallistov came in search of dogs or cats. Uncle Vasya called for a bowl of soup. He looked terrible. Komarovich called—the leading expert on Dostoyevski—in the hope that we would stand him some rusks. But misfortune had come upon us even before then.

Letter no. 2

Dear Valya! This letter is a continuation.

And so, the worst month was January. I can't remember whether there was any bombing or shelling in January: we couldn't have cared less. No one paid any attention to them. No one went out to the air-raid shelter, which had been made into a mortuary. Our friends and relations were dying one after another. Zina's father had a hard death all alone. She used to visit him and barter his belongings in the street, buy him food, but it was too late; he didn't want to eat, and when the desire for food is gone, it's the end. He died with food in the sideboard.

We were forced to barter our belongings at the market: a samovar for 100 grams of duranda, a few dresses for 200 grams of peas, etc. We had no regrets over anything and it kept us alive.

My brother Yura left in January; my father developed heart trouble, but we couldn't find a doctor. Finally we offered a paediatrician who lived nearby 200 grams of peas to call. He examined Father, but we couldn't get medicine as the chemists were closed. By that time I was walking with a stick and my legs were shaky. There was a corpse on the stairs and another outside the house. We couldn't sleep at night because of lack of food. One's whole body ached and itched—that was the system consuming its nerves. A mouse ran about our room in the dark, couldn't find any crumbs and died of hunger. I went to a special diet canteen, where I met your father, and there I carried out an 'operation': I exchanged a lunch coupon for a groats coupon, and used that for lunch next day. In that way we could sometimes have soup without wasting potatoes. Those hours in the canteen were awful. The windows were broken and blocked up with plywood. People ate in the dark and snatched one another's bread, potatoes, coupons. Once I dragged a dying man up the stairs to the canteen and it weakened me considerably. In general, it only took the slightest physical exertion for you to be noticeably weaker and you only had to eat a piece of bread for strength to be noticeably regained. It was hard to put your coat on, and especially to do up the buttons: your fingers wouldn't obey—they were 'wooden', they didn't 'belong' to you. At night the side you slept on became numb and paralysed.

In February the supply situation eased somewhat and standpipes were set up here and there in the streets. Zina and Tamara now went for water not to the Neva but to Pushkarskaya *Street*. The children went outside for ten minutes or so through the back entrance, but not down the main stairs where dead bodies lay. They behaved like heroes. We introduced a rule: no talking about food, and they obeyed! At table they never asked for food, were never naughty, but were terribly adult, slow-moving, serious, sat close to the *burzhuyka* warming their hands; we were all chilled to the marrow by a sort of internal cold.

Winter seemed incredibly long. We used to tell our fortunes for the coming week: would we see it out or not! On the first of March my father died in fearful torment. We couldn't bury him; we took him to the mortuary in the garden of *Narodny Dom* on children's sledges and left him there among the dead. To this day the memory of that journey and that mortuary preys on my mind. At the end of the month I went into the Institute for ration cards; I was no longer being paid, as there were no wages clerks—they'd all died. The building was terribly empty, and there was only the elderly porter, dying, and warming himself by the boiler. A lot of people later died without trace, leaving the Institute and never reaching their homes. Once I fell in the street and scarcely managed to get home.

In March I went into a 'dystrophy clinic' in the *Dom Uchenykh*, where they gave me rather more to eat, which merely increased my desire for food. I never stopped thinking of food, day or night, the whole month that I spent there. We slept in our clothes there and ate in the canteen at a temperature of –minus fifty Celsius. Outside the window on the Neva we could see the explosions of the renewed, springtime shelling. The ice was breaking. The citizens that were still alive began to clean the streets and remove the refuse, but their hands couldn't yet hold spades. The meat ration was increased.

In April the no. 12 tram began to run, then the 7, the 3 and later the 36.

Bathhouses opened. There I caught sight of myself for the first time and was horrified, as was your father when he saw me.

By May I was writing articles and going round the canteens 'acquiring' potatoes, although Zina did most of that sort of thing. The children went out a little. Tamara brought us orach, dandelion leaves and nettles from where she was working digging trenches.

Thus we survived the winter, but I can't describe it all.

Greetings to your family.

Prorabotki[202]

The object of this chapter of my memoirs is not to rehearse the history of *prorabotki*, which has occupied three decades and had a prehistory and a post-history. That would require reference to documents, possibly such shorthand reports and other materials as have survived, newspapers and magazines of the time. My task will not call for explanation of the meaning of *prorabotki* or their ideological basis; in my view they contained much nonsense, inspired solely by the desire of the Party organisations to demonstrate their power, their resolve and their preparedness to deal with things that they really didn't understand.

In this chapter I shall touch upon, fundamentally, the techniques of *prorabotki*, their psychological effect on the 'unorganised mass' of academics and non-academics, teachers and pupils. *Prorabotki* were the pinnacle of the informer's art, giving free rein to malice and envy. It was the culmination of evil, the triumph of all manner of foulness, when people (at least, some of them) even strove to gain the reputation of villains, seeking consolation in the horror that was suggested by what surrounded them. It was, in its way, a mass spiritual sickness which gradually tightened its grip on the whole country. People weren't ashamed of being informers, but even hinted at their special power.

The *prorabotki* of the decades from the '30s to the '60s grew into a definite system for the destruction of the Good, and were, to some extent, the ghost of the model processes of the late '30s and took into account their 'experience'. They were a kind of reprisal against academics, writers, artists, restorers, theatricals and other members of the intelligentsia.

At whatever cost admissions of guilt, if only partial ones, had to be beaten out of the victims of *prorabotki*. No proof at all was required after an admission (as was the case after the admissions of those accused during the great terror), it wasn't important. That was the 'juridical' revelation of the 'academic' Vyshinski[203]. Even, therefore, in the model *prorabotki* of the intelligentsia the victim of the torture had to be demoralised, reduced to such a condition that nothing mattered to him any more, all he wanted was to renounce everything and be off the stage quickly.

Therefore the presence of a crowd in the hall or auditorium where a *prorabotka* took place played into the hands of the tormentors. Even if that crowd was on the side of the victim, disagreed with the charges, was indignant, sympathetic—all the same, to become an 'objective' of the spectacle was extremely wearing. Thousands of students gathered at *prorabotki*, simply out of curiosity; well-known people were to be 'carved up', the authors of numerous works, who were accustomed to gratitude from their listeners and readers. It was no longer of any importance if one of the speakers tried to reduce the charges, or defined his position by words that had already been heard. By the very fact of their participation they demoralised the accused.

I remember one such incident. The well-known expert on Russian folklore and ethnography Mark Konstantinovich Azadovski was undergoing *prorabotka* in the *Pushkinski Dom*. A prominent folklorist sitting beside me was indignant. The celebrated *prorabotchik* I. P. Lapitski—a Reader in the University—was called as a witness, and he read a personal letter of Azavodski's which had been intercepted and opened by his student P. G. Shiryayeva. My neighbour was furious: "What a swine! What a swine!" After Lapitski the president called my neighbour. She strode vigorously to the witness-box and—I couldn't believe my ears!—accused Azadovski. Then she returned to her place and asked me "Well, how was that?" I said "I thought you were going to stand up for Mark Konstantinovich!" She replied indignantly "No use defending him—everybody's doomed already. But I didn't say anything new, you know, I merely repeated what had already been said. "

This was the *prorabotchik's* essential task—to let people say what they wished as long as they upheld the charge, yea but a little. This was the 'voice of the people', in its way the antique chorus of Greek tragedy.

Every effort was made for people near to the accused to speak at the hearings: friends, pupils, post-graduates, undergraduates—that was most painful of all for him. Those present would whisper to one another "What, him as well?" and so on. And the halls were packed with informers. One of the purposes of *prorabotki* was to try to break the disobedient in the masses. Almost in the same way as new arrivals were broken in the camps.

Hardly any of those accused withstood the pressure. Only a decisive rejection of the accusations could lead, if not to victory, then at least to the failure of the charges and the embarrassment of the accusers. The organisers of *prorabotki* were therefore very afraid that the accused wouldn't accept the charges. Discussions often took place in the Party offices with the person designated to be accused; he was asked to adopt a 'self-critical' attitude towards his work and lectures so as not to bring down the wrath of the area committee on his institution. No one really knew the substance of the charges at that stage, but they were prevailed upon to plead guilty and were promised 'mercy to the fallen'. Defence was rendered difficult because any that defended were genuinely under threat of victimisation. Disaster affected not merely individuals who had dared somehow to distinguish themselves from the common herd, but also the whole 'school', the whole tendency (be it even the narrowest and most severely specialised).

I knew already, from my own personal experience of associating with the counter-revolutionaries of the late '20s, the meaning of such an acknowledgement of one's guilt. Essentially, Vyshinski had invented nothing new in his theory of the self-sufficiency of public acknowledgement of guilt; he had merely set on a theoretical basis what already existed in practice. The *prorabotchiki* beat acknowledgement out of those in intellectual occupations in the same way that (by different means) the investigators of Cheka, OGPU and NKVD had done.

If a victim of *prorabotka* refused to acknowledge that he was a cosmopolitan (anti-patriot, formalist, follower of bourgeois ways or whatever) he was supposed to be considered 'an evil opponent of the

Party line', and merely un-selfcritical only in fortunate instances. But even if he did acknowledge his guilt and in detail (to acknowledge guilt fully was all but impossible, as that would have been tantamount to betrayal of the Motherland) there still remained the charge of 'lack of self-criticism' and a burden of guilt remained, though not sufficient to drive him out of all employment and to stop him being printed.

B. M. Eykhenbaum, who simply did not appear at the 'judgement' on his work, was dismissed and reduced to living on the voluntary contributions of his friends. They would go to see him and take a big pie, a cake or something else to eat.

The ostracism of Anna Akhmatova went on and on, and she was regularly taken food by the Tomashevskis; they even took her soup in a milk-container.

But let's get back to the procedure (more exactly, ritual) of *pro-rabotki*.

The statements of accusers of cosmopolitanism (Indo-europeanism, Marrism, etc.) were uniform even in their turns of phrase. As in the investigations of OGPU also, a single fact would be seized upon, a single quotation, and interpreted in the way the accuser required. Naturally, no proof was demanded, because neither did there exist the 'sins' ascribed to the academics. Accusations were as a rule formulated as follows: "Deliberately confirms...", "X agreed that...", "It is understandable that for X...", "X admits that...", "X cannot conceal his...". Seldom did anyone present demand a full quotation of the words taken out of context, an account of the circumstances, the subject, the time. That would have amounted to a show of solidarity with the accused. Accusers would often cite words from quotations with which X himself would argue, and ascribe them to him. Pages of books or articles would be indicated for 'accuracy'.

In the tense atmosphere of the hall it was hard for the accused to remember everything that had been said and to check. Usually he was allowed to speak after all the depositions, without any right to reply to each separately. An attempt was made to put him off by shouting and the sound of 'indignation', etc. The president would stop only the accused. And should the accused finally admit something of his own accord (though not everything) in order to appease his tormentors, this partial admission would be considered total and in his concluding address the president would declare that X had "admitted", "confessed", "agreed", "pleaded guilty" and so on, repeating everything that had been said by the others and reading out what had previously been prepared in meetings of the 'cells', the 'bureaux', the 'commissions' and the rest.

So that the charges of *prorabotki* should not be forgotten special wall-newspapers were published. The significance of this 'wall-literature' was very great. The content of articles was controlled by the Party organisations, and in them the *prorabotchiki* could range even wider than in meetings or in the local or national press. The victims of *prorabotki* were subjected to abusive mockery, featured in cartoons and slogans saying "Root 'em out!" and the like. In particular students and friends suffered in these, as did academics who were merely honourable and tried to come to the aid of the persecuted.

On one occasion Tomashevski and I went up to our Institute wall-newspaper, in which the routine exhortation "Uproot Formalism once and for all" (or words to that effect) was proclaimed in large letters. Tomashevski ran his short-sighted eyes over the contents of the paragraphs and the slogan, sighed, and said out loud "Before the Revolution it used to be simpler: 'Beat the Jews, save Russia!'". Informers were swarming around the paper (immediately after it had come out), studying the reactions of readers, and he naturally knew that...

People looked forward to the appearance of each issue: the direction to be taken by the next 'drive' was defined.

Among the leading *prorabotchiki* in the *Pushkinski Dom* were L. A. Plotkin, B. S. Meylakh, P. Shiryayeva and I. P. Lapitski, the Leningrad University Reader, famous outside its walls.

So, Plotkin fired off an article against M. M. Zoshchenko[204] in *Leningradskaya Pravda* after which Zoshchenko waited uneasily for his arrest. He packed a bag with essentials and went out of the main door of his house after midnight so as not to be arrested in front of his wife... Meylakh placed a huge pogrom-style article against Eykhenbaum in the *Pushkinski Dom* wall-newspaper, in which exaggerated importance was attached to the one sentence in *Moy vremennik* [My Chronicle] in which he indirectly admits to being Jewish (I don't propose to restore it to memory now). The paper with this article was hanging in the first-floor corridor in the *Pushkinski Dom* when Eykhenbaum died suddenly in the *Dom Pisateley* [Writers' Club] during the proceedings in honour of A. Marienhof, and the coffin with his body had been placed in the Writers' Union. No one thought to take down that wall-newspaper, a fact that is universally known thanks to R. O. Yakobson's obituary notice. He is, however, in error when he states that the wall-newspaper was on the same premises as Eykhenbaum's coffin. Even the coffin wouldn't have been accepted in the *Pushkinski Dom*—it was a rather purer place than the Writers' Union...

And how did people generally behave in the hall during *prorabotki*? The participants were as a rule disposed as follows: 'honoured' academics sat at a table on the stage in 'festive' manner, together with Party men and leaders of local Party society, their faces deeply pensive. In the front row of the hall sat those 'academics' upon whom lay the onus of expressing approval or bringing charges. Farther back, the rest of the hall, waiting in horror and sympathising with the wretch, was quietly (or sometimes loudly) indignant. Informers kept watch everywhere.

Were people prepared for speeches contrary to the Party aims? Yes, and such things happened. Most often people made speeches mitigating the accusations, but there were also firm rebuttals. Everybody remembered, for example, the speech of N. I. Mordovchenko in defence of G. A. Gukovski in Leningrad University. Mordovchenko announced that he couldn't believe in Gukovski's evil intentions and flatly refused to condemn him. Rapid retribution didn't follow, but Belchikov, Director of *Pushkinski Dom,* took over a year to ratify the defence of his doctoral thesis. Mordovchenko was very depressed: how do you explain to your students why the Higher Attestation Commission refuses to award you your doctorate? I myself don't really know to what extent it was an act of personal spite on the part of Belchikov, all-powerful on the HAC for philological sciences, or whether it was the result of instructions from the Party organisation. There were actually rumours that he would soon be arrested. As a result of his depression, Mordovchenko developed cancer, and was admitted to the Oncological Clinic in Beryozovaya alleya on Kamenny island. P. N. Berkov and I were at the time in the Gastric Sanatorium not far away. I decided not to go to say goodbye to him (his wife Yelena Dmitriyevna was constantly at his bedside) but I went every day to enquire about his condition at the information desk. One morning, instead of the usual bland reply, I was taken aback by a question in return: "What relation are you to him?" I realised what this meant and asked "He's dead?" The reply was in the affirmative...

The defence of Gukovski cost Mordovchenko his life. But Gukovski himself, after the *prorabotka* (conducted in his absence, as he was on holiday), was arrested and shot, or, in official version, 'passed away'.

I too had to appear in the defence of an accused. What happened was this: N. F. Belchikov was Director of the *Pushkinski Dom*, endowed with special powers plenipotentiary to clear the Institute of cosmopolitans. He usually came up from Moscow, where he lived permanently, for two or three days and stayed in his room off the courtyard of the main building of the Academy of Sciences, where the dental branch of the Academy clinic is now. All the Institute scum flowed together there to 'confer' with him. He dashed between Moscow and Leningrad and was mainly concerned with the vigilant preservation of literary studies and the discrediting of academics in that field. Everything was intensified by his pathological inclination to falsehood. The direct and candid Berkov went and told him exactly what he thought (and what the majority of his colleagues in the *Pushkinski Dom* thought too). The most wicked and laconic character-sketch of Belchikov was that by Tomashevski: "The only thing straight about Belchikov is his rectum, and he's had that out!" (he'd had an operation for cancer of the rectum). Of course, Berkov didn't repeat that shaft of wit to Belchikov's face, but he did speak bluntly about his 'academic assistants'. He listened in silence to all that Berkov said and decided not to organise an immediate *prorabotka*; he was, after all, a coward. Belchikov (or as Eykhenbaum used to call him, Belchichikov[205]) hated Berkov, and although there was no instruction from the area committee, he organised a long article attacking him in *Leningradskaya Pravda*, from the pens of two youngsters from the University Faculty of Philology, Yelkin and another whose name I forget.

After the appearance of that vile article there was to be a discussion on it in the *Pushkinski Dom*—so it was proposed—and Belchikov remained, as it were, in the clear. A session of the Academic Soviet was convened, and Tomashevski and I decided to defend Berkov and worked out our tactics: I would speak last but one in the session, and Tomashevski would be last, as the role of final speaker was always very important. And so we did. When Berkov was supposed to be invited to speak and 'repent' I asked to speak and proved in detail that in Yelkin's article words ascribed to Lenin were the opposite of what he'd written, and that the accusation against Berkov of 'bibliographic method' was illiterate, as bibliography was a science, not a method. My speech could scarcely have made any difference had it not been for the reference to Lenin. I knew that, and therefore spoke in a very forthright manner. Belchikov announced that because of its importance the session couldn't be concluded and proposed that it be continued the following week. I don't remember much about the second session, although towards the end Tomashevski spoke with very powerful arguments, and brilliantly, as he always did. Belchikov was forced to call a third session of the Soviet. What he was hoping for I don't know. The writers of the article didn't appear: they were too un-authorlike to speak in public—such writers as they only 'received attention' in letters and articles.

I remember Tomashevski meeting me in the lavatory (dirty as usual) on the first floor of the Institute and saying "This is the only place in the *Pushkinski Dom* where you can breathe easy!"

And so, the third session on the discussion of the work of Berkov... Either his nerve had broken, or one of his 'well-wishers' had persuaded him, but without a word of warning to Tomashevski or myself Berkov spoke out and half-admitted his errors. Tomashevski gave a howl, and when the whole packed hall, which had been expecting truth to prevail, was dispersing in bewilderment, he said to me out loud over the heads of the departing people "Dmitri Sergeyevich, why did we try?" I remember his words precisely.

Belchikov disliked me even more and began in his turn to 'try', but with different methods.

Belchikov had a pathological passion for making people quarrel. In Moscow he assured N. K. Gudzi that Likhachev hated him, and in Leningrad he told me that Gudzi had that same attitude towards me. Fortunately Gudzi and I knew each other well, so this [didn't have] the consequences that Belchikov had anticipated. I knew that Gudzi was a very straightforward man who would never dissimulate. When, therefore, Belchikov arrived from Moscow and told me that Gudzi had been cursing me and had some grudge against me, I said at once that it was out of the question. Gudzi in Moscow behaved similarly.

Belchikov wanted to stir up the Party men in the Institute against me, and said to them "Likhachev's the son of a millionaire property-owner, well known in Petersburg. That's the sort we've got working here!" I met him shortly afterwards and said "If you want to know who my father is you can read about him in my dossier, and for confirmation there's the 'All Petersburg' handbook". All he said was "But I thought..."

It became more and more difficult to work, and M. P. Alekseyev and I decided finally to submit to the academic secretary of the Department of Language and Literature, V. V. Vinogradov, a petition for Belchikov to be relieved of the post of Director of the *Pushkinski Dom*; when everyone's fighting everyone else no work is done. We decided to go and see Vinogradov in Moscow. Belchikov refused to send us officially, but we got tickets (which wasn't easy) and set off on 'absence without leave'. I had warned Vinogradov by telephone that we were coming.

With the passage of time my memory of certain details has been obliterated, and I can't recall whether Alekseyev was with me at the Department of Language and Literature, or whether I went to Moscow twice—once with Alekseyev and once by myself (but in that case how did the first conversation end? Failure of memory!)

In any case, I arrived at the Department and discovered that Belchikov was already there in Vinogradov's study. That meant he'd beaten me to it. I asked to be received. Vinogradov said "But I'm seeing Belchikov." I replied "Excellent! Otherwise I'd have been obliged to make my representations in his absence." Vinogradov said "Yes, and the Party organisation secretary, Barkhudarov, is here at present too." I replied "Good; we shall be able to resolve all the questions straight away." We sat down, and in front of all three of them, with Belchikov present, I told them how he 'organised' the work of the Institute and brought colleagues into conflict, adducing concrete examples. Vinogradov phoned the personnel department of the Presidium of the Academy of Sciences in our presence and said "I've got Likhachev here, and he's explained to me in the presence of the Director of the Institute why he can't work with him. In my view he's right!" To put it in a nutshell, the Belchikov question was soon dealt with: he was dismissed from the Directorship. A collective Directorship was established for the time being with V. P. Adrianova-Perets as Deputy Director.

I myself suffered *prorabotka* repeatedly. I had never been a formalist, an antipatriot, a cosmopolitan, or belonged to any of the tendencies that usually received this treatment. It was hard to find anything anti-Soviet in my work, and yet I was clearly not 'one of theirs': I hardly ever quoted Lenin and Stalin. Particular attention was paid to that when my book *Vozniknovenie russkoy literatury* [The Origins of Russian Literature] came out. I was made to write an introduction and a conclusion with appropriate reference to the 'beacon of all sciences'. After Yakov Solomonovich Lurye was appointed to the Section the fault-finding became incredible. Lapitski, lecturer in the Faculty of Philology, soon emerged as chief accuser, while in the His-

275

torical Faculty, where I worked (I was simply not admitted to Philology), there were Stepanishchev, Urodkov and Karnatovski.

I'll tell you about a few *prorabotki* in which I myself was the accused.

In the spring of 1952 or '53 there was to be a special discussion in the Institute of the *Poslanie Ivana Groznogo* [The Epistle of Ivan the Terrible]. I recall that the book consisted of a straightforward edition of the text, with an article by me on Ivan the Terrible as a writer and a commentary by Lurye.

About a week before the discussion an event took place which must have been a shock to my ill-wishers—I was awarded a Stalin Prize (second class) for my work on the *History of the Culture of Ancient Rus'*. By all the Party rules that made me, at least for some time, untouchable. In this instance, however, the discussion of the book was not removed from the agenda.

Our *Pushkinski Dom* was supervised on the area committee by Vorobyova-Smirnova, who later became an editor at the Leningrad branch of the publisher *Khudozhestvennaya literatura* [Fiction]; she was a pupil of M. O. Skripil, and that gentleman of honourable years went to her to inform on me. Not only did she order the discussion to take place, but made the opening speech herself—contrary to the rules, as area committee staff didn't take part in *prorabotki*—accusing the book of 'objectivism' and more besides. The Party organisation had done the appropriate 'work' among the academics, and a number of solid colleagues (or those considered solid) were ready to support the charges. The small hall of the *Pushkinski Dom* was packed, with many standing. Congratulation on the Stalin Prize was such an original idea that many came out of curiosity.

It began as usual. The chairman addressed a few complimentary remarks to me (Lurye wasn't mentioned) and called upon those present "not to succumb to the fascination of merit" and to speak all the more critically, as Likhachev's work will have more effect on the reader. That is, it was all for the sake of my work! The crucial point in the *prorabotka* was Skripil's speech. Contrary to his usual practice he read it, and in a soft, furtive, almost gentle voice. Among the accusations there was heard, rattled off very quickly, "It is no surprise that Dmitri Sergeyevich sympathises with that betrayer of the Motherland, Prince Kurbski[206]". Having given voice to his accusations Skripil handed his text to the shorthand writer. In the circumstances of the time such a speech could only result in arrest. I realised that the speech had been a summary of the conversations between Skripil and Vorobyova-Smirnova on the area committee, and that it was on that that I needed to concentrate in my reply. So I did. I expounded in detail my treatment of Kurbski's defection and demonstrated at the same time that my 'seeking refuge in textual criticism from the real political tasks of the present' was sheer fabrication, all the stranger as Skripil was deeply interested in textual problems. The discussion led to nothing, and even Lurye kept out of it and wasn't dismissed from the Institute; I asked him not to speak either in the Writers' Soviet or in the *Pushkinski Dom*.

In September or October 1950 I was taken ill with a perforated ulcer and had to stay in bed. A mass public 'carving up' of writers took place in the *Pushkinski Dom*. I had only been accepted into the Union on the recommendation of Zhirmunski and Orlov, and couldn't imagine that the *prorabotka* would have to do with me. But it did! In his huge, pogrom-like speech Lapitski subjected my work to 'criticism'. I decided to respond and appeared at the continuation of the writers' meeting, which was held in the big hall in the presence of a mass conflux of people. I had made careful preparations.

Lapitski made a second speech, this time in my hearing, and in the course of it lambasted Lurye too. In the interval, before Lapitski's second speech (in which he again attacked us both over the publication of *The Epistle of Ivan the Terrible* in *Literaturniye pamyatniki* [Literary Monuments]), Lurye came up to me saying over and over "It's all up, it's all up!" The well-known 'character assassin' Komsar Grigoryan was walking behind Lurye and listening. In the end, not wishing our 'conversation' to be made known to Lapitski, I went to the lavatory to get away, but Lurye ran after me, and Grigoryan after him...

After the interval I spoke and, I think, refuted Lapitski on all points, exposing the mistakes in his quotations not only from Lurye and myself, but also from the 'Marxist classics'. It seemed that the matter was clear, and I received congratulations on winning, but the chairman, a member of the area committee staff, formulated his conclusion in words such as "It's a specialised matter and will have to be investigated, but it's impossible that in Lapitski's accusations there should be absolutely no correct statements". From my place I shouted "There are none!"—and the session was closed.

Of course, the attitude of the management of the Institute and the area committee didn't change (and it couldn't really), but now the main attacks on me began to take place in the History Faculty of the

University, and there went on for quite a long time—as long as I was teaching. At every session of the Board of Studies of the History of the USSR somebody spoke against me, and Lapitski began to attend them although he had no official connection. His sole purpose was to slander me somehow. I stopped going.

One day I went to the University cash-desk and noticed that I was receiving a smaller salary than usual. I asked the cashier about this, and she replied "That's the usual salary for a junior lecturer"; I was by then a corresponding member of the Academy of Sciences. It was to be inferred that I had been demoted to junior lecturer without even being notified of the fact. It was quite obvious that I was being pushed out of the History Faculty. I refused to accept the junior lecturer's money and without, in my turn, notifying the Board of Studies, ceased teaching in the Faculty...

Hot on my track came an article by Lapitski, printed in the *Vestnik* [Bulletin] of the University, in which I was accused of every deadly sin: I was a monarchist, a Socialist Revolutionary, a Trotskyist and I know not what besides. My telephone conversation with the then Rector of the University, A. D. Aleksandrov, led to nothing. He defended Lapitski's right to his opinion...

In the spring of 1994 I was at a meeting in memory of I. P. Yeremin in the Philology Faculty of the University. In the cloakroom V. Kholshevnikov reminded me that on those premises Yeremin and I had undergone a *prorabotka* at the hands of one Rozhdestvenskaya, Lapitski and F. A. Abramov, who had not previously managed to know anything about cases of 'state ideology'. Later on, when we were sailing together to Solovki on the steamer Tatariya, he came up to me and, in the middle of a conversation about the beauties of the North, suddenly said "I thought you weren't going to talk to me", and reminded me himself of his speech in the *prorabotka* at the University. By that time I'd completely forgotten about it, so used was I to such 'thrashings'. By the way, I had gone to the discussion of our work merely out of solidarity. I could have not gone, as I didn't teach in the Philology Faculty—they wouldn't have me.

Rozhdestvenskaya was particularly repulsive during the *prorabotka*. She was an unusually thin (the result of malice?) and ugly woman, of slovenly dress. She attacked everyone, but didn't stand up for anything. Her speech, as Kholshevnikov reminded me, began: "I've been studying Ancient Russian Literature for three whole weeks, and I've come to the conclusion that neither Likhachev nor Yeremin knows a thing about it..." Perhaps he was laying it on a bit, but he'd got the general drift.

Her speech surprised no one. Everyone was used to her, as they were to Lapitski's insults as he wound his painful way through his speeches.

In 'Romanov' times *prorabotki* assumed other forms. In October 1975 I was due to talk in the Assembly Hall of the Philology Faculty about the *Slovo o polku Igoreve*[207]. When, an hour before the talk was to start, I left my flat, a man of medium build with an obviously false moustache attacked me on the landing and punched me in the solar plexus. I was, however, wearing a new double-breasted over-coat of thick material, and the blow didn't have the desired effect. The stranger then hit me in the region of the heart, but in my inside pocket was the file containing my text (the *Slovo* protected my heart) and once more the blow was ineffective. I rushed back into the flat and called the police. Then I went downstairs, where a driver was waiting for me (clearly, from the same organisation) and I rushed off to look for my assailant in the neighbouring streets and alleys. But he, of course, had by that time changed his cap and shed his false mous-tache. I went and delivered my paper.

My appeal to a detective in the police had the same result as in 1976, when my flat was burgled.

There was a period in 1976 of arson attacks on the flats of dissi-dents and left-wing artists. We'd gone to the dacha for the May holi-day, and on our return we found a policeman wandering about the flat. The windows in the balcony door had been broken. The police-man asked us not to be upset, he'd been waiting for us to arrive. It turned out that at about three o'clock the previous morning our alarm had gone off and the block had been woken by the noise. Only one man had rushed out onto the stairs, a scientific worker who lived underneath us; the rest had taken fright. The arsonists (that's what they were) had hung a canister of flammable liquid on the front door and tried to pour it into the flat through a plastic hose, but it wouldn't go through as the gap was too narrow. Then they began widening the gap with a crowbar. The burglar alarm, of which they hadn't known (it had been installed in my son-in-law's name) began to howl wildly and the arsonists took to their heels, leaving at the door both the canister of liquid and the fragments of plastic with which they'd tried to block the crack so that the liquid wouldn't run back, and other 'technical items'.

The investigation was conducted in an odd manner: the canister was destroyed, the composition of the liquid was not established (my younger brother, an engineer, said that from the smell it had been a mixture of paraffin and acetone), and the fingerprints (the arsonists had fled, wiping their hands on the painted walls of the staircase) were washed off. The case was passed from one to another until, finally, a woman detective said in encouraging fashion "Don't even ask!"

In any case, fists and arson weren't just the final arguments in attempts at subjecting me to *prorabotka*, they were also malice against Sakharov and Solzhenitsyn.

The attack on the landing took place on the very day when M. B. Khrapchenko, who had taken over from Vinogradov as academic secretary (by none-too-reputable means) had phoned me from Moscow and asked me to join the members of the Presidium of the Academy of Sciences in signing the famous letter censuring A. D. Sakharov. "By that you'll be cleared of all accusations and dissatisfaction." I replied that I wouldn't sign it, even without having read it. Khrapchenko's last words were "Well, you can't be sued for saying no". He was wrong: action taken laid all the same—more precisely, 'lynch-law'. As for the May arson attack, that was probably to do with my writing the draft of the chapter on Solovki in *Arkhipelag GULAG*. I won't give a full account of everything that I had to endure when I saved from demolition the Putevoy Palace at Srednyaya Rogatka and the churches at Sennaya and Murino, saved the trees in the park at Tsarskoye Selo from being cut down, the Nevski Prospekt from 'reconstruction' and the Gulf of Finland from pollution, etc., etc. It will suffice to look at the list of my articles in newspapers and magazines to realise how much time and effort the struggle in defence of Russian culture has caused me to divert from my work.

A Trip to Solovki in 1966

My time on Solovki was for me the most significant period of my life. It was natural for me to be interested in the fate of the people that I met there, and in the fate of Solovki itself. I dreamed of going there one day and abandoning myself to my recollections.

After the death of Stalin this became possible, but one had to obtain permission and travel via Arkhangelsk; this was difficult in my position, and furthermore I was often ill. My duodenal ulcer wouldn't let me go. In 1966 an opportunity to go to Solovki arose when I was invited to a conference in Arkhangelsk on Monuments of the culture of the Russian North, to be followed by excursions. One of these was to be by the steamer Tatariya to Solovki. I decided to go to the conference and afterwards to stay for a while on Solovki, where by then the museum was being organised. I'd only been to Arkhangelsk once—just after the British left in 1921, with a party from school. I had retained a visual memory of the amazing bell-tower which closed the view of the main street, and of the grandiose Gostiny Dvor: two symbols of the ascendancy of Arkhangelsk in the North—one spiritual, the other economic.

V. I. Malyshev flew with me to Arkhangelsk, and from Moscow came A. A. Zimin, with whom my relations had cooled after several years of friendship; I had tried to persuade the Academy of Sciences to print his work on the *Slovo o polku Igoreve*. My efforts were not successful and Zimin reckoned that I did not try hard.

The conference aroused very great interest in Arkhangelsk, all the more so as at that time the first open-air museum of wooden architecture in the country—Noviye Korely—was being set up. It was the height of summer and the weather was marvellous. The hall was full for my paper; I was the only one present that had served a sentence on Solovki, and people had come to see the 'old Solovki hand'.

The title of my paper was 'The tasks of the study of the Solovetski historico-cultural complex', which could not fail to be of interest to historians of the Russian Middle Ages. Zimin sat in the first row from the front by the middle gangway, conspicuously opened a newspaper, held it out into the gangway and immersed himself in reading. That was a protest and one that was out of place, especially as people had come partly in order to greet the prisoner of Solovki.

I didn't take offence as I understood that in those years Zimin's interests were centred on his idea of a later date for *Slovo o polku Igoreve*.

Next day I bumped into him surrounded by his friends. I said good morning—they went straight past. Naturally, neither on the steamer Tatariya nor on Solovki itself did I go near them, and they deprived themselves of the opportunity of finding out something more than the archaeologist that was guiding the party told them. There was much that was puerile in Zimin.

281

On Solovki I was met by Svetlana Veresh[208] (née Nevskaya) who had been at the Academy of Arts with my daughter Vera. She'd had a hard life. She'd married a Hungarian from Romania and gone off with him to Bucharest. They had a son by that time, but she soon realised that he, being half-Russian and half-Hungarian, wasn't going to be able to live in Romania, and she decided to come back to the USSR. But where could she live? The only job with a flat was that of curator of the historico-cultural museum-sanctuary on Solovki. Restoration work had already begun there, and volunteers came in summer—students in the main. A lady from Moscow was in charge of the restorations, who considered, as do many restorers, that restoration should be carried out 'for a given moment in the life of a monument'. That has often spelt ruin for the monument. I have always thought that Grabar's point of view was much sounder, that restoration is the prolongation of the life of a monument and the preservation of all that is valuable in it.

One of the museum staff gave up her room for me. It was a former six-man cell in no. 4 company. I asked to be left to my own devices and walked a lot by myself, remembering places and being amazed at the changes which had taken place over the years when SLON had been transformed into STON[209]. The traces of STON were much more fearsome that those of SLON: there were iron bars on the windows of even the buildings which, in SLON days, had been considered unfit for habitation, such as the loop-holes of the Nikolskaya bastion. In camp times this bastion had only been a store, but under the prison regime it had been a huge common cell without sanitation or real heating. Iron bars had even appeared on the sick-bay. The Onufriyevskaya church had been burnt down. The roofs of the principal churches had been burnt (for the second time), with the exception of the Annunciation. A few of the Trudkoloniya barracks were intact. The Krimkab office was in perfect order.

I took a rowing-boat to Bolshoy Zayatski island, where I'd never been during my imprisonment, when the terrible women's punishment cells had been there. I walked over to Muksalma, where I saw the barracks in which the 'numbered children' had been kept—the children of 'enemies of the people', who had been deprived of their surnames and had numbers stuck on their backs by which the guards knew them and roughly addressed them if need arose. One of those 'numbered' later turned up in Sverdlovsk, travelled to Solovki and recognised the place on Muksalma where he'd been imprisoned in childhood. Those were dreadful years, the crimes of which must not be forgotten.

I went with a group of museum staff to Anzer, where almost all the monuments had suffered fearful damage. I was particularly upset at Golgofa [Calvary] and the Troitski skit [Trinity Monastery]. I was struck by the pencil graffiti on the walls—people had wanted to leave some memory of themselves at least... I saw the same in the *sekirka*. I also looked at the damage inflicted on the monuments by the Cadet School that was there during the war.

My principal difference of opinion with the restorers was over the completion of the Preobrazhenski Cathedral. The point was that before the fire of 1921 the Cathedral had had a huge 'onion' cupola with greatly distended sides. It was obvious that such a cupola couldn't have been constructed before the late seventeenth century. Furthermore, the shape of the windowed drum below the cupola was very odd: it was sharply tapered upwards. For that very reason the cupola had had to have very distended sides—wider than the base of the drum. Even Nazimov, under whose direction I'd worked for several days at general tasks in 1925, had suggested that it wasn't a drum but the bottom stone section of a tent-roof. The existence of a high, obviously two-section tent-roof, the top part in wood and the bottom in stone, was confirmed by a number of illustrations of the Solovetski monastery in seventeenth century miniatures and icons. Such a tent-roof had been needed in order greatly to increase the height of the church, which was meant to serve as a navigation mark for shipping bound for the monastery. And indeed, after my departure Svetlana inspected the drum and came upon a very important detail: the deep sockets to hold the beams of the second, wooden part of the tent-roof. The restorer, however, wouldn't accept the conflicting argument and categorically refused to erect a tent-roof and instead put an inelegant cupola (inelegant, that is, for the church in question). The question of the removal of the Holy Gates—the outer part of them—had not yet arisen at that time. I achieved a modest success in one thing only: I persuaded them not to clean the very beautiful red lichen off the huge boulders of which the monastery walls are built. For some reason the restorers thought that the lichen would damage the stone...

Another idea concerning Solovki entered my head and has never left it yet. The monastery is essentially built on a dam, partly a mound of sand, partly stone. In the sixteenth century this permitted the raising of the level of Svyatoye Ozero for a variety of technical purposes: water ran through channels and pipes and worked machines in the laundry, the bakery, etc. The builders of the monastery allowed for the instability of the banked-up soil and made the wide footings for the walls of the cathedrals, which give the Solovki buildings their characteristic appearance, and the slope of the walls, thinner towards the top. The seaward slope of the whole monastery area is especially noticeable on the square by the Preobrazhenski Cathedral. This is because the upper part of the Cathedral is positioned with a distinct eastward orientation, towards the lake, and rests on the massive sanctuary wall and two pillars; that is to say, the construction of the Cathedral takes account of the seaward slope of the whole monastery site.

In brief, the whole monastery is built like a gigantic hydraulic installation, and at the same time is multifunctional. Now, my idea was to preserve the monastery unaltered as not only a religious and historical-natural monument, but also as the only museum in the country of Russian technology of the sixteenth and seventeenth centuries. To this one could add the monastery smithy, the brick-works, the agricultural buildings, etc.

I arrived on Solovki when the island was wrapped in a thick mist. The Tatariya hooted at regular intervals so as not to collide with another vessel. Only when we had come right up to the quay did the USLON building become visible. And I left Solovki in marvellous sunny weather, with the whole length of the island visible. I won't describe the feelings which filled me when I recognised the grandeur of that mass grave—not only of people, each of whom had his own spiritual world, but also of Russian culture—the last representatives of the Russian 'silver age', and the best representatives of the Russian Church. How many have left no trace, for those that remembered them are dead. The 'solovchane' hadn't rushed southwards, as the song had it, but for the most part had died either here or on the islands of the archipelago, in the North, in the wilderness of Arkhangelsk oblast or in Siberia.

My Last Time on Solovki

My last visit to Solovki was with V. B. Vinogradov's television film crew to make a film about me. I recall:

Everything went well. A delightful, friendly, youthful film crew, wonderful summer weather, and, in my opinion, successful filming—but Solovki left me with a heavy heart. The Holy Gates of the Kremlin had been demolished, there was less orange-red lichen—a clear indication of poorer air quality, as there were now motors—there were houses on the Onufriyevskoye cemetery, including a light blue one on the site of the 1929 executions. The road to the Parley Stone had become too wide, and in places on it there had appeared quarries for the extraction of sand. On Bolshoy Zayatski island the Petrovskaya church had lost its panelling, which had been torn off for fuel. Extraordinary damage had been done to the monuments on Anzer and Muksalma and in Savvatiyevo.

Restoration had progressed. Shingled onion cupolas, differing in size but uniform in shape and not suiting the monumental Solovki churches had appeared on the drums of all the remaining churches, and that made the monastery look featureless, flat. The Solovki monastery, Solovki camp, Solovki prison had all receded farther still into the realm of oblivion. The single monument to all the hundreds of graves, ditches, pits, in which the thousands of corpses were heaped which had been opened since my last visit to Solovki couldn't fail, in my view, to emphasise yet more the homogenisation of the past, the disregard for it, the obliteration of it. Alas, there is nothing to be done about it. One must evoke one's memory, for there is no one left that can remember the past of Solovki.

NOTES

1 RGIA (*Rossiiski Gosudarstveni Istoricheski Arkhiv* [Russian State Historical Archive]). Fond 1343. Op. 39. Delo 1777.

2 A town to the east of Vologda, some 600 km east of St Petersburg.

3 A permanent covered market, the St Petersburg equivalent of the Muscovite GUM.

4 *Peterburgski nekropol*, St Petersburg 1912–13, vol. 2 pp. 676–7.

5 The *sobor* in honour of the miracle-working icon of the Mother of God of Vladimir.

6 See the file headed *Materials concerning funeral* in the papers of A. G. Dostoyevskaya (*Gosudarstvennaya Biblioteka Lenina* [Lenin State Library]. f. 33, sh. 5. 12, l. 22).

7 TsGIA (*Tsentralni Gosudarstveni Istoricheski Arkhiv* [Central State Historical Archive]). F. 40, Op. 1 D. 35 1882, L. 462.

8 In Finland at the time of the narrative, but now in St Petersburg near the Kareliya Station.

9 Ispolnitelny komityet [Executive Committee]. In effect, the city council.

10 In Belarus, south-west of Minsk.

11 The Old Believers were those members of the Russian Orthodox Church that refused to accept the liturgical reforms of the Patriarch Nikon in the 1650s. Several Old Believer sects were formed, some of which still exist.

12 Nikolay Alekseyevich Nekrasov (1821–78) was a poet, as was Aleksey Koltsov (1809–42). Afanasi Nikitin was a merchant of Tver who left an account of his travels between 1466–72.

13 'The assembly of the nobility', a gentlemen's club.

14 Vsevolod Yemilevich Meyerhold (1874–1940?) was a distinguished theatrical producer, director and actor, associated at various times with the Moscow Art Theatre and the Mariinski and Aleksandrinski theatres in St Petersburg/ Leningrad.

15 Nikolay Semenovich Leskov (1831–95) and Dmitry Mamin (1852–1912)—Sibiryak is a pseudonym—were novelists; Vladimir Semenovich Solovev (1853–1900) was 'the first Russian philosopher'.

16 A literary magazine. The word means 'field'.

17 Small biscuits made in the shape of a knot.

18 The first hydroelectric station in USSR, built in 1926 on the river Volkhov near the town of the same name in north-eastern Russia.

19 The New Economic Policy which replaced War Communism in 1921. In 1929 it was superseded by the series of Five Year Plans.

20 Tsar Pavel I was murdered by some of his officers in 1801.

21 Fodor Ivanovich Shalyapin (1873–1938), the famous operatic bass.

22 Anna Akhmatova is the pseudonym of the poetess Anna Andreyevnan Gorenko (1888–1966).

23 A pre-metric measurement, equal to 3,500 feet or slightly more than a kilometre.

24 The Russian Zelenogorsk.

25 Russian novelist (1853–1921).

26 The first was the *Talvisota* [Winter War] of 1939–40, the second the *Jatkosota* [Continuation War] 1941–44. I am indebted to Prof. Michael Branch of the School of Slavonic and East European Studies for assistance on various points concerning Finland (Translator's note).

27 Vasili Andreyevich Zhukovski (1783–1852), poet.

28 A town on the upper Volga, NNE of Moscow. Between 1946–57 it was known as Shcherbakov and from 1957–84, Andropov.

29 The battle fought against Napoleon in 1812 to the west of Moscow. Mikhail Ilarionovich Kutuzov (1745–1813) was the Russian Commander in Chief.

30 Ilya Mechnikov (1845–1916), an associate of Pasteur, who shared the Nobel Prize in 1908 for work on immunology.

31 A Russian bat-and-ball game similar to rounders.

32 Author's note: The name of this station was derived from two large villages in the vicinity, Strugi and Byelaya. Later it became known as *Strugi Byeliye* [White Strugi], which appears more grammatically correct, and in the Revolution the name was changed to *Strugi Krasniye* [Red Strugi].

33 A military corps instituted by Ivan IV.

34 Russia has been known by various names at different times. The early medieval state based on Kiev was *Rus'*. With the rise to prominence of Moscow the name *Rus'* gave way to *Rossiya*. After the establishment of Soviet power the country was briefly *Sovyetskaya Rossiya* until in 1922 it was renamed *Sovyetski Soyúz* [Soviet Union].

35 Founded by Potr I The Great in 1703, the city had been known as St Petersburg (*Sankt Peterburg*). The name was changed to Petrograd in 1914 in order to remove an evident Germanism during the war, and on the death of Lenin (1924) was changed to Leningrad because of its association with his revolutionary activity. The original name was resumed in 1992.

36 Anatoli Vasilevich Lunacharski (1875–1933) was prominent in cultural matters in the early Communist era.

37 The Russian Orthodox Church split in 1922 when Stalin prohibited the election of a new patriarch on the death of Tikhon. Vvedenski was a prime mover in the 'Renovated' Church, which persisted with governmental support (despite its lack of popularity) until the Second World War.

38 *Obedinyeniye Gosudarstvennykh Izdatelstv* [State Publishing Association].

39 The Elzeviers were a Dutch firm, chiefly remembered for their fine pocket editions of the Classics. The Aldine press was established in Venice in c. 1498 by Aldus Manutius (Manucci) (1450–1518) and was kept in being by his family.

40 Aleksandr Radishchev (1749–1802). This work, much influenced by Laurence Sterne's *Sentimental Journey*, dates from the 1780s.

41 A Ukrainian active in Moscow in the reign of Potr I (1672–1725). He was responsible for putting into effect the church reforms of the day, and wrote both prose and verse.

42 Sergey Aleksandrovich Yesenin (1895-1925), poet of peasant origins. From 1923-24 he was married to the American dancer Isadora Duncan.

43 Aleksey Remizov (1877-1957), novelist and short-story writer.

44 Aleksey Nikolayevich Tolstoy (1883-1945), novelist.

45 Aleksandr Aleksandrovich Blok (1880-1921), Symbolist poet.

46 Grigori Yevseyevich Zinovev (1883-1936), chairman of the Comintern 1919-36 and allegedly writer of the famous 'Zinovev Letter' to the British Communist Party in 1924. He shared power with Stalin and Kamenev after the death of Lenin but was purged in Stalin's first show trial.

47 Tradition had it that Peter the Great had stood on this supposed meteorite to command the foundation of St Petersburg. It was later taken to the city.

48 1605-13.

49 Aleksandr Vvedenski (1904-45), not to be confused with the Renovationist Metropolitan of the same name, was a poet of the OBERIU school (*Obyedinyeniye realnogo isskustva* [Association of Real Art]), which flourished briefly in the late 1920s. Formal experimentation, which rendered their work baffling, was the OBERIU tendency. Many of its members suffered badly in the purges of 1934-38.

50 The Polish poet Cyprian Kamil Norwid (1821-83).

51 The stage name of Konstantin Sergeyevich Alekseyev (1865-1938), actor, producer and teacher, founder of the 'method' school of acting. He was associated with the Moscow Arts Theatre from 1898, and the autobiographical work referred to here was published in 1924.

52 William James (1842-1910), American psychologist and philosopher.

53 'Beau' Brummel (1778-1840).

54 Mikhail Kuzmin (1875-1936), novelist and essayist.

55 *Fakultet obshchestvennykh nauk* and *Fakultet ozhidayushchikh nevest*, respectively.

56 *Obshchestvenno-pedagogicheskoye deleniye.*

57 Nikolay Yakovlevich Marr (1865-1934), linguist, archaeologist and ethnologist. Georgian by birth, he was favoured by Stalin and his 'monogenetic' theory of language, based on Marxist principles, was dogma even after his death. It was, of course, without serious foundation and was denounced by Stalin in 1950.

58 Higher education courses for women established in 1879 by K. N. Bestuzhev-Ryumin.

59 French art historian, 1862-1964.

60 Leonid Vitalevich Sobinov (1873-1934), a renowned operatic tenor.

61 Marshak (1887-1964), a well-known writer of children's books, founded *Detgiz*, the Children's State Publishing House. He was also noted as translator of Shakespeare's sonnets and some of the works of Burns.

62 This is not a standard term in the history of Russian culture. It is used by Anna Akhmatova in her *Poema byez geroya* [Poem without a hero] (1940-62, published 1976) and clearly refers to a period starting in the late century and ending about 1914.

63 A proverbial symbol of impending doom.

64 *Obshcheye gosudarstvennoye politicheskoye upravleniye* [General State Political Directorate], successor to the Cheka and forerunner of the NKVD; the Secret Police.

65 A reference to Dostoyevski's *Crime and Punishment*.

66 *Dom predvaritelnogo zaklyucheniya* [House of Preliminary Confinement].

67 *Khudózhestvenno-literatúrnaya, filosófskaya i nauchnaya akademiya* [Artistic-literary, Philosophical and Scientific Academy].

68 Principal executioner and assassin to Ivan IV. This murder took place late in 1568; Filipp's remains were buried on Solovki and moved to the Uspenski Cathedral in Moscow Kremlin on his canonisation in 1652.

69 *Kommunisticheski soyuz molodosti* [Communist League of Youth].

70 September.

71 All Russians have three names: christian name, patronymic and surname.

72 *Kosmicheskaya akademiya nauk*.

73 Greek: Guardian of the Record.

74 Modern Pushkin.

75 A literary example of this sort of thing will be found in Aleksandr Kuprin's novelette *The Garnet Bracelet*.

76 *Narodny komissariat vnutrennykh del* [People's Commisariat for Internal Affairs], the name of the Secret Police after OGPU.

77 *Dom Predvorityelnovo Zaklucheniya* [House of police custody].

78 A profiteer during the period of the *NEP, Novaya Ekonomicheskaya Politika* New Economic Policy, which encouraged private enterprise from 1921–29, when it was superseded by Stalin's series of 5-year plans.

79 *Urka* is camp slang denoting a non-political prisoner.

80 Traditional felt over-boots, worn in snowy conditions.

81 'Ka-er' = KR, short for *kontrrevolutsionny*.

82 A monk who has taken the strictest vows, known as *skhima*.

83 An anchorite, a member of the monastery living in solitude.

84 A small member of the cod family.

85 *Upravleniye solovetskikh lagerey osobogo naznacheniya* [Directorate of the Solovkí Special-purpose Prison Camps]. By an odd coincidence the Russian *slon* means 'elephant'.

86 A slightly alcoholic drink produced from the fermentation of rye bread.

87 The 'Holy gates' (*Svyatiye vorota*) are sometimes referred to as the 'Fire gates' (*Pozharniye vorota*) for this reason.

88 'Children's Colony' and 'Labour Colony' respectively.

89 'The Solovetski islands'.

90 Aleksandr Fedorovich Kerenski (1881–1970), Minister of War and later Premier in the Provisional Government that followed the abdication of Nikolay II.

91 Founded in 1469 by St Zosima, the monastery grew to be one of the largest in Russia and one of the most important centres of the region.

92 *Skit* is a small and secluded monastery.

93 A force of *streltsy* from Moscow eventually overcame the monks' resistance and religious reforms were enforced.

94 Where the representatives of the monastery held talks with the commander of the British fleet which bombarded it in 1854, in the early days of the Crimean War, on account of its military significance.

95 Author's note: this was the most terrible punishment cell, on Mount Sekirnaya. Few returned from it alive.

96 *Kriminologicheski kabinet* [Criminology office].

97 Author's note: It was my exclusive good fortune that thanks to the good offices of Father Nikolay Piskanovski and *vladyka* Viktor Ostrovidov I found employment in the Criminological office. In his memoir *Thoughts on What Was* N. P. Antsiferov writes: "I dreamed of working in the Krimkab, where they collected the drawings, letters and verses of criminal prisoners. In that way, I thought, I would come to understand the psychology of the people of Dostoyevski's *The House of the Dead*" (p. 346). He doesn't say that it wasn't just a matter of understanding criminals. He wanted to work there because so did his friends A. A. Méyer, K. A. Polovtseva, A. P. Sukhov etc. —DSL.

98 By Yevgeni Zamyatin (1884–1937).

99 Anti-hero of Turgenev's *Fathers and Sons*.

100 An inferior tobacco, the sort commonly used for *papirosy*.

101 The forerunner of OGPU.

102 A type of paper used for drawing and printing engravings, named after its inventor.

103 Author's note: After speaking on television about Kozhevnikov's case I received a letter from Safin Mansur, serving in the Home Fleet. He wrote: You were talking about the (partisan) army commander Innokenti Kozhevnikov, who fought in the Prikamye during the Civil War. There were several thousand Chelnintsy, people from my part of the world, in his forces. There is an exhibition on the brave commander Innokenti Kozhevnikov in the local history museum but, unfortunately, absolutely no material relating to his later life after the Civil War, nor any reference to his being in Solovkí—DLS. *Chelnintsy* are citizens of Chelny, a town on the Kama, known from 1930–82 as *Naberezhnye Chelny* and from 1982 as *Brezhnev*.

104 Author's note: In an excerpt from my *Memoirs* printed elsewhere I erroneously named Kazarnovski as author of this slogan.

105 The White Sea-Baltic Canal project.

106 *Sever* 'north'; *yug* 'south'.

107 An anti-Soviet movement in Central Asia.

108 A thin metal plate used for framing icons.

109 Andrey Rublev (?1365–1430), most renowned of all Russian icon painters.

110 A type of large and important monastery. This one is in the modern Zagorsk.

111 Author's note: Before his arrest (thanks to his small size) Ivanov had been in service with the Metropolitan of Novgorod, and then became an anti-religious activist. In some of the accusations made against him he had 'slandered' the Novgorod Party organisation. He was convicted in particular for the theft of many church valuables. His 'works' are full of fab-

rications, mostly for anti-religious purposes. They can in no way be trusted.

112 *Riza* means either a chasuble or the metal mounting of an icon.

113 Short for *Kommunisticheski Soyuz Molodosti* [Communist League of Youth].

114 'Living Antiquity' and 'Russian Speech'.

115 Tsarist predecessor of the Cheka.

116 *Soyuz ukrainskoy molodosti* [League of Ukrainian Youth]; *Soyuz vyzvoleniye Ukrainy* [League for the support of Ukraine].

117 That should read *Belomorobaltiski*.

118 Author's note: I was told that the marvellous library of books sent to prisoners was also destroyed—burnt—on his orders. However, the blame obviously lay with higher authority—DSL. The islands were the training centre for the Northern Fleet during 1939-47.

119 Mikhail Yurevich Lermontov (1814-41).

120 Writer (1893-1984).

121 A sort of tap-dance.

122 'The Twelve' (1918), a revolutionary verse of Aleksándr Aleksándrovich Blok (1880-1921), in which twelve drunken Red Army men symbolise the Apostles with Lenin, not Christ, at their head.

123 Author's note: For B. M. Lobach-Zhuchenko (son, it is thought, of Marko Vovchok) see the memoirs of his son B. B. Lobách-Zhuchénko *Na perekrestkakh sud'by* [At the crossroads of Fate] in *Raduga*, 1900, no. 1, pp. 109-126—DSL.

124 *Kobza* is a Ukrainian stringed instrument, *kobzar'* its player.

125 Dmitri Sergeyevich Merezhkovski (1865-1941), philosopher and writer, founder of the Symbolist school, and his wife Zinaida Nikolayevna Hippius (1869-1945), writer. They had emigrated to Paris in 1919 and 1920 respectively.

126 Author's note: Stromin was an Estonian and for that reason, perhaps, lacked the requisite degree of sensitivity in Russian.

127 Author's note: By the way, he was the son of that Mishanchik who is often mentioned in *Trubetskoy's Zapiski kirasirov* [Notebooks of the cuirassiers] printed in the magazine *Nashe naslediye* [Our Heritage].

128 Author's note: The distinction between criminals and counterrevoultionaries (Ka-er) was by this time developing, but had not produced perceptible results at the end of the '20s.

129 'On the right to myth'. In: *Filosofskiye sochineniya*. Paris 1982, pp. 96-100.

130 *Leonid Fedorov. His Life and Work.* Rome, 1966.

131 a poet, writing mainly on religious and philosophical themes. Much influenced by the German philosphers of his youth and by Solovev, his grandiloquent style earned him the sobriquet 'the Magnificent'.

132 'The Catholic Search for God and Marxist Atheism' (Rome, 1941).

133 Nikolay Berdyayev (1874-1948), philosopher.

134 Petr Arkadiyevich Stolypin (1862-1811), Tsarist statesman and from 1906 Minister of the Interior. The railway cars used for prisoner transport were introduced in his period of office.

135 Nikolay Derzhavin (1743–1816), the major Rusisian poet of the eighteenth century. Yevgeni Baratznski (1800–44) is often rated as second only to Pushkin among Russian poets of the ninteenth century.

136 Osip Mandelshtam (1891–1938), poet of the Acmeist school.

137 Andrey Bely was the pseudonym of Boris Bugayev (1880–1934), writer of the Symbolist school of which Valeri Bryusov (1873–1924) was a leading figure.

138 Maksimilian Voloshin (Kirienko-Voloshin) (1877–1932), minor poet.

139 'World of Art', a luxury journal founded in 1898 by Sergey Diagilev and others. It ran until 1904 and the Merezhkovskis and Mikhail Kuzmin were among its contributors.

140 Nikolay Grech (1787–1867), described by his opponents as a 'literary shopkeeper', was a writer and publicist, involved with Faddey Bulgarin and others in the nineteenth century journals *Polyarnaya zvezda* [Pole Star] and *Severnaya pchela* [Northern Bee].

141 The Slaavilainen Kirjasto [Slavonic Library] of Helsinki University was a legal deposit library for all publications in Russia from 1828, and holds a full set of *Solovetskiye ostrova*.

142 Russian human rights organization with an archive.

143 Vorkuta is in the Komi Republic, then Komi ASSR.

144 Prisoners were deprived of civil status for the duration of their sentence and might not therefore address others, or be addressed, as 'comrade'.

145 A thorough account of this article of the Criminal Code can be found in Solzhenitsyn's *Gulag Archipelago*. Broadly speaking, it considered any action or inaction directed at the weakening of State power to be counterrevolutionary.

146 Near Ukhta in the Komi Republic.

147 Mikhaylo Kotsyubinski (1864–1913), leading Ukrainian novelist and short-story writer.

148 'The smart man follows fashion' and the tune 'Forgotten, abandoned'.

149 On release some prisoners were not free to live where they chose, but certain towns and cities—usually the important centres—were barred to them.

150 Igor Severyanin was the pseudonym of Igor Lotarev (1887–1941), futurist poet.

151 Nikolay Stepanovich Gumilev (1886–1921), Acmeist poet and husband of Anna Akhmatova.

152 'Life', 'biography', but in practice the word is restricted in use to Lives of Saints.

153 The Protopop Avvakum Petrovich (1620/21–1682), leader of the opposition to Patriarch Nikon. Exiled to Transbaikalia in 1653 he was recalled in 1662, but exiled again in 1667 to Mezen (NE of Archangelsk) and spent his last fifteen years in the remote Pustozersk, where he wrote this autobiographical work. For a full account of his life see Janko Lavrin's *A Panorama of Russian Literature* (London UP, 1973) pp. 26–30.

154 Nikolay Nikolayevich Yudenich (1862–1933), Tsarist military commander who led anti-Soviet forces in Estonia in the Civil War.

155 The three ships had previously belonged to the monastery.

156 There are two SS Herman: Herman Contractus ('The Cripple') (1013–54) and Herman Joseph (1150–1241).

157 The celebrated violinist Yasha Heifetz (1901–87) emigrated with his family to the USA in 1917, becoming an American citizen in 1924.

158 White bread made from sifted flour.

159 The tea itself is unsweetened, and the drinker holds a lump of sugar in his mouth. If the tea is sweetened, one drinks *vnakladku*.

160 Faddey Bulgarin (1789–1859), writer and journalist. An associate of Grech in *Severnaya pchela* and *Polyarnaya zvezda*.

161 *Avtorski list* 'royalty page' is a publisher's unit of 40,000 ens, used for the calculation of royalties.

162 Lev Borisovich Kamenev (Rosenfeld) (1883–1936). A prominent Bolshevik, he was expelled from the Party in 1927, re-admitted, re-expelled and finally shot after a show trial.

163 Igor Vladimirovich Ilinski (1901–), an actor well known for his comic roles. He came to prominence in Meyerhold's experimental productions of the '20s.

164 A town in Kemerovo oblast, SE of Barnaul in SW Siberia.

165 Sergey Mironovich Kirov (Kostrikov) (1886–1934), a close associate of Stalin, reputedly murdered on Stalin's orders. A wave of reprisals followed.

166 Special shops.

167 From *teply* [warm]. The *teplushka* was a kind of heated goods vehicle used for carrying people.

168 *Kulak* [fist] means a well-to-do peasant. The class was fiercely attacked and destroyed in the process of the collectivisation of agriculture, with the resulting loss of much managerial skill and not a few lives.

169 Author's note: The peasant is mispronouncing and misunderstanding *zaem* [loan] as *s"em* [I will eat you].

170 *Sotsialnoye i Ekonomicheskoye Izdatelstvo* [Social and Economic Press].

171 *Institut Istorii Materialni Kulturi* [Institute of the History of Material Culture].

172 Lucien Levy-Bruhl (1957–1939), French philosopher. He took a special interest in the psychology of primitive peoples and published on the subject.

173 Nikolay Vasilevich Krylenko (1885–1938). Chief State Prosecutor 1918–31; later People's Commissar of Justice [*narkomyust*]. He was shot in 1938.

174 Giacomo Quarenghi (1744–1817), Italian-born architect who acquired a great reputation in Russia under Catherine II. Aldo Rossi (1931–), Italian architect and theorist strongly influenced by Neo-Clasicism.

175 [The language of the Yellow Uygurs], a Turkic people of NW China and Siberia. This was eventually published—the translator has a copy!

176 *Rayonny komitet* [Regional Committee].

177 A bronze memorial, sculpted in 1862 by Mikhail Mikeshin.

178 *Oblastnoy komitet* [Oblast Committee], roughly the equivalent of County council.

179 [The bottom] or [Gloom].
180 It is said that only eight persons survived the whole war in Novgorod.
181 A kind of fish soup.
182 This refers to the author's wife Zina (Zinaida Aleksandrovna), not his own mother.
183 A vehicle factory.
184 Presumably a reference to the sinking of the battle-cruiser HMS Hood on 24 May 1941. Russian history distinguishes between the Great Patriotic War (referred to here) dating from the German invasion of 1941, and the Second World War beginning in 1939.
185 'White ticket men', persons exempt from military service.
186 'First Aid'—the ambulance service.
187 *Burzhuyka* was a small home-made cooking-stove using solid fuel.
188 Author's note: I've had occasion to say more than once that under interrogation people were made to sign even statements that they hadn't made or written, didn't support or which they considered perfect rubbish. At the time when the authorities were preparing Leningrad for surrender a mere conversation between two people about what they should do, how they should hide, if the Germans took the city was considered little short of treason. I didn't therefore think of blaming Gukovski in the least, nor the numerous others who signed under duress whatever the interrogator-torturer wanted. I could only sympathise with them. It was the first time that Gukovski had been arrested, and he evidently didn't know that one should either refuse to answer the interrogator's questions or say as little as possible. I can imagine his conversation with the interrogator: Interrogator: Are you aware that Koplan is waiting for the Germans? Gukovski: What rot, he's scared to death of them. Interrogator: (pretending to be naive) Why? Gukovski: He's Jewish. Interrogator: Not at all, he's Orthodox. Gukovski: If the Gestapo had any sense they'd realise that he couldn't be a Zionist. Interrogator: Thank you for defending your comrade. Sign this report. Gukovski: This is wrong, I didn't say "the Gestapo have got some sense", I said "If..." Interrogator: Let's not quarrel over a couple of letters. The important thing is, you've defended your comrade from slander. Gukovski signs and is taken away satisfied that he's defended his comrade.
In the report there are three bases for accusation. Against Koplan there are two: he was inclined to panic and was ideologically prepared to go over to the enemy: to betray the ideology of Soviet man and to lean politically on religion. Against Gukovski there is one: he acknowledges 'sense' in the Gestapo, or at all events the possibility of it.
I haven't made it all up: that is just how interrogations were carried out, and such accusations were brought.
189 A heroic figure of Russian folklore.
190 The author sees a play on words with *kanalya* [villain] or the French *canaille* [low life].
191 Ivan Sergeyevich Turgenev (1818–83), novelist and poet; Konstantin Nikolayevich Batyushkov (1787–1855), poet; Petr Yakovlevich Chaadayev (1794–1856), philosopher.

192 The 'Dream' and the 'Ball' are excerpts from Pushkin's *Yevgeni Onegin*. Aleksey Niklolayevich Pleshcheyev was a minor poet, whose best-known work in the West is the text of Tchaikovski's famous 'Legend' (op. 54 no. 5).

193 Revelation 3:16. Therefore because thou art lukewarm, and neither hot nor cold, I will spew thee out of my mouth.

194 Author's note: Wrong! In 1958 they turned out to be alive and living in New York. Zhura is married to a rich man, travels in Europe, sings songs of her own composition under the name of Komaro (she was ashamed of her Russian surname). The gnawings of conscience, it would seem, are insignificant.

195 'Who will make the reckoning? (Leningrad. The blockade. The children).'

196 *Zhirinka* is a diminutive of *zhir* [fat], *dovesochek* of *dovesok* [make-weight].

197 The feast held after the funeral.

198 'House of Scientists', the scientists' club.

199 Short for *zhilishchno-arendoye kooperativnoye tovarishchestvo* [Housing Lease Cooperative Society].

200 A play on *griva*, which can mean 'mane' or 'ridge'.

201 Short for *zaveduyushchi khozyaystvom* [person in charge of the economy] [or bursar].

202 There is no real English equivalent for this colloquialism, and details of its implications will emerge in the text. It consisted of the orchestrated public 'hauling over the coals' of an academic for (alleged) departures in his work from Communist Party notions of political correctness. As will be seen, this practice could have very serious consequences for the victim, and presented a golden opportunity for the settling of scores. To translate it as 'criticism' (Smirnitski) or 'slating' (Oxford) would dilute the menace inherent in the term; I prefer to leave it in Russian.

203 Andrey Yanuarevich Vyshinski (1883–1954), lawyer and diplomat.

204 Mikhail Mikhaylovich Zoshchenko (1895–1958), a very popular humorous writer.

205 *Chichikov* is the crafty 'hero' of Gogol's novel *Dead Souls*.

206 Prince Andrey Mikhaylovich Kurbski (1528–83) had been a successful military commander under Ivan IV 'The Terrible', to whom he was distantly related. He rose to the rank of *boyar* but fell out of favour and fled to Poland-Lithuania, where he fought against Russia, although concerning himself with the welfare of the Orthodox Russian population of the country. He conducted a lengthy and acrimonious correspondence with Ivan from Lithuania and wrote religious works and a history of Ivan's reign.

207 'The Lay of Igor's Campaign', one of the oldest works in Russian literature, tells of the war campaign waged by Prince Igor Svyatoslavich of Novgorod-Seversk against the Polovtsians in 1185.

208 Thus transcribed from the Russian. The Hungarian must be either Vörös or Veress.

209 *Solovétskaya tyurmá osóbogo naznachéniya* [Solovki special purpose prison]. The Russian word *ston*, appropriately enough, means 'groan'.